Out of the Red

Out of the Red

Investment and Capitalism in Russia

John T. Connor
with Lawrence P. Milford

WILEY

John Wiley & Sons, Inc.

Published by John Wiley & Sons, Inc., Hoboken, New Jersey.
Published simultaneously in Canada.

For general information on our other products and services or for technical support, please contact our Customer Care Department within the United States at (800) 762-2974, outside the United States at (317) 572-3993 or fax (317) 572-4002.

Wiley also publishes its books in a variety of electronic formats. Some content that appears in print may not be available in electronic books. For more information about Wiley products, visit our Web site at www.wiley.com.

Library of Congress Cataloging-in-Publication Data:
Connor, John T., 1941-
    Out of the red : investment and capitalism in Russia / John T. Connor ; with
Lawrence P. Milford.
        p. cm.
    Includes bibliographical references and index.
    ISBN 978-0-470-26978-7 (cloth)
        1. Investments—Russia (Federation)   2. Capitalism—Russia (Federation)   3. Russia
    (Federation)—Economic policy.   I. Milford, Lawrence P., 1975-   II. Title.
    HG5580.2.A3C66   2008
    330.947—dc22

                                                                    2007047648

Printed in the United States of America
10 9 8 7 6 5 4 3 2 1

The book is dedicated to Arkady Volsky, who embodied the best in the transition from the old regime to the new. The Founder of the Union of Industrialists and Entrepreneurs, Russia's leading business lobby, he was, earlier, a young Soviet factory manager who became economic advisor to the leader of the USSR. Arkady was smart, honest, patriotic, hard working, effective, and dedicated to excellence in Russian business policy and practice.

Contents

Foreword

Russia's transition from a component of the Soviet empire to independence and from a planned economy to a market system with the majority of productive assets under private ownership is one of the most remarkable transformations of the last hundred years. The new Russia possesses the potential for the most promising investment opportunities of the twenty-first century.

That potential, of course, is not yet a full reality. Russia's stock market has been subject to wide fluctuations, although its currency is now fully convertible and the market for it stable. And the runaway inflation of the early 1990s (largely the product of the monetary imbalances created in the last years of the Soviet period) has given way to steadily declining inflation, down to manageable levels. The more serious problems and uncertainties that Russia faced in the 1990s, such as lower prices for oil, its major export, a persistent budgetary deficit, fears of currency instability, and a lackluster effort to complete its reform process, have given way to a high price for oil, continuing reform, and solid monetary and fiscal management. In fact, Russia, which continues to enjoy large trade and budgetary surpluses, has proven to be one of the world's most conservative fiscal and monetary regimes.

Tax collection has increased dramatically after Russia's tax reform was implemented, including a low 13 percent flat personal income tax rate. Investment in the stock market has broadened and deepened as more companies go public and as domestic pension funds and other investors join foreign investors. Russians are still finding their way to and in a capitalist market system, and individuals are not yet accustomed to building retirement funds in equity assets. This, however, is a worldwide trend, most noticeable in the United States, and it therefore seems likely (though by no means assured) that Russians will also join the parade. If Russian productivity begins to grow and financial markets become more stable, their attraction for Russians and foreigners alike will grow.

John Connor has been active in Russia for 30 years. Unlike most financial specialists who took an interest in Russia only after independence, Connor understands the Soviet system and period as well, which provides historical depth to his judgments. His involvement since 1993 has been particularly intense: In that year he founded an insurance company in Russia and has been an active participant in the Russian stock market since 1996.

For those considering investments in Russian securities, John Connor's book is a godsend. I know of no other work that describes so well the companies offering securities to investors in the Russian stock market. Both readable and concise, it provides just the sort of information potential investors need to have.

JACK F. MATLOCK JR.
Former U.S. ambassador to the USSR
Special assistant for national security to
President Ronald Reagan

Preface

At the end of the nineteenth century, Russia sported the world's fastest-growing economy; business was flourishing. Then came the Red Revolution, and "business" disappeared. Looking at that nation's "financial statements," Stalin and the Soviet era leadership added substantial assets to the balance sheet—through forced industrialization. The Soviet Union's income statement, by contrast, was characterized by inputs exceeding outputs. In short, Enterprise Soviet Russia operated at a loss (or in the red, some may say).

With the disintegration of the Eastern European Soviet empire in the early 1990s and the subsequent dismemberment of the Soviet Union itself, Russia was back and business reappeared. A modern constitution was adopted, patterned on that of France, and democratic institutions were created. From Boris Yeltsin leading the rise of Russian democracy to Vladimir Putin leading the rise of the Russian economy, the transformation of the Soviet Union into modern Russia has created a wealth of opportunities for business.

Americans continue to be fascinated with what is going on in Russia. After nearly a half century of living through the Cold War, watching the former bastion of communism emerge as a democratic nation is a story that resonates in the West. This book looks at Russia's fast-growing and highly profitable business economy, and what it means for global markets.

Part One sets the stage for the investor or more general business/ economics reader to understand Russia in terms of traditional risk/

reward analytical categories, including recent historic developments informing these judgments.

When approaching the subject of business in Russia, it is hard not to address up front the overwhelming concern that the average reader evinces about crime and corruption and the rule of law in Russia, so Chapter 2 provides some further background.

Part Two discusses how conditions were ripe for business to flourish in the 1990s and focuses on the new businesses in Russia's free market economy that have grown up over the last 15 years, as well as on the so-called oligarchs who are the first generation of owner-operators. Some businesses were built from the privatized bits and pieces of former Soviet ministries and some are purely private start-ups like the cell phone companies. Chapters 4 through 8 discuss the leading companies in the main sectors of the Russian economy today. Chapter 9 briefly steps away from the discussion of Russia to look at the countries of Ukraine and Kazakhstan and at a few companies there.

Part Three challenges the reader to move beyond the traditional misconceptions about modern-day Russia and look toward its future. Chapter 10, titled "Discovering the Real Russia," highlights the evident negativity among U.S. elites toward many of these recent developments in Russia. Chapter 11 looks forward briefly toward possible future developments in Russia.

Earlier writings for the Third Millennium Russia Fund (TMRFX) focused more on the mechanics of investing in the Russian stock market, which are by now well understood. In fact, Russia has become mainstreamed, as most global financial firms are well represented in Moscow. So this book is an attempt to put investing in Russia in the broader context of the companies that have grown up, their leaders, and the macroeconomic and political developments that form the present-day environment for doing business in Russia.

The Third Millennium Russia Fund can be viewed on a daily basis at Yahoo! Finance and other Internet sites and at www.tmrussia.com. The Third Millennium Russia Fund is a series of The World Funds and can be reached at 1-800-527-9525. The Fund covers all the countries of the Commonwealth of Independent States (CIS). Now that Russia has entered a dramatic domestic growth phase, we hope its stock market will continue to outperform world stock markets, but past results are never an indicator of future performance.

The contents of this book pertaining to markets and specific companies come mainly from the research conducted by Third Millennium Russia Fund. This research has been aided by the research departments of various brokerage firms that cover Russia and the Commonwealth of Independent States (CIS). We would like to especially thank UBS for its extensive research resources for the region.

Part One

FREE MARKETS AND DEMOCRACY ARRIVE IN RUSSIA

Chapter 1

Today's Russia

The Russians have endured generally abysmal leadership for long periods of time. In the nineteenth century, Tsar Alexander II freed the serfs, but Josef Stalin in effect again enslaved the population in the second quarter of the twentieth century. As a result, the Russians are long-suffering and more than a little cynical about their leaders. If you want to hear something unfavorable about Russia and its leaders, you do not have to go to Washington, D.C. Just ask a Russian and you will hear it at length. You do not have to read an American journalist; just pick up a Russian newspaper.

Russia has a tremendous number of daily newspapers, and readership continues to be among the highest in the world. The expression and range of opinions in the Russian media are very great. If it is favorable coverage you need for your business or political purposes, just buy it, it's for sale. Broadcast media? That's another story as it is under the Kremlin's thumb.

Rebuilding Russia is now the challenge. For the past 15 years, the country has been depleting its Soviet-era legacy infrastructure: the roads, factories, proven oil reserves, and so forth. Now the era of inadequate new investment is over and a period of domestic growth and expansion has been launched, a la post–World War II Japan and the United States. Public–private partnerships, including toll roads, a new Priority National Projects program, and company-funded capital expenditures (capex) are all in prospect.

Russia's Transformation into a Free Market Economy

Before assessing the risks and rewards of investing in Russia, let's look at how the centrally planned, communist economy from the Soviet era became the free-market economy of today's democratic Russian Federation.

Gorbachev, Yeltsin, and Putin: Three Transformational Leaders

Like its stock market, the recent history of Russia has been volatile. But net, Russia's market has also been up over 1,000 percent[1] since the 1998 collapse of the economy (the "Crisis"). Mikhail Gorbachev, Boris Yeltsin, and Vladimir Putin have each been transformational leaders, contributing greatly to fast progress and positive change.

Mikhail Gorbachev, of course, presided over the ceding of an empire by letting go of Romania, Bulgaria, Poland, East Germany, the Czech Republic, and Hungary. Not one person died in the process. For this he is greatly esteemed outside of Russia, but not in Russia. If he had decreed Soviet tanks to roll into central Prague, people would have run for cover, as in the past. But he did not do so. He let it all unravel.

He was a true believer in communism, and still is. He thought he could give communism a new face, a renewed lease on life. But, as a product of the system, enjoying the confidence of the Politburo right up until it was too late for the ancient regime, he oversaw the dismantling of Russia's international empire.

In the process, he sat down with President Ronald Reagan, who well appreciated the historic opportunity and who, it turned out, hated nuclear weapons and the threat they posed to humanity and negotiated the most substantial arms control agreements ever. This accomplishment alone assures Reagan of his place in history. Although he recognized the overall possibilities with Gorbachev and certainly sought to promote the end result ("Mr. Gorbachev, tear down this Wall"), his more triumphalist supporters want to give him sole credit for the end of the "Evil Empire." (For more, please read *Reagan and Gorbachev* by former Ambassador Jack Matlock Jr., who assisted President Reagan at the Reykjavik Summit in Iceland.)

But Gorbechev, who dismantled the Eastern European Soviet empire, did not intend the disintegration of the Soviet Union itself, the former Russian empire. Boris Yeltsin (see Figure 1.1), not esteemed at present anywhere, stepped up on a tank and oversaw three historic developments:

1. Russian Independence
2. Democracy
3. Free Markets and Privatization

Figure 1.1 Boris Yeltsin, First President of the Russian Federation
Courtesy of Fotosearch.

Russia: Free at Last

As a Russian nationalist, Yeltsin understood that it would be an unnecessary burden for Russia to continue to carry the weight of the other generally resource-poor former Soviet republics. Great Russia itself is the largest country in Europe. When Siberia is added to the map, a region that has the same population as Canada, with its people also clinging to its southern border, even European Great Russia looks small.

It took only one meeting of the Communist Politburo for hands to wave in the air when Yeltsin asked for volunteers to lead each of the constituent Soviet republics into independence. In general, those Soviet-era leaders grabbed and held their presidencies long after each republic declared its independence. This process generally unfolded smoothly. As for Ukraine, though, there was particular chagrin. In the 1950s, Nikita Khrushchev, who was from The Ukraine, as it was then called, gave The Crimea, which had no particular historic tie to Ukraine, to that Soviet republic. The painful realization of the modern implications of that gratuitous decision are now apparent to Russia as it is currently fighting a legal battle with the government of independent Ukraine to ensure the Russian Navy's continued access to its important warm-water port, a need Russia has pursued since the reign of Peter the Great.[2]

Most of us are familiar with the White House of Russia, the offices of the Supreme Soviet of the RSFSR (the Russian Republic, a constituent of the Soviet Union). This is the location of Boris Yeltsin's famous mounting of the tank during the attempted coup against Gorbechev. And, later, it was the site of the brief hostilities when the Yeltsin forces shelled the White House and the recalcitrant Communist-led Supreme Soviet (the national legislature adopted the historic *Duma* name later with the new democratic constitution) was forced to surrender. Subsequently, a fine new democratic constitution was adopted to replace the Soviet-era constitution-in-name-only (the Communist Politburo had run the country dictatorially).

My office was just across the Moscow River from the White House and, during my years of living in Moscow, I watched its early stages of construction as the seat of government for the RSFSR, never dreaming that one day it would in fact house the government of the new, independent Russian Federation. Since, in typical Soviet construction style, it took 10 years to be completed, this transition in fact took place not long after its completion. Today, it is surrounded by a heavy, iron fence, so storming it would not be easy.

The Establishment of Democracy

As the first president of an independent Russia, Boris Yeltsin set up the institutions of democracy. He oversaw the drafting of a new constitution, based on that of the French Fifth Republic, which has well served France since 1958, and serves the Russian Federation today.

Boris Yeltsin was a genuine, backslapping, smiling, people-to-people politician. Americans are not the only voters who appreciate a leader possessing the "common touch." Russians can also tell when a candidate likes people, enjoys being among them, and simply asks for their votes and support. This Yeltsin did admirably, moving around the country in two election cycles (1992 and 1996), and the Russian people responded. Unlike Putin, Yeltsin had always been a populist leader, well known to the public.

The 1996 Presidential election and the State Duma election were of course critical to the continued progress of Russia toward democracy and free markets. Although the threat of a Communist Duma has now receded to the point of being very unlikely, the Communists had been nothing but obstreperous in the early days of the new, independent Russia. They had a significant bloc in the State Duma, and from 1995 to 1999, they stopped tax reform and other necessary changes.[3] In the 1996 election cycle it was the financial and organizational support of the oligarchs—who had profited so much from the privatization program—that saved the day for Yeltsin and helped contain the size of the Communist bloc in the Duma going forward so that tax and other reform programs could be enacted.

Free Markets and Privatization

Yeltsin's third historic achievement, in January 1992, freed prices to fluctuate with the market under acting Prime Minister Igor Gaidar and shepherded by his brilliant young privatization director, Anatoly Chubais. Then shops, apartments, and enterprises were privatized to their occupants, workers, and managers.[4] Russia's business sector today is more private than that of Italy or France. Chubais's animus was simply to get everything out of the hands of the government, which had made such a mess of it.

The tricky part was the privatization of clearly valuable companies, such as oil companies. No one had funds to pay market prices, so were they to be auctioned off to foreigners, or to Russians? Fifteen years later, even after the Yukos affair and the clawing back of assets by the state, the Russian oil industry is still about two-thirds privately owned as measured by output. Since government-owned oil companies are more fully valued in the market due to less perceived risk, on a market-cap basis the public/private ratio is closer to 50/50.[5]

It was during these pre-1998 years that the United States was of tremendous help to Russia. Laws, including securities laws, were enacted with U.S. assistance. Americans can take great pride in the material assistance we gave Russia; and the government of Russia eagerly sought and accepted that advice and assistance. It was during this period that the idea that our two countries were great friends and allies took hold. Now, many U.S. commentators, instead of building on the base of the many positive developments we engendered in Russia, seem intent only on hectoring and lecturing Russia on its many real and apparent shortcomings (more on this in Chapter 10).

Learning the Hard Lessons of Capitalism: The 1998 Crisis

The year 1998 brought with it events that have continued to shape Russian politics and economic policy. On the surface, the end of 1997 looked like it was going to be a turning point in the grand Russian free market experiment. The United States and the International Monetary Fund (IMF) were working closely with the Central Bank of Russia (CBR) to bring in foreign loans and assist in creating effective controls over the economy, and this assistance seemed to be working. The country was reporting its first annualized growth (0.8 percent) in gross domestic product (GDP) since the collapse of the Soviet Union.[6] At the same time, Russian blue chip stocks were showing huge gains on the Russian Trading System (RTS), some stocks recording gains as high as 1,500 percent,[7] as Western and Japanese investors flocked to the Russian market in search of the hefty gains that seemed a sure thing.

The price of oil, Russia's primary export, was holding steady at then-record levels of around $23 per barrel, bringing in added revenues to the Russian economy and the Russian government. Thanks in part to the help of the IMF and the United States, this impressive turnaround came with a reduction in inflation, a number that reached a high of 2,600 percent in 1992, down to 11 percent in 1997. These improvements, though, seemed to convince most people involved that the Russian economy was sound and that the economic warning signs that were evident at the time could be ignored as merely, as then–World Bank head James Wolfensohn stated, "a bump in the road."[8]

Although 1997 appeared to be a breakthrough year for the Russian economy, the underpinnings of economic disaster were already becoming evident. The first sign was the Asian currency crises of 1997 that began with the Thai baht crisis in Thailand, where currencies in many Asian countries, and their economies, were devastated by speculators betting huge sums of money on the potential of their currencies devaluing while their central banks spent huge sums of money to protect the value of those currencies.

The Asian currency crisis had a major impact on Russia's exports, as it relied on many of these Asian markets as trading partners. This crisis also put pressure on the price of crude oil, which eventually fell to around $11 per barrel in 1998 on the potential for decreased demand. The financial pressure, along with poor government decision making, was taking its toll on the Russian economy. This is evidenced by the fact that by the end of 1997 only about 40 percent of Russian workers were being paid on time and in full.[9]

The pressures on the Russian economy and the Central Bank of Russia (CBR) had finally proven to be too much for the fledgling Russian economy to bear, and by August of 1998 the crisis had come. The Russian stock market, as measured on the Russian Trading Systems (RTS), the main stock market in Moscow, fell from a high of 571 down to 37. The Russian government devalued its currency, the ruble, by removing it from its controlled range of 5 to 6 rubles per U.S. dollar and by letting it become a free floating currency. The ruble quickly responded by dropping in value down from 6 rubles per U.S. dollar to 25 rubles per U.S. dollar. The government then also defaulted on its short-term debt and, eventually, most of its debt. Not only did the government default on its Eurobonds, but on its domestic treasury bills, called GKOs. These GKOs constituted the bulk of the assets at the life insurance company I founded in 1993, ROSGAL, as, at that time, they were one of the only investments an insurance company could legally make. This mass default of government debt dealt our life insurance company (and much of the Russian economy) a death blow.[10]

Government Policy during the 1998 Crisis

A good deal of the blame for the 1998 crisis can be put on the actions of the Russian government and the CBR during and leading up to the crisis. One of the primary factors leading to the economic collapse was the government's insistence on keeping its currency overvalued. From 1992 until the crisis in 1998, the government allowed the ruble to float against the U.S. dollar in only a narrow range of between 5 to 6 rubles per U.S. dollar. This level of valuation of the ruble was considered adequate at the time because during the Soviet era, the ruble was maintained at a completely artificial exchange rate of 0.6 rubles per U.S. dollar. It was thought that a strong ruble was a sign of a strong Russia, but it turned out that keeping the ruble strong was the main factor leading to the weakening of the Russian economy.[11]

Following the Asian currency crisis in 1997, many investors felt that it was inevitable for the ruble to be allowed to depreciate against the dollar. In order to keep the ruble from depreciating, the CBR was forced to use its foreign currency reserves to buy rubles on the open market. In November 1997, investors staged the first serious attack on the ruble by selling large numbers of rubles on the foreign currency markets to create a large supply with the intention of causing the ruble's value to depreciate. The CBR successfully thwarted this attack by purchasing rubles with its U.S. dollar reserves, but spent $6 billion of its foreign currency reserves to do so. April and May of 1998 brought similar attacks on the ruble, as investors saw the Russian government's weakness as a sign that the ruble was vulnerable to devaluation. The CBR was also successful in counteracting these attacks, but was left with only $8 billion in foreign reserves to continue propping up the ruble.[12]

The government's efforts were not helped by the public relations missteps that occurred early in 1998. In May of 1998, the then-head of the CBR, Sergei Dubinin, was giving a periodic fiscal update to government ministers when he warned of possible serious debt crisis in the near future if quick actions were not taken to correct the debt situation. His comments were not meant to instill fear in the public but to impel the government ministers to start taking positive actions concerning the government's fiscal problems. He did not realize when making the statement that reporters were in the room, and word of his statements quickly got out to the public. The problem was made even worse by a statement later that month from newly appointed Prime Minister Sergei Kiriyenko, who told press that due to low levels of tax collection that the government was "very poor."[13]

These statements worked to further shake investors' confidence, as well as solidify in their minds that the ruble would need to be allowed to depreciate in the near future. This also had an effect on Russian citizens, who rushed to buy U.S. dollars fearing that their savings would be worthless if kept in rubles. Deposits made in rubles in Russian banks increased by a mere 1.3 billion rubles in 1998, compared to 29.8 billion in the year before.[14] This helped lead to decreased demand for rubles, making the CBR's job of keeping the ruble's value between 5 and 6 U.S. dollars even more difficult by the day.

Low tax payments and heavy spending on interest payments on government debt were also causing a cash crunch for the government. The country had recently installed a short-term debt system similar to that of the U.S. Treasury in which short-term debt instruments, called GKOs, were sold weekly at auctions to finance its debt service needs. This system worked well for a short period of time, but as the crisis worsened, the investors for these securities demanded more interest be paid in order to compensate for the perceived risk of government default. In 1998, the interest rate had to be raised to over 50 percent for the government to be able to sell the bonds at all.[15] This increased interest payments that the government needed to make and quickly spiraled to make the situation worse instead of better.

By May of 1998, the CBR was not selling enough bonds to cover its upcoming debt obligations, and soon after the demand was so low the auctions were canceled altogether. This made the government's position untenable, as it had begun using the GKO auctions not only for debt service, but also to finance cash flow needs. At the same time, the CBR increased lending rates to banks from 30 to 50 percent, then again to 150 percent hoping to increase deposits in rubles. This not only did not increase ruble deposits, but also worked to destroy lending in the country as banks were certain that at such rates business loans would not be repaid that they basically stopped lending altogether.[16]

The Role of the Private Sector

The blame for the economic collapse cannot be laid completely on the government. Although its policies were the major factor leading to the crisis, Russia's private industry did much to harm the economy as well. One of the most important sectors of a developing free market economy is banking. By taking deposits and lending a portion of these deposits out, banks create money supply and create growth in the economy. Russian banks during this time were doing just the opposite; they were taking state money given to them as seed money to spur lending and using it to make currency bets against the ruble.[17] To this day, the commercial banking sector in Russia has not properly developed its intermediation role, and good corporate credits often get directed to the global credit market instead of borrowing from domestic banks.

One can also look to the country's other businesses as a source of disappointment. Many of the privatized companies were handed over to old-guard Russian managers often referred to as *red directors* who cared little about corporate profits and more about lining their own pockets at the expense of the companies they ran and their employees. Many of the newly minted oligarchs were of little help as well. They took most of their newfound riches and quickly invested them in other countries. Pleas by Yeltsin for them to start investing in Russia fell on deaf ears.[18]

The country's elite did not have the institutional memory or experience base or regulatory, fiscal, or monetary policies necessary to make correct decisions when facing questions of first impression.

The Lasting Effects of the 1998 Crisis

The financial crisis of 1998, although economically devastating for the fledgling free market experiment in Russia, has taught Russia some valuable lessons on fiscal management that the country has taken to heart. Much of what is seen today in how Russia controls its economic policies can be traced back to lessons learned since the crisis. From the fall of the Soviet Union until the 1998 crisis, the Russian government followed most of the advice given to it by Western "experts." This advice came from many different sources, from the International Monetary Fund (IMF) to Harvard professors. The problem was that, at times, this advice was contradictory or inconsistent but not necessarily wrong. It is important to get advice from different viewpoints, but it is also important to be able to vet the advice given and choose which advice to take, requiring an experience base that Russia did not have. Making choices and correct decisions is the basis for competent leadership.

The process of sorting through all of the advice being given was something that the Russian government was not prepared to do at the time. Russia had been a communist state for most of the twentieth century and had very little in the way of competent free market economic and fiscal expertise. This led to many inadvertent errors in decision making that helped lead to the 1998 collapse. Since that time, Russia has made a large effort toward developing the free market expertise needed to guide the country's economy into the future. This training began at Western schools and has now been transferred into Russia itself with schools such as Moscow State University Higher School of Economics and New Economic School, both considered world-class economics institutions. This emphasis on developing the internal expertise to manage its own economy has led to an excellent record of fiscal management and an increased confidence in Russia's ability to rely on its own judgments.

This newfound confidence in managing its economy, coupled with its impressive recent track record, has led Russia to veer slightly from the course of development most favored by the West. This course correction, while mostly accepted in the European Union, has met with skepticism in the United States. Many believe that the government's recent decisions on retaining some government control in industries such as oil and natural gas represent backsliding from free-market reforms. In the view of the Russian government, these moves are deemed as important as a way to help insulate their economy from mismanagement or misuse of the country's all-important natural resources.

The country is determined not to have a repeat of the 1998 crisis, and some of these moves can be seen as a way to help shield them from such a reoccurrence. The management of economic policy in Russia can also be seen as a way for the country to reestablish its national identity. Although they are adamant about continuing democratic and free market reforms, and "public/private" is clearly the Kremlin's governing ethic today, Russia is just as adamant about doing it the Russian Way. This conflict manifests itself between Finance Minister Kudrin's emphasis on fiscal discipline and the desires of the "siloviki" (Russian for "power," commonly used to describe ex-military and KGB officers now in government positions) to spend resources on military and other government projects which would be more inflationary.

The Putin Era

Vladimir Putin (see Figure 1.2) is Russia's third transformational president in a row. He is not a politician. He did not work his way up the Communist Party apparatus, as did Gorbechev and Yeltsin. He is capable

of personal charm, as his early relations with his opposite number U.S.
president demonstrated. Evidently,
he possesses a visible soul. But he
is a limp-wristed, no eye contact,
one foot in front of the other, no
drinking at lunch career bureaucrat.
What he is—is competent. After
the chaotic, somewhat lawless, and
oligarch-wild Yeltsin years, Russians
are happy to have more stability,
order and competence, and professionalism in the execution of the
nation's affairs.

Figure 1.2   Vladimir Putin, Second President of the Russian Federation

Putin has been very highly esteemed at home. But, as the Russian economy has progressed into the busting-its-buttons phase of its growth and Russia is asserting its interests as it sees them, he has come to be less esteemed abroad. When Russia aspired only to become a normal country, everything was fine. Now that Putin has decided Russia needs to be once again a great power, international relations have suffered. Not a crowd crawler, Putin exercises his media prowess by appearing on TV to take hours of questions from voters across the country, and Russians are wowed by his grasp of detailed issues of day-to-day government and his professionalism.

The Putin years have been characterized by a public/private model, fiscal discipline, ruble stability, superb macroeconomic management, dramatic GDP growth—and backsliding on first-amendment–type rights. There can be no defense of the Kremlin's smothering of objective news reporting on TV. But, there was a history here. Many of the TV stations had been acquired by individual oligarchs during the free-wheeling 1990s as a bully pulpit and the government ended up inheriting these assets one way or another.

But appointing, rather than electing, governors is discretionary under the Russian constitution, based on the French model. Elected regional governors had frequently proven to be corrupt or incompetent or both. Hopefully, in a *federal* system (not a unitary government, as in France) for a country so large, authority will be allowed to devolve to the regions through local elections in the future. Fiscal relations among local, regional, and national governments are extremely complex, even in the United States. As to actual power and responsibility, in a meeting with the Tver Governor Zelinin, he maintained that the center has asked the regions to take on more responsibility for health and education, for example, and has also supplied the necessary funding. So there is today more local authority in some areas critical to people's day-to-day lives than has ever been the case in Russia.

From Bankrupt to Boom: Economic Management in the Putin Era

The management of Russia's economy under Putin's leadership has been a point of constant criticism in the West due to what is perceived as increased government control of business. Although this has been true in certain sectors of the economy, especially natural resources, it is actually far from the truth in the overall economy. The Russian economy is now more privatized than most of the emerging markets in the world, as well as some of its Western European counterparts such as Italy or France.

Putin's two terms as the president of the Russian Federation have been marked by fundamental improvements in the Russian economy and its fiscal management. Under Putin's leadership, Russia has become one of the most conservative examples of fiscal management in the emerging markets, if not the world (for example, in the European Union, Italy, Portugal, and Greece frequently sport theoretically impermissibly large budget deficits). In fact, Russia is one of the only oil-exporting nations that is not endemically corrupt. (But, see Chapter 2.) Instead of the oil revenue received from today's high oil prices going to line the pockets of a handful of royals or to help prop up a dysfunctional government, Russia has created a *Stabilization Fund* to hold the government's sizable portion of the oil revenues. This fund, created in 2004, acts a receiver for the government's oil profits tax that takes nearly 90 percent of all oil profits when the price of oil exceeds \$25 per barrel.[19] This money is put into the Stabilization Fund to help keep inflation low by not spending it and to provide a rainy-day fund for domestic projects.

The Russian government, under the direction of Putin, has been continuing to work on divesting the government's stake in many industries. The most notable example of this divestiture has been the Russian utility sector. The Russian government has been working to privatize the electricity sector in Russia, including large generation companies and distribution companies, by slowly reducing the ownership stake it holds in electricity companies and selling more shares on the open market. The country has also been working toward complete privatization of the wireline telephone industry (the cell phone companies have been private start-ups from the beginning).

Priority National Projects

Flush with fiscal surpluses and huge monetary reserves from nine straight years of economic growth, in 2006 to 2007 Russia began to focus on spending some of this surplus on domestic priorities. This new focus was probably in no small part due to the upcoming elections for the State Duma in December 2007 and for president in March 2008. This focus on domestic priorities is evidenced by what the Kremlin refers to as its Priority National Projects (PNP). These projects are designed to alleviate some of the social and economic deprivations that still face Russians years after the transition to a capitalist economy. The four areas of focus for the Priority National Projects are (1) public health, (2) education, (3) housing, and (4) agriculture. Putin has elevated the PNPs by creating a Presidential Council for Implementing Priority National Projects, headed by First Deputy Prime Minister Dmitry Medvedev, who was designated by Putin to succeed him as President.[20]

Health Care The first Priority National Project is improving health care in the country. Russia currently has a declining population, falling at a rate of almost one-half of one percent per year, or about three-quarters of a million people per year. The major reason for this declining population is an extraordinarily high death rate, especially among working-age males, who make up 80 percent of working-age deaths. The life expectancy among women in Russia is a respectable 74, but for males it is only 60. This can be attributed to high rates of cardiovascular disease, alcoholism, and often dangerous workplace conditions. The country also suffers from a prevalence of malignant diseases, especially tuberculosis and HIV/AIDS, which the current health care system cannot adequately manage.[21]

The priority health care initiative is designed to bring better-quality health care to all Russian citizens. The health care plan envisions creating more advanced medical facilities in all of Russia's regions to handle medical specialties, including cardiology and oncology. These new first-class facilities will serve as the backbone for a completely reorganized health care system in Russia. The country has already begun this reorganization by changing the way hospitals and clinics are funded, from being funded based on the number of beds and staff they employ to funding based on the number of patients that are treated. To ensure citizens are able to take advantage of these new facilities, the country wants to increase the number of people eligible for federal-funded aid by 400 percent by the end of 2008.

The health care plan also envisions a more efficient primary care apparatus where more people are able to receive quality care from local doctors. Russia has a very high per capita rate of doctors in the country, but the utilization of these professionals has been inefficient and centered in Russia's largest cities. The country plans to push for reorganization of these primary care physicians to provide for a more even distribution of health care services throughout Russia's cities and rural areas. Part of this plan encompasses increases in pay for all medical professionals, from doctors and nurses to emergency responders. To help increase the effectiveness of emergency respond-ers, the government plans to increase the number of first aid vehi-cles, modernize the fleet of existing vehicles, and install a modern communications system for the medical first responders.[22]

The PNP of modernizing health care goes along with the focus of solving the demographic problem that is plaguing Russia. According to Vladimir Putin, the country's declining population threatens "the survival of the nation" and he describes the problem as "one of the most alarming that the country faces." The primary solution to this problem is the improvement of health care in the country, which is one reason that the responsibilities for demographic programs have been shifted to the Presidential Council for Implementation of Priority National Projects. Putin has also become more aggressive in calling on businesses to improve safety conditions at workplaces to reduce the number of injuries and deaths of working-age men. The government has started programs to encourage women, through financial inducements, to have more than one child, as well as pro-grams to take care of Russia's 200,000-plus orphan population.

The first program enacted provides for *childbirth certificates* and monthly financial aid for mothers of newborns. The childbirth cer-tificate amounts to 3,000 rubles (about $120) for mothers having their child in a pregnancy center or 7,000 rubles (about $280) for mother having their child at a maternity home. This childbirth cer-tificate is designed to help offset the cost to the mother of medicines, healthcare, and baby supplies. The mother is also eligible for financial aid from the government of 40 percent of salary for working moth-ers and up to 3,000 rubles per month for nonworking mothers. This monthly aid is paid until the child reaches one and one-half and is designed to make it easier on families to decide on having children by defraying some of the financial costs.[23]

The second program instituted for fostering childbirth is the *maternity capital* program. This program gives an incentive to families to have a second child. The maternity capital program provides for a one-time payment to the mother of 250,000 rubles (about $10,000), soon to be increased to 400,000 rubles (about $16,000), after the child reaches the age of three. The mother has the option of having the money deposited directly into her pension account or taking it as a payment. The payment option is designed so that the family can use the money for a variety of needs, including home improvements, the purchase of a new house, or child educational expenses.[24]

Russia currently has a very large orphan population and, adding to the demographic problem, more orphans are adopted into foreign countries than are placed in Russia. To assist in finding homes for the 200,000-plus orphans currently in Russia, in addition to improving the orphanage conditions, the government is working to expand the benefits it pay to foster families and adoptive parents. This program consists of increasing the monthly payments to foster parents to 4,000 rubles (about $160) and increasing the state-paid wage of foster parents, a second source of payment, to 2,500 rubles (about $100). The plan also calls for an increase in the one-time payment to the foster family to 8,000 rubles (about $320) regardless of the situation in which the child is taken in.[25]

Education Education is another of Russia's PNPs. Although the Russian education system has produced a population with a literacy rate of 99.6 percent,[26] the country is facing a lack of graduates with the necessary skills to compete in Russia's fast-changing, global economy. The first step in this program has been to bring technology into all schools in Russia. The government plans to have all of its schools connected to the Internet with high-speed access by 2008.[27] The plans include a new pay scale for primary teachers and headmasters that would make teaching more attractive while providing for bonuses to the best teachers to help reward and retain the country's best instructors. Also outlined is a plan to work with businesses and schools to create vocational education schools that would provide skilled workers with the input of the companies helping to create the programs and ultimately, employing the students.[28]

Higher education is the major point of emphasis for the education PNP. The Kremlin would like to see university students graduate with more relevant and useful educations. The government plans to create a new nationwide consortium of universities that would focus on world-class business and economics classes, scientific research and education, and technology research and education. These schools will be formed as a public–private model with the government supplying funds in conjunction with business interests in the country who would help build relevant curriculum and fund research initiatives. The government would also like to make higher education more attainable to more of the population through a combination of grants to talented young scientists and a government effort to create incentives for banks to provide low-cost student loans, as well as provide for competitive secondary education in the military system.[29]

Housing Russia's housing situation is also of particular concern to Putin. He has repeatedly stressed the importance of making modern housing available to more of the population. A vast majority of the population of Russia still live in old, Soviet-era, apartments that provide only a basic standard of living. As Putin stated in his Annual Address to the Federal Assembly in 2004, only 10 percent of Russians currently live in modern housing. His goal is to have at least one third of the population in modern housing by 2010.[30] The first part of the plan that the government is currently working on is efforts to ease the license and tax burdens that prove to be an obstacle against private owners making investments into their current homes, as well as rewriting licensing, zoning, and tax code to make it easier for apartment owners to form homeowners' associations to provide for shared upkeep and maintenance of the properties. In his 2007 Annual Address, Putin requested that the government create a program to spend 150 billion rubles to help finance home repairs, plus another 100 billion rubles (about $400 million) to help people move out of dilapidated housing.[31]

The primary focus of the PNP on housing is the creation of new, modern, energy-efficient homes that are affordable for more of the population. The government plans to achieve this goal not through government spending, but by creating an environment of lower interest rates. Lower interest rates on mortgage loans will make mortgage payments more affordable for the average Russian. The government hopes that by making mortgage rates lower for buyers and by making mortgage lending more attractive to banks, they can triple the amount of mortgage loans in two years. The Kremlin would also like to put into effect a system that provides for incentives to spur home ownership by new families and military personnel. This would be accomplished through special loan programs, government housing subsidies, or a combination of both.[32]

Agriculture The final PNP is the project focusing on agriculture in the country. One of the goals of this project is to increase spending on housing programs to lure young, educated graduates to move to the rural regions in an attempt to populate and increase the economic viability of Russia's rural regions, reversing urban migration, though this might prove to be whistling in the wind. The primary goal of the agriculture project is to provide for low-cost loans for agriculture businesses.[33] Along with low-cost loans, the government would like to remove the bureaucratic hurdles involved in registering farm land as private property.[34] It is hoped that these measures will spur private investment in farmland to make the country's agriculture more productive, more efficient, and more competitive in the European market.

Russia's Crumbling Infrastructure Aside from the four primary PNPs, there are a number of smaller projects assigned to the Presidential Council for Implementation of Priority National Projects. In addition to the demographic problem already discussed, the country has embarked on a substantial project to improve the country's infrastructure. In his 2007 Annual Address to the Federal Assembly, Putin outlined the improvement of the country's transportation infrastructure as a project of prime importance because the poor state of the country's current infrastructure is costing Russia at least 3 percent of its GDP annually. The government plans to invest in better rail transit and has already begun a project to improve the country's strategic airports to make it easier to travel within the country. An important part of the project on infrastructure is, for the first time, using toll roads to finance the construction of much-needed highways in the country.[35]

President Putin has also repeatedly stressed the importance of creating what he calls *an effective state*. He has pressured the government, especially local governments, to take a leading role in battling corruption by increasing efforts to investigate and prosecute corruption in all levels of government as well as private businesses. He strongly believes that corruption not only reduces public trust in the government, but hinders the country's development as a free-market economy.[36] Along with tackling corruption, the Kremlin plans to finance projects that help to modernize and diversify the economy through incentives for investments in modern production equipment and for high-tech research and development.

The final important domestic project for Russia is the modernization of its armed forces. Contrary to the beliefs of many in the West, Russia by no means wants to prepare for a new cold war, as it feels it is more important to spend its money on social programs. The Kremlin does, however, want to upgrade its neglected military to become a smaller, more modern, globally capable force. To meet this goal, the country has been increasing spending on refurbishing some of its Soviet-era equipment, increasing education and housing for soldiers, and has decreased the mandatory conscription from 18 months to 12 months. Defense Minister Sergei Ivanov's stated goal was to have every young Russian male receive basic training, then supplementing the army by a professional career core force.

The PNPs, along with other domestic projects, form a very large pledge from the Russian government to increase spending on social projects. The important aspect of many of these pledges, one that is often overlooked, is that they focus on creating public–private partnerships to solve the problems facing the country. This fact shows the growing importance of the private sector in Russia's development. The government's plan calls for partnerships with Russian businesses for education programs as well as calling on banks and government to work together to provide for loans that will finance programs such as student loans, agriculture lending, and low-cost mortgage lending. The Priority National Projects, then, are focused not just for their benefit to society in general, but also for their economic value citing the potential for positive returns on investments.[37]

President Putin highlighted the importance of domestic projects in his Annual Address to the Federal Assembly in 2007. In his speech, he stressed the importance of implementing these projects as soon as possible and backed up his words with pledges to increase funding to these domestic priorities. In his 2007 Annual Address, Putin for the first time hinted at the possibility of using money from the Stabilization Fund to finance domestic initiatives. The government has also decided to split the Stabilization Fund into two separate funds, the Reserve Fund and the Fund for Future Generations. The Reserve Fund will initially be set at 10 percent of Russia's GDP and will replace the Stabilization Fund as the country's rainy-day savings account to help insulate the economy from sharp drops in the price of oil or natural gas. The Fund for Future Generations will be financed from excess revenues from oil exports that are not included into either the Reserve Fund or the federal budget. This fund will be used to finance domestic projects as well as create an extra savings to cover the government's growing pension liabilities.[38]

Dmitry Medvedev

As mentioned, the Priority National Projects have been the responsibility of First Deputy Prime Minister Dmitry Medvedev (Figure 1.3)

Figure 1.3   Dmitry Medvedev, First Deputy Prime Minister of the Russian Federation and Chairman of the Board of Gazprom
Courtesy of Gazprom www.gazprom.com.

who is slated to succeed Putin as President. Medvedev was born in St. Petersburg, formerly named Leningrad, in 1965. He graduated with a degree in law from Leningrad State University in 1987 and attained a Ph.D. in private law from the school in 1990. After obtaining his Ph.D. in law, Medvedev served as an assistant law professor at the school he graduated from, now called St. Petersburg State University, from 1991 until 1999. He co-authored a civil law textbook used in the state university system. From 1990 to 1995, Medvedev also contributed to the City of St. Petersburg as a legal expert for the city and acted as an expert consultant to the Mayor's Committee for External Relations, which was then headed by Vladimir Putin.[39]

In 1999, after Boris Yeltsin stepped down and appointed Vladimir Putin to replace him, Medvedev found himself headed to Moscow as part of the new administration. He started out as the deputy chief of staff to the Government of the Russian Federation, soon becoming the deputy head of the presidential administration in January 2000. In January 2000, Medvedev also became the head of Putin's presidential election campaign headquarters, helping to orchestrate Putin's successful election bid. Following Putin's election, Medvedev was appointed first deputy head of the presidential administration and, in 2003, the head of the presidential administration. He served in this position until late 2005, when he became first deputy prime minister of the Russian Federation.[40]

In his position as a first deputy prime minister, Medvedev has been put in charge of the Priority National Projects as well as other domestic projects under the purview of Presidential Council for Implementing Priority National Projects. He is considered by most as a protégé of Putin, although considered slightly more pro-Western and pro-business, and would bring with him to the presidency a political ideology that he describes as European.

Medvedev also has been chairman of the Board of Gazprom, Russia's largest public company and third largest in the world. During his tenure at Gazprom, Medvedev has helped oversee the company's rapid growth and modernization. In 2001, Gazprom had total revenues of just over $20 billion. By 2007, the company has shown a fourfold increase of revenues to an estimated $80 billion, along with a fifty-nine-fold increase in net profits.[41]

The Challenges of Democracy

The recent death of a truly transformational figure, the first president of the Russian Federation, Boris Yeltsin, is a reminder that Russia's road from communism to democracy has not been smooth, straight, or easily traveled. The current state of the Russian political system seems to evidence this fact. To the dismay of the West, and many of its own people, Russia's political system has gradually backslid on first amendment-type rights since Putin succeeded Yeltsin as Russia's president. The Yeltsin years produced great changes in Russia's political landscape and allowed for free press and open media. Yeltsin's reforms, though, also went uncontrolled and led to huge abuses by newly minted oligarchs and crime syndicates, a time seen by many as somewhat lawless and chaotic. A small amount of assertion of power by the federal government was to be expected by Putin as he sought to bring law and order to the country.

Looking at Russia leading up to the State Duma elections in late 2007 and presidential election in early 2008, it became obvious that state control has continued to increase in all facets of Russian society. The Russian government has gained control of the three major television stations in Russia, either through direct ownership or through ownership by government-controlled natural gas giant Gazprom, and has severely limited any anti-government sentiment on these channels. The government has also worked to reign in one of the few independent television stations, REN-TV, by pressuring it through its investment bank to lighten up on negative coverage of the government. The state control of television in Russia led Mikhail Gorbechev, the former Soviet leader known for *perestroika,* to remark, "The one thing I can say is that it's pointless today to watch television."[42]

Television has been the first, and most successful, target of the Russian government, which is now working on gaining more content control of other media outlets as well. As elections came up on the horizon, the Kremlin asserted its control over some radio stations. One station, Russian News Service, the largest independent radio news network, was told by its new ownership that it was to report at least 50 percent good news, that opposition leaders were not allowed to be mentioned on air, and that the United States was to be portrayed as an enemy of Russia.[43] With Russian Internet usage rising at nearly 100 percent per year, the Kremlin has been attempting to find ways to control the content of Internet news sites and to monitor dissent on chat room and Web forums. The government has had some limited success in this area by having the Federal Security Service of the Russian Federation (FSB) question those who post anti-government messages on the Internet. These people can often be difficult to track down, so the government has been increasingly putting pressure on

Web sites to control their content and limit anti-government messages. Failure to comply can lead to a Web site being taken offline, or the government putting pressure on the host of the Web site, essentially paving the way for the site to be taken offline.

This was the case when the Web host for anticompromat.ru, an anti-Putin Web site, was forced to find a U.S. host after its Russian host was pressured by the government to stop hosting the site. The Kremlin has also been trying to pass legislation that would formalize this already somewhat enforced ban on "extremist" content on the Internet. The Russian Parliament recently passed a law imposing prison sentences of up to three years for "vandalism motivated by politics or ideology." This law is already being tested, as Moscow prosecutors are attempting to try a case against a person who posted remarks critical of a Parliament member on a Web site.[44]

The Kremlin has also been exerting its control over open demonstrations of political opposition. This is evidenced by the actions of the government toward protests by an opposition group called *Other Russia*. Other Russia is a political group formed by a coalition of anti-government groups that is led by former chess champion Garry Kasparov and former Russian Prime Minister Mikhail Kasyanov. In December 2006, the group held its first rally in Moscow called the "March of the Discontented." The group held a second rally in March 2007 in St. Petersburg, which drew a limited following. In April 2007, the group held two rallies over one weekend in both Moscow and St. Petersburg.[45]

Both of these demonstrations were broken up with federal riot police. The demonstration in Moscow was broken up with brutal force, with Garry Kasparov and Mikhail Kasyanov both being arrested and questioned by the FSB. The government's official reason for the strong-handed response to the demonstration was that Other Russia did not have a permit to march because a pro-Kremlin youth group happened to get a permit minutes before Other Russia applied. Although Other Russia had a permit for a rally, the fact that some supporters walked a few blocks turned it into a *march,* leading to a violation of their permit.[46] Days after the weekend demonstrations, the National Bolshevik Party, a small fringe group that is part of the

Other Russia coalition, was stripped of its official party status and labeled an *extremist organization.*

The Kremlin's tough stance against dissent has not been limited to domestic groups. It has turned its attention to nongovernmental organizations (NGOs) operating inside Russia. The first action by the government was to impose strict new rules on NGOs requiring all foreign NGOs to reregister with the government and provide detailed information about their activities and financing sources.[47] As part of the government crackdown, police raided the offices of the Educated Media Foundation, an NGO funded by U.S. and European interests that focuses on fostering independent news media, and seized documents and computers. Some of the computers were being used to host Web sites that encouraged free press, causing these sites to be shut down.[48]

Days before the December 2007 Duma elections, I met with seven leading Russian intellectuals from various think tanks, consultancies, and the Academy of Sciences (Sociology). The consensus seemed to be that Russia could never be a democracy because it had once been ruled by a tsar; that Russians needed a strong hand at the top. Still, they displayed a wide range of condemnations of current government policy and practice. Free speech abounded, but negativity in general reigned. I believe I discovered the prime source drawn upon by Western media and think tanks for negativity on Russia.

Summary

The West currently has some serious misgivings about Russia's recent backsliding on political freedoms (first-amendment–type rights) and many of these misgivings are well founded, while others are not (more on this in Chapter 10). One can look at Russia's political landscape as a pendulum, with government (public) control on one side and business (private) control on the other. For decades, under the Soviet system, the pendulum was stuck all the way over to the government control side. During the period of rapid privatization in the early to mid-1990s, business owners, the newly minted oligarchs, came to control most of the major media outlets while corruption and influence allowed them control over government, pushing the pendulum rapidly over to the business side.

Polls showed the Russian public outrage at the oligarch's excesses. Unfortunately, this was also the period during which democratic institutions were introduced. What is happening now can be seen as a possible overreaction to this earlier swing, pushing the pendulum beyond equilibrium toward the government control side. As the Russian democracy continues to grow and evolve, it is possible that the pendulum will work its way toward the middle.

Russia's putative next President Dmitry Medvedev delivered a progressive manifesto to the 2nd All-Russia Civic Forum congress on January 22, 2008. Stressing investment in human capital and the PNPs' main elements, he appeared to signal a greater degree of self-government, at least locally, and personal freedoms going forward. We shall see. Please read the Medvedev manifesto, posted on www .tmrussia.com.

Chapter 2

Investing in Russia: Risk/Reward

Before exploring Russia's rebirth as it affects Russians' daily lives, in the places where they work to earn their rapidly rising incomes, we should set out the usual framework foreigners use when approaching any market for investment. Whether you are an individual portfolio investor looking for the superior returns from global investing or investing in emerging markets or you work with an international company contemplating a direct investment in the Russian market, you (and your management) will want to assess any such opportunity in terms of risk and reward.

Risks of Investing in Russia

Given the huge run-up in the Russian stock market in recent years, the reward part of the equation is problematic: Can Russian investments possibly continue the returns experienced in the recent past? Hopefully, this book will help clarify these prospects.

On the risk front, three categories of risk are central to any decision to go into Russia: (1) currency risk, (2) oil risk, and (3) political risk.

Currency Risk

One of the major causes of the 1998 financial crisis was the government's attempt to keep the ruble's exchange rate pegged at an unreasonably high 5 to 6 rubles per U.S. dollar. A major step forward in allowing the Russian economy to grow was allowing the ruble's exchange rate to float freely against the U.S. dollar. This step was very difficult at first because it was painful both psychologically and physically as Russia's GDP per capita plunged, but it has yielded great rewards. The former high exchange rate made Russian exports more expensive on the world markets, while, at the same time, making imported goods cheaper on the Russian market.

Once the ruble was allowed to depreciate significantly against the dollar, Russian exports became much cheaper and more competitive in the world markets, while Russian goods became competitive against imports in the Russian market. This has helped lead to nearly a decade of consistent growth in the Russian economy, while instilling confidence in the ruble. The government has done an impressive job in managing its currency, with currency reserves that now top $440 billion,[1] the third largest currency reserves in the world, after Japan and China. This has made the ruble a nearly impregnable currency by world standards, with the Central Bank of Russia (CBR) having an immense amount of resources at its disposal to overcome nearly any eventuality.

This newfound confidence in the ruble is very important for the country moving forward. In the past, uncertainty over the ruble's stability and the future of the economy meant that most Russians would quickly exchange their rubles for dollars and would generally hide these dollars under the mattresses. Now that the ruble has been relatively stable for nearly a decade—in fact, it has been appreciating against the dollar by nearly 10 percent per year[2]—a majority of Russians are becoming comfortable depositing their money in the banks as rubles (and a foreign investor, such as a U.S. mutual fund, also stands to enjoy these returns). This trend works to continue economic expansion as more rubles deposited in Russian banks correlate to more rubles that the banks have available to lend to businesses and consumers, creating even more growth and leading to an advantageous cycle of growth.

In recent years, due to the continuing economic strength of the Russian trade surplus and economy, the ruble has appreciated against the dollar continuously. Many foreign currencies have proven to be good investments in and of themselves in an environment of the weakening dollar, given the continuing trade deficits of the United States.

The Government of Russia has limited its direct expenditures on social programs in an attempt to control inflation. As a result, it has not expended its surpluses, which have built up smartly. Also, in recent years, given the high price of oil, the windfall profits regime in place has taken much of the upside away from private oil companies and has resulted in the Stabilization Fund increasing as well. The result has been a Central Bank of Russia with enough reserves to provide a great deal of leeway to control Russia's currency, and, in turn, inflation, as well as a large Stabilization Fund to provide a cushion against oil-price fluctuations.

The bottom line is that the Russian ruble is currently one of the world's strongest currencies and currency risk is therefore among the least in the world. In fact, if the past is prologue, investors can count on a nice floor to any investment in Russia, the currency delivering a modest but dependable return in and of itself year after year.

Oil Risk

A major misconception by investors in the Russian market is that Russian oil companies are directly impacted by swings in the price of oil. Although this is true to a limited extent, a government tax imposed in 2002 makes the effects much less pronounced on company earnings. The tax code gives the government about 89 percent of all revenue from exported crude at prices above $25 per barrel.

At the current price levels of oil (2007 saw price levels of $70, $80, even $90 per barrel, and oil actually hit $100 a barrel at the beginning of 2008), the impact of small price swings on Russian oil companies is much less dramatic than financial markets would generally assume. The tax code also stipulates a tax of about 73 percent on all exported refined products. This is an attempt by the government to promote the production of more value-added products as well as help insulate the country's refining businesses. Russia currently exports approximately 70 percent of the crude it extracts from the ground, and almost half of it (44 percent) is exported as refined product.[3] Most exports are to CIS countries and, of course, domestic sales are price controlled.

The government takes the money it receives from the oil tax and deposits it into the Stabilization Fund, briefly discussed in Chapter 1. The fund serves two purposes: It keeps much of the oil money from going back into the economy, and it provides a rainy-day fund. In 2007, the Stabilization Fund held more than $140 billion,[4] or about 10 percent of the country's gross domestic product (GDP). The Stabilization Fund will be discussed in greater detail later in this chapter.

The numbers highlight the main reason for the fund: to keep money out of the economy. This much money entering the Russian economy would put enormous pressure on inflation, causing it to soar, which would cause massive problems for a country whose citizens still have a long way to go before they reach average European wages and living standards. Taking money out of the economy is referred to as *sterilization*.

The second part of the Stabilization Fund's purpose is to provide a safety net for the economy should oil prices fall dramatically. The Kremlin has stated its desire to move the Stabilization Fund from being solely dependent on oil to becoming a more inclusive of the entire economy by indexing it to GDP instead of oil prices. This shows that the Russian economy is quickly diversifying as oil's share of GDP is becoming smaller every year—not because of lack of growth in the oil industry, but because of rapid growth in domestic consumer industries.

Political Risk

Words that are on the tips of peoples' tongues when they hear about Russia are *crime* and *corruption,* so before moving into a discussion about Russian businesses, a little background on the topic of perennial interest is in order. This has been a moving target, but it is possible to make some general points.

After the fall of the Soviet Union, the first "crime wave" of which I was aware, in the early 1990s, was Chechen gangs coming up into Moscow and committing horrible and brutal crimes. This was well before the first Chechen War and this fact, of course, did not endear Chechens to Muscovites.

Next, since nothing was for sale in the state-run shops in existing structures as privatization had not yet taken place, masses of kiosks appeared on the curbsides, and the protection rackets started. These first two developments were often interrelated.

The mayor of Moscow quite rightly objected to taxpaying shops being sidelined and, after privatization of these shops to their managers and employees, the kiosks were removed by ordinance.

There have always been complaints about petty bribe taking among low-level bureaucrats and this goes back generations in Russia as in many other places. Read *The Inspector General* by Nikolai Gogol (1842). Notorious examples are cited in the press about border guards accepting bribes to let terrorists through and onto airplanes, but the most ordinary experience the average person has is with the traffic police who fine violators on the spot. This is a legal system in many countries. My own personal experience has been that the two fines I paid were deserved, since I had committed the infraction and the amount was not much. I leave it to the reader to assess whether this is official corruption. In Prague, Czech Republic, I was also fined on the spot, where the officer tore pages out of a chit book conferring a receipt for my payment on the spot. Maybe, if Russians adopted this receipt device, some of the perception of police corruption would be ameliorated.

The activities of organized crime in Russia appear to be focused on gambling, prostitution, and drugs, not on areas directly affecting

businesses. There have been numerous gangs and official corruption—
and the patterns shift. Just as corporate corruption has abated thanks
to tax reform and an attempt by the Putin administration to reduce
the burdens involved in licensing and permitting (always an opportunity for bribe taking), higher-level bribe seeking in government seems
to be increasing. This is probably due to any given deputy minister's
envy for Russia's young billionaires ("He took it; why not me?").

Many of Russia's oligarchs got their start with some pretty brutal
conduct, including murder. Assassinations are still too frequent, not
just of journalists, but also among business rivals. Fortunately, the government of Russia apprehended the banker who hired the assassins of
Deputy Central Banker Andrei Kozlov, who had done yeoman work
cleaning up the banking business, including yanking the license of
the aggrieved murderer.

Political risk, of course, also relates to the world arena and international relations, between Russia and the United States, between
Russia and its neighbors, the *near abroad,* between Russia and the
European Union, Great Britain, China, and the other nations of
the world. Many issues in these arenas are of prime interest to think
tanks and others mentioned in Chapter 10, "Discovering the Real
Russia." Russia has not done a great job in managing the various
criticisms directed at it, some deserved, some not. Clearly, this international dimension affects investors' appetites for Russia securities,
as in the major British sell-off when Russia refused to extradite to
Britain a suspect in the notorious Litvinenko case. Generally, though,
this arena is beyond the purview of this book.

The heightened political-risk discount imputed to Russian stocks
in the first part of 2007 does seem to stem more from Russia's inadequate handling of the public relations dimensions of various international friction points with the United States, Great Britain, Estonia,
Georgia, and other countries. As mentioned, like any major player,
be it British Petroleum or the City of New York, criticisms are constantly thrown and must be fielded competently. Assuming, on merits,
the various friction points have solutions, still Russia has frequently
overreacted and made matters worse.

Perhaps, ironically, Russia's international standing would have been higher had President Putin decided to answer the call of his countrymen for a third four-year term as president of Russia. After all, when his time in office seemed lengthy, his focus was simply on Russia becoming a normal country. Only after he began to contemplate his limited tenure in office did he begin to worry about his legacy and decide to kick it up a notch, to make Russia, "once again, a great country." This self-start toward greatness has not gone well internationally. At home, however, polls indicate the Russian people applaud such efforts.

Rule of Law

The rule of law takes a generation or more to instill in this or any population, but the Putin administration has placed considerable emphasis on promoting it by increasing the professionalism of judges. This does not come naturally to a population that has been brutalized for decades and has never experienced being able to defend their civil rights through due legal process.

You can spend time negotiating a contract, but when a problem develops, the instinct of a Russian businessman is not to ask what the governing document says but to pick up the phone and say: "Igor you got me into this mess; get me out of it." Whether business culture will develop along rule-of-law lines and whether a highly legalistic culture is in anyone's best interests anyway, only time will tell. Better to do your level best to maintain good working relations with the other side in any transaction so problems can be dealt with amicably. (On the international level, the conservative would be the school of thought that says that treaties can only remain in force when they continue to be in each country's national interest.) The written word may not mean much.

Many of the new laws in the corporate arena and the Civil Code, as with the Constitution, are fine. American experts were frequently there to help in this effort over the last 15 years. The future will bring questions of interpretation and enforcement.

As to the role of the security services in Russia, this is a very troubling subject. In many formerly communist countries, these people have all been drummed out of government service. Generally, this has occurred in Central Europe, in occupied or conquered countries after World War II, and those acting in league with a foreign country (namely, the Soviet Union) are seen as in no way performing a loyal act.

In the case of Russia itself, as mentioned, it gave up on communism and was not solely defeated by the United States or anyone else. The old system was dysfunctional, and continuing on the communist path was simply not in the national interest. Presumably, leaders in the security services shared this estimate. Putin himself served in the KGB in East Germany over a period of years and studied the workings of its business economy. Evidently, he has put these lessons to use and, in that regard, he, like Peter the Great, performs a great service to his nation.

However, members of Department 5 of the KGB routinely performed unspeakable acts of cruelty and abuse against their fellow citizens, and I would hope that many of these people have been sent packing. Quite candidly, my perception is that my own business, our life insurance business—which prospered for several years—was adversely impacted by the security services, so I am reluctant to speak further on this subject—not that I have any specific information, in any event.

Regulatory Atmosphere

As mentioned, in the 1990s, we Americans were of material assistance to the Russian Federation in the establishment of its securities markets and regulatory systems, which, as in our own case, depend heavily on self-regulation by the professional securities industry participants. It is not an exaggeration to state that the Russian Trading System (RTS) has established a level of trust and confidence that puts it at an upper tier, certainly among emerging markets. More work needs to be done, like setting up a central depository regime such as our DTC (Depositary Trust Company), but improvements are constant.

The yearly timetable for disclosure by Russian public companies bears a heavy resemblance to what we see in U.S. markets: 10K-type annual reports, 10Q-like quarterly reports complete with teleconferences with the CFO, proxy statements, annual meetings, and so forth.

As we have seen, much of the progress in corporate transparency and disclosure owes more to the Yukos affair and tax code reform, but regulatory effectiveness by the independent Federal Securities Market Commission has played an important role. Also, effective in addressing corruption and financial irregularities in general has been the Federal Financial Monitoring Service (Russia's anti–money laundering agency). President Putin's commitment to this work and to attacking corruption in the government services is highlighted by the September 2007 appointment of Viktor Zubkov as Russia's new prime minister. This appointment was an interim appointment and Vladimir Putin himself appears set to become the next Prime Minister under a Dmitry Medvedev Presidency.[5]

Viktor Zubkov

Who is Viktor Zubkov? This was the question in the minds of most observers, including those in Russia, when President Putin named him to replace Mikhail Fradkov as prime minister in September 2007. Viktor Zubkov, born in 1941, gained his degree in economics from the Leningrad Agricultural Institute in what is now St. Petersburg. Following his degree, he was drafted into the Soviet Army to serve an obligatory 18-month term. After his term ended in 1967, he managed collective farms in the Leningrad area.[6]

Viktor Zubkov's political career began in 1985, when he left the collective farms to pursue a career with the Communist Party in the Leningrad region, eventually becoming the first deputy chairman of the Party's Leningrad Region Executive Committee in 1989. In 1992, he began his work with Vladimir Putin in the St. Petersburg Mayor Office as a deputy chairman of the External Relations Committee and later becoming the city's chief of the Department of State Tax Inspection.[7]

His work in the Saint Petersburg government earned Zubkov his first federal government post in 1998, becoming the chief of the St. Petersburg branch of the Tax Ministry and later the deputy tax minister of the Northwestern region of Russia. After a failed attempt to become elected as governor of the Leningrad Region, Zubkov was named first deputy finance minister of Russia and chairman of the Financial Monitoring Committee, later renamed the Federal Financial Monitoring Service, in 2001. In this position, Zubkov has been a strong force against money laundering in Russia, taking on a number of Russian banks that were involved in the facilitation of money laundering.[8]

Rewards

Understanding the risks involved in investing in Russia is an important part of forming a complete investment decision. To get a complete understanding of the investment opportunities, it is also important to understand the rewards that can be received from taking on the risks discussed in this chapter. The Russian market has provided investors with immense rewards for those willing to take on some of the risks involved with Russia's developing economy. The rewards associated with investing in the Russian market include (1) strong GDP growth, (2) economic diversification, and (3) internal reinvestment.

GDP Growth

Since the 1998 financial crisis, the Russian economy has been a story of tremendous growth. In 1999, the total output of the Russian economy as measured by GDP was less than $200 billion,[9] which is comparable to the GDP of state of Connecticut in the United States. Russia's economy has now surpassed the $1 trillion mark in GDP, more than quintupling in seven years. It is now expected that, by the end of 2008, the Russian economy will surpass the $1.5 trillion level of GDP.[10]

The impressive growth of the Russian economy, averaging about 7 percent a year, has been felt throughout the entire economy, with one of the primary beneficiaries being the Russian people, whose disposable incomes have been rising along with GDP. The 1998 financial crisis was particularly devastating to the Russian people, who saw their incomes drop by about 30 percent as measured by GDP per capita to $1,350 in 1999. Since that time, the Russian people have seen their averages wages grow impressively, with a per capita GDP growing from $6,800 in 2006 to over $8,700 in 2007, or a 28 percent increase, and expected to increase to over $10,200 in 2008, a 17 percent increase.[11] This trend is expected to continue for the near future as Russia's economy continues to diversify and increasing domestic consumer demand, fueled by income increases, continues to feed demand for retail goods, services, travel, cars, and homes.

The rapid expansion of disposable income is working to move Russia away from being a purely oil and natural gas exporting economy toward becoming a truly modern economy that is based almost as much on domestic demand as it is on export demand, allowing the Russians to be able to fuel much of their own growth. Although Russia's stock market index, the RTS, is around 60 percent oil and gas,[12] these industries only form about 25 percent of Russia's GDP.[13] This means that the country's impressive growth is coming from more than just these industries and is more diversified than most believe.

Economic Diversification: Domestic Boom Town

There is an old adage that states, "A rising tide lifts all ships." This adage is as true in Russia as it is anywhere else. Although the country sports a class of oligarchs and 36 billionaires that have a combined wealth that totals a hefty percentage of the nation's annual GDP, the country's wealth still remains more evenly distributed than that of the United States.[14] The main driver of this shared prosperity is the rising wages of the average Russian worker. The average wages of Russian workers have been rising at approximately 28 percent per year during the protracted Russian economic boom.[15] This newfound money is finding its way back into the Russian economy, transforming it from what most people believe is a pure oil and natural gas economy into a modern, diversified economy that is increasingly driven by domestic consumption.

The increasing wages of average Russians provide ample opportunities for educated investors to find significant returns in a market where oil and natural gas companies have found their stock prices stabilizing recently. Russians are no different than anyone else in that they have both needs as well as wants, both of which offer areas of high growth and increasing levels of importance in the Russian economy and Russian market. Some of the best corporate growth stories in Russia are in the retail sectors, especially in food and multi-format retailing. To take advantage of the investment opportunities that are arising from the rising disposable incomes of the ever-increasing Russian middle-class, an investor should take a *bottom-up* approach.

To profit from investing in the consumer sector, one needs to look at the effects of rising personal incomes on the average Russian. Just like anyone else, the average Russian would first ensure that they spend their newfound disposable income on better quality food. This opens up opportunities for the country's large food retailers that are seeing huge increases in revenues and are in the early stages of buying up smaller competitors and consolidating their market shares. For many, the next step is communication services—standard telephone and cellular telephone, each offering promising investments in well-run companies.

Once the average consumers have satiated their desire for good food and the ability to stay in contact with their friends and family, they start looking at other ways to improve their living conditions. A primary way to do this is to improve their surroundings by moving out of an old, dilapidated, Soviet-era apartment and into one of the new apartments or single-family homes being constructed at breakneck pace by the country's real estate developers. In addition, Russians' desire for new cars is rising rapidly. A Russian law states that all vehicles sold in Russia will have to have 50 percent local content by 2010,[16] leaving Russian automobile makers in a good position to benefit from this rapidly growing market.

Internal Reinvestment

With Russia in its ninth consecutive year of rapid economic expansion, the old Soviet-era infrastructure it has relied on has been showing its age and is beginning to reach the end of its serviceable life. This includes roads, railroads, and bridges, as well as homes and buildings. For Russia to continue its economic expansion in the future, it will have to greatly improve its infrastructure, especially in the area of transportation. The government has made infrastructure improvements one of its domestic priorities and has begun allocating significant government budgetary resources toward this goal.

The country's emphasis on redeveloping its internal infrastructure can provide investors with interesting opportunities to take advantage of the government's increased spending in this area to invest in companies that will be the main beneficiaries of the infrastructure projects. Two of the main industries that will benefit from infrastructure projects are the cement and steel industries. Whether the projects are buildings, homes, roads, bridges, or railroads, there are two things that are inevitably needed: cement and steel. This is also a good time for investors to take a good look at companies involved in building roads and bridges, as there are a few companies that have very large positions in the race for infrastructure investment dollars.

In 2007, Russia enjoyed $275 billion investment in its $1.2 trillion economy: $145 billion in debt financing, $55 billion in new equity, and $75 billion from reinvested corporate earnings. Capital flight became history as the country enjoyed $57 billion in capital inflows.

In terms of investment in Russia's stock market, proportionately over time, the weight of oil and gas will continue to decline as the consumer sector grows dramatically.

Summary

There are many risks to consider when investing in Russia. When the country is studied on its merits, and when compared to opportunities elsewhere, the risks are acceptable in proportion to the potential rewards that can be gained. Russia has the third largest currency reserves in the world, and the chances of a sharp decline in the price of oil have to be assessed in terms of the prospects for continuing growth worldwide and the supply constraints and geopolitical tensions in the Middle East. The rewards are very much evident in Russia, especially when compared to other emerging markets such as China and India, as Russian equity valuations continue to be comparatively conservative. This leads to the prospect of continued growth as a new wave of internal reinvestment helps to diversify Russia's economy and create new opportunities for investors.

Part Two

RUSSIA AS A RISING ECONOMIC POWER

Chapter 3

An Overview of
Business in Russia

This chapter is designed to give readers an overview of some of the most prominent investable Russian public companies. This overview section is not meant to be a complete list of investable Russian companies, nor does it attempt to evaluate these companies as to their suitability for your investment portfolio. As always, be sure to do your own research and/or consult a financial professional before making any investment decisions.

Russia as an Emerging Free Market

If you were to meet someone who asserted that it does not matter much who is in power in Washington because our country is all about business, that everyday life is a struggle to earn a buck to support the family and our way of life—how many readers would take issue? But somehow Russia is seen as being a country run by the mafia and a new autocracy and, as many would say, by a modern-day tsar, or the oligarchs, or is it the KGB?

This disconnect is simply not factual. Russia is in the midst of an economic boom, with rising standards of living and consumer disposable income. Russians today are all about homes and cars, cars and homes, just like us. While there is still corruption in Russia—in fact the nature of corruption has changed dramatically over the last 15 years—the United States has had its own problems with Enron, WorldCom, and other major corporate scandals. Formerly esteemed American business leaders are now being paraded to court and doing time here at home. We all know about endemic corruption in India, China, and Nigeria; even in Germany we now see prosecutors going after bribery-to-get-contracts schemes at large companies such as Siemens, which have in fact been in place for many years.[1]

Today, Wall Street and America's investing public have been entertaining a love affair with both India and China as being the jewels of the emerging markets. This amorous relationship is fueled by two powerful forces in America: investors looking to capitalize on the rapid growth in these countries and by the close business ties between these countries and U.S. corporations looking for cheap supplies of labor and goods. Partly as a result of the effective intermediation function of Washington's vast array of lobbyists, this has led to these countries enjoying friendly relationships with both the American media and with the American government. Ironically, certainly in comparison with the People's Republic of China, Russia can be considered a democracy and a free enterprise economy. Whether it is due to our tense past relations or current lack of strong business ties and any evident lobby clout, most news presented in the United States about Russia is negative news. Perhaps, though, if Russian-flagged tankers filled with oil began to appear regularly at American ports, some of this negativity might eventually abate.

Table 3.1 presents basic financial information about Russia that should be evaluated when making investments in Russian-owned corporations.

Table 3.1   Russia: 2007 Info and Estimates[2]

Currency	ruble (Rub)
Exchange Rate	Floating, approximately 25 Rub/USD
Exchange Reserves	$485 billion
GDP	$1.25 trillion
GDP per Capita	$8,725
GDP Growth YOY	7.5%
Inflation YOY	10%
Unemployment	5.8%
Primary Exchange	MICEX
Country Ticker Code	RU

Oil Revenue Leads to Economic Growth

The reality is that Russia is on track to be one of the first oil-dependent economies that is not endemically corrupt. The fiscal management of its trade surplus resulting from its commodities exports—the world's biggest—has been extremely conservative. This fiscal discipline has resulted in Central Bank reserves that now exceed $440 billion—the world's third largest, as mentioned in Chapter 2—and enough to cover the amount of goods Russia imports for nearly two years,[3] while the international standard is to have enough coverage for four months. The government has also taken the wise step of creating the Stabilization Fund, now over $140 billion,[4] roughly 10 percent of Russia's annual gross domestic product (GDP), which helps shield the economy from sudden losses of export revenue. This fund also helps shield the economy from inflationary pressures that can be caused by such large inflows of foreign money from the country's exports.

Bolstering the fact that Russia is becoming less an oil-dependent economy and more a diversified modern economy (except for commercial banking and insurance), the government recently announced plans to peg the Stabilization Fund to a percentage of GDP, slated to be between 10 and 15 percent, instead of the price of oil. The government also said that it is going to split this fund into two funds: a Reserve Fund to cushion the economy against any shock caused by drops in the price of oil, and the Future Generations Fund, which will serve as their fund to cover any shortfalls in national priority projects. As mentioned, the sound fiscal policies put in practice by the Kremlin have led to the ruble becoming a nearly impregnable currency.

The Russian economic boom has been one of the most amazing success stories of any emerging market. The economy has been growing at a rate of around 7 percent per year when calculated in ruble terms. When the effects of the appreciation of the ruble are considered and this growth is converted into U.S. dollar terms, the resulting growth rate is about 25 percent per year. This impressive growth has not been limited to the government and a few lucky oligarchs; the Russian population has been experiencing similar income and purchasing power growth. Disposable incomes have been rising at a similar rate to GDP, boosting the Russian population from one quarter middle class to one half middle class over the next few years. This rise of the middle class has led to a retail boom in Russia with sales increasing nearly 30 percent per year.[5]

The business of Russia, it seems, is business. Make no mistake, Russia is still a poor European country and once you get outside of Moscow and St. Petersburg, many of the cities and towns are pretty bleak with limited services. But, the increases in real wages and the disposable incomes of average Russian citizens is on pace to bring the country up to European standards within a decade, an amazing accomplishment for one generation. Malls and high-end stores are popping up everywhere, while cell phone usage and consumer goods sales are exploding. The wealthiest Russians, as with the end of the nineteenth century, when the upper classes invested in the French Riviera, are buying up London flats and Riviera beachfront. Would that they invest instead in southern Russia, it should enjoy the kind of growth we have seen in the southeast and southwest United States during recent generations.

Yukos Affair Actually Led to an Improved Business Environment

The year 2003 was a turning point year for Russia. The national legislature, the State Duma, was up for election in December with the presidential election to follow in March 2004. The Kremlin did pre-election polling and discovered that, life still being hard, the people were ready to vote Communist, and they also reviled the oligarchs "who stole Russia." The Kremlin knew that from 1995 to 1999, when the Communists had a large bloc in the State Duma, reform legislation in the Duma was blocked.[6] From 1999 to 2003, by contrast, tax reform, reorganization in the telecommunications sector, the beginning of reforms in the utilities sector, and many other reforms had taken place. The Kremlin was very concerned.

Then their savior appeared. Mikhail Khordokovsky, the founder of Yukos, had earlier placed his Bank Menatep into bankruptcy, mysteriously finding the necessary funds to buy the Russian oil company Yukos. He did a terrific job of building up what became one of Russia's very best companies, at one time Russia's largest oil company. He became a multibillionaire who took to lecturing Putin on how the country should be run. He pictured himself as a future president of Russia. He was also liberal in his expenditures of influence buying in Moscow and in Washington, D.C., where several politicians were quick to come to his defense.[7]

The prosecution of Mikhail Khordokovsky, known in the West as the Yukos Affair, played out as a modern-day parable for the Russian business elite. Picture nine cars speeding down the turnpike at 90 miles per hour with a state trooper on the side of the road, able to pull only one car over. Then he sees the leader in a small red sports car flip him the bird. Guess who gets pulled over? All were breaking the law. As in New York, prosecutors in Russia do have discretion, and exercise it every day. Their staffs are simply not large enough to bring to trial all perpetrators, so in this case they focused on one offender. The prosecution of this oligarch for fraud and tax evasion was extremely popular in Russia and played a big part in winning elections and, together with tax reform, bringing order out of corporate chaos.

Tax Reform Up until 2003, many of Russia's biggest companies practiced massive tax evasion schemes called *transfer pricing*. Their factories sold their output at cost to their fully owned international sales companies located in low-tax countries, which then resold the products to their final customers and realized all the real profit from the manufacture of the product, collecting the proceeds abroad. These actions, of course, were a tax avoidance technique designed to circumvent the still Soviet-era tax regime that was nearly impossible to navigate and took a disproportionate chunk out of company profits.

In 2003, two coincidental developments helped revolutionize Russian business practices. The first was a new tax regime implemented, where a reasonable corporate rate of 24 percent was put in place and an extraordinarily low 13 percent personal flat tax rate took effect.[8] This overhaul of the tax code made tax avoidance less compelling, as it made it unquestionably simpler for individuals to file and pay their taxes while, at the same time, making corporate taxes less burdensome. The net effect, surprising even to the Kremlin, was that tax collections from both individuals and corporations soared almost overnight as tax schemes quickly became taboo.

Order Out of Chaos The second development, as mentioned, was the Yukos Affair, which, like a biblical parable, provided a new lesson on how Russian business leaders were expected to act. Put into the past was the chaos of billionaires exercising outsized influence on government policies. Polls showed the Russian public found this intolerable. It also cemented the position of the Russian government and Russian law as the regulatory authority for Russian business. The Russian government essentially told oligarchs that the laws of the country applied to everyone, even them. While foreign journalists were wringing their hands about the lack of legal due process for Mr. Khordokovsky, the business leaders in Russia "got the message." The result of these two developments was a dramatic transformation in corporate Russia. Corporate entities were consolidated into logical business units, transfer pricing was abated, and PriceWaterhouseCoopers, KPMG, Deloitte, and others were called in to do full audits according to international financial reporting standards (IFRS). Companies religiously paid their taxes (and for some, dividends) and, *voila,* the Russian economy sprouted a bevy of world-class, year-on-year fundamentally performing, investable companies.

Today we see a new generation of founder-operating managers totally focused on making profits and creating growth. Consolidations, geographic expansion to serve underserved markets, and resuscitation of moribund Soviet-era industries have produced one of the fastest-growing and best-managed economies in the world. When you visit plants all over the country, you are treated to an English-language Power Point presentation by English-speaking investor relations professionals and are able to freely ask questions of the senior, Russian-speaking managers.

Russia: Not Just Oil and Gas

We will consider Russia's business economy on a number of levels. First, we will focus on several of the most promising sectors, each of which reflects different aspects of Russia today. Steel is a major export sector but, unlike oil, it was an industry given up for dead worldwide as companies everywhere went under. Its revival in Russia has been an entirely private-sector effort, as new investors picked up existing assets on the cheap and used the cash flows from this recovering sector to invest in new plant and equipment. We will look at contrasts to the aluminum industry.

Oil and gas are what most people think of when they hear about the Russian economy, and we will look at the more public–private experience in this sector. Indeed, *private–public partnerships* is the current governing policy. Modest public funds are seeding private leverage as investors step up to these new programs.

Also of more recent vintage, as described in Chapter 1, are the new Priority National Projects (PNPs) for education, medical services, housing, and agriculture. Substantial sums have now been earmarked from the huge Stabilization Fund, but the government is acting in a more managerial capacity and is looking to local levels of government and private-sector participation to pick up much of the operational responsibility.

Emerging Industries

The continuing growth and diversification of the Russian economy is creating new opportunities for Russian businesses in various fields. Two fields that the Russian government has declared priorities are aeronautics and technology. The government plans to invest in these areas through a special Development Fund to be financed by the Stabilization Fund. The Development Fund will be controlled by a major bank instead of the government, in the hopes that a bank will be better able to analyze and finance emerging businesses in these fields.

The government's drive to become a global player in the aeronautics sector will be getting a boost from its decision to combine the various government-controlled design bureaus into one publicly traded company, Unified Aircraft Corporation. The government has promised to provide over $700 million over the next three years to help the company modernize its facilities and become competitive globally. Russian aircraft design has been world-class for decades, with names such as Irkut, Mig, and Sukhoi, who have continued to design and build high-quality aircraft but have often lacked both the scale and management expertise to compete in a capitalist environment.

It appears that United Aircraft will be built around the already public aerospace company Irkut, which designs and manufactures fighter planes and an aircraft that scoops up huge water loads to dump on forest fires. Irkut is a well-managed, profitable company, and a well-regarded stock. It is slated to be folded into United Aircraft and so should form the core around which a large commercial enterprise can be built. Once all of the Russian design bureaus have been consolidated into Unified Aircraft Corporation, the company has the opportunity to become a major player in the global aerospace sector. On the other hand, United Aircraft is definitely a siloviki project and so runs the risk of being calcified by government bureaucracy.

Russia has also been active in the technology sector. With a drive to become a global player in the high-technology sector within the next decade, Russian companies have already started focusing on this sector. Two Russian Internet technology (IT) companies completed IPOs in 2007. The first was Sitronics, the former technology arm of Russian conglomerate Sistema. The second was Armada, which was spun off from RosBusinessConsulting (RBC) as a way to differentiate the company's technology business from its media business. With government support, the Russian technology sector will continue to show more growth and opportunities for investors. The Kremlin will also promote biotech for future development.

Sergei Ivanov

The man put in charge of implementing the government's lofty goals of improving Russia's competitiveness in new sectors is First Deputy Prime Minister Sergei Ivanov (see Figure 3.1). Ivanov was born in 1953 in what was then called Leningrad, now St. Petersburg. After receiving his education in English and Swedish from Leningrad State University, he went on to study law and counterintelligence and began a career in the KGB in 1976. Ivanov served as Vladimir Putin's deputy while Putin served as the director of the Federal Security Services (FSB), the new iteration of the old KGB.

Figure 3.1   Sergei Ivanov, First Deputy Prime Minister of the Russian Federation, Also Has a KGB Background

Once widely considered to be one of the leading candidates to succeed Vladimir Putin as Russia's President in 2008, Ivanov was given a much higher public profile in 2007. Ivanov began his political career in 1999, when Boris Yeltsin appointed him as secretary of the Security Council. Serving as the country's first civilian defense minister from 2001 until early 2007, Ivanov was promoted to first deputy prime minister, putting him on equal political footing as Dmitry Medvedev until Putin picked Medvedev to run as president in the 2008 elections.

Sochi 2014 Olympics

In July of 2007 it was announced that the Russian city of Sochi, a southern resort city on the Black Sea, would host the 2014 Winter Olympics (see Figure 3.2). This is an important milestone on the road to Vladimir Putin's goal as president of Russia of making the Sochi area a global tourist destination. Putin himself led the effort to woo the Olympic Committee to choose Sochi over its competitors. On the day of voting, Putin flew to Guatemala where the voting was taking place

Figure 3.2   View of Sochi, Site for the 2014 Winter Olympics

and is said to have impressed the delegation by explaining, in English and French, why Russia's Sochi would be the perfect host for the winter games. So what does this mean to investors?

Preparing for the Olympic Games in Sochi will involve substantial investments in infrastructure, hotels, and stadiums. President Putin stated that over $12 billion will be expended in preparation. Investors can take advantage of these projects by focusing on companies that will be the primary beneficiaries of the development in the area. Among publicly traded companies, the large investments in building roads and bridges will, for example, benefit Mostotrest, Russia's leading bridge and overpass builder, as it has strong connections to the area as well as the modern equipment, scale, and proven track record to be a strong choice to receive prime contracts for the area's development. The influx of workers for these projects will mean more housing, and Olympic guests will need hotel rooms.

Open Investments is currently a real estate developer with significant projects in the area, already working on a project for a large housing community and a high-class hotel in Sochi. Open Investments currently has significant land holdings in the area and will benefit from property prices in the area that are already beginning to rise dramatically.

The immense building projects envisioned in preparation for the Olympic Games provide other opportunities for investors as well. Concrete will be in great demand for roads, bridges, homes, hotels, and stadiums. As of now, concrete is a difficult sector to invest in, as the companies are highly illiquid. This may change as early as mid-2008 if Russian leader Evrocement, with over half of all production in European Russia, goes ahead with its IPO. With all of these building projects, there will also be a large demand for steel. Most construction will require steel rebar and beams, which will benefit Russian leaders Evraz and Mechel. Construction will also require, to a lesser extent, flat steel, which would primarily be supplied by Severstal and Novolipetsk.

With construction work beginning and tourism expected to begin picking up well before the Olympic Games, more and more people will be traveling to and from Sochi, as well as to and from Russia from other countries. The primary beneficiary of this increased travel will be Aeroflot, Russia's leading airline with a near monopoly on international flights and the only carrier with three direct flights per day to Sochi from Moscow. More people in the area will also lead to a drastically increased need to communications. A beneficiary will be Southern Telecom, the incumbent phone provider in the southern region. The company will be working to increase value-added high-speed Internet services throughout the region, as well as benefit from increased call traffic through the 2014 Olympics.

Increased demand for communications services will not be limited to the local fixed-line operator; cellular communications will also increase with the influx of workers and tourists. Beneficiaries of an increase in cellular usage will be Russia's Mobile Telesystems (MTS) and VimpelCom. People will also need a place to shop for food and other necessities while they stay in the region, and the main beneficiary of this will be Russian food retailers, such as Magnit. The company currently operates more than 60 stores in and around Sochi and is headquartered in Krasnodar, near Sochi. It is also worth noting that much of the project financing will come from loans, most notably benefiting Sberbank and VTB.

The Olympics has the potential to boost the economic growth of Russia, especially in the Sochi area, as the government rapidly develops an area that has been lagging the central region of the country. The largest contribution to Russia by the 2014 Olympic Games in Sochi will be increased focus on Russia by tourists, investors, and news sources. The Sochi Games give Russia an excellent opportunity to focus news flow on the positive aspects of the country. Domestic investors also played a role in the stock market in the days after the decision was made. The awarding of the Olympic Games to Russia gives the Russian people a confirmation that they are, and will continue to be, an integral member of the international community.

Summary

The discussion in this chapter has highlighted the progress Russia has made toward emerging as a world power. This reemergence is not based on military might as in the past, but now is based on becoming a true world economic power. Although many have commented that Russia's progress has been marred by government control of certain industries, Russia is certainly on the path to becoming a formidable free market economy. The fact that it chose to remake its economy the "Russian Way" should not detract from the fact that significant progress is being made.

Chapter 4

Metals and Mining

Resources to Spare

Russia has vast reserves of mined resources and a variety of metals essential to global production. Russia is currently the fifth largest producer of coal in the world and sits on the second largest reserves in the world with 17 percent of global reserve supply. The country also has 17 percent of the global reserves of iron ore, giving it the second largest supply in the world. Russia also accounts for 13 percent of the global supply of primary aluminum, with 100 percent of the country's total controlled by RUSAL.[1]

Russia also has large supplies of other metals. Russian production accounts for about 20 percent of the global production of nickel, 90 percent of which is produced by Norilsk Nickel. Russia also provides 50 percent of global palladium production, a metal that is an essential component of automotive catalytic converters. The country also supplies 15 percent of the world's platinum production as well as 10 percent of its magnesium. Norilsk Nickel enjoys a majority market share in platinum and palladium, while VSMPO-Avisma has a large market share in magnesium. Russia also provides around 30 percent of global titanium output, with VSMPO-Avisma owning a monopoly in Russian production of the metal.[2]

Risks:
- The Russian metals and mining industries are subject to international pricing for metals, leaving them exposed to price fluctuations on the global markets.
- Most exported metals sales are transacted in U.S. dollars or euros, presenting companies with decreasing ruble-based revenues as the ruble appreciates against these currencies.
- Russian metals and mining companies are part of the global supply/demand of metals, and increased supply from countries such as China (one of Russia's largest consumers) can lead to lower prices and decreased demand for Russian products.

Rewards:
- Continued global economic expansion should lead to high demand for metals for the near future, leading to continued high metal prices.
- Consolidation within the Russian metals and mining industries is set to continue as global prices remain high, leaving room for scale and efficiency improvements.
- Russia's large contribution to global metals production should continue to secure its position as a world leader in this area.
- Domestic infrastructure and construction will continue to drive demand for steel products.

Steel

Just ask anyone and they will tell you, Russia's economy is characterized by oil and natural gas. Although these two industries have contributed the most to Russia's rebirth, the first Soviet-era industry to be reborn was the Russian steel industry. The steel industry's awakening from a nearly bankrupt somnolence has helped to propel

Russia into becoming the world's largest exporter of commodities. Driven by many factors, Russia soon became the Saudi Arabia of steel. And by putting to work substantial cash flows generated from steel sales in a recovering market to replace outdated plants and equipment, the owners of New Russia's steel industry demonstrates the best in modern business practices. These owners were not handed mines or wells with vast resources. They were given companies with outdated equipment that were mired in debt, which they turned into world-class steel companies.

Background

To understand how Russia has emerged as a global powerhouse in the steel industry, it is important to understand how the industry got to the point where it is today. Russian steel producers first entered the world markets in the 1730s, and by the 1770s had become a world leader in steel exports. In fact, in the period between 1770 and 1800, Russia supplied Great Britain with nearly 50 percent of all of the steel used.[3]

This period of global dominance was short-lived as protectionist policies and war came together to put Russian steel exports at a competitive disadvantage. In 1790, Great Britain began imposing a tariff on Russian imports that was increased annually to allow for the development of its own fledgling industry. This effect was amplified by the Napoleonic Wars that both created periodic trade embargos and a massive distraction for the Russian iron centers located in the European area of the country. Even after the Napoleonic Wars ended in 1815, Russia's place as a preeminent global supplier of metals rapidly eroded as tariffs were increased and competitive global production increased. It was not until a new period of Russian industrialization that the Russian nation reemerged as a steel-producing giant.[4]

Stalin

The industrialization of Russia was started by Lenin in the early 1920s, but emerged as a major national priority under Josef Stalin.

In 1928, Stalin replaced Lenin's New Economic Policy with the first of his Five-Year Plans that violently propelled the country toward true central planning. These plans included the collectivization of farming, in part to help supply food to factory workers that were part of Stalin's *forced industrialization*.[5]

Stalin was born on December 18, 1878, as Iosif (Josef) Vissarionovich Dzhugashvili in the Georgian city of Gori, part of the Russian Empire. At the age of 14, he graduated first in his class and was offered a scholarship to the Seminary of Tiflis (now Tiblisi), the capital of Georgia. His mother had always hoped that he would become a priest, even after he became the leader of the Soviet Union. Stalin had other plans. According to official records, he was expelled from seminary in 1899 just before his final exams. But prevailing wisdom is that he quit so that he could pursue his activism for the Socialist movement. He worked for the next decade with the Georgian political underground, being arrested numerous times and getting sent to Siberia on one occasion.[6]

Dzhugashvili, by 1912, had become a member of the Socialist's Central Committee and, soon after, decided to change his name to help hide his Georgian heritage. He decided to keep his first name of Josef and change his last name to Stalin, which is derived from the Russian word for steel, *stal*. Following the Revolution of 1917, Stalin became the people's commissar for nationalities affairs and the editor of *Pravda*, the official Communist newspaper. In 1922, he became the general secretary of the Soviet Communist Party and, after Lenin's death in 1924, won a power struggle with Leon Trotsky, a Revolution hero, to become the leader of the Soviet Union, a position he kept until his death in 1953.[7]

Stalin made massive contributions to the Soviet Union's steel industry. In 1928, he scrapped the New Economic Policy for the first of his Five-Year Plans. Stalin's primary focus in these Five-Year Plans was to transform the Soviet Union from a primarily agrarian economy to a modernized, industrial powerhouse. One of the main beneficiaries of these plans was the steel industry, as nearly every aspect of industrialization required steel. Steel was required for massive building projects including railroads, buildings, and bridges, as well as for manufacturing projects that included automobiles and industrial machinery.[8]

Cold War

The importance of the steel industry waned briefly after the death of Stalin in 1953, when Nikita Khrushchev took over the reigns of power and started a period of *de-Stalinization*. This process included the attempt to move more industrial assets toward the production of consumer products in an attempt to make life better for average Russians. This shift was short-lived due to the rise of the Cold War and the ensuing military buildup. The refocus of the Soviet Union on military spending reaffirmed the position of the steel industry as one of national preeminence, with steelworkers becoming Russian icons.[9]

Post–Soviet

By the time of the Soviet Union's collapse in 1991, the steel industry had suffered years of decreasing government spending. This reflected less demand from not only the military, but also from infrastructure projects, automobile manufacturing, and other consumer and domestic projects. This decrease in demand, coupled with Soviet-era management teams that were never focused on profits or efficiency, led to long-term neglect of vital industry infrastructure improvements. This caused Russian steel plants to become highly inefficient, relying on old and outdated technologies and processes.[10] This soon changed as a new era of post-Soviet ownership came to the floundering industry.

Industry Turnaround

The collapse of the Soviet Union and subsequent transfer of steel companies to private ownership came at an opportune time. The Russian steel industry was able to revive itself quickly with the help of surging global demand lead by China's economic boom, creating a large market for rolled product for automobile production and for long product to feed China's booming high-rise building construction. Coupled with China's growing market for steel was the lagging ability of China to produce the product domestically. This caused the global price of steel to soar, creating an excellent opportunity for Russia's steel industry to take advantage of its ability to leverage relatively low production costs and its proximity to this huge market to quickly stake a claim as major steel exporter. Now that China has developed a large domestic steel industry, internal price controls on steel has caused Chinese manufacturers to export their products at higher global prices leaving a significant market for Russian steelmakers.

Reinvestment

During this period of high global demand for steel, the industry was further aided on the world markets by Russia's relatively low costs for product inputs, including labor, gas, and electricity. Unlike many other industries where Russia's new corporate owners lined their own pockets with company profits, as Boris Berezovsky was very adept at doing, the steel industry was nearly unique in its overall reinvestment of profits back into the business. Reinvestment took two forms: the first by purchasing both suppliers and sellers to vertically integrate their businesses and increase cost efficiency. Second, by heavily investing in new, modern steelmaking oxygen-reduction furnaces that could do in 40 minutes what took the outdated Soviet-era open-hearth furnaces about 7 hours to complete, Russia greatly increased productivity.

Global Reemergence

The Russian collapse of 1998 actually provided an added benefit to the Russian steel industry. With Russian steelmakers exporting over half of total production, the devaluation of the ruble following the collapse proved to be a huge boost to the competitiveness of Russian steel on global markets, leading to demand in many countries for Russian steel. As a result, on the prodding of the U.S. steel industry lobby, the U.S. president introduced steep tariffs ranging from 13 to 30 percent on imported steel exceeding 5.4 million tons per annum. But the Russian steel industry prospered as continued soaring demand from China was coupled with growing domestic demand from infrastructure improvements, automobile manufacturing, and construction projects.[11]

The Russian steel industry today is in very healthy shape, as many of the positive global factors that helped lead to the industry's resurgence are still in place. China continues to have an insatiable appetite for imported steel, with no signs of an impending slowdown in import demand. The domestic demand for steel continues to rise as the Russian automotive industry, including foreign manufacturers in Russia, is growing very quickly, fueled by domestic demand for automobiles. The Russian government has also announced ambitious plans to invest in the country's infrastructure, with specific emphasis on rail lines, which will be yet another major driver for the Russian steel industry.[12]

This comes at a time when Russian steelmakers still enjoy relatively low costs for labor, electricity, and gas. The industry's past and ongoing investment in more efficient production equipment continues to improve the cost competitiveness of Russian steel. The industry's vertical integration of suppliers, including mining and coking facilities, has increased the competitiveness of Russian steelmakers by providing for insulation from extreme cost fluctuations. In 2004, the top five steelmakers in Russia accounted for well over two thirds of the country's total production. This consolidation leads to much lower comparative costs, as companies are able to lower fixed costs while reducing supply costs using their greater leverage with suppliers. At the same time, quality improvements caused by the industry's massive capital improvements enable the companies to produce steel of a quality comparable to any in the world, allowing them to sell steel on the world market at prices that continue to be buoyed by high global demand.[13] Finally, these five companies are expanding internationally, including into the United States, such that 15 percent to 19 percent of their revenue now comes from North America.

Severstal

Symbol	CHMF
GDR	SVST.LI
GDR Ratio	1:1
Market Cap	$14.06 billion
Shares Outstanding	1.01 billion
Estimated Freefloat	17.3 percent

An excellent example of the revival of the Russian steel industry is the company Severstal, who's name is derived from the Russian words *sever,* for northern and *stal,* for steel, or Northern Steel. The history of Severstal begins in 1955, when the Soviet Union opened a steel plant in Cherepovets as the Cherepovets Iron and Steel Complex. This plant has enjoyed continuous operations since opening and is currently the fifth largest single steel plant in the world. Severstal officially became a public company on September 24, 1993, when the president of the Russian Federation signed a decree that converted the Cherepovets Iron and Steel Complex into the new joint-stock company Severstal. The company quickly followed its privatization with a series of acquisitions, including a producer of iron-ore pellets in 1994 and a mining and processing plant in 1995.[14]

Severstal, under the adept leadership of young owner/manager Alexei Mordashov, followed up these acquisitions with a comprehensive program of restructuring and modernization. This program greatly reduced the company's reliance on old, outdated open-hearth furnaces and replaced them with the latest technologies in oxygen converters and electronic arc furnaces. This program has been very successful in increasing the quality of the finished products, as well as decreasing the time and costs of production. Severstal has also gained considerable cost advantages from its acquisitions. The company is capable of supplying 100 percent of its core material needs from its mining assets, as well as providing for about 45 percent of its electricity through its electricity-generating assets. The company also enjoys the benefits of being in the world's largest natural gas–producing country, paying well below international prices for this important manufacturing input, adding an additional cost advantage.[15]

In 2002, Severstal became the Severstal Group. This new structure reflected its expansion into mining, coking, and auto making,
among many other secondary endeavors. The company has recently
used some of its profits for overseas acquisitions, becoming the
first Russian steelmaker to make the leap into global expansion. In
2004, the company bought the assets of Rouge Steel in Dearborn,
Michigan, and rebranded it as Severstal North America. Severstal
North America now supplies about 8 percent of the steel used in
the United States' auto industry. The company followed this with a
2005 purchase of Lucchini, an Italian steelmaker with operations in
Italy and France. This acquisition further increased Severstal's global
presence, while giving the company even greater exposure to the
higher-margin automotive and other finished steel products. This
adds to Severstal's large automotive portfolio in the United States
and Russia as Russia's largest supplier of automotive steel.[16]

In terms of global production and revenues, Severstal is Russia's
largest steelmaker. Severstal is also one of the world's top ten
steel companies. Locally, the company is currently the third largest domestic producer in Russia, behind Novolipetsk and Evraz
Group. The company, while having some transparency problems in
the past, is now a model for good corporate governance in Russia.
The company is pursuing a renewed focus on its core businesses by
slowly divesting some of its noncore assets. The company has spun
off its large automotive unit, Severstal-Avto, while working to divest
units such as its insurance company, banking unit, and other unrelated assets. A good example of the company's focus on continual
improvement is the Severstal Corporate University, founded by the
company in 2001 to provide training to both managers and employees in subjects ranging from general training and health/safety to
economic efficiency and business.[17]

Alexei Mordashov The main driver behind Severstal's rise to
becoming a world-class company has been the young, dynamic Alexei
Mordashov (see Figure 4.1). Mordashov was born in Cherepovets
in 1965, 10 years after the Cherepovets Iron and Steel Complex
opened. While he was growing up in Cherepovets, both of Alexei's

Figure 4.1 Alexei Mordashov, CEO of Severstal, Combines Industry Heritage with Financial Acumen

parents worked at the steel plant. After Mordashov studied economics at the Leningrad Economics Institute, he returned home to take a job at the Cherepovets plant as an economist. By 1992, at the age of 27, Mordashov was promoted to chief financial officer of the plant. He used this insider status to take full advantage of the privatization of the factory in 1993 by raising money to buy as many shares as possible. In 1996, he was named chief executive of Severstal, a position he still holds today.[18]

Alexei Mordashov was never the standard, old-guard, Soviet-era manager. His promotion to an officer position coincided with the company's attempt to save itself by bringing in top young talent that the locals referred to as the *Iron Boys*. Soon after, the era of privatization began and Mordashov used his position in the company and industry contacts to orchestrate taking control of the company, not a small task considering at the time they were battling investors in Moscow that were looking to buy assets and quickly turn a profit. Unlike many managers during this turbulent time, Mordashov did not siphon off the company's profits, but instead reinvested them into the company to make it more efficient and more competitive in the world markets. He sees Severstal's expansion into the United States and elsewhere as providing a "strong global platform" for growth.[19]

Novolipetsk Steel

Symbol	NLMK
GDR	NLMK.LI
GDR Ratio	1:10
Market Cap	$17.68 billion

| Shares Outstanding | 5.99 billion |
| Estimated Freefloat | 11.9 percent |

Novolipetsk Steel is one of Russia's largest steel producers and a leading global supplier of steel slab and electrical steel. Exports account for more than 50 percent of the company's revenues, with exports to Europe, North America, the Middle East, and Asia. Novolipetsk Steel, with its high reliance on exports, purchased a controlling stake in Russia' fifth largest seaport, located on the Black Sea, to help reduce transportation costs. The company also has a large domestic market share in the automotive, construction, and steel pipe industries. The company is 50 percent self-sufficient in coking coal and 100 percent self-sufficient in coke production. Novolipetsk Steel has produced impressive financial results, remaining one the world's most profitable steel companies, and continues to increase production and gain global market share.[20]

Evraz

Symbol	Not Listed In Russia
GDR	EVR.LI
GDR Ratio	NA
Market Cap	$14.94 billion
Shares Outstanding	350.71 million
Estimated Freefloat	14.3 percent

Evraz, majority-owned by Roman Abramovich's Millhouse Capital, is Russia's largest domestic steel producer. Evraz also has steel-making assets in the Czech Republic and Italy. Evraz is 86 percent self-sufficient in iron ore, with controlling stakes in some of Russia's largest iron ore producers. Evraz is also 100 percent self-sufficient in coking coal, owning Russia's largest and third largest mines. The company also owns a seaport in the Far East region of Russia as a way to reduce transportation costs. The company enjoys a near monopoly in long steel used for railroad tracks and in railroad car wheels used in the Russian railway industry, an enviable position as Russia increases its government spending on the expansion of its railroad infrastructure. The company also has a leading market share in long steel products using in building and construction, including rebar and H-beams, at a time when the Russian government is pushing both residential construction and infrastructure building.[21]

Mechel

Symbol	MTLR
ADR	MTL.US
ADR Ratio	1:3
Market Cap	$5.25 billion
Shares Outstanding	416.27 million
Estimated Freefloat	23 percent

Mechel is Russia's sixth largest steel producer by total output and second largest long steel producer. The company is also heavily invested in mining assets, being a net seller of coking coal. The company is 100 percent self-sufficient in coking coal, 80 percent self-sufficient in iron ore, and 50 percent self-sufficient in electricity. Mechel also owns a nickel mine, where it has benefited from high global prices for that metal. The company saves on transportation costs by funneling much of its exports through its own port in the Far East region of Russia. The company has pursued a two-pronged approach to its business model by focusing not only on improving steel production, but also expanding production at its mining assets. The company plans to become nearly 100 percent self-sufficient in iron ore by 2009, allowing it to sell more raw materials to other steel producers.[22]

TMK

Symbol	TRMK
GDR	TMKS.LI
GDR Ratio	1:4
Market Cap	$8.21 billion
Shares Outstanding	873 million
Estimated Freefloat	21.2 percent

TMK is Russia's largest producer of large-diameter (LD) steel pipe. This pipe is mainly used for the oil and natural gas industries to transport their products large distances. TMK's main customers are Russia's natural gas giant, Gazprom, and Transneft, the state-controlled company responsible for the country's petroleum pipeline system. The company has shown impressive sales growth as it continues to benefit from Russia's increased spending on its commodity infrastructure, adding new pipelines and refurbishing old Soviet-era pipes.[23]

Aluminum

It can be said that the Russian aluminum industry, while very similar to the steel industry, has been taking a much different path since the privatization of the Russian economy. As with steel, Russia is one of the largest aluminum exporters in the world. In the Soviet era, the main customer for domestically produced aluminum was the military aviation sector. These orders dried up as military spending plummeted with the fall of the Soviet empire, and now domestic demand for aluminum is only one-sixth of what it was during Soviet times. The aluminum industry has made up for this loss in domestic demand by exporting their aluminum production globally where demand continues to remain very high.[24]

The problem that has plagued the Russian aluminum industry has been endemic corruption and internal transfer pricing. At one point before the 1998 financial crisis, transfer pricing became so endemic that Estonia, a country with no natural aluminum industry, had become one of the world's top aluminum exporters.[25] This problem has been abated in the industry and replaced with a more challenging problem, lack of transparency. The country's aluminum industry has been almost completely controlled by two companies, RUSAL and SUAL.

Both of these companies are privately owned and, therefore, are not required to publish financial or operating results. To make matters worse, the Russian government continues to hold on to a Soviet-era ideal of not releasing industry data such as production amounts, due to the claim that it is a state secret. This lack of transparency looks to have no end in sight, as the two largest aluminum producers have agreed to merge to create United Company RUSAL, which will control nearly the entire aluminum industry in Russia, creating the world's largest aluminum producer.[26]

Oleg Deripaska

The owner of the world's second-largest aluminum producer, RUSAL, is Oleg Deripaska (see Figure 4.2), the richest and the youngest

Figure 4.2 Oleg Deripaska, Owner of RUSAL, Cannot Obtain a U.S. Visa

Russian oligarch. Deripaska was born in 1968 on a small farm in southern Russia. He graduated with honors from Moscow State University in 1993 with a degree in engineering. In 1996, he obtained his master's degree from the Plekhanov Economics Academy. During his time at Moscow State University, Deripaska served as the financial director for an investment and trading cooperative formed under Gorbechev's new rules for small private businesses. In 1992, he became CEO of newly formed Rosaluminproduct, his first foray into the aluminum industry.[27]

In 1994, Deripaska became the head of one of Russia's largest aluminum plants, the Sayansky Aluminum Plant in Sayanogorsk, Russia. The Sayansky Aluminum Plant became the base of a new industrial group, Siberian Aluminum. Deripaska became CEO of RUSAL, Russian Aluminum, a company that consolidated most of Russia's aluminum manufacturing assets.[28] Deripaska, along with Roman Abramovich, bought RUSAL, and then Deripaska eventually purchased Abramovich's 50 percent stake for $2 billion to cement control over the company. He also owns stakes in other large manufacturing companies, including Russian truck maker GAZ. He recently bought a 30 percent stake in

STRABAG, the sixth largest construction business in Europe.[29] In 2001, he started an investment company, Basic Element, which specializes in capital management and private equity. Basic Element is now one of the largest private equity companies in Russia, with over $10 billion in assets.

Oleg Deripaska is considered by many as the oligarch best connected to the Kremlin under the Putin administration, and he loyally stays out of the Russian political arena. In 1999, he was awarded the Order of Friendship of Peoples for his work in business and his contributions to the Russian economy. The same year he also was named entrepreneur of the year in Russia.[30]

The aluminum business in Russia has been considered as one of its roughest industries. This notoriety has followed the man who made it to the top of the industry, with the United States twice rescinding his visa to travel to the United States due to alleged ties to criminal activity. Deripaska was able to get a visa in 2005 with the help of Senator Bob Dole's lobbying firm in Washington on the condition he meet with the FBI for questioning. His visa was again denied in 2007 when attempting to travel to the United States because the U.S. Justice Department believed that he was not candid when answering its questions.[31]

Mining

As previously mentioned, when looking at Russia's wealth of natural resources, most people look at the country's staggering reserves of oil and natural gas, but these are not the only areas in which the country enjoys natural resource wealth. Russia also enjoys vast natural resources including metals, coal, and other mined products.

VSMPO-Avisma

Symbol	VSMO
ADR	NA
Market Cap	$3.34 billion

| Shares Outstanding | 11.53 million |
| Estimated Freefloat | 26.6 percent |

VSMPO–Avisma, also known as Verkhanaya Salda Metal, is the world's largest vertically integrated producer of metallic titanium, providing about 30 percent of global supply. VSMPO–Avisma also produces half of Russia's magnesium output, accounting for around 5 percent of global production. The company's main customers for semifinished titanium products are in the aerospace industry, with VSMPO–Avisma being the number one supplier of titanium products to Airbus and the primary supplier to Airbus's new super–jumbo A380 project. VSMPO–Avisma is also the second–largest supplier of titanium products to Boeing, with whom they created a joint venture to become the primary supplier for Boeing's popular 787 Dreamliner project. With global demand for titanium continuing to increase, the company has been focusing on technological and efficiency improvements that will allow it to leverage its dominant position in the industry to add more finished product to its portfolio and continue revenue growth of nearly 10 percent per year.[32]

Norilsk Nickel

Symbol	GMKN
ADR	NILSY.US
ADR Ratio	1:1
Market Cap	$39.31 billion
Shares Outstanding	190.63 million
Estimated Freefloat	45.4 percent

Norilsk Nickel is Russia's largest integrated metals and mining company and a global metals and mining leader. The company boasts nearly 20 percent of the world's total nickel production, accounting for 90 percent of Russia's total. Norilsk Nickel also produces 12 percent of the world's total platinum, 50 percent of the world's palladium, and nearly 3 percent of the world's copper. The company has been expanding its reach globally, taking advantage of record high global prices for its main metals, especially nickel. In 2006, Norilsk

Nickel took advantage of high gold prices to create Polyus Gold as a spin-off of its gold mining assets. Polyus Gold is now Russia's largest gold producer. Norilsk Nickel purchased a 56 percent stake in U.S. metals miner Stillwater Mining and has bought a controlling stake in Canada's LionOre, a global mining company that would have the potential to increase Norilsk Nickel's nickel output by 20 percent and give it a global presence with operations in Australia, Botswana, and South Africa.[33]

Norilsk Nickel is a vertically integrated company. The company controls the production of metals from mining to refining. The company has also become 100 percent self-sufficient in electricity after its purchase of OGK-3, one of Russia's six large wholesale electricity generation companies. Norilsk Nickel has acquired an impressive portfolio of electricity generation assets in addition to its ownership of OGK-3. The company has large stakes in 13 different electricity companies in Russia, some completely dedicated to their production facilities, as well as a 3.5 percent stake in the Russian national electricity generation company, Unified Energy Systems (UES).[34]

Norilsk Nickel plans to combine its power assets to create a separate electricity generation company, Norilsk Power. The only power generation assets not to be included in Norilsk Power will be four generators that are considered strategic assets for the company's production facilities. Norilsk Power assets will be spun off from Norilsk Nickel so as not to provide a distraction for the company's core business. Norilsk Power will be one of Russia's largest electricity generation companies with over 4,500 Megawatts of installed generating capacity spread across 34 plants, including OGK-3, TGK-1, and TGK-14, covering Central Russia, the Northwest, the Ural region and Siberia[35] (more on types of electricity generators in Chapter 8).

Norilsk Nickel has been owned by Interros, an investment company founded by Russian billionaire oligarchs Vladimir Potanin and Mikhail Prokhorov, since 1995. When purchased by Interros, Norilsk Nickel had over $4 billion of debt, was shedding over $2 million of cash on a daily basis, and its workers had not been paid in four months. Two years later, under the direction of Interros, Norilsk Nickel had become current on its debt, paid its employees, increased employee wages twofold, and went from losing over $800 million a year to showing a profit. Today, Norilsk Nickel is considered one of the best-run Russian companies and a global leader in the metals and mining industry. It is also a leader in corporate governance and financial transparency.[36]

Norilsk Nickel continues to work to expand its global presence. In 2006, it acquired a 35 percent in U.S.-based Plug Power, Inc., a company that develops and manufactures hydrogen fuel cells. Norilsk Nickel hopes fuel cell technology will bring a new revolution to power generation that it could use to provide power to its operations in the Arctic Circle, as well as expand the global uses for platinum and palladium, two key metals in the production of fuel cells.[37]

Vladimir Potanin

Vladimir Potanin, president and co-founder of Interros Investment Company (Figure 4.3), was born in 1961 in Moscow to a well-

Figure 4.3   Vladimir Potanin, President of Interros Investment Company and Majority Owner of Norilsk Nickel
Courtesy of Interros (www.interros.ru).

connected family. Potanin graduated from Moscow's State Institute of International Relations, considered a stepping stone to a career at the Ministry of Foreign Affairs, the KGB, or the Kremlin. After graduation, Potanin worked at the Soviet Department of Trade and, in 1991, formed Interros as a nonferrous metals trading company. Potanin used the profits from Interros to purchase UNEXIM Bank, as well as to found MFK bank. From August 1996 until March 1997, Potanin held the position of first deputy prime minister of the Russian

Federation and still remains involved in the Russian government, being a member of the board for Russian Federation Governmental Council on Entrepreneurship and the Russian Union of Industrialists and Entrepreneurs.[38]

Together with his former partner, Mikhail Prokhorov, Vladimir Potanin has grown Interros into an investment giant with over $10 billion in investments. The direct ownership of companies by Interros contributes about 1.3 percent of Russia's GDP and includes Norilsk Nickel, the country's largest metals and mining company; Open Investments, one of the country's largest real-estate developers; Rosbank, one of the country's largest banks; as well as a small petroleum company, media companies, and an electricity generation equipment company.[39] Potanin is considered one of the leading businessmen in Russia and is consistently ranked in the top 10 of the most influential Russian businessmen and is one of the only oligarchs to be free of any charges of unsavory business practices in Russia.[40]

Vladimir Potanin has been a prolific contributor to charitable causes in Russia, founding the Vladimir Potanin Foundation in 1999. Through the Foundation, Potanin has focused on improving education in Russia and preserving Russia's cultural heritage. The Vladimir Potanin Foundation has created a number of programs to help promote education throughout the country. The Foundation awards over 400 grants and 2,300 scholarships annually to help exceptional students pay for higher education. The Foundation also provides grants to exceptional teachers and separate grants for promising young teachers. The Foundation started a scholarship program in 2003 to help increase the prestige of serving in the armed services by providing 200 scholarships annually to exceptional military cadets that wish to pursue a higher education.[41]

The Vladimir Potanin Foundation has also been active in funding programs related to Russian culture, working with the Russian Ministry of Culture to fund programs that promote the Russian language and programs that preserve Russian arts and culture. Potanin, himself, has been active in promoting Russian culture, helping to show Russian art abroad as well as using his personal funds to purchase historical Russian art for use by the Russian Ministry of Culture. Potanin donates more than $1 million annually to the Guggenheim

Foundation and is on the board of trustees of the Guggenheim Museum. In January 2007, Potanin was named an officer of the Order of Arts and Literature, a prestigious honor bestowed by the French Ministry of Culture and Communications, for his work on preserving culture.[42]

Polyus Gold

Symbol	PLZL
ADR	OPYGY.US
ADR Ratio	1:1
Market Cap	$8.22 billion
Shares Outstanding	190.63 million
Estimated Freefloat	45.4 percent

Polyus Gold is Russia's largest gold producer and the tenth largest in the world. The company was created in March 2006 when Norilsk Nickel spun off its gold assets. Norilsk Nickel left Polyus Gold in an enviable position to begin its life as an independent company with no outstanding debt. This has left the company with well over $2 billion in cash to finance acquisitions and increase production at existing fields. The company's management has an ambitious plan to become one of the top five global gold producers by 2015.[43]

Uralkaliy

Symbol	URKA
GDR	URKA.LI
GDR Ratio	1:5
Market Cap	$5.56 billion
Shares Outstanding	2.12 billion
Estimated Freefloat	20.0 percent

Uralkaliy is Russia's second largest potash producer and a leading global supplier. The company mines its own ore and processes it into potash, a potent fertilizer. The company's primary export markets are China and Brazil. China is increasingly using potash fertilizer to increase yields on its crops as its population continues to increase and its farmland continues to decrease. Uralkaliy recently signed a lucrative deal for the continued supply of potash to China. Brazil uses potash fertilizer for its sugarcane fields, which are coming under increasing demand as the country continues to lead the world in refining and using sugarcane as biofuel. The company will continue to benefit from rising global populations and the increasing use of crops as biofuels. The company will also benefit from the fact that it is expected to account for up to 40 percent of the increase in global potash production through 2011.[44]

Chapter 5

Oil and Natural Gas

Fueling Russia's Growth

Oil Industry

Russia is currently the world's largest producer and exporter of oil after Saudi Arabia. In 2005, Russia accounted for about 12 percent of global oil production. After enjoying production increases for five straight years between 2000 and 2005 of nearly 8 percent annually, production growth has slowed to around 2.5 percent per year since 2005 as older wells and equipment make increasing production both expensive and difficult.[1]

Risks:
- A primary risk to the oil industry is the volatility of oil prices. If oil prices decline, the oil companies will receive less revenue while still incurring steady costs.

- Ruble appreciation is another risk for the oil industry, as nearly all oil transactions are denominated in U.S. dollars, while expenses are almost solely denominated in rubles. As the ruble appreciates, the industry's U.S. dollar–denominated sales are worth fewer rubles that are used to cover costs.
- Russia's oil fields have finished their easy-growth phase and oil is becoming more difficult to extract. At the same time, many of the oil rigs in Russia are nearing the end of their useful lives. This requires that oil companies increase their spending on both equipment replacement/upgrades as well as additional exploration and extraction costs.
- There is always the political risk associated with Russia's oil industry. The government considers oil as a *strategic industry,* and has shown a tendency to favor state-controlled Rosneft.

Rewards:
- The oil industry in Russia enjoys a prime position in the eyes of the government, which will be sure to protect the nation's ability to export oil.
- Russia enjoys one of the largest reserves of oil in the world. In fact, reserves may be greatly understated. Global expansion–led demand for oil has the potential to keep the price of oil high for the foreseeable future.
- As oil fields become more expensive to develop and oil exports continue to decline as a portion of Russia's GDP, it is possible that the country's oil industry could enjoy some form of tax relief from the Russian government. Greenfield development and largely depleted oil fields have recently been given tax relief.
- Russian oil stocks are currently valued at a considerable discount to similar developed-market and emerging-market companies, leaving the potential for further growth.

Oil Introduction and History

The Russian oil industry has been one of the country's main economic drivers. Russian oil production actually reached its peak in

1987, before the collapse of the Soviet Union. Years of neglect and underutilization at oil fields left the industry with greatly reduced production by the time capitalism came to the country in 1991. In 1992, the privatization of the oil industry began with many of the assets of the state being transferred into private hands. This first round of privatizations did very little to increase the production of oil, as the assets were generally acquired by large financial businesses that had little knowledge of the oil industry.[2]

The pace of industry reform changed drastically for the better in 1999 to 2000. A second round of privatizations occurred when the government sold considerable portions of its control positions in the industry to private holders. This round saw the creation of now-familiar Russian oil companies, including Surgutneftegaz, Sibneft (now a subsidiary of Gazprom, called Gazprom Neft), LUKoil, TNK (now part of a joint venture with British Petroleum, TNK-BP), and the famous Yukos.[3]

The last round of privatizations and consolidations in the oil industry in 2000 led to a more structured and professional approach to the oil industry in Russia. The newly formed companies used this period of post-consolidation to begin renovations of their previously neglected assets. These improvements, which encompassed nearly every level of production, led to the industry increasing production at an average rate of 7.8 percent per year between 2000 and 2005. Russia's oil production now is nearly back to 1987 levels.[4]

Present/Future

The future of Russia's oil industry looks very bright. The country is currently the second largest producer and exporter of oil in the world to Saudi Arabia. Russia is said to contain more than 6 percent of the world's oil reserves, a number that many analysts assess to be greatly understated. There have been a number of projects to extract new oil reserves in Russia recently, moving away from the traditional Ural Mountains region where the oil is very high in sulfur, expensive to refine, and mostly depleted, to oil fields in Siberia and the Far East.[5]

One notable, and very promising, extraction project is in the Far East region of Sakhalin Island. This project promises huge reserves potential within easy shipping to oil-hungry markets. Russia is currently in a process of expanding and upgrading its pipeline networks to ship more oil to the China market and the European market. At the same time, Russian oil companies have been investing heavily in exploring new fields and improving their extraction technology. These developments should help Russia continue to improve its position as a dominant exporter of oil, both crude and refined product, for many years to come. In addition, as the government's Stabilization Fund moves away from being primarily reflective of oil revenues and toward a broader interpretation of the economy, oil companies stand to benefit, as the oil tax could drop considerably.

Oil in the News

When people think of the Russian oil industry, many point to the recent problems surrounding Royal Dutch Shell's problems at the Sakhalin Island project as reason to be suspicious of the government's role in the industry. Shell has been working to develop this project on Russia's Pacific coast since 1994 and was recently forced to give up half of the project to the Russian company Gazprom. Observers opined that this was just another example of the Russian government usurping the rights of foreign companies and working to consolidate the oil industry into government control. Although this may be true, the Russian side of the story should be heard.

The deal between the Russian government and Shell was completed in 1994 to develop this vital project. Part of the deal was that Shell would be exempt from Russian taxes on the project until its investment was recovered, which was agreed by the company to be no more than 10 years. By 2005, the costs had more than doubled, and Shell said it would not recoup its investments—therefore not pay taxes—for at least an additional 10 years. When the Russian government decided this was unacceptable, it attempted to renegotiate the contract, believing that Shell was not living up to its end of the deal. When negotiations failed and Shell refused to start paying taxes, the government stepped in and forced Shell's hand by giving a controlling stake in the project to state-controlled Gazprom. Notably, this project had been the only one in the emerging world without a local partner.[6]

Rosneft

Symbol	ROSN
GDR	ROSN.LI
GDR Ratio	1:1
Market Cap	$82.88 billion
Shares Outstanding	10.57 billion
Freefloat Estimate	8.6 percent

Rosneft is Russia's largest oil company, both by amount of reserves and by market capitalization. The company is considered to be the Russian government's *state champion* of the oil industry. In keeping with its status as the state champion, the company is more than 75 percent owned by the Russian government. In a May 2007 decree, the government has classified Rosneft as a *strategic asset,* meaning the government cannot sell any of its stake in the company. Rosneft derives over 80 percent of its revenue from exports, with over 60 percent coming from exports of unrefined crude.[7]

The company has been able to acquire the most lucrative assets of Yukos through state-run auctions of the bankrupt company's assets. The consolidation of former Yukos assets has made Rosneft the leader in the Russian oil industry, surpassing LUKoil. These assets also contain refining capacity that forms a base of the company's plans to sell more refined product as a way to increase the company's margins.

LUKoil

Symbol	LKOH
ADR	LUKOY.US
ADR Ratio	1:1
Market Cap	$63.75 billion
Shares Outstanding	851 million
Freefloat Estimate	58.6 percent

LUKoil derives its name from the three oil companies that were combined in its formation; Langepasneftegaz, Uraineftegaz, and Kogalymneftegaz. The company was incorporated as LUKoil in 1992, making it one of the oldest public companies in Russia. LUKoil is Russia's second largest vertically integrated oil company. The company produces over 18 percent of Russia's total oil output and controls oil assets that range from exploration and extraction to retail sales. The company is, by far, the

Figure 5.1 LUKoil Gas Station in the United States
Courtesy of Fotosearch.

most privatized of any Russian oil company, with 100 percent of the company being owned by shareholders. Of that amount, more than 20 percent is owned by company management and nearly 20 percent is owned by ConocoPhillips (see Figure 5.1).[8]

LUKoil has consistently been named one of Russia's top companies for corporate governance. This is evidenced by the fact that the company has had an American Depository Receipt (ADR) in the United States since 1996 and was the first Russian company to obtain a full listing in London in 2002. The company has also received praise for its corporate governance within Russia. In 2001, the company's retirement pension plan was named the best among Russian companies. In 2005, the president of LUKoil, Vagit Alekperov, was presented a Fourth-Class Order "For Services to the Country" by Vladimir Putin.[9]

The company extracts oil reserves mainly from the Western Siberia area and Kazakhstan, while it is aggressively pursuing reserves in the North Caspian Sea. LUKoil also has exploration and production facilities in nine other countries, including Egypt, Saudi Arabia, Colombia, and Iraq. LUKoil also recently signed a memorandum of understanding with Qatar for exploration and production. The company has vast natural gas reserves, with plans to become Russia's second largest supplier behind Gazprom.[10]

LUKoil not only extracts oil, but also owns significant refining capacity. In fact, LUKoil has enough installed refining capacity to process over half of its total oil production. LUKoil currently has refineries in Russia, Ukraine, Bulgaria, and Romania. The company became the first in Russia to produce the new, environmentally friendly Euro-4 grade diesel in 2004, and in 2005 was the first to produce Euro-3 grade gasoline. The company benefits from a high level of refining capacity, as the Russian tax on refined product is considerably less than that on crude oil.[11]

The company distributes much of its refined product to its retail outlets for final sale. The company owns approximately 1,700 retail outlets inside Russia and more than 4,100 outlets internationally. LUKoil's most notable retail acquisitions were the purchases of the Getty retail gas station chain in 13 U.S. states in 2001 and ConocoPhillips retail stations in Pennsylvania and New Jersey in 2004. The first former Getty station to be branded with the LUKoil brand occurred in New York in 2003 and its opening ceremony was attended by Vladimir Putin. The company now has close to 2,000 LUKoil branded stations in the Northeast United States.[12]

Vagit Alekperov The president of LUKoil, Vagit Alekperov, is a lifelong oilman (see Figure 5.2). Born in 1950 in Baku, Azerbaijan, Alekperov followed in his father's footsteps by starting his working career in the oil industry. In 1974, he graduated from the Azerbaijan Oil and Chemistry Institute, working as a drilling operator for the Caspian oil company Kaspmorneft during his studies. His early work with the company involved working on offshore oil platforms. On one occasion, he was blown off a rig by an explosion, forcing him to swim for his life. He continued to work for the company after graduation, moving up from drilling operator to engineer and, eventually, to deputy head of production.[13]

Figure 5.2   Vagit Alekperov, President of LUKoil, Ably Guides this Multinational Giant
Courtesy of LUKoil www.lukoil.com.

In 1979, Alekperov left Azerbaijan for Western Siberia, where he worked for Surgutneftegaz until 1985. By the time he left Surgutneftegaz, he had risen to the post of first deputy general director of the Bashneft subsidiary of Surgutneftegaz. After working as general director of another oil production company, Alekperov was appointed deputy minister of the Oil and Gas Industry of the Soviet Union in 1990. During his time in this position, he championed vertical integration of oil companies as a way to promote more efficient operations and aid in coordinating the efforts of the many different companies operating in various sectors of the oil and gas industries.[14]

Alekperov's position poised him to put his belief in vertical integration into action by merging the assets of Langepasneftegaz, Uraineftegaz, and Kogalymneftegaz ("LUK") into a single, integrated oil company in 1991. When privatization of state-owned oil assets came in 1993, the company he helped form was renamed LUKoil, with Alekperov assuming the role of the company's president, a position he still holds today. Since rising through the ranks at Surgutneftegaz, Alekperov has been considered an oil industry expert in Russia. His early adoption of vertical integration, even before free-market forces came to Russia, has made LUKoil one of the world's premier oil companies.[15]

Under Alekperov's leadership, LUKoil has become the world's sixth largest producer of hydrocarbons, as well as becoming the first Russian company to buy a company in the United States with the acquisition of Getty Petroleum in 2000. In July 2007, Alekperov showed his belief in the future of LUKoil by doubling his stake in the company up to 19 percent. This increased stake also ensures that between his holdings and those of top management, the management of LUKoil will continue to control the company he founded.[16]

TNK-BP

Symbol	TNBP
ADR	NA
Market Cap	$26.61 billion
Share Outstanding	15.83 billion
Freefloat Estimate	5.2 percent

TNK-BP is a 50/50 joint venture that combined the assets of oil companies Alfa Group and Access/Renova with a share of capital owned by British Petroleum (BP). The alliance with BP brings the company a wealth of experience in the oil industry, both through technological expertise and through Western management style. TNK-BP currently ranks as the third largest crude oil producer in Russia and is also a minor producer of natural gas in the country. TNK-BP is a vertically integrated oil company, owning assets that follow oil production from exploration and extraction to final retail sale. In fact, TNK-BP currently owns the only refinery with a direct pipeline to Moscow, giving the company a 30 percent retail market share in the nation's capital. TNK-BP has enough refining assets to convert about one third of its crude into finished products.[17]

The company has a network of roughly 2,000 retail gas stations throughout Russia and Ukraine that it is in the process of converting to Western-style gas stations. The company's primary advantage is its access to the technological expertise of BP. Much of TNK-BP's oil reserves are located at fields that had been neglected for years or decades. The company has been able to upgrade many of these fields and is continually working on ways to increase production. TNK-BP has been able to post double-digit increases in production for the past few years and the company expects to achieve above-average output growth through at least 2008.[18]

Surgutneftegaz

Symbol	SNGS
ADR	SGTZY.US
ADR Ratio	1:50
Market Cap	$39.30 billion
Shares Outstanding	35.73 billion
Freefloat Estimate	44.0 percent

Surgutneftegaz is Russia's fourth largest vertically integrated oil producer and the country's third largest producer of natural gas. The company has over 6 billion barrels of proven oil reserves and also significant refining capacity, allowing it export refined oil products accounting for 20 percent of its revenues. The company receives most, over 60 percent, of its revenues from exporting crude oil. It is difficult to assess Surgutneftegaz in comparable performance to other companies in the sector because it has not released Western-audited financials since 2001 and the company continues to be better at producing oil than at corporate governance. In fact, its management exhibits disdain for shareholders' concerns and fails to plan for the utilization of its large (over $12 billion) cash hoard.[19]

Natural Gas

Russia is the world's leading natural gas producer. When gas and oil are totaled, Russia is the world's leader in energy exports. The country boasts 27 percent of the world's proven natural gas reserves and accounts for nearly a quarter of global production. The European Union relies on Russia for 28 percent of its consumption of natural gas. The country currently uses natural gas for about 70 percent of its electricity production and domestic heating through cogeneration is based on natural gas. The country has been gradually increasing by about 10 percent per year, the domestic prices of natural gas a commodity that had been previously subsidized to protect citizens from dramatic price increases.[20]

Risks:
- Political tensions in Europe stemming from unease about state-owned Gazprom shutting off gas supplies to Ukraine and Belarus is causing EU countries to consider diversifying supplies of natural gas.
- European natural gas sales, Russia's largest export destination and the most profitable, are denominated in U.S. dollars or euros. As the ruble appreciates against both currencies, the amount of revenue received in rubles is decreased and most expenses of production are paid in rubles.

- Political risk is evident in the Russian natural gas industry as it is deemed a "strategic industry" by the Russian government, with state-run Gazprom being considered the *state champion*.
- There is a possibility of increased taxation on natural gas extraction by the Russian government. Currently, oil extraction is taxed heavily, resulting in considerable tax revenues. Discussions have been underway for some time for a way to increase natural gas companies' contribution to the government.

Rewards:
- The size of Russia's natural gas reserves and its extensive existing pipeline network virtually ensure the country's importance to Europe in the foreseeable future. In fact, projections show that Russian natural gas will increase to about 75 percent of EU consumption.[21]
- The domestic tariffs for natural gas are rising at over 10 percent for households and industry. With Russia producing over 70 percent of its electricity from natural gas, the industry should benefit from consistent demand and increasing prices.[22]
- Russian natural gas producer stocks are considerably undervalued compared to emerging and developed market peers, leaving the potential for further appreciation.

The oil industry has been given a majority of the credit for the resurgence of the Russian economy since the country emerged from the Soviet era. This may be true, but one of the primary drivers for the country's rapid growth has been the natural gas industry. Russia has since grown to become a global powerhouse in the natural gas industry. Natural gas is used throughout Europe and Russia for heat, a fuel for industrial producers, and as a source of fuel for electricity producers. The main beneficiary of Russia's immense natural gas wealth is Gazprom, which will be discussed later in this chapter.[23]

As to domestic demand for the product, natural gas is used heavily in Russia for home heating and industrial production, especially in the steel industry. One of the most important domestic markets for the country's natural gas industry is the country's electricity generators.[24]

Since the formation of the Russian Federation and subsequent capitalization of the economy, the government has heavily regulated the prices for natural gas.

This has helped insulate not only electricity generators and manufacturers from hefty price increases, but also Russian citizens who use natural gas to heat their homes during the cold winters. This price control has been to the detriment of domestic sellers, primarily Gazprom, which accounts for 87 percent of domestic supplies. In the past, suppliers were forced into a situation where they had to supply domestic customers at a net loss to allow people and businesses time to adjust to increased prices. This is slowly changing, as the government has been raising the price companies can charge, called a tariff. Natural gas prices are expected to be fully market-determined by 2011.[25]

Future

The Russian natural gas industry is already a giant in global terms, but the future looks even brighter. The country's share of European Union consumption is set to expand from 28 percent in 2005 to about 47 percent by 2020. The industry should also benefit from international concern over climate change caused by carbon dioxide emissions. Natural gas–fueled power plants, although somewhat more expensive to operate compared to coal- or fuel-oil-based plants, operate with considerably less carbon dioxide and other emissions. It is projected that by 2030, natural gas will account for 24 percent of global fuel demand, up from 19 percent in 2005.[26]

This gradual increase in global demand comes at a time when Russia is working to open its first LNG facility at the giant Sakhalin Islands oil/gas fields. LNG, liquefied natural gas, is simply natural gas that is cooled until it is in liquid form so that it can be compressed and stored for shipping. This opens up the markets of the world to Russia's massive natural gas reserves.[27]

Internal market reforms in Russia's natural gas industry will also greatly improve the efficiency of the country's natural gas producers. Currently low domestic market prices can, at times, make it cheaper for companies to *flare* (burn off excess production into the atmosphere) their production rather than pay pipeline transport costs to sell the product at a loss. This is done because, due to government production license requirements, companies must produce a minimum amount of natural gas or risk losing their extraction license. It is estimated that Russian companies flare about 27 percent of their total production every year.[28] As the domestic market becomes more attractive and exporting opportunities grow, the need for flaring natural gas should greatly decrease. This will only lead to increased revenues for all of the companies in Russia's natural gas industry.

Gazprom

Symbol	GAZP
ADR	OGPZY.US
ADR Ratio	1:4
Market Cap	$234.37 billion
Shares Outstanding	23.67 billion
Freefloat Estimate	39.2 percent

Gazprom has a near monopoly on the natural gas industry in Russia, controlling nearly 90 percent of domestic sales and 100 percent of export sales. The company also controls the nation's natural gas pipeline systems that transport natural gas both internally and externally. In 2005, Gazprom produced 20 percent of the world's total natural gas production and accounted for the entire 28 percent of European Union consumption that Russia provided. The Russian government owns over 50 percent of the shares in the company, giving it majority control of the company's operations.[29] Dmitry Medvedev, the probable successor to President Vladimir, currently acts as both Russia's first deputy prime minister and as the chairman of Gazprom's board of directors.

Gazprom's near-monopoly status and close relationship with the government have not stopped it from pursuing a truly capitalist approach to doing business. The company is currently the fourth largest publicly traded company in the world with a market capitalization of $234 billion. Although the government owns over a 50 percent stake in the company, the public owns a substantial portion as well. This makes it the most traded blue chip stock on the Russian market. The company is fairly transparent in financial reporting and has had PriceWaterhouseCoopers as its auditor.[30]

The company has been aggressively investing in growth through acquisitions and through capital improvements. The company's main natural gas sites in West Siberia are being depleted and the company is currently investing in making these sites more efficient. One of the company's major expansion projects is at the Sakhalin Islands site where it is working on developing its capacity to create and deliver liquefied natural gas to global markets. This is an integral part of Gazprom's drive to become a global natural gas company. Gazprom currently owns portions of natural gas companies in over 25 countries throughout Europe and is currently working on joint-venture deals in other countries including Brazil.[31]

Gazprom is often in the news for all of the wrong reasons. In the beginning of 2006, Gazprom and the Russian government were on the receiving end of a great deal of criticism for shutting off the natural gas supplies to Ukraine. At the surface, this seems like a strong-arm tactic by the Russian state to use energy as a tool of coercion. In reality, the natural gas supply contract for Ukraine was up for renewal on January 1 of that year, and failure to reach a pricing agreement is what led to the natural gas cutoff. Ukraine was paying about $45 per million cubic meters at the same time that Gazprom was selling the same gas in Western Europe for about $250 per million cubic meters. Natural gas was restored quickly when Ukraine agreed to an increase to a little over $100 per million cubic meters, still less than half of the price in most of Europe.[32] Russia and Gazprom received similar criticism in the beginning of 2007, when the same issue arose in the respect of Belarus. Again, the issue was solved quickly with Belarus still enjoying pricing of less than half of the rate in Western Europe. On the other hand, both Ukraine and Belarus cited the fact that Russia, too, was paying less than market value for the Turkmen natural gas that is a primary supplier to these countries.

Novatek

Symbol	NVTK
ADR	NVATY.US
ADR Ratio	1:10
Market Cap	$15.15 billion
Shares Outstanding	3.04 billion
Freefloat Estimate	24.1 percent

Novatek is currently Russia's second-largest natural gas producer. The company's market capitalization of $15 billion pales in comparison to Gazprom's $234 billion, and Gazprom owns nearly 20 percent of Novatek's shares. Novatek is also Russia's fastest-growing independent natural gas producer with an increase in production of 15 percent from 2005 to 2006 and an estimated 10 percent annual growth through 2010. The company's relationship with Gazprom gives it an advantage when it comes to access to the country's domestic natural gas pipeline distribution system. Gazprom is increasingly relying on Novatek to supply its obligations in the domestic market. The company intends to capitalize on the increasing tariffs in the domestic market to become a more significant domestic player as Gazprom continues to look more toward international markets for revenue growth.[33]

Chapter 6

Information and Communication as a Business

The New Russia

Cellular Telecom

The cell phone industry in Russia, almost nonexistent in the Soviet Union, is now approaching Western countries in terms of cell phone usage. This is partly due to the still low availability of home phone lines and also due to the fact that owning a mobile phone is not only a convenience but also a status symbol. The country has been slow to implement technology enhancements to mobile phones, mostly due to the focus on expanding the customer base. Now that the Russian mobile phone market is highly utilized, the country is moving quickly to implement new cellular technologies such as 3G. The country's cellular industry is dominated by wireless giants MTS and VimpelCom, both private start-up companies. This is another area where Russian companies have had an enormous advantage over foreign companies, mostly due to the complications in getting licenses for wireless communications.[1]

Russian wireless companies have been exceptionally successful at expanding their market shares, both inside and outside of Russia. Russia's two premier wireless operators, Mobile Telesystems (MTS) and VimpelCom, have significant presences throughout the Commonwealth of Independent States (CIS, the organ formed by many of the former Soviet republics, which are now independent). These companies are using both their geographical and cultural closeness to this region to gain large footholds into economies that are growing very rapidly.

Risks:
- The largest risk to Russian wireless companies is the high penetration of mobile phones in Russia, causing wireless operators to rely more on revenue growth from existing customers and volatile CIS countries for growth.
- Russian wireless operators are facing increased competition from fixed-line companies offering mobile phone services.
- Wireless companies also face political risks as they are required to obtain licenses from the Russian government to operate.

Rewards:
- Russian wireless companies are beginning to work toward 3G services including mobile Internet and television, providing for increased revenues from existing subscribers.
- As disposable income skyrockets, revenues per subscriber (ARPU) are increasing.
- Continued operating improvements have allowed Russian wireless companies to increase their profitability considerably.

- Russian wireless carriers enjoy large market shares in fast-growing CIS countries.
- Government licensing provides a large barrier for entry by foreign companies.

VimpelCom

Symbol	VIMP
ADR	VIP.US
ADR Ratio	1:0.25
Market Cap	$22.29 billion
Shares Outstanding	205.13 million
Estimated Freefloat	45.1 percent

VimpelCom, Russia's second largest cellular phone provider after Mobile Telesystems, has been an excellent example of a successful private start-up company in Russia. Formed in 1992 by a group of Russian scientists who had previously worked on advanced radio technology and defense projects in the former Soviet Union, VimpelCom has grown to become a world-class mobile telecommunications company. The company now boasts over 50 million subscribers and nearly $5 billion in annual revenue.[2]

VimpelCom now earns roughly 10 percent of its revenues from the Ukraine market alone, where it operates under the Beeline brand and is one of the fastest-growing cellular companies in Ukraine. VimpelCom also has licenses for the entire countries of Kazakhstan, Uzbekistan, Tajikistan, Georgia, and Armenia.[3] VimpelCom also recently announced a joint venture to enter Vietnam in an attempt to take advantage of the lucrative Asian markets. The company has recently begun a pilot program in Tajikistan to take advantage of the newly granted 3G license by offering Internet access services in that country for the first time. This program is both an attempt to increase per-user revenues by adding more value-added services and a subtle way of prodding the Russian government to grant similar licenses for Russia.

Mobile Telesystems (MTS)

Symbol	MTSS
ADR	MBT.US
ADR Ratio	1:5
Market Cap	$19.55 billion
Shares Outstanding	1.99 billion
Estimated Freefloat	47.2 percent

MTS is Russia's largest cellular phone provider with over 70 million subscribers in Russia and the CIS, a coverage area with a population of 230 million. The company's presence in the CIS includes its operations in Ukraine, under the UMC brand, where it holds the number two position in market share to Ukraine's own Kyivstar. MTS has also expanded into the CIS countries of Belarus, Turkmenistan, and Uzbekistan. MTS is majority-owned by Russia conglomerate Sistema with 52.8 percent of the company. The rest is freefloat.[4]

MTS has traditionally grown through mergers and acquisitions (M&A) in Russia and the CIS, as compared to organic growth and widening margins. Management has turned its attention to increasing organic growth and increasing profitability, and the results are just now beginning to show as the company continues to beat analysts' estimates for profitability. The company also plans to benefit from the acquisition of one of Russia's only 3G licenses that will allow it to provide more value added services and mobile Internet services for the first time. MTS plans to continue to focus on increasing its market share in its existing markets, some of which was lost to VimpelCom, and increasing per-customer profitability.[5]

Wireline Telecom

The Russian fixed-line industry was successfully reorganized into seven *super regional* companies, each licensed to a dedicated region of the country, plus one company (Comstar/MGTS) responsible for the Moscow area, with Svyazinvest holding a 51 percent stake in each company while the rest is publicly traded. But the government has been too slow in moving toward full privatization, with the government still holding control of the companies in this sector through its holding company Svyazinvest (*Svyaz* meaning communications). Some speculate that this delay is due to the alleged hidden interests of Communications Minister Reiman, which are currently being investigated by the authorities in the British Virgin Islands. Partly, this is due to the government's belief that it needs to slowly bring phone rates up to market standards to give the population time to adjust to the rising rates.[6]

These recently formed companies are Center Telecom, Comstar/MGTS, Far East Telecom (also called Dalsvyaz), Northwest Telecom, Sibertelecom, Southern Telecom, Uralsvyazinform, and Volga Telecom. These companies are all majority-owned by the state-run company Svyazinvest. There is also a separate company for long-distance service, Rostelecom, that now competes with a private company, Golden Telecom, in the long-distance market.[7]

The fixed-line industry in Russia is still plagued by long delays in installing lines into consumers' homes. Some of the regional companies have lines connecting only about 20 to 25 percent of their licensed consumer base. This is a problem these companies have been working to rectify and will provide them with a large revenue growth driver for years to come. The Russian government has also been working to increase the amounts that companies are allowed to charge for their phone service in preparation for the eventuality of allowing phone rates to be determined by market forces.[8] To supplement their revenues, Russian fixed-line operators have been adding more services to their offerings. Internet DSL service is becoming very popular in the country—the number of broadband-connected households increased by 98 percent in 2006 and is expected to continue to increase by over 50 percent per year for the near future.

Risks:
- Fixed-line telephone reorganization is still a work in progress, with considerable debate continuing inside the Russian government as to the fate of Svyazinvest.

- Fixed-line operators are still working to install phone lines to a majority of their customers. With cellular service available in most of the country, the fixed-line operators run the risk of suffering from substitution of mobile phones.

Rewards:
- Russian fixed-line companies are connecting residential customers at an increasing rate, adding additional revenue.
- Regional telecoms have been adding value-added services with high margins, such as high-speed Internet and cable TV.
- Government-regulated tariffs on phone services are set to continue to increase until they are brought to market levels, adding an additional revenue growth driver for fixed-line companies.

Comstar

Symbol	CMST
GDR	CMST.LI
GDR Ratio	1:1
Market Cap	$3.72 billion
Shares Outstanding	417.94 million
Estimated Freefloat	33.0 percent

Comstar is one of the largest fixed-line telephone operators in Russia. Comstar is majority-owned by the giant Russian conglomerate, Sistema. One of the core businesses for Comstar is its MGTS subsidiary, which is one of the regional telephone companies spun off during the government's privatization process. MGTS is solely responsible for the city of Moscow, where the company enjoys the advantages of having a population with higher incomes than most areas of Russia, as well as having a very high level of phone service penetration compared to most of the country.[9]

Comstar operates mainly in the city of Moscow as well, servicing the large number of corporate clients as well as providing telephone-related services such as broadband Internet, where it supplies about 30 percent of Moscow's total broadband access. Although the company has a heavy presence in the Moscow market, it has the flexibility and the desire to begin working on acquiring business outside the city and throughout Russia. Comstar believes that gaining a presence throughout Russia will be a prime growth driver in its future.[10] A very large advantage that Comstar has over its rivals in Russia is that it owns a 25 percent stake in Svyazinvest. The Russian government is determined to complete the privatization of the telephone industry, the only sticking point to completion being the method of privatization. The leading plan for privatization at this point seems to be to turn Svyazinvest into a publicly traded company, with the government retaining a controlling stake. This course of privatization would be very beneficial to Comstar, potentially giving the company the opportunity to become a controlling shareholder in the new, privatized version of Svyazinvest. This would give Comstar nationwide reach instantaneously, as well as give the rest of the regional companies much-needed liquidity.[11]

Golden Telecom

Symbol	Not Listed in Russia
ADR	GLDN.US
ADR Ratio	NA
Market Cap	$2.04 billion
Shares Outstanding	39.92 million
Estimated Freefloat	32.0 percent

Golden Telecom is a Russian phone company that promotes itself as an alternative to the incumbent, formerly state-run, regional telephone companies. One of the company's main focuses has been in business telephone services, which accounted for 58 percent of total revenues in 2005. The company is also making a strong push into the Russian long-distance market, where it is licensed to offer services throughout the entire country. Golden Telecom offers consumers a viable choice for long-distance services putting pressure on the state-run former long-distance monopoly, Rostelecom.[12]

The company offers much of its services through what is called an *overlay network* in which it uses satellite and other means to bypass the existing Rostelecom network. The company has also been focusing on providing competitive, value-added services in Russia, especially Internet services. Golden Telecom has been very aggressive in establishing fiber-optic networks throughout Russia, with the focus on creating a more efficient high-speed Internet network. The company has recently completed construction of the largest wireless Internet network in Europe to cover the city of Moscow. The company also operates as a cellular phone company in Ukraine and is actively expanding into other countries of the CIS.[13]

Far East Telecom

Symbol	ESPK
ADR	FEEOY.US
ADR Ratio	1:2
Market Cap	$611.0 million
Shares Outstanding	95.58 million
Estimated Freefloat	61.9 percent

Far East Telecom, also known as Dalsvyaz, is the regional fixed-line incumbent in the Far East region of Russia. The company has an 85 percent market share in this region for both wireline services and Internet services. The company has the highest proportion of value-added services among fixed-line incumbents, including Internet services and mobile phone service. The company was able to increase its DSL Internet subscriber base by nearly 300 percent between 2005 and 2006, as management has focused on developing this profitable market segment in the fixed-line industry.[14]

Southern Telecom

Symbol	KUBN
ADR	STJSY.US
ADR Ratio	1:50
Market Cap	$769.92 million
Shares Outstanding	2.96 billion
Estimated Freefloat	61.8 percent

Southern Telecom is the regional wireline incumbent for the southern region of Russia including the Black Sea area. The company has shown impressive operating performance improvements, mainly by reducing the overall debt burden and aggressively reducing costs. The company has an 89 percent market share in the southern region of Russia, as well as an over 50 percent market share in Internet services. The company's main growth drivers are increased regional tariffs and increases in value added services such as Internet services, which it plans to increase by 800 percent by 2011.[15]

Rostelecom

Symbol	RTKM
ADR	ROS.US
ADR Ratio	1:6
Market Cap	$7.62 billion
Shares Outstanding	728.69 million
Estimated Freefloat	62.0 percent

Rostelecom is the leading long-distance and international calling services organization of Russia. The company has a majority share of the country's long-distance market, although competitors such as Golden Telecom and MTT are slowly eroding Rostelecom's dominance in this market. Rostelecom does own 11 percent of its main competitor, Golden Telecom, as well as a 31 percent stake in a wholesale ISP provider. The main driver for this stock is the anticipated breakup of Svyazinvest. One prevailing scenario for this breakup would create a new privatized entity with Rostelecom at the center, with a controlling position in the country's fixed-line industry.[16]

Media

The Russian media market is expanding rapidly on the rise in consumer spending and increased Internet access. The primary sources of access for investors into this fast-growing market are through television and Internet companies. On the television side, rising consumer demand and competition among retailers to capture this demand has led to advertising revenue increases of over 35 percent per year for television stations, who control nearly 50 percent of Russia's total advertising market. As high-speed Internet usage rapidly expands in Russia, up over 50 percent per year, Internet companies are enjoying increased prominence in attracting advertising dollars.[17]

Risks:
- While growth rates are high, Russian media companies are valued relatively high against emerging market peers.
- The Russian media industry is still in its infancy and competition from large conglomerates is a potential threat.
- Political risk is very large in Russian media companies as the Kremlin watches media outlets very closely for any hint of criticism against the government.

Rewards:
- The country's continued economic-expansion-led domestic consumption growth should continue to push media advertising revenues up at over 35 percent per year.
- The Russian media industry is still fragmented, leaving opportunities for continued consolidation.
- The media industry, still very young, has room for innovative ideas that can bring additional market penetration and advertising revenue.

CTC Media

Symbol	Not Listed in Russia
ADR	CTCM.US
ADR Ratio	NA
Market Cap	$41.11 billion
Shares Outstanding	151.54 million
Estimated Freefloat	25.0 percent

CTC Media is Russia's fourth largest television broadcasting company, operating an entertainment station (CTC) and a female programming station (Domashny). It boasts total television market share of about 10 percent. The company's CTC station is entertainment only, staying away from news in favor of series shows and movies. The company's Domashny station features programming geared toward a female audience. The company has been one of the beneficiaries of the increased spending on advertising and has seen its revenues from advertising increase by over 30 percent per year, a trend the company sees continuing through 2010.[18]

Rambler Media

Symbol	Not Listed In Russia
GDR	RMG.LN
GDR Ratio	1:1
Market Cap	$617.18 million
Shares Outstanding	15.02 million
Estimated Freefloat	18.96 percent

Rambler Media is one of Russia's largest media companies. The company owns the country's second largest Internet search engine, rambler.ru, as well as some of Russia's most popular Web sites. Rambler Media also owns a mobile content provider, an advertising agency, and the Internet service provider (ISP) Rambler Telecom. Prof-Media, a company owned by the giant Interros investment fund, recently purchased the television asset of Rambler Media. Prof-Media followed this acquisition with a purchase of a controlling stake (48.8 percent) in Rambler Media. The acquisition by Prof-Media of a controlling stake in Rambler Media will instantly provide Rambler with the scale it has lacked to take full advantage of the opportunities in the Russian media industry.[19]

RBC Media

Symbol	RBCI
ADR	RINFY.US
ADR Ratio	1:1
Market Cap	$1.09 billion

Shares Outstanding   119.26 million
Estimated Freefloat   39.2 percent

Formed in 1993, RBC (RosBusinessConsulting) was the first public Russian media and IT company. The company gains most of its revenue, over 70 percent, from media and television advertising, and the rest comes from IT services. In 2003, RBC Media launched Russia's first business television station, RBC TV. RBC has also expanded into print media, mainly focusing on business and financial news, with publications in Russia and Ukraine. RBC Media has recently expanded its offerings by acquiring EDI S Press Holding, a company that specializes in trendy magazines and informational Internet sites. The company has shown an impressive track record of continued revenue growth of over 41 percent per year, which the company intends to continue through 2011.[20]

Chapter 7

The Rising Russian Consumer

Retail

One of the most exciting sectors of Russia's economy for investors is the emerging retail sector. With the average Russian's disposable income rising at about 27 percent every year since 2000[1] (and expected to continue rising at 20 percent or more), a large market is developing to provide Russian citizens the opportunity to spend some of this newfound wealth. Russia is expected to surpass Germany as Europe's largest consumer market by the end of 2008. In light of this rapid growth, it is surprising to most that foreign retail giants have been slow to enter the Russian market. Although there are many foreign retailers in the large population centers of Moscow and St. Petersburg, with stores such as Ikea and Ralph Lauren, expansion into big-box retailing, food retailing, and expansion into areas outside of the major cities has been almost nonexistent.

This is mainly due to the complexities of the Russian consumers as people of different regions of Russia have both different income levels and different product preferences. This makes it difficult for foreign companies to implement "one size fits all" approaches to Russian retail, and they suffer from lack of local knowledge of customer desires. This has been a boon to domestic retailers in Russia, as they have been able to secure precious market share and profit from the exceptional growth of the country's retail sector.

Risks:

- Consumer companies are driven by personal consumption, and any drop in consumer confidence can have a negative impact on the sector.
- If the Central Bank of Russia cannot contain inflation, disposable income rises will slow, leading to reduced consumer spending gains.
- Large foreign retailers could enter the market in the future.
- Consumer sector companies' aggressive expansion plans are putting pressures on their margins.

Rewards:

- Continued consolidation in the industry is creating economies of scale for the market leaders, as well as increasing their revenues at a rapid pace.
- Consumer spending continues to rise as the increase in Russians' disposable incomes continues to outpace inflation.
- The complexities of the Russian market outside of the main cities provide a barrier to entry for foreign retailers.
- There are signs that many Russian retailers are beginning to pursue methods of expansion that are less destructive to margins.
- There is still plenty of room for consolidation of Russia's retailers. X5, Russia's largest food retailer, accounts for only 3 percent of the market.

X5

Symbol	Not Listed In Russia
GDR	FIVE.LI
GDR Ratio	NA
Market Cap	$6.41 billion
Shares Outstanding	216.48 million
Estimated Freefloat	25 percent

X5, a chain founded by the merger of Russian food retailers Pyaterochka and Perekrestok, is the largest Russian retailer (see Figure 7.1). X5 can still claim to be Russia's largest food retailer, but has recently begun to expand into other areas of retail goods. X5, formerly almost entirely confined to the Moscow and St. Petersburg

Figure 7.1   X5 Grocery Store
Courtesy of X5 Retail Group.

areas, is now aggressively expanding into the entire country, including regions with lower incomes but exceptional growth prospects. The largest area of expansion has been in what are called *hypermarkets,* under the Frank brand.[2]

These hypermarkets can be compared to a smaller version of Wal-Mart. These stores combine a complete grocery store with a retail store that provides a wide variety of products from everyday needs to larger items important to Russian households. This focus has enabled X5 to show revenue growth of over 40 percent per year, with no slowdown apparent in the near future. The company plans additional acquisitions in the near future, with a high probability that it will exercise its purchase option on Russian hypermarket chain Carrousel, a company with nearly $1 billion in annual sales. X5 also recently signed an agreement with Sistema-Hals, a major real estate developer, to jointly develop shopping centers in Russia.[3]

Magnit

Symbol	MGNT
ADR	NA
Market Cap	$3.16 billion
Shares Outstanding	72 million
Estimated Freefloat	19 percent

Russia's second largest food retailer, Magnit, started with a different approach to the Russian retail sector. Magnit has focused almost entirely on food retailing, making it a pure grocery chain. The company has also focused on small stores in cities with populations of 500,000 or less. The company targets these areas with a customized approach to each individual store, tailoring its product offerings and pricing based on the local incomes and shopping patterns. The company consistently reviews the incomes and shopping patterns of its regional stores and changes product offerings based on local needs. This approach has made the company the sole retailer in many of the regions it serves, giving the company a large foothold in the growing economies of the smaller cities.[4]

Seventh Continent

Symbol	SCON
ADR	NA
Market Cap	$1.94 billion
Shares Outstanding	75 million
Estimated Freefloat	25 percent

Seventh Continent is Russia's sixth largest retail chain, with exposure to luxury stores, hypermarkets, and convenience stores. The company's main store format (over 40 percent) is traditional grocery stores. The company currently has about a 1 percent market share in the Russian food-retailing sector, but is growing rapidly. Seventh Continent continues to show revenue growth of nearly 35 percent per year and is aggressively working to expand through acquisitions. The company has also been expanding its presence in the hypermarket sector, both through acquisitions and through new store openings.[5]

Wimm-Bill-Dann

Symbol	WBDF
ADR	WBD.US
ADR Ratio	1:1
Market Cap	$3.16 billion
Shares Outstanding	44 million
Estimated Freefloat	33.7 percent

Wimm-Bill-Dann is Russia's largest food company, producing dairy products, baby food, and beverages. The company is Russia's largest dairy producer, with 31 percent of the country's market share. The company's dairy products include milk, yogurt, cheese, and desserts. Wimm-Bill-Dann is also Russia's second largest beverage maker. The company produces juices and bottled water, with a 19 percent market share in this category. The company also produces baby food, an area where it enjoys a 22 percent market share as Russia's third largest producer. The company has been shifting its focus to high-end dairy products, baby food, and beverages and away from milk because raw milk prices have been rising at about 15 percent annually. Wimm-Bill-Dann has been continuing its respectable growth rate at nearly 20 percent per year and increasing its margins due to product mix adjustments.[6]

Baltika Brewery

Symbol	PKBA
ADR	NA
Market Cap	$7.96 billion
Shares Outstanding	161.54 million
Estimated Freefloat	11.8 percent

Baltika Brewery is Russia's largest brewer, with an impressive 23 percent market share. When combined with other brewers of its parent company, Baltic Beverage Holdings, the total market share is 35 percent. The company produces its market-leading Baltika brand, as well as Fosters. The company has also formed a joint venture with Scottish Newcastle and Carlsberg Company to produce their worldwide brands at Baltika facilities. The company has experienced growth of about 20 percent per year, but that growth is expected to slow as the beer market has reached relative maturity, with the top five producers controlling more than 80 percent of the market.[7]

Kalina

Symbol	KLNA
ADR	NA
Market Cap	$375.46 million
Shares Outstanding	9.75 million
Estimated Freefloat	70.0 percent

Kalina is a market leader in the Russian personal care market. The company gains a majority of its revenue from the manufacture and sales of cosmetics in Russia, Ukraine, Kazakhstan, and Belarus. The company produces cosmetics, oral hygiene products, detergents, household chemicals, fragrances, and grooming products. Kalina has a 24 percent market share in the Russian cosmetics market and a 10 percent market share in the oral hygiene market. The personal care market has been rising at about 13 percent per year in Russia, with Kalina being a primary beneficiary. The company has recorded sales gains of nearly 30 percent annually since 2002. Kalina bolstered its product lineup in 2005 by purchasing a controlling stake in the German company, Dr. Scheller. Russia's average spending on personal care products is still less than half that of Western Europe, leaving Kalina with a great opportunity for continued growth.[8]

Pharmacy Chain 36.6

Symbol	APTK
ADR	NA
Market Cap	$720 million
Shares Outstanding	8 million
Estimated Freefloat	30.6 percent

Russian retail growth has not been limited to the food retailers. Another Russian hometown retail success story has been in the pharmacy industry. Pharmacy Chain 36.6 is the largest Russian pharmacy chain and has been growing rapidly in recent years, securing market share throughout the country to take advantage of the still-underserved Russian prescription and over-the-counter drug markets. Russia is currently the second fastest growing pharmaceutical market in the world following Brazil, with annual growth of 35 percent in 2005 and 37 percent in 2006.[9]

Even with Russia's impressive growth in the pharmaceutical sector, Russian consumers are still relatively underserved in this market. As disposable incomes continue to rise, this gap is getting smaller, aided by the government's inclusion of medical care as part of its Priority National Projects. This emphasis on medical care, including making drugs accessible to those who need them, will help fuel pharmaceutical growth.

This provides an excellent opportunity for Pharmacy Chain 36.6, unquestionably Russia's largest pharmacy, to take advantage of this growth through its nationwide retail network which it expects to increase by 70 percent to about 1,450 stores by the end of 2007.[10] Pharmacy Chain 36.6 has also implemented an aggressive strategy of overhauling its stores to resemble something along the lines of Walgreens in the United States. This will allow the company to benefit from higher-margin retail sales of beauty products, health care products, and other common retail products that consumers could buy to take advantage of the convenience of one-stop shopping.

Pharmstandard

Symbol	PHST
GDR	PHST.LI
GDR Ratio	4:1
Market Cap	$2.34 billion
Shares Outstanding	37.79 million
Estimated Freefloat	43 percent

Another company benefiting from the rapid increase in pharmaceutical spending in Russia is Pharmstandard. Pharmstandard is a Russian manufacturer of both prescription and over-the-counter drugs, as well as medical supplies. The company currently manufactures and distributes 241 different generic drug formulations, as well as two original drug formulations. The company is currently one of the top Russian producers of pharmaceutical products, and its market share in this segment continues to grow. Russia's current pharmaceutical market is dominated by foreign powerhouses, contributing to about 75 percent of domestic sales. Russian manufacturers have been turning the tide and have been steadily taking market share away from the foreign manufacturers, not by regulatory roadblocks, but by increasing quality and efficiency.[11]

Pharmstandard's growth has been robust, increasing sales of existing product lines at an average rate of over 25 percent per year since the company's creation in 2004. The company currently has over 50 different drug formulations in the pipeline pending regulatory approval in Russia and has been aggressive in obtaining growth through new products and acquisitions of other manufacturers. Pharmstandard, as well as other health-care-related companies in Russia, stands to reap large benefits from the Priority National Project focusing on health care that is designed to increase federal spending on prescription drug reimbursements to citizens and make pharmaceuticals more widely available.[12]

Roman Abramovich The majority owner of Pharmstandard, and one of Russia's richest and most notable oligarchs, is Roman Abramovich (see Figure 7.2). Abramovich was born in 1966 in Saratov, Russia. His mother died when he was an infant and his father died in a construction accident when he was four. He was raised by his grandmother in Moscow and his uncle in Ukhta, a small Siberian town 700 miles north of Moscow. He began attending Moscow's Industrial Institute, but was drafted into the Soviet Army. Following his compulsory military service, Abramovich attended the Moscow State Auto Transport Institute but chose to pursue business interests instead of completing his education.[13]

Abramovich first entered into private business in the late 1980s. Gorbachev had permitted the establishment of small businesses, called *cooperatives,* and Abramovich took advantage of this opportunity to begin his entrepreneurial activities by opening up an auto parts cooperative after a brief stint as a child's doll salesman. After the fall of the Soviet Union and the privatization of the economy, he founded five separate businesses focused on the resale of products and developed an expertise in oil product trading, working for a Swiss trading company.[14]

Figure 7.2   Roman Abramovich, Russia's Richest Oligarch, Is a Governor and, as Owner of England's Chelsea Football Club, a UK Celebrity.

Roman Abramovich's fortunes took a dramatic turn for the better when he befriended Boris Berezovsky in the mid-1990s. Berezovsky brought Abramovich into Yeltsin's inner circle, and he soon became personal friends with Yeltsin himself. When Berezovsky obtained a majority stake in Sibneft, one of Russia's largest oil producers, he made Abramovich a member of the company's board of directors. He later became the manager of the company's Moscow offices. During Yeltsin's presidency, Abramovich and Berezovsky were able to secure a 26 percent stake in Russia's largest airline, Aeroflot, as well as a 50 percent stake in the country's largest aluminum producer RUSAL.[15]

After Yeltsin's presidency ended and Putin's began, Abramovich kept his ties to the government by breaking camp with his friend Berezovsky to become close to the Putin administration. When Berezovsky was forced to flee Russia, he sold most of his assets to Abramovich at a heavy discount. Sometimes referred to as "Putin's favorite son," Abramovich cemented his relationship with the Kremlin by giving to the government a gift of Berezovsky's ORT television station, one of the largest in Russia.[16]

Abramovich had been able to continue his close relationship with the Kremlin, having steered clear of Russian politics. But he then won a seat in the state Duma from the Chukotka region and was elected governor of the region, a poor, remote region in Russia's Far East that is most notable for reindeer farming—12 time zones away from his home in London and just across the Bering Strait from Alaska. He found the Chukotka region's low taxes to be an opportunity to relocate the headquarters of his oil company Sibneft to the region's capital city of Anadyr. Through this arrangement, Sibneft saved hundreds of millions of dollars in taxes, some of which was invested directly back into the community to pay for homes, hospitals, a movie theater, and a radio station, and, as a result of transfer pricing, some of the wealth went to further enrich the owners.[17]

Since becoming governor of the region, Abramovich has invested more than $200 million[18] of his own fortune into the region and created Pole of Hope, a charity organization to benefit the people of Chukotka, to help improve standards of living and diversify the economy, earning him the Russian Order of Honor award. In 2005, Putin abolished the election of governors in the regions. Putin has continued to appoint Abramovich as governor of the Chukotka region, despite repeated requests to be relieved of this duty.

With his partner, Eugene Shvidler, in 2001 Abramovich founded Millhouse Capital, an investment company that they still manage together in London to control and manage their large holdings in Russian companies. In the period between 2002 and 2005, Abramovich and Shvidler, through Millhouse Capital, sold their stake in Sibneft to Russia's natural gas giant Gazprom for $13.1 billion, 65 times what was paid for it, and their stake in RUSAL to Oleg Deripaska for $2 billion. Millhouse Capital also sold a large stake in Aeroflot for an undisclosed amount, and now has a controlling stake in Pharmstandard.[19] Millhouse Capital is also the majority shareholder in Russia's second largest steel company, Evraz, and has numerous other business interests in Russia.

Formerly known as the *stealth oligarch* due to his reclusive nature (a Russian tabloid once offered 1 million rubles for a picture of him), Abramovich has recently become a well-known public figure.

In 2003, Abramovich made headlines by purchasing London's Chelsea Football Club. He quickly became a fan favorite by spending his own money to bring in top-tier players and bringing the team, formerly a noncontender, up to the level of a yearly playoff team. Prior to the sale of Sibneft to Gazprom, the company was the primary sponsor for Moscow's CSKA team, a team that became the first Russian team to win a major European soccer competition by winning the UEFA cup. Abramovich is also known as a large benefactor of Jewish causes. He has funded vast projects in Jerusalem and Tel Aviv as well as being the largest donor to the Jewish organization Chabad-Lubavitch, a Hasidic group that works to provide services to Jewish communities around the world.

Abramovich has also been raising his public profile by becoming a lavish spender, becoming the world's largest spender on luxury yachts. He now owns 3 of the 20 largest yachts in the world. He also has a fleet of aircraft, a convenience for someone who must fly across 12 time zones to get to Chukotka. Since his arrival in London, Abramovich has become a large sponsor of art exhibitions. According to the Russian Space Agency, he has offered $300 million to become the first lunar space tourist on a trip around the moon sometime after 2010. In a rather short period of time, the stealth oligarch has become a front-page celebrity.

Veropharm

Symbol	VRPH
ADR	NA
Market Cap	$420 million
Shares Outstanding	10 million
Estimated Freefloat	50 percent

Veropharm is a leading Russian manufacturer of generic pharmaceuticals, bandages, and over-the-counter drugs. The company is majority-owned by Pharmacy Chain 36.6, Russia's largest pharmacy chain. The company produces over 100 different pharmaceutical products and over 100 different types of bandages. Veropharm continues to benefit from increased Russian spending on health care, along with increased government spending from its health care Priority National Project. Veropharm has been recording revenue increases of about 30 percent per year while increasing its profitability through product mix changes, increasing its focus on prescription medication.[20]

Real Estate

The real estate market in Russia is a relatively new concept in a country that has not had private ownership of property for nearly a century. After the fall of the Soviet Union, the country began liberalizing the property markets, and the property market is beginning to boom. This real estate boom is not universally spread throughout the country, though. The booming economy has led to huge property value increases in the main cities such as Moscow and St. Petersburg. In the majority of Russia's rural regions, though, the boom has yet to materialize.[21]

Of course, this is advantageous to the residents of these rural areas that are beginning to experience home ownership for the first time. One of the signs of this is the huge increases in mortgage lending in Russia. Russia's overall amount of mortgages has been increasing at a rate of over 100 percent per year. Considering that the country's amount of mortgages in relationship to GDP is amazingly low, about 0.7 percent of GDP, this shows the potential for outstanding growth as more Russians become comfortable with the stability of the Russian banking system.[22]

The real estate boom in Moscow has been a very interesting development, with office space price-per-square-foot rivaling leading Western European cities, including Paris, Zurich, Rome, and Milan. This is true even though the Moscow city government has been dragging its feet for years on the implementation of privatization for property ownership in the city. Most real estate in Moscow is still leased, with leases extending up to 49 years. It is assumed that privatization will occur in the near future, as the process was intended to be completed by now.

Based on the plans for privatizations, current leaseholders will have first rights to the properties they occupy, but the final price they will have to pay is still a mystery. This has not stopped investors from capitalizing on the city's amazing property boom. There are now a number of investment companies that operate in the area, and throughout the country, building and renovating office and retail space as well as building residential communities for the growing middle class. Some of the Russian companies involved in this growing market include Sistema Hals, Open Investments, and Mirland.

Risks:

- Property prices in Moscow are high even by European standards due to a lack of available property. An overbuilding of the Moscow area can negatively impact valuations of real estate developers.
- The construction and infrastructure boom in Russia is creating a supply shortage for construction materials such as concrete and rebar, with corresponding price increases on the domestic market. These price increases have the potential to erode real estate developers' profits.
- Any loss of consumer confidence or banking confidence could lead to a decline in housing demand, although this scenario is unlikely due to the shortage that exists.

Rewards:

- Russia has a very large housing deficit to overcome. Government focus on reducing this deficit should lead to continued demand for improved residential housing.
- The rapid rise in disposable income among Russian will continue to fuel demand for improved living quarters.
- Rapid expansion plans of the country's top retail chains are driving the demand for stores and shopping centers.

Mirland Development

Symbol	Not Listed In Russia
GDR	MLD.LN

Market Cap	$1.17 billion
Shares Outstanding	100 million
Estimated Freefloat	30 percent

Mirland Development, established in 2004, is one of Russia's youngest real estate investment and development companies. The company brings with it years of experience in real estate through its ownership by IBC, one of Israel's largest real estate companies. Mirland Development focuses on developments in Moscow and Saint Petersburg, as well as the largely untapped markets in Russia's regions. The company develops a mix of residential housing, retail stores, and office buildings. The company has shown impressive growth, with revenues increasing from $40 million in 2006 to an estimated $218 million in 2007.[23]

Open Investments

Symbol	OIVS
ADR	NA
Market Cap	$2.89 billion
Shares Outstanding	11.55 million
Estimated Freefloat	40 percent

Open Investments is a leading Russian real estate investment and development company. Open Investments is owned by Interros, the investment company of Norilsk Nickel owners Vladimir Potanin and Mikhail Prokhorov. The company's main area for investments is in the Moscow region, where real estate prices and incomes continue to outpace the rest of Russia. The company has recently expanded its developments to the fast-growing cities of Samara, Tver, and Sochi. Open Investments' main focus has been on upscale residential housing, accounting for 54 percent of 2006 revenues, and the company is looking toward investments in standard residential housing to take advantage of the government's drive to improve the quality of Russian housing.[24]

Open Investments also invests in other areas of real estate, including office buildings, hotels, and resorts, as well as acquiring prime land for future development. The company's ownership by Interros gives Open Investments a good track record of shareholder relations and corporate governance. Open Investments has had impressive performance, increasing total equity from $250 million in 2005 to $1.3 billion in 2006 due to acquisitions and rising valuations in the Moscow region.[25]

Sistema-Hals

Symbol	HALS
GDR	HALS.LI
GDR Ratio	20:1
Market Cap	$2.69 billion
Shares Outstanding	224.34 million
Estimated Freefloat	20 percent

Sistema-Hals is a major Russian real estate investment and development company created from the real estate holdings of the Sistema conglomerate. In fact, Sistema-Hals is run by the 28-year-old son of Sistema's controlling shareholder, Vladimir Evtushenkov. The company invests in and develops residential apartments, office buildings, retail stores, and residential cottages. The company has expanded its focus from Moscow to include the Russian regions and CIS countries. The company has shown impressive growth, with revenues increasing from $93 million in 2005 to $246 million in 2006.[26]

Banking

One of the primary drivers of Russia's real estate boom has been a wholesale transformation of the Russian banking industry. During Soviet times, and for some time after, banks were generally small operations that were set up for such activities as laundering money and hiding assets from taxation. This lack of real banking led to the development of a strictly cash economy. This has slowly changed as the government has cracked down on such banks by pulling the operating licenses of the offenders, well over 100 since 2004.

The government, in 2003, set up a Federal Deposit Insurance Agency to insure depositors against bank insolvency. This amount insured began at 100,000 rubles and was raised to 300,000 rubles in 2007.[27] The actions of the government's central bank and the ongoing economic growth have caused Russians to gradually gain more trust in the banking system. This is evident by the tremendous growth of the Russian banking sector. Assets held in Russian banks have increased by 350 percent since 2002, over 37 percent in 2006, and that growth rate is set to continue for the near future.[28]

This growth in Russian banking assets, along with the growth in trust of Russian banks, has led to the introduction of new banking products to consumers such as credit cards, mortgages, and auto loans. The facilitation of these loan products is aided by the fact that Russian banks have seen a tremendous increase in the amount of deposits held in rubles and not U.S. dollars. After the economic crisis in 1998, when the ruble fell dramatically against the dollar, depositors were adamant to keep their deposits in U.S. dollars.

Now, after more that eight years of ruble appreciation and steady economic growth, Russians are quickly moving their deposits to rubles, and most new deposits are made in rubles. This makes it much easier for banks to provide loans, which are generally made in rubles, as they do not have to worry about exchanging currency to provide the loans. As Russians become more comfortable with using the banking system and their incomes continue to increase, the banking sector continues to see rising use of these loan products. These loan products are helping to fuel the continuation of the boom in the Russian economy because people are becoming able to buy houses with mortgages, cars with auto loans, and consumer goods with credit cards.[29]

Risks:
- Political risk in the banking sector appears in a different form than in other sectors. The main political risk in the banking sector is the possibility that banks will be forced to make less than economic loans to help finance domestic priorities.

- A sharp correction in the ruble or a financial scare could reverse the trend of increasing ruble deposits in Russian banks.
- The lack of an effective nationwide credit tracking systems increases the risk of nonperforming loans as consumers loans continue to increase.
- Declining interest rates, albeit a very slow decline, puts pressure on Russian banks to increase efficiency and cut costs.

Rewards:
- The Russian banking system continues to grow at a breakneck pace as retail deposits increase at over 35 percent per year.[30]
- Increased Russian incomes and faith in the banking system are driving demand for consumer loans.
- The Federal Deposit Insurance Agency has tripled its deposit insurance to 300,000 rubles in 2007 and is set to increase further to 400,000 rubles.[31]
- Business spending on capital expansion projects is creating a growing market for corporate lending.
- Russian banks continue to remain highly profitable while expanding their operations.

Sberbank

Symbol	SBER
ADR	NA
Market Cap	$82.46 billion
Shares Outstanding	21.59 million
Estimated Freefloat	39.4 percent

The primary beneficiary of the meteoric rise in the Russian banking system's fortunes has been Sberbank. This should come as no surprise, considering that the company has been instrumental in pushing along banking reforms in Russia. Sberbank is, by far, Russia's largest bank, with over 20,000 branches throughout the country and more than 50 percent of the total banking system deposits. The company was formerly the government's National Savings Bank; now it is the largest publicly traded banking stock in Russia and has the third–largest market capitalization of any publicly traded company in Russia. Its history dates back to 1841.[32]

Despite its past as the former Soviet National Savings Bank, Sberbank has displayed excellent management for growth and cost-cutting. The company was able to slash its number of branches from 36,000 to the current level of just over 20,000 without sacrificing market share. The company has also continued to maintain its dominant position in the Russian banking sector, not just from sheer size, but from becoming a leader in product innovations.

Sberbank not only accounts for over half of all deposits in Russia, but also dominates the loan sector as well. The company has provided over 40 percent of all consumer loans in 2006, as well as over 30 percent of all corporate loans during the same period. The company has also been aggressively pursuing the expansion of financial products such as auto loans and mortgages, while working with consumers to help them become more comfortable with banks in general and move them away from the urge to continue operating under the assumption that "cash is king." The money has been moving from under the mattresses to the country's banks.[33]

One of the more ambitious recent projects of Sberbank has been the introduction of its consumer credit cards. Although credit cards are used in Russia often as a debit card, where employees receive their wages to the card and are able to pay their bills and make purchases from this card, actual revolving credit cards are a relatively new concept for most of the population. Sberbank is attempting to change this status and make standard revolving credit cards more widely accepted and used in the country, which would allow the company to reap huge returns from leveraging its dominant position in the market to gain a large portion of the credit card market early in its creation.

VTB

Symbol	VTBR
GDR	VTBR.LI

GDR Ratio	1:2000
Market Cap	$38.69 billion
Shares Outstanding	6.95 billion
Estimated Freefloat	23 percent

VTB, the former Russian Foreign Trade Bank, is currently Russia's second largest bank to Sberbank. VTB held its initial public offering in May 2007, raising $8 billion in what was called the *people's IPO,* as shares were sold in Russia at less than one U.S. cent. The bank plans on using the proceeds from its IPO to increase its market share and continue to be a consolidator in the Russian banking industry. The company plans to increase its market share in retail deposits from the current 3.2 percent to 10.5 percent in 2010. The bank currently focuses on corporate loans to large businesses for about 80 percent of its business, normally an unprofitable segment in Russia.[34]

Transportation

For the purpose of this discussion, we are including airlines and automobile manufacture in the transportation sector. Russia has been experiencing a boom in both categories. As disposable income rises among average Russians, the desire to buy decent, reliable vehicles continues to increase and, just as in the West, increasing incomes leads to the desire for more upscale models. The country has also seen air passenger traffic increase at rates of around 20 percent per year because Russians are enjoying more time and money to travel abroad and to visit the treasures within their own country. In the airline industry, Russian carriers have a near monopoly on air travel, while the Russian automotive industry faces challenges from foreign manufacturers, who enjoy 75 percent of the Russian market.[35]

Risks:
- High fuel prices are a very large factor in both the airline and the automotive industries. High fuel prices decrease airline profitability,

while changing the purchasing habits of vehicle consumers. Russia currently caps the domestic automotive fuel prices, but there is a strong push to significantly raise these caps.

- Foreign competition is very strong in the automotive industry, owning 75 percent of the Russian market.
- Russia's road and highway infrastructure is very poor at the moment, limiting the demand for vehicles.
- The political risks in the industry can be evidenced by Aeroflot's attempted bid for Alitalia, which was pushed by the Russian government, but would have been an uneconomic acquisition for the company.

Rewards:
- Airline passenger traffic continues to increase unabated, as rising disposable income gives people the opportunity to vacation away from home.
- Car ownership continues to increase rapidly in Russia as it becomes more attainable to the average Russian.
- Automobile loans by Russian banks continue to increase, giving more people the ability to own cars.
- Russian government investments in infrastructure and the development of public/private toll road partnerships should increase demand for vehicles.
- Russian law states that, by 2010, 50 percent of vehicles' components must be manufactured in Russia, giving domestic producers a strengthened position in the market.

Aeroflot

Symbol	AFLT
ADR	NA
Market Cap	$3.04 billion
Shares Outstanding	11.10 billion
Estimated Freefloat	19 percent

Aeroflot, Eastern Europe's largest airline, continues its Soviet-era role as Russia's national airline. Aeroflot is majority-owned (51 percent) by the Russian government. The company boasts a 25 percent total market share in Russian air travel, with a 30 percent share of international traffic and 17 percent share in domestic traffic. The company also earns about 10 percent of its revenue from cargo transportation throughout Russia and the CIS. The company has been aggressively modernizing its fleet to both better serve passengers and to create a more efficient and competitive fleet. This fleet modernization and growth in passenger levels has enabled Aeroflot to continue to post impressive financial improvements.[36]

Aeroflot already operates multiple Airbus models for domestic and international service, as well as Boeing 767s for international travel. The company plans to completely eliminate its fleet of older Tupolev domestic aircraft by 2010, some of which are to be replaced with Sukhoi's new Superjet 100 as well as the modern Ilyushin Il-96 for international routes. In 2014, Aeroflot will start receiving its new generation of aircraft. The company has signed purchase agreements for the Airbus A350 for short- to medium-range routes and the Boeing 787 Dreamliner for medium- to long-range routes.

Auto Industry

The Russian auto industry has been very heavily criticized in the West for the quality of automobiles produced during the Soviet era. In contrast to the general perception of Russian automakers, they have consistently improved their product offerings to provide for regional competitiveness of their vehicles. Russia's oldest automobile manufacturer, GAZ for Gorkovsky Avtomobilny Zavod (Gorky Automobile Plant), can trace its formation back to America's oldest automaker, Ford. GAZ was created in 1929 as part of Stalin's first Five Year Plan of Soviet industrialization.

To help jump-start the Soviet Union's auto industry, Stalin brought in Ford as a joint venture with the Soviet government. By 1932, the first Soviet-made vehicles began rolling off the production lines. The first vehicles made by GAZ were called the NAZ A, based on the Ford Model A. The most famous vehicles in the minds of foreigners are the Lada vehicles produced by AvtoVAZ during the

Soviet era. These cars were designed to be the Russian Volkswagen, a simple, inexpensive car for the masses. These cars were the epitome of basic in styling and function, but were within the reach of many Russians.

The automobile industry in Russia is at last making some progress. In fact, Russia will soon become the number two car market in Europe. Joint arrangements with global automobile manufacturers have helped boost the level of technological innovation, bring in modern production practices, and assist in helping the Russian automakers become more self-sufficient. The various companies in the Russian auto industry have formed partnerships in varying degrees with companies such as General Motors, Fiat, and Isuzu. The Russian automobile market, growing at an average of 8 percent per year due to rising disposable incomes, has also attracted competitors such as Ford and Toyota to set up domestic manufacturing capabilities. Even with the foreign competition coming in, the domestic companies will enjoy significant protection from the government because of the law that requires that by 2010 half of a vehicle's components will need to be produced locally.

Boris Berezovsky

Boris Berezovsky was born in 1946 in Moscow as an only child to a Jewish family. His father was a factory worker and his mother was a pediatric nurse. He graduated from the Moscow Forestry Engineering Institute in 1967 with a degree in electronics and computer science, he even schemed to obtain a Nobel Prize. It was not until 1983 that he obtained his Ph.D. in mathematics and physics. He was never considered to be an accomplished scientist, as he has since admitted publicly. In 1969, he got a job as an engineer at the Scientific Research Center for Hydrometeorology and later became a manager before his departure in 1987.[37]

Boris Berezovsky has been the most recognizable name in the Russian automobile industry. This fame is not based on excellent earnings results or adept management skills, but rather, from his early rise as one of Russia's first billionaire oligarchs and subsequent fallout with the Kremlin. A student of forestry and doctorate of applied mathematics, Berezovsky began his business life in 1989 when, under *perestroika,* he was able to buy vehicles from AvtoVAZ and resell them at a profit. In 1992, he was able to formalize this business as LogoVAZ, an exclusive dealer for AvtoVAZ.[38]

Berezovsky's financial fortunes peaked during the 1990s due to his close personal and professional relationship with then–president Boris Yeltsin. During this period, he was able to buy large stakes in privatized companies, including auto manufacturer AvtoVAZ, airliner Aeroflot, oil company Sibneft (now part of Gazprom-controlled Gazprom Neft), large aluminum holdings, and stakes in two large television networks.[39]

Berezovsky's ownership of the nation's largest and most influential television network enabled him to provide significant support to Yeltsin's 1996 presidential bid. In 1999, Berezovsky was elected to a seat in the country's lower house of parliament, the Duma. This influential position was short-lived, as the election of Vladimir Putin in 2000 signaled an end to his free-wheeling times. Although Berezovsky used his influence to help aid Putin's presidential campaign in 2000, Putin was intent on cracking down on the oligarchs that were a symbol of the chaos of the previous administration. Not long after the election of Putin, Berezovsky fled the country and now resides, with political asylum status, in Great Britain.[40]

Berezovsky is accused of many schemes to avoid taxes and hide profits. In the case of AvtoVAZ, he sold the company's vehicles to his distributor company LogoVAZ at cost to hide the profits and increase his ability to take money out of the company. This greatly reduced the competitiveness of AvtoVAZ, because there was little or no money left for improvements and maintenance to plant equipment. He was charged with running similar schemes at his other companies and of defrauding the region of Samara of over $2 billion, the main reason for his self-imposed exile.

Boris Berezovsky, although in exile in London, did not go silently into the night. Now calling himself Platon Elenin, *Platon* being Russian for Plato and *Elenin* being the name of his wife, Berezovsky has been a vocal opponent of the Putin administration.

Berezovsky owned, until 2006, an influential publishing company in Russia that publishes the daily *Kommersant,* literally translated as *The Businessman,* which is still a widely read newspaper in Russia that has maintained its critical stance against the Putin administration. In political protest to Putin's administration, he once sent 100 silver limousines to park outside the Russian Embassy in London. Since that protest in 2004, his rhetoric has become more direct and forceful, calling for a change in Russian leadership.

In April of 2007, Berezovsky set off a media storm when he stated that he was financing and supporting revolution in Russia, claiming that "It is not possible to change this regime through democratic means" and "There can be no change without force, pressure." He later followed these remarks with a statement in which he said that all of the methods he would back in Russia "would be bloodless," but in the same statement also stated that he was "calling for a revolution, and revolution is always violent." These statements have caused the Russian government to ask for Berezovsky's political asylum status in Great Britain to be reviewed.[41]

AvtoVaz

Symbol	AVAZ
GDR	AVVG.GR
GDR Ratio	1:1
Market Cap	$4.08 billion
Shares Outstanding	27.19 million
Estimated Freefloat	36.5 percent

AvtoVAZ (Volzhskiy Avtomobilny Zavod, meaning Volga Automobile Plant) is Russia and Eastern Europe's largest automobile manufacturer. The company is currently controlled by the Russian governments' import-export company, Rosoboronexport. The company produces Russia's most popular passenger car, the Lada, as well as General Motors joint venture production of the Chevy Nina and the Chevy Viva. It is currently in talks to produce GM's Opel Corsa. AvtoVAZ has also been working with Fiat to produce the popular

Italian company's vehicles in Russia. AvtoVAZ gained another international partner when Oleg Deripaska, owner of Russian aluminum monopoly RUSAL, purchased Canadian auto parts manufacturer and vehicle assembler Magna International, Inc. The companies intend to implement a joint venture in Russia to produce low-priced compact cars.[42]

GAZ

Symbol	GAZA
ADR	NA
Market Cap	$2.72 billion
Shares Outstanding	18.52 million
Estimated Freefloat	28.2 percent

GAZ (Gorkovsky Avtomobilny Zavod, meaning Gorky Automobile Plant) was Russia's first automobile manufacturing company. Set up by an agreement with Ford Motor Company, the company began producing the Ford Model A under the name GAZ A in 1932. GAZ, now owned by Russian billionaire Oleg Deripaska, is Russia's second largest automobile manufacturer. The company produces a wide range of vehicles, including small passenger cars, sedans, light trucks, SUVs, and commercial vehicles. The company produces the popular Volga sedan and, in 2006, purchased the equipment and rights to produce Chrysler's Sebring. The company's largest market share is in light trucks and commercial trucks, such as delivery vehicles and cargo vans.[43]

Severstal Avto

Symbol	SVAV
ADR	NA
Market Cap	$1.15 billion
Shares Outstanding	34.27 million
Estimated Freefloat	42 percent

Severstal Avto is a leading Russian automotive manufacturer that is made up of the automotive assets of the Russian steel giant

Severstal. In 2007, Severstal's owner, Alexei Mordashov, sold his controlling stake in the company to Severstal Avto's Chairman of the Board, Vadim Shvetsov. This transaction solidified Severstal Avto's independence from Severstal and gave Shvetsov a large stake in the company's success. Severstal Avto continues to be Russia's most profitable automotive manufacturer, with a profit margin of over 13 percent. The company specializes in off-road vehicles, SUVs, and commercial trucks. The company produces the popular Russian 4×4 UAZ Hunter and UAZ Patriot, as well as South Korean SsangYong SUVs. Severstal Avto also produces and distributes passenger cars from Fiat, as well as the Russian OKA *city car,* a small and affordable compact car. The company also produces light and commercial trucks from Fiat and Isuzu.[44]

Chapter 8

Electricity and Infrastructure

Powering the Rebuilding of Russia

Russia's Energos

The most far-reaching of Russia's continuing privatization plans is the effort to privatize the country's electric utility system. Russia's electric power grid spans 11 time zones and is connected by nearly 70,000 kilometers of transmission lines. In 2006, Russian electricity generators supplied the country with over 960 million megawatt hours of electricity. Of the country's electrical output, nearly 16 percent was from nuclear power plants and an additional 9 percent was produced by hydroelectric plants. The rest of the country's electricity comes from power plants that burn natural gas, coal, or fuel oil. Russia, sitting on top of about one third of the world's natural gas deposits, generates much of its electricity from natural gas, accounting for over 70 percent of fuel used for generating electricity.[1]

The Russian electricity market is still highly regulated, with relatively low electricity prices for consumers. The government has been slowly raising allowed prices to both residential and commercial consumers, with the goal of having market-driven pricing by 2011 to 2012. This arrangement was officially formalized in April 2007, when the government issued Decree Number 205.[2] The current prices and increases are based on the area of the country in which the electricity is generated and consumed. The regions with lower incomes are brought up more gradually, while regions with high generating costs are being brought up more quickly to compensate for these costs. This action has been required by the government to allow for the gradual adjustment from formerly subsidized electricity consumption to true free-market rates. This gradual price adjustment is also allowing Russian businesses time to make adequate adjustments to prepare for the increases in rates.

The process of privatizing the country's electrical power grid is unparalleled in its complexity. The initial, and most complex, portion of the process—breaking up the grid into viable public companies—has already been completed. The current structure has Unified Energy Systems (UES), a government-controlled holding company, as a majority owner of all of the assets subject to privatization. Not subject to privatization are the few local generating companies that are already privatized and operating outside of UES, which amounted to about 14 percent of electricity generated in 2005. The only other holdings not included in UES are the country's nuclear power plants, which are going to continue to be operated and 100 percent owned by state-controlled Rosenergoatom (Russia Atomic Energy).[3]

The process of creating independent companies out of Russia's electrical systems has formed a number of companies, which will be discussed in more detail in the coming pages. They include generating companies, distribution companies, and a transmission company. These companies have been separated based on the type of plant used to generate their electricity and the market in which the electricity is sold. The companies created include 14 regional generation companies called TGKs (from the Russian for Thermal Generating Company), 6 wholesale generation companies called OGKs (from the Russian for Wholesale Generating Company), and HydroOGK, which encompasses the country's hydroelectric plants.

The last stage of privatization will be to break up Unified Energy Systems and allow all of the newly formed companies to operate independently from UES. This process is scheduled to be completed by the end of 2008. UES is currently a publicly traded company, with the Russian government holding a 51 percent controlling stake in the company. Once the privatization process is complete, UES will cease to exist as a holding company and shareholders in the company will get pro-rata shares in the companies owned by UES. One of the caveats that these companies will be forced to abide by is the government's requirement to spend a specified amount on capital expansion (capex) to ensure that the country has adequate electricity resources in the future.[4]

To help finance some of the capex needs of the companies that are going to be separated from United Energy Systems, UES stated in April 2007 that it would forgo paying a dividend for 2006 operating income so that it could instead use the money to reinvest into the assets before they are going to be spun off. Also in April 2007, the government presented its preliminary plan for investments in new electrical grids and generating assets through 2020.[5] The government plans to increase the use of nuclear power from 16 percent to 20 percent of the country's total and also increase the use of coal from 23 percent to around 35 percent by 2020.[6] The government's initial plan calls for around $500 billion to be spent between the government and the privatized electricity companies through 2020 to increase the country's generating capacity and power reliability.

Risks:
- Electricity privatization may stall or the terms may be changed in a way that negatively affects minority shareholders.

- The Russian government may require capital expansion programs that are not economically justifiable, leaving the costs of such projects to be borne by shareholders.
- Russian electricity generators are 70 percent reliant on natural gas,[7] and profitability can be negatively impacted by a sharp rise in the cost of fuel or any interruption of supply.

Rewards:
- Russian electric utilities are, as a whole, still considered to be undervalued compared to international peers.
- The liberalization of the electricity market will provide true competition among electricity companies, leaving open the potential for large improvements in efficiency.
- The Russian hydro generators will be consolidated into a single company, HydroOGK, that will control nearly 10 percent of the country's capacity and will be able to sell electricity at market prices with a lower cost of production.[8]

Unified Energy Systems (UES)

Symbol	EESR
ADR	USERY.US
ADR Ratio	1:100
Market Cap	$55.89 billion
Shares Outstanding	41.04 billion
Estimated Freefloat	26.3 percent

Unified Energy Systems (UES) is a state-run holding company that is currently the largest electric utility in the country. As previously discussed, UES has a majority stake in most of Russia's electric utilities, including generators, distributors, and sales companies. Investment in UES shares gives investors the opportunity to gain exposure to most of Russia's electricity generation and distribution industries in one share. The current plan has UES slated for complete dissolution by the middle of 2008. Upon breakup, shareholders in UES will receive pro-rata shares in the companies controlled by UES.[9]

Zhigulevskaya Hydro

Symbol	VLGS
ADR	NA
Market Cap	$1.77 billion
Shares Outstanding	3.87 billion
Estimated Freefloat	NA

Zhigulevskaya Hydro is one of Russia's largest hydropower generators with a total installed capacity of 2,300 megawatts. The company is located in southern Russia in the town of Zhigulevsk near Samara and gets its power from the Volga River. Zhigulevskaya Hydro will be integrated into the giant HydroOGK by mid-2008 when shares in the company will be converted into shares of the new HydroOGK. Electricity market liberalization will allow HydroOGK to sell electricity at the same prices as fossil fuel generators with a significantly lower cost of generation.[10]

TGKs

The core of Russia's electrical generation grid consists of the country's TGKs. The breakup of the country's electrical grid included the formation of 14 TGKs, each responsible for a prescribed area of the country and named TGK1 through TGK14. The only exception to this naming pattern has been TGK3, which renamed itself Mosenergo as it provides power to the Moscow area. The TGKs are driven by natural gas, coal, or fuel oil, with the exception of TGK1, which gets over one third of its electricity from hydroelectric plants outside of HydroOGK control.

The country's TGKs are also responsible for providing heat for their respective areas. Throughout the years, due to its extremely cold climate, Russia has invested heavily in combined heat and power plants (CHPs). These CHP plants generate electricity using fossil fuels and use the heat created during the electricity-generating process to create additional electricity, as well as heat for the surrounding area. The CHP plants do this by capturing the exhaust heat from the generation process and using it to run a steam generator.

This is referred to as *co-generation* in the West. This heated liquid is then fed through a local system and used to heat residential buildings and industrial plants. These CHP plants are one of the most efficient ways to produce electricity by fossil fuels available in most circumstances and make up a majority of the TGKs' generating assets.

OGKs

Another creation of the privatization of the nation's electric grid was the OGKs. The government created 6 OGKs, named OGK1 through OGK6, as electricity producers for the wholesale electricity market. Russia has an extremely efficient electric transmission grid, enabling electricity to be transferred to different areas of the country as needed. The wholesale electricity market was designed to take advantage of this ability by creating companies that can sell their electrical-generating capacity to industries and also to TGKs as demand requires.

Irkutskenergo

One of the only independent electricity producers in Russia is Irkutskenergo, which supplies electricity and heat to the Irkutsk region in Siberia. Irkutskenergo is majority-owned by RUSAL, the privately held Russian aluminum monopoly, with no ownership by United Energy Systems.[11] Irkutskenergo is the only other major hydroelectric producer in Russia outside of HydroOGK and TGK1, producing nearly 70 percent of its power from hydroelectric generators, and producing about 6 percent of the country's total output.[12] The company is considered vertically integrated, due to the fact that it owns all of the assets involved with electricity production and distribution from generation facilities to power lines and distribution facilities.

HydroOGK

HydroOGK is the company formed through the privatization process to control the country's hydroelectric plants. The only hydroelectric plants that will not be controlled by HydroOGK will be those already owned by another utility, mainly by TGK1 and Irkutskenergo. Once fully consolidated after the breakup of UES, which currently owns 100 percent of HydroOGK, the company will control 23 hydroelectric plants located throughout Russia, including two currently under construction. This will give HydroOGK the largest installed capacity, with over 23 gigawatts of potential output. Because of seasonal river flows, HydroOGK can realize only about 40 percent of this capacity consistently, making it the second largest electricity producer behind Rosenergoatom, Russia's nuclear energy holding. This large generating capacity will make HydroOGK the second largest hydroelectric company in the world to Hydro Quebec.[13]

HydroOGK will be operating in the wholesale electricity markets competing directly with the OGKs. HydroOGK will be able to sell its electricity at the same prices as the country's OGKs, giving it a significant advantage in the market as its costs for electricity production are much lower than its fossil fuel fired competitors. This cost advantage will only grow as over 70 percent of Russia's fossil fuel power comes from natural gas, the price of which is expected to rise considerably over the next few years as the government works to bring the domestic natural gas market prices up to market levels.[14]

Rosenergoatom

Rosenergoatom is the Russian government's 100 percent–owned nuclear energy holding that, although not subject to privatization, should be included in any discussion of Russian electrical generation. Rosenergoatom is the country's top supplier of electricity, nearly doubling the output of the consolidated HydroOGK. Nuclear power generation is an export business, as Russian expertise in this sector is sought around the globe. Russia has been actively developing its nuclear power technology and has been recently working on a floating nuclear power plant that has the capacity to also desalinate seawater to provide both electricity and drinking water.

Anatoly Chubais

As the head of Unified Energy Systems, Anatoly Chubais (see Figure 8.1) is playing a pivotal role in the privatization of the Russian electrical grid. The privatization of state-owned assets is nothing new to Chubais, who led the privatization efforts of the 1990s. Born in 1955 in Belarus, Anatoly Chubais graduated from the Leningrad Institute of Economics with a Ph.D. in economics in 1977. He stayed with the school, first as an assistant lecturer then as an assistant professor, until 1990. His time at the school was formative for Chubais, as he made a conscious effort to make sense of the Soviet Union's economic system. His study of

Figure 8.1 Anatoly Chubais, Spear-Headed Russia's Privatization and Now Heads Unified Energy Systems (UES)

the Soviet economic model quickly led to disillusionment because he could not understand how such a state-run model could have any chance of operating with economic efficiency. He expressed his disillusionment with official economists at the time, stating, "You have fire in your home but what they discuss at this conference is maybe we should change the color of the walls and it would become better."[15]

Chubais was able to find some like-minded scholars at his institution and formed a discussion group to research economic policies, including Lenin's New Economic Policy, which was an activity strictly prohibited during the Soviet era. Chubais was able to overcome this prohibition by disguising the group as a pro-Soviet Young Scholars' Committee and offering the KGB falsified meeting notes before they were requested so as to defer any questioning.

This proactive approach granted the group considerable goodwill with the local KGB office, which helped give them the breathing room they needed to continue their discussions. Using the pro-Soviet Young Scholars' Committee moniker also allowed the group access to school facilities and research materials that would otherwise be out of reach. The group used this front to help set up Young Scholars' Committees at other universities throughout the Soviet Union, helping to spread the idea of alternative economic thought. When Gorbachev initiated his plan of perestroika, these committees became the foundation of the local Perestroika Clubs, where new economic directions became openly discussed.

The fall of the old Soviet system and emergence of democracy in the new Russian Federation led to a quick rise for Chubais. Already an economic advisor for the mayor of Leningrad (changed to St. Petersburg in 1991), Chubais found a perfect position in the new government as a deputy prime minister for the Ministry of Privatization in 1992, where he served until 1994. These two years were pivotal in the formation of New Russia. In his post, Chubais was responsible for the process of breaking up state-owned industries into private companies.

He is most noted during this time for his plan to help spread the wealth of privatization to Russian citizens. His plan provided vouchers to every Russian citizen that represented an average per capita share of the country's wealth, which amounted to 10,000 rubles at the time. These vouchers could be exchanged for shares of newly privatized companies at the voucher holders' discretion. These vouchers were an efficient and relatively fair way to disperse the country's wealth, but poor management of *voucher funds,* where people deposited their vouchers to be invested as a kind of voucher mutual fund, poor decision making by voucher holders, and some unscrupulous operators stripped most voucher holders of their value. For this, Anatoly Chubais is still blamed, albeit unfairly. Also, he instituted the "loans for shares" program as a means of privatizing major oil companies, and is still criticized for this.

This was not the end of Chubais's career, as he followed his tenure at the Ministry of Privatization with a stint in the Duma and, in 1996, became chief of the presidential administration for Boris Yeltsin. He was then quickly promoted in 1997, becoming first vice-premier and Minister of Finance and director of the Russian Federation to the World Bank's International Bank of Reconstruction and Development (IBRD). It is in this position that he was responsible for bringing in billions of dollars in foreign aid to the Russian Federation and was known to outsiders, including the IMF, as the man to see in the Russian government to get things accomplished. His tenure here was short-lived, as he became a casualty of Yeltsin's government purge in 1998.

His unemployment was brief, however. About one month after his dismissal, he was appointed chairman of the board of Unified Energy Systems, a position he still holds today, where he is now charged with yet another challenging privatization process.[16] Chubais is one of the great men of New Russia. He predicts a further substantial increase in the market caps of Russia's Energos as a result of the final, Spring 2008, privatizations.

Infrastructure

The improvement of Russian infrastructure is a primary domestic priority of the Russian government. The country's aging and incomplete Soviet-era infrastructure is in vital need of upgrading and replacement. President Vladimir Putin, in his 2007 Annual Address to the Federal Assembly, stated that the country's poor infrastructure is costing Russia up to 3 percent of its GDP.[17] Russia still lacks a cross-country highway, and many existing roads are in dire need of repair. Highway fatalities are high. The government is beginning to spend significant budgetary money to help solve the problem of the country's infrastructure and is working on public/private partnerships to help speed the construction of a nationwide highway system.

Risks:
- One of the largest risks in this segment is the reliance on federal money. If oil revenues unexpectedly fall, the government will not have the money to finance its ambitious programs.

- As progress in this sector continues, the prices of inputs are sure to increase, to the detriment of profitability.
- The possibility of temporary supply shortages from rapidly increasing demand is a real risk as the government puts more money into these projects.
- Most stocks in this industry are relatively illiquid and trade only on the Russian exchanges.

Rewards:
- The government's focus on infrastructure improvements and realization that the country's infrastructure is hurting the country's economic health should continue to drive these projects forward.
- Public/private partnerships will help speed the development of the country's infrastructure.
- The companies in this sector are experiencing rapid growth and increasing profitability.

Evrocement

Symbol	EVCG
ADR	NA
Market Cap	$7.50 billion
Shares Outstanding	0.50 million
Estimated Freefloat	NA

Evrocement is Russia's largest cement producer, accounting for 45 percent of the country's total cement production. The country's next largest competitor is Siberian Cement, with about 7 percent of total production. The company also controls 80 percent of the Central Federal District, which includes the hub of Russian construction, the city of Moscow, and the surrounding region. Evrocement owns 13 cement plants in Russia, as well as a number of plants in Ukraine. The company also operates concrete mixing stations throughout the country and a building materials plant. The company boasts a nationwide sales network where its large scale allows it to essentially dictate cement prices and delivery terms throughout Russia.[18]

Evrocement continues to benefit from cement shortages in Russia, causing prices to remain high, owing to the extensive building projects across the country. The company has continued to enjoy a leadership position allowing it to set the prices of cement throughout Russia and even won a case against the Federal Antimonopoly Service protecting this right. The company has very limited liquidity, but this will be aided by an IPO expected to occur in late 2008 or early 2009.[19]

Siberskiy Cement

Symbol	SCEM
ADR	NA
Market Cap	$2.82 billion
Shares Outstanding	30.35 million
Estimated Freefloat	14.24 percent

Siberskiy Cement, also known as Siberian Cement, is Russia's second largest cement producer, headed by a dynamic young executive, Andrey Muraviev. The company, with four cement plants in the Siberian region of Russia, accounts for about 7 percent of Russia's total cement production. The company also has ambitious expansion plans as it looks to take advantage of the boom in construction from building projects and infrastructure projects in Russia. Siberskiy Cement plans to open a fifth plant in Siberia, as well as a plant in Kazakhstan. The company's new plants will be its first to use *dry technology*, a more efficient process of producing cement, and these plants will add about 50 percent to the company's capacity.[20]

Mostotrest

Symbol	MSTT
ADR	NA
Market Cap	$423.87 million
Shares Outstanding	1.24 million
Estimated Freefloat	20 percent

Mostotrest is Russia's largest construction company focused on building and repairing railway and highway bridges and overpasses. The company was recently acquired by Severstaltrans, the transportation arm of Russian steel giant Severstal. The control by Severstaltrans promises to give Mostotrest the benefits of greater scale, more transparency, and better corporate governance. The company's focus on bridge building and repair gives it a leading position in the most profitable part of the road-building process. In a country where there is still no cross-country highway, the company stands to benefit from increased government focus on infrastructure improvements. The possibility of public/private partnerships to build toll roads will only boost the opportunities for Mostotrest.[21]

Power Machines

Symbol	SILM
ADR	NA
Market Cap	$1.23 billion
Shares Outstanding	7.21 billion
Estimated Freefloat	19.6 percent

Power Machines is Russia's leading manufacturer of electric power equipment. The company produces electric turbines and generators for heat, hydroelectric, nuclear, and gas electricity production facilities. The company also produces co-generation equipment as well as other generation-related equipment. Power Machines is 25 percent owned by the German conglomerate Siemens, allowing it access to Siemens' advanced generation technology. Another 25 percent of Power Machines is owned by the state-run electricity holding, UES. This stake is set to be sold in early in 2008 as the breakup of UES takes place. Interros, owners of Norilsk Nickel among many other assets, also owns 30.4 percent of the company, with the remaining 19.6 being freefloat. Russia has repeatedly blocked Siemens' efforts to buy a larger stake in the company, considering it a strategic asset. Power Machines will be a major beneficiary of the breakup of UES that mandates Russian generation companies spend billions of dollars on upgrading their capacities.[22]

Chapter 9

Ukraine and Kazakhstan

Ukraine

2007 Information and Estimates[1]

Currency:	Hryvnia (UAH)
Exchange Rate:	Fixed at 5.05 UAH/USD
Exchange Reserves:	$22 billion
GDP:	$110 billion
GDP per Capita:	$2,275
GDP Growth YOY:	6.5 percent
Inflation YOY:	11 percent
Unemployment:	8 percent
Primary Exchange:	PFTS
Country Ticker Code:	UZ

Ukraine, with a population of over 45 million, is the largest (after Russia) of the former Soviet republics to become an independent state. Prior to the breakup of the Soviet Union, Ukraine had the highest per capita GDP of any region of the Soviet Union. The country had a difficult time following its independence, losing 60 percent of its GDP between 1991 and 1999. Ukraine's GDP per capita is currently only about one quarter of that in Russia, approximately $2,275 compared to about $8,750 in Russia. The country has enjoyed rapid growth since 2000, currently experiencing GDP growth of nearly 7 percent annually.[2] Its main stock index, the PFTS, climbed 100 percent in the first half of 2007[3] despite what can be best described as a dysfunctional government situation.

With the breakup of the Soviet Union, Ukraine inherited the world's third largest nuclear arsenal and a large standing army. The country has given up its nuclear arsenal and trimmed its military, officially declaring itself a neutral country. Ukraine has been a member of the Commonwealth of Independent States (CIS) since its formation in 1991. The country has more recently been working with NATO and is currently working toward World Trade Organization (WTO) membership and more integration with Europe.

Risks:
- The single biggest risk in Ukraine is the often volatile political situation. Ukraine's president and prime minister are political foes who have been continually wrangling for control of the country.
- Ukrainian equities are very illiquid, and corporate governance generally leaves plenty to be desired.
- Transfer pricing is still a common occurrence in Ukraine as companies exploit their convoluted cross-ownership structures to the detriment of minority shareholders.
- Much of Ukraine's stock price rise is a byproduct of limited free-float of stocks combined with large amounts of money flowing into its speculative market, making it susceptible to correction.

Rewards:
- Ukraine is set to continue its rapid economic growth, albeit from a low base, with GDP growth between 6 percent and 7 percent.[4]
- The PFTS has increased over 130 percent in 2007, following a 47 percent increase in 2006.[5]

- Ukrainians, like Russians, are experiencing a rapid rise in their disposable income, leading to demand for homes, cars, and retail items.
- Ukraine's relatively low wage base and proximity to Europe, coupled with nearing WTO entry, make it a natural exporter to Europe.

Azovstal

Symbol	AZST
ADR	NA
Market Cap	$2.67 billion
Shares Outstanding	3.65 billion
Estimated Freefloat	2.3 percent

Azovstal is Ukraine's third largest steel producer, with 15 percent of the country's total steel output. The company is a large exporter of steel slabs and steel billets. The company also supplies steel strips to steel pipe producers throughout the CIS. Azovstal is a large producer of other long steel products, including railways and beams. The company is majority-owned by Metinvest, the metals company that is wholly owned by Ukrainian business conglomerate System Capital Management (SCM). This alliance gives Azovstal access to materials through SCM-owned coking coal producers and iron ore producers. Azovstal also benefits from this alliance on the sales side, from its SCM connection with one of the largest pipe makers in the CIS, Khartsysk Pipe. Azovstal also benefits from a favorable location near Black Sea ports, reducing the transportation costs of exports.[6]

Motor Sich

Symbol	MSICH
GDR	BC21.GR
GDR Ratio	10:1
Market Cap	$401.20 million
Shares Outstanding	2.08 million
Estimated Freefloat	23.4 percent

Motor Sich is Ukraine's only producer of aircraft and helicopter engines. The company is the primary supplier to the former Soviet, now Ukrainian, design bureau Antonov. The Antonov design bureau produces passenger aircraft and cargo variants with two new aircraft recently certified for passenger traffic, the An-140 short-range aircraft and the An-148 regional passenger jet. Motor Sich also supplies engines to the Russian Tupolev design bureau for many older aircraft still in service, as well as the new Tu-334 regional passenger jet. Motor Sich is in a good position to benefit from Russia's military modernization plan, as it supplies most of the helicopter engines for Russia's producers, with modernization of Russia's helicopter fleet a leading priority. The company also benefits from repairing and rebuilding most of the engines in Russia's helicopter fleet, as well as the Antonov and Tupolev aircraft still in service.[7]

Raiffeisen Aval

Symbol	BAVL
ADR	NA
Market Cap	$6.40 billion
Shares Outstanding	29.90 billion
Estimated Freefloat	4.7 percent

Raiffeisen Bank Aval was created in October 2005 when Austria's Raiffeisen International Bank Holding, AG, bought a 93.5 percent stake in one of Ukraine's largest banks, Aval. At the time, Raiffeisen International was operating Raiffeisen Bank Ukraine, one of the top 10 banks in Ukraine, which it then sold to Hungarian OTP bank. Raiffeisen Bank Aval is currently Ukraine's second largest bank, both by assets and number of retail outlets. The company has 8.2 percent of the total Ukraine banking market and has more than 1,400 retail outlets. The company has enjoyed the rapid growth in the Ukraine banking sector, with deposits growing 44 percent between 2005 and 2006 and retail loans expanding 141 percent during the same period.[8]

Stirol

Symbol	STIR
GDR	SVX.GR
GDR Ratio	1:1
Market Cap	$435.08 million
Shares Outstanding	27.12 million
Estimated Freefloat	9.9 percent

Stirol is Ukraine's largest chemicals and pharmaceuticals producer. Stirol is also the only producer of polystyrene in Ukraine. The company is one of the world's largest producers of ammonia, 60 percent of which the company uses to produce fertilizers. The company exports a large portion of its production to the United States, Europe, and the CIS. Stirol has the advantage of being connected to an ammonia pipeline that transports its products to shipping ports on the Black Sea, greatly reducing the transportation costs of its exports. Stirol's owner–operator, Nikolay Yankovsky, is a member of the national legislature, the Rada, and a scientist in his own right.[9]

TMM Real Estate

Symbol	Not Traded In Ukraine
GDR	TR61.GR
GDR Ratio	NA
Market Cap	$895.34 million
Shares Outstanding	51.79 million
Estimated Freefloat	14 percent

TMM Real Estate is one of Ukraine's leading real estate development companies. The company's main focus is residential and commercial real estate in Ukraine's capital, Kiev. Ukraine's population continues to migrate in large numbers to Kiev, fueling demand for residential and commercial property while pushing the prices for real estate to world levels. TMM also has significant properties in development in Kharkiv, one of Ukraine's largest cities, and Yalta, on the Crimean coast, where Ukrainians and Russians are increasingly flocking to purchase vacation homes. The company benefits from its vertically integrated approach, providing its own development, design, construction, and post–construction services.[10]

Ukrnafta

Symbol	UNAF
GDR	UKAA.GR
GDR Ratio	1:5
Market Cap	$5.15 billion
Shares Outstanding	54.23 million
Estimated Freefloat	8 percent

Ukrnafta, majority-owned by the state-owned Naftogaz Ukrainy, is the country's largest oil company. The company accounts for 74 percent of Ukraine's crude production along with 16 percent of the country's natural gas production. The company has benefited from the high global prices for crude oil, with revenues increasing nearly 33 percent between 2005 and 2006. Ukrnafta has plans to become a vertically integrated company, working to acquire assets from refining to retail filling stations. The company is also working on exploration deals with Nigeria and Middle Eastern countries on joint exploration and production deals, as well as looking at using offshore wells on Ukraine's potentially oil-rich shelf.[11]

Ukrtelecom

Symbol	UTEL
GDR	UK1.GR
GDR Ratio	1:30
Market Cap	$4.26 billion
Shares Outstanding	18.73 billion
Estimated Freefloat	2.1 percent

Ukrtelecom is Ukraine's fixed-line telephone incumbent. The company provided fixed-line telephone services as well as long-distance service. The company has over 10 million fixed-line telephone customers and a near monopoly on long-distance service in Ukraine. The company is also rapidly expanding its profitable Internet services. The company was recently awarded the country's only 3G cellular telephone license, signaling a reentry into the country's wireless telephone market after selling its stake in the cellular telephone provider UMC to Russian Mobile Telesystems (MTS).[12]

Kazakhstan

2007 Information and Estimates[13]

Currency:	Tenge (KZT)
Exchange Rate:	Floating, about 122 KZT/USD
Exchange Reserves:	$22 billion
GDP:	$95 billion
GDP per Capita:	$5,650
GDP Growth YOY:	10.5 percent
Inflation YOY:	8 percent
Unemployment:	Not Available
Primary Exchange:	KASE
Country Ticker Code:	KZ

Far from its less-than-glamorous depiction in the recent movie *Borat,* Kazakhstan is a rapidly expanding economy. The country is the fastest-growing economy of the former Soviet Union, with GDP growth of over 10 percent annually, thanks to a large surplus of oil and related hydrocarbons. This rapid increase in the country's wealth is finding its way down to the average citizen, providing for a continued broadening of the economy's diversification. Consumer demand continually outpaces GDP growth, showing that the average person is feeling the effects of the country's economic expansion. Bank deposits have been growing at over 50 percent per year,[14] bringing more of the economy out of the *gray market* and providing more capital for banks to loan to businesses and consumers. The country has a stable, although not completely open, political system with President Nursultan Nazarbayev enjoying broad support.

Risks:

- Although the economy is diversifying, it is still in the early stages and heavily dependent on oil and hydrocarbon exports. This makes the country susceptible to global oil prices.
- Kazakhstan equities are generally illiquid and carry with them the risk that minority shareholders' rights are not of primary concern.
- Nazarbayev enjoys large popularity in Kazakhstan, but his decision to exempt himself from mandatory term limits when his term expires in 2012 could spark political backlash.

Rewards:

- The country is enjoying annual GDP growth of more than 10 percent, much of which is funneling down to average citizens, sparking economic diversification and increased consumer demand.
- Kazakhstan enjoys a prime position for oil and hydrocarbon exports in Central and Southeast Asia.
- Kazakhstan has an oil industry that is experiencing output increases much higher than surrounding countries thanks, in part, to its constructive relationships with Western oil companies.
- Nazarbayev's tenure as Kazakhstan's president has brought stability that should continue through his current term, which ends in 2012.

Kazakhmys

Symbol	Not Listed in Kazakhstan
GDR	KAZ.LN
GDR Ratio	NA
Market Cap	$11.73 billion
Shares Outstanding	467.47 million
Estimated Freefloat	33.5 percent

Kazakhmys is the world's tenth largest vertically integrated producer of copper. The company mines, processes, smelts, and refines copper primarily for export. The company is also 100 percent self-sufficient in electricity, owning two coal-fired power plants.

Kazakhmys relies on copper and copper products for 82 percent of its revenues, but also mines and sells silver, zinc, and gold. Kazakhmys has experienced rapid growth due to production expansion and increases in the global price for metals, showing revenue growth of over 100 percent between 2004 and 2005.[15]

Kazakhtelecom

Symbol	KZTK
GDR	KZTA.GR
GDR Ratio	2:1
Market Cap	$4.37 billion
Shares Outstanding	10.92 million
Estimated Freefloat	50 percent

Kazakhtelecom is Kazakhstan's incumbent fixed-line telephone services provider. The company currently enjoys a 90 percent market share in the country's fixed-line market. The company also owns 49 percent of Kazakhstan's largest wireless company, K-Cell, which enjoys a 60 percent market share. Kazakhtelecom has been losing long-distance market share due to competition from market deregulation but has been increasing market share in value-added services such as Internet access.[16]

Kazkommertsbank

Symbol	KKGB
GDR	KKB.LI
GDR Ratio	1:2
Market Cap	$7.75 billion
Shares Outstanding	575 million
Estimated Freefloat	41.0 percent

Kazkommertsbank is the largest bank in Kazakhstan with nearly 25 percent of the country's market share in both deposits and loans. The company also has a successful operation in Russia, Moskommertsbank, as well as operations in Kyrgyzstan and Tajikistan.

Kazkommertsbank has also been looking into expansion into the fast-growing market of Turkey. Kazkommertsbank has been a prime beneficiary of Kazakhstan's rapid economic growth. The bank has seen deposits and loans grow at 30 percent annually as more Kazakhs put their money into the country's bank. The company is rapidly expanding its retail branch network throughout the country to continue to gain domestic market share.[17]

KazMunaiGas

Symbol	RDGZ
GDR	KMG.GR
GDR Ratio	1:6
Market Cap	$9.45 billion
Shares Outstanding	70.22 million
Estimated Freefloat	40 percent

KazMunaiGas is Kazakhstan's incumbent oil production company. KazMunaiGas has some of the most mature oil assets in Kazakhstan, limiting the company's production to about 200,000 barrels per day. The company is, by law, required to sell 30 percent of its production in Kazakhstan, which nets lower prices than global markets. The company does benefit from the government-granted right to buy a stake in any oil asset in Kazakhstan at market price. KazMunaiGas recently used this right to buy into KazGerMunai and is looking to buy into PetroKazakhstan and Karazhanbasmunai, which will help the company attain a greater efficiency from scale, as well as increased exposure to international markets.[18] The company also benefitted from the resolution of a dispute concerning the world's largest oil discovery in 30 years, the Kashagan oil field. The field's main operators—Italian Eni, French Total, Royal Dutch Shell, and U.S. companies ExxonMobil and ConocoPhillips—will be forced to face fines and allow KazMunaiGas to more than double its stake in the project from 8.3 percent to 16.8 percent as compensation to the Kazakhstan government for repeated delays in implementing the project.[19]

Part Three

THE FUTURE OF INVESTING IN RUSSIA

Chapter 10

Discovering the
Real Russia

Washington, D.C., is the primary locus of negative animus toward Russia. Across the United States there are those who are suspicious of Russia for a variety of reasons. But in Washington, there are institutional and career bets being placed daily, and criticizing and hectoring Russia is the way to go. Their clients, U.S. senators and presidential candidates, bet on it, too. It is easy, and there are no consequences. No local lobbies to contend with.

Think tanks, which are advocacy groups and do not pretend to engage in detached and objective analysis, practice this art, as do some military and intelligence planners—in general, the local crowd whose insight and analysis brought us the Iraq War. And, lest we forget, when the Soviet Union collapsed and the objective light of day was brought to bear on its autopsy, we discovered its remnants to be an emaciated carcass, not the robust body our intelligence estimates had posited as the basis for our own military expenditures.

Many need to have an enemy and plan for confrontation. Real men do not do diplomacy. That's for wimps. Real men use weapons. History teaches that successful empires, such as the Venetian Republic, which was by definition not an autocracy, can also survive and prosper and grow for long, long centuries by diplomatic means and not always at the point of a sword. It is imperative for America to be aggressive and stand for something, and free markets and democratic institutions, human rights and rule of law are what we stand for, but these goals must be implemented locally, with local adaptations, as in India, and now, yes, progressively, Russia. There is no template, American or other. We do have, and will continue to have, enemies. Russia is not one of them.

Until the summer of 2007, China, where there is very limited religious freedom, little political freedom, and not a whole lot of copyright protection, had been getting a relatively free pass from the hateful crowd: the think tanks and the U.S. media. The names and places are hard to remember and pronounce, and we really do not understand the Chinese culture. Well, we understand that their retail "investors" are inveterate gamblers, that many of their projects are state-mandated Potemkin villages, that bad debts are piling up gigantically in the state banks, which are ordered to loan to those projects and, most of all, that their currency is managed in a predatory manner, doing real harm to our own businesses and workers due to an artificially low-priced flood of imports. Their accomplishments in the recent past are staggering and, hopefully, their carbon emissions can be reduced. As to the odds of their making a successful political transition to a more democratic system, don't hold your breath. When it comes to giving the populace a choice through competitive political parties, ala Russia's managed democracy, they are clueless. As of mid-2007, however, massive product recalls due to dangerous lead levels and other problems, have caused closer scrutiny.

When China sought admission to the World Trade Organization (WTO), the huge lobby in Washington of U.S. importers quashed any opposition, and we said, "Come right in." Years have gone by, and China has still not lived up to commitments it made in the WTO admission process to allow U.S. banks and other financial services access to the Chinese domestic markets.

A real enemy to our way of life, though, is generally never mentioned among the hateful crowd or the media. Saudi Arabia, where women are not even allowed to drive a car, finances the construction of mosques all over the world and staffs these "gifts" with mullahs preaching the Wahabbi messianic message of hate and intolerance against Christians and Jews. But the oil lobby in Washington would not permit any mention of this threat to our way of life, to our values of civilization, feminism, democracy, and religious freedom.

In Washington, with one bright exception, Russia has no such lobbies. If we are serious about diversifying our sources of oil and if Russia begins to directly import meaningful quantities of oil into the United States, perhaps that will change. As of now, Russia is still not a member of the "World" Trade Organization; it is the only large country left out. And the Jackson–Vanik Cold War legislation is still on the books. It is mean-spirited and short-sighted, unless Russia is still your enemy.

This chapter was not written in an attempt to disparage Western media outlets, the U.S. government, or think tanks. This chapter is meant to be an attempt to show the reader that, when looking at reporting on Russia, it is important to understand that there are biases that can affect the tone and content of news articles and research reports dealing with Russia. Russia also receives a great amount of criticism from respected publications such as *The Economist,* which in a recent article advised on expelling Russia from the G8 and continuing NATO expansion,[1] and *National Review,* among many other news organizations, which seems, for seemingly unknown reasons, to hold a strictly one-sided bias in all reporting of events related to Russia.

One need only look at how many common bonds there are among the different think tanks, both in funding and in membership, to realize that their viewpoints are probably not all that dissimilar. It is also important to note that many media outlets get their information and quotes from these same organizations, so this bias can be easily transmitted to traditional media. It is hoped that the reader will be impelled to do further research on subjects relating to Russia to get both sides to any story. There are some reliable media outlets that report on Russia and can be used as a counterbalance to traditional Western media outlets. Some of these include the *Moscow Times, Kommersant,* and *Johnson's Russia List,* just to name a few.

A bright spot in Washington specializing in enhancing business ties between U.S. and Russian companies is the U.S.–Russia Business Council (USRBC). Under the able leadership of Gene Lawson, who was awarded the Order of Friendship by Vladimir Putin, the USRBC is a leader in promoting bilateral business interests and assisting U.S. companies looking to do business in Russia. The USBRC assists in providing support for member companies in doing business in Russia, as well as providing timely, unbiased information about business and political matters in Russia.

Think Tanks: The Hateful Crowd

If it is negative news on Russia you are looking for, look no further than the so-called think tanks based in the United States. These organizations provide what they purport to be objective policy study that is designed to help shape the direction of U.S. policy and mold the terms of public discourse. These organizations provide reports for public consumption, quotable "expert commentary" for stories related to Russia, and provide reports to Congress and Washington policy makers to highlight the problems in Russia. The main problem with the think tanks is that, all too often, the pursuit of objective facts is abandoned for the sake of providing a consistent editorial bent. It is not uncommon for alleged research papers from prominent think tanks to ignore any facts that would run counter to the overall message that they are attempting to convey. Whether these omissions are due to lack of knowledge of the facts, or for the purpose of pushing forward their agendas, we will leave up to the reader to decide.

Freedom House

One of the most prominent Washington think tanks is the nonprofit Freedom House. Freedom House was founded in 1941 by a group of concerned individuals, notably including Eleanor Roosevelt, to provide an intellectual counterweight to the spread of Nazism in Europe.[2] Freedom House retains its prominence in Washington circles due to its direct link to the U.S. government. The organization receives approximately 75 percent of its funding via U.S. government grants from the National Endowment for Democracy, USAID, and the U.S. State Department. The organization's nongovernmental funding includes a number of foundations, most notably the Soros Foundation, the Sarah Scaife Foundation, the Lynde and Harry Bradley Foundation, and the Smith Richardson Foundation. Freedom House has attracted some notable board members that include Donald Rumsfeld, Paul Wolfowitz, Otto Reich, Steve Forbes, Dan Quayle, and former CIA Director James Woolsey Jr.[3]

Since its inception, Freedom House has had an impressive record of supporting democracy both at home and abroad through public discourse and the support of democratic movements across the globe. Freedom House states that it "functions as a catalyst for freedom, democracy, and the rule of law through its analysis, advocacy, and action." The 1940s saw the organization push for the Marshall Plan and the formation of NATO. The 1950s saw it fight against McCarthyism, while in the 1960s, Freedom House sided with the Civil Rights movement. Starting in the 1970s, the organization's efforts became more focused on anti-communism. The organization has been active in the Solidarity movement in Poland and the Orange Revolution in Ukraine, and supports activities in Kyrgyzstan and Serbia as well. Freedom House has also been active in supporting rights in countries around the world, where the organization states, "It has championed the rights of democratic activists, religious believers, trade unionists, journalists, and proponents of free markets."[4]

Freedom House is most notable for its annual publication, *Freedom in the World,* which ranks countries on a scale of 1 to 7 in various categories of freedoms. In the most recent of these publications, as well as special reports on press freedom and nations in transition, Freedom House consistently rates Russia as "not free." The organization is, however, even in its criticism of "not free" countries, harshly critical of China and Saudi Arabia. It can be wondered whether all the work Freedom House has done through the years fighting against communism has somewhat tainted its view on Russia, one that it shares with the press at every opportunity. In its 2006 edition of *Freedom in the World,* Freedom House levied some serious charges against the country, stating that the direction of Russia paints a "bleak picture" for the region. It also goes on to state that Russia now "serves as a role model for authoritarian-minded leaders in the region and elsewhere."[5] Is the legacy of Freedom House in jeopardy? Have the neocons taken it over?

The Heritage Foundation

The Heritage Foundation—another think tank that has been known to be considerably one-sided when it comes to Russia and many other issues—is guided by its mission to "formulate and promote conservative public policies based on the principles of free enterprise, limited government, individual freedom, traditional American values, and a strong national defense." Founded in 1973 by Joseph Coors of the Coors Brewing family, the Heritage Foundation has been led since 1977 by former House Republican Study Committee Staff Director Edwin Feulner Jr. The organization's staff has included such names as L. Paul Bremer, Elaine Chao, and John F. Lehman. A majority of the organization's funding comes from conservative donors and foundations, including the Sarah Scaife Foundation and the Lynde and Harry Bradley Foundation. The Heritage Foundation also receives funding from many corporations, including ExxonMobil, Ford Motor Company, General Motors, and GlaxoSmithKline, among others. The organization has also received nearly $1 million from the Korea Foundation, which is primarily funded by the government of South Korea, and is linked to lobbying activities for Malaysian interests.[6]

The Heritage Foundation has garnered considerable political clout among Washington's conservative circles through innovative packaging of "research" and consistent public relations, considered to be the basis for a majority of today's think tanks. The Heritage Foundation has seen its influence rise to the top levels of government, and was a driving force behind Newt Gingrich's 1994 Contract with America. Most notable to our discussion is the organization's position as an inspiration behind the policies of the Reagan administration. The Heritage Foundation was influential in Reagan's policy of labeling the Soviet Union as the *Evil Empire* and aiming for the eventual demise of the nation instead of continuing a policy of containment. Heritage was also influential in Reagan's Strategic Defense Initiative, commonly referred to as the Star Wars program.

The Heritage Foundation has continued its criticism of Russia well into the post-Soviet period. The organization has continued to work to highlight the deficiencies in today's Russian government. The Heritage Foundation has released research reading that includes an article on how the United States should confront "Putin's Anti-U.S. Crusade," one assaulting Russia's NGO law as "an attack on freedom and civil society," and articles outlining the questions of property rights following the Yukos Affair and articles highly critical of Russia's democracy.[7] Russians will tell you that they too suffered under the Soviet Union, and that today's Russia is not the Soviet Union. Is the Heritage Foundation stuck in first gear?

The Jamestown Foundation

The Jamestown Foundation, founded in 1984, is yet another think tank that devotes a considerable amount of its resources toward what it sees as problems in the evolution of Russia toward democracy. Touting itself as delivering material "without political bias, filter, or agenda,"[8] The Jamestown Foundation has strong political and financial connections to Washington conservatives. The organization receives a majority of its funding from conservative foundations, including the Sarah Scaife Foundation, the Earhart Foundation, the Lynde and Harry Bradley Foundation, and the Smith Richardson Foundation, among others. The Jamestown Foundation's board includes former CIA Director James Woolsey Jr., Barbara Buchanan, and Patrick Gross, while having high-profile former board members such as Dick Cheney.[9]

The Jamestown Foundation began its work in 1984 after its founder, William Geimer, spent time working with the highest-ranking Soviet official ever to defect to the United States, Arkady Shevchenko. Since that time, The Jamestown Foundation has worked against communism and, more recently, against radical Islam and any government where it feels that freedom is at risk. The organization provides nearly daily updates on the problems in Russia through its *Eurasia Daily Monitor*, which is consistent in its criticism of the Russian government.[10] The Jamestown Foundation also has strong links to other think tanks that have a consistently negative view of Russia, which could leave one wondering, exactly how independent is the organization?

The Hudson Institute

The Hudson Institute, founded in 1961 by a group from the RAND Corporation, is "committed to building an America where freedom, opportunity, prosperity, and civil society flourish" (www.hudson.org). The Hudson Institute shares its funding sources with many other conservative think tanks, including the Sarah Scaife Foundation, the Lynde and Harry Bradley Foundation, and the Smith Richardson Foundation, as well as Eli Lilly and Company, DuPont, and Procter & Gamble, among others.[11] Owing to its mission, the organization has had as its primary focus domestic policy. The Hudson Institute does continue to devote considerable focus to Russia and Eurasia, however, where it helped to advise former Soviet countries on economic liberalization.[12] The Hudson Institute has consistently been highly critical of Russia's government under Putin's leadership. One could only guess as why the editorial line from the Hudson Institute is equivalent to the editorial line of the other think tanks that share the same funding sources.

American Enterprise Institute

Arguably the most influential think tank under America's current administration is the American Enterprise Institute. The organization, founded in 1943, has to its credit a veritable who's who among conservatives in its list of current and former scholars and fellows. These names include John Bolton, Lynne Cheney, Newt Gingrich, Alan Keyes, Richard Perle, and Fred Thompson, among others. The organization also shares its funding sources with other prominent think tanks, including the Sarah Scaife Foundation, the Lynde and Harry Bradley Foundation, the Earhart Foundation, and the Smith Richardson Foundation. The American Enterprise Institute also gets considerable funding from corporate donors, including from ExxonMobil for work to critique reports about global climate change, Coors Brewing Company, and Microsoft Corporation.[13]

When it comes to reporting on Russia, the American Enterprise Institute follows the line of most think tanks and stresses in its reports the negative aspects of Russia's current government and political climate. The organization has been highly critical of Putin's presidency in terms of the rollback from democracy and his economic policies. The American Enterprise Institute, in a 2005 report "Democracy in Russia" citing the Republican Party of Russia (RPR), claimed that "the Russian people are receiving less and less of the 'oil-soaked' economic pie." The article goes on to state that "outside the commodity sector, expansion has been modest and slowing."[14] This despite the fact that average incomes are rising considerably faster than GDP and that Russia's national income is distributed more evenly than that of the United States, as well as the fact that some of the fastest-growing industries in Russia are retailers, banks, and real estate companies. Of course, as evidenced by its work to critique global climate change on a grant from ExxonMobil, it is possible that the American Enterprise Institute can be swayed in its editorial content by its sources of funding, which it shares with many think tanks that are consistent in their anti-Russian bias.

Other Think Tanks

The aforementioned think tanks are the most pervasive and persuasive of those who hold sway in the halls of Washington, but they are not the only ones who devote time and energy to push an agenda of

negativity toward Russia. The Foreign Policy Research Institute, with
funding from conservative donors like the Sarah Scaife Foundation,
the Smith Richardson Foundation, and the Lynde and Harry Bradley
Foundation,[15] works to bring "the insights of scholarship to bear on
the development of policies that advance U.S. national interests"
with articles such as the March 2007 "Russia under Putin: Toward
Democracy or Dictatorship?"[16]

The important aspect for the reader to take away from this discussion is that many of these self-proclaimed independent think
tanks are beholden to the same funding sources. Whether this affects
their independence and impartiality, it is for the reader to judge. It
is imperative to remember, though, that many of these organizations
lend themselves to public comment in the media on these issues with
the intended effect of swaying public opinion in their direction. These
think tanks are often able to get their "analysts" featured in articles
and news reports simply as "Russia experts." The donor lists of these
organizations consistently have the Sarah Scaife Foundation, the
Lynde and Harry Bradley Foundation, and the Smith Richardson
Foundation, among others, at the top of their lists.

Jackson–Vanik

If you were to ask most people, they would tell you that the Cold
War is long over. But all you need to do is look at the fact that the
Jackson–Vanik amendment is still in effect for Russia to see that
remnants of the Cold War still remain in the halls of Washington.
The Jackson–Vanik amendment was passed in 1974, at the height
of the Cold War. This amendment was designed to prohibit countries
that restricted emigration from enjoying permanent normal trade
relations (PNTR) with the United States. PNTR status with a country ensures that goods imported from that are given the lowest rates.[17]

The main focus of the Jackson–Vanik amendment was to punish
countries that did not allow for the emigration of Jewish citizens out
of each respective country. This has not been a problem in Russia
since the fall of the Soviet Union in 1991. From that time, emigration has not been an issue, as people are allowed to leave the country

unencumbered, which would seem to make the Jackson–Vanik amendment a relic of the past. The U.S. government has insisted in keeping Russia from enjoying permanent normal trade relations under the auspices of the Jackson–Vanik amendment, instead opting to grant one-year normal trade relation status every year since 1992. In fact, the United States has found Russia in compliance with the terms of the amendment since 1994,[18] but this yearly absolution process is deemed humiliating by a Russia, which deeply resents it.

The U.S. government hopes that by keeping the Jackson–Vanik amendment in force, it can use the hope of permanent normal trade relation status as a way to keep pressure on Russia to continue democratic reforms. In fact, the amendment has become a sticking point in U.S.–Russian relations, as Russia is insulted that it is still included in the relic of Cold War legislation. Even Israel's Minister for Immigration and Absorption, Ze'ev Boim stated, "There is no need for the Jackson–Vanik amendment. Russia has changed, and the need for amendment is no longer there."[19] Boim said that the amendment should be scrapped as soon as possible. To add to the insult, permanent normal trade relations were extended to the former Soviet republics of Kyrgyzstan and Georgia in 2000 and Ukraine in 2006.[20] To further exacerbate the issue is the fact that the People's Republic of China, a truly communist regime with strong restrictions against emigration, was removed in the late 1990s as a way to ensure China's entry into the World Trade Organization, an organization that Russia is still attempting to join.

Recent U.S. Stance

The Jackson–Vanik amendment is not the only sticking point in U.S.–Russian relations. Recently, the U.S. government has opted for more overt criticism of the Russian government, as evidenced by recent U.S. State Department reports on the present and future conditions of U.S.–Russian relations. As the U.S. State Department celebrates the 200th anniversary of U.S.–Russian diplomatic relations, it has issued two reports on human rights with unprecedented focus on Russia, followed with its five-year strategic plan that devotes a significant portion of its agenda to Russia.[21]

The first document released by the U.S. State Department, in March of 2007, was the agency's annual report on international human rights that devoted significant space to discussing the problems of democratic rights and freedom of expression in Russia. The State Department's findings include a criticism citing that Russia has one of the highest rates of incarceration in the world at 685 incarcerated per 100,000 citizens, without mentioning that the only country with a higher incarceration rate is the United States, at 701 incarcerated per 100,000 citizens.[22] The second document, titled "Supporting Human Rights and Democracy: 2006," contains some similar criticisms of Russia's recent record on freedom and democracy, but is also the first to hint at the fact that the United States is prepared to use its influence to promote free elections in the region.[23]

The third document that emerged is titled "Strategic Plan—Fiscal Years 2007–2012." This is the U.S. State Department's outline of priorities and challenges it plans to tackle in the upcoming five-year period. This new iteration of the document, released in April 2007, spends a great deal of space discussing future challenges with Russia. The report outlines many channels of potential positive relations between the United States and Russia, such as economic, scientific, and political ties. The report also discusses the many potential problems the United States sees in the U.S.–Russia relationship, stating, "We will engage with Russia where we can do so productively, while continuing to stand firm—with the support of our European and other allies—for the values of democracy, human rights, and freedom and to push back on negative Russian behavior."[24]

Part of the negative Russian behavior that Washington sees is compiled in a list included in the report, which includes "increasing centralization of power, pressure on NGOs (nongovernmental organizations) and civil society, a growing government role in the economy, and restrictions on media freedom." The report also views increasing Russian weapons sales to countries such as Syria, Iran, and Venezuela as a source of "major concern" for the U.S. government. Although previous versions of the Strategic Plan offered significant space to the U.S.–Russia relationship, this latest version is the first to devote a special section to Russia.[25]

Areas of Tension

There are many areas of disagreement that underlie the difficulties in the U.S.–Russia relationship. One of the major areas of contention, and one that provides for an undercurrent of distrust on the Russian side of the relationship, is the real and perceived encroachment of the United States into Russia's former sphere of influence. After the fall of the Soviet Union and the formation of the Russian Federation, there was an unwritten understanding between Russia and the United States that the United States would not provoke Russia by infringing on its sphere of influence, especially as it pertained to former Soviet republics. Since the formation of the Russian Federation, the Russians have seen the European Union and NATO expand right up to the Russian border. NATO has admitted the countries of the Czech Republic, Poland, and Estonia, and is currently, to the great dismay of Russia, working on the admission of Ukraine.

The European Union, meanwhile, has managed to add to its membership the countries of Estonia, Latvia, Lithuania, Poland, and the Czech Republic. This has caused Russia to have the feeling that it has been surrounded on its Western border by the EU and NATO. The feeling of being caged in can be understood with the realization that during the Cold War, Russia was the power broker in the region. Now Russia is left watching a Western encroachment up to its western borders. The United States has also been actively arming and funding the southern former Soviet state of Georgia in its battle against the country's rebels. Right or wrong, Russia has been backing the rebels, which has led to an almost Cold War–style proxy battle between the United States and Russia, with Russia viewing the United States as encroaching on its southern borders. To make matters worse, the United States has decided to install components of its missile shield in Poland and the Czech Republic, further adding to the unease of the Russian government. Although ostensibly a shield against missiles from rouge states such as North Korea and Iran, the locations of the interceptor missiles create uncertainty in Russia as to their intended target of deterrence.

Of course, the United States and the West have legitimate grievances with Russia. One of the major sticking points in Russia's relations with the West is the perceived consolidation of power toward the Kremlin at the expense of political freedoms and first amendment–type rights as such backsliding has clearly occurred. This tension was heightened leading up to the 2007 State Duma elections and 2008 presidential election. The Kremlin has been quick to quell dissent leading up to elections. In April 2007, the Kremlin sent riot police to violently disperse anti-government protests in both Moscow and St. Petersburg by the fringe Other Russia group (it is actually a collection of very small groups) led by former chess champion Garry Kasparov and former Russian Prime Minister Mikhail Kasyanov, who were both arrested and questioned by the Federal Security Service of the Russian Federation (FSB). Shortly after the demonstrations, the National Bolshevik Party, a small member of Other Russia, was declared an extremist organization and delisted as a political party.[26]

It is also seen in the West that the Russian government has been increasing its control over media outlets leading up to the election. The government has already cemented its control of television outlets through ownership of major stations and intense scrutiny of independents. The government has also been working to push its message through radio channels and is trying to find ways to control the message on Internet sites, where it has limited success by pulling Web sites and putting pressure on service providers to monitor content. The Russian government has also been putting pressure on NGOs operating in Russia, creating new rules and forcing existing NGOs to reregister with the government and provide detailed reports on their activities and financing. However, over half a million NGOs have sprouted up. The government said *nyet* to even a garden club in Soviet times, but very few NGO registrations have been rejected by the Russian government.

Summary

The West continues to have serious misgivings about Russia's real and perceived backsliding from some of the democratic reforms established during the Yeltsin era. Many of the concerns raised in the West are justified, such as Russia's hard-handed dealing with political demonstrations. Other concerns seem to stem from either a misunderstanding of the facts or from ulterior motives. To be fair, Russia also has its concerns about the intentions of the West. Nowhere is this more evident than the U.S. plans to install interceptor missiles near Russia's Western border. Russia's path to democracy, although slower than many in the West would like, is only a little over 15 years old and should be given time to develop naturally.

"Still, for a 15-year-old democracy, Russia is doing well," points out Vyacheslav Nikonov, head of the Politika Foundation in Moscow. "In Germany, they elected Hitler exactly on the 15th year of democracy," after years of hyperinflation during the failed Weimar Republic. He notes that political structures are still developing, the rule of law is shaky, and people in power do not have accountability. Again, it will be the leaders who mold, top down, until the middle class is ready to assert itself, bottom up.

Vladimir Putin pleads for patience. "The road is not simple. It takes time and the right groundwork and conditions. We need to ensure that our economic transformations bring about the growth of the middle class, which is to a large extent the standard bearer of [democracy]. This is something that takes time and cannot be achieved overnight."[27]

In late November and early December 2007, I was in Moscow and observed the elections held for the national legislature, the State Duma. The negativity of many foreigners towards these elections was highlighted by the OSCE. In its report on the 2003 elections in Russia, which greatly credited the Elections Commission there for the very professional results of over a million officials and volunteers in administering the vote for such a large country, the OSCE gave Russia an overall flunking grade due to the incumbents' purported unfair media access. This year, I saw the leaders of each of the four major parties on TV repeatedly, but the minor parties, most of which polled at very low levels and got one percent or less of the vote, were not given such access.

The fact is Russia continues along the road of maturing free market democracy, with a high voter turnout and four political parties to be represented in the next Duma. The substantial increase in the next Duma for President Putin's United Russia party, from about 37 percent in the present Duma, to about 63 percent, reflects the high level of confidence Russians have in the policies of his administration, which have brought prosperity to ever-increasing numbers of the Russian people. The political stability that this vote of confidence reflects will be a strong plus for investors going forward.

Chapter 11

What's in Store for Russia and Its Investors?

Many of us wonder, "What will Russia look like in the future?" "What are Russians really like?" Each of us is, of course, the net of our plusses and our minuses. And every country is in a state of constant evolution, not least the United States of America. Many countries now wrestle with serious endemic problems—the Muslims in France, and questions of identity in Japan.

The English tradition of the commonweal, where we care not just about ourselves and our families, but about our communities, our states, and the country, is still important in America. We have great media that help police honesty and integrity in government, but most public officials are honest and dedicated to begin with.

In this regard, Russia has many historic legacies to overcome, and polls indicate that the populace does not esteem democratic values. But they do like to vote and are offered meaningful choices.

So the role of leadership in Russia will be critical. Will a civil society develop? Will we see that kind of leadership from its religious communities? That's a long shot.

Who Will Lead?

The business community has leaders who are effective in managing public companies and playing by a set of rules that are certainly recognizable to us. In fact, the norms in Russia today can be said to be those of the international community of world-class companies. Will these business leaders be community leaders?

It is true that many seem more focused on making an impact in France, on their beaches, and on their ski slopes, than in Russia. But many business leaders are art collectors, with voracious appetites for anything from the historic Russian past. And there are signs of charitable and community spirit. The government of Russia clearly expects business to assume broader responsibilities. Our first president, George Washington, observed that our Constitution laid the foundations of our new country, but that "the community at large must raise the edifice of our society."[1] What kind of civil society will Russia's business community and others erect? We shall see.

Not long ago, it was universally said that Vladimir Putin would change the Russian Constitution to fit his fancy and give himself a third term. After all, how many politicians worldwide enjoy the kind of popularity he does? But, trained as a lawyer, he gets it: Russia is not to be a banana republic; it is to be a serious, stable participant in a global community. He did not change the Constitution. What an example he has set and, for that matter, followed, from Boris Yeltsin. That he should use his prominence to take a leading role in the recommendation to the people of the man to follow him in office is seen as an abuse by some. More properly, it is what his countrymen expect him to do, want him to do. They have that kind of respect for his judgment and leadership.

Do the grouping of Gorbachev, Yeltsin, and Putin, who did not much care for each other, amount to the grouping of Washington,

Jefferson, and Hamilton, who also did not always see eye to eye? I think so, and judge the Russian Federation fortunate in the founding fathers of modern and democratic Russia, a free market economy, and responsible participant in the global community.

As for Russia in its neighborhood, relations with the "near abroad" will continue to be difficult, but Russia does have justifiable cultural, as well as political, aims and objectives. The English language is by far the world's number-one second language, partly as a result of the British Empire, and its demise. The recent demise of the Soviet empire has left the Russian language as the number-two second language in the world, and the Kremlin has recently appointed Vyacheslav Nikonov to head the "Russian World Foundation" with the mission of promoting Russian language and culture around the world. His agency will join the USIA, British Council, Alliance Française, and Goethe Institute as a quasi-governmental soft approach to influencing opinion and policy by cultivating friends. Vyacheslav Nikonov's has been an objective, moderate voice as head of the Polity Institute.

Predictions for the Future

Before summarizing what we hope the reader will derive from this book, here are a few speculations on the future:

- Southern Russia will enjoy massive infrastructure development and population growth. Sochi 2014 will be a major stimulus.
- Uneconomic Siberian towns, such as Mirny, the location of the world's largest open-pit diamond mine, will be seen more as offshore platforms with workers flown in and out, rather than uneconomic permanent towns, with 9 out of 10 residents performing support roles.
- Yes, the Russian population will start to grow as soon as Russian men learn that marriage is a team sport. State subsidies for second children will help.
- No, the Orthodox Church will not become more tolerant of other Christian denominations that expect to proselytize local populations.

- Russians will not be accepted in the Baltics. Poland will continue to dislike Russia. If Kosovo is broken off from Serbia, Georgia will not recover Abkhazia (Pitsundi and Sukhumi on the Black Sea).
- The Chechans will go on and on in their resistance, and tourism there will be about as popular as visiting drug-lord-dominated parts of Colombia.
- Moscow's casinos will be co-opted into districts successfully.
- Russia will not continue to completely shut down between New Year's and Orthodox Christmas.
- Single-family home ownership, baseball, and mass transit will prosper.
- Russia will follow the lead of its older brother, Ukraine, into the European Union, but will not join NATO, which will become less important to its European members but still afford the United States a vehicle for coordination of its military policy.
- Russia will not be our enemy in this century. Our military planners need to posit an enemy(s) for planning purposes and, evidently they have put Russia in that category and, of course, certain think tanks are the cheering section for that. And Russia will have its own national interests which its leadership must pursue outside of NATO. But cooperation—in nuclear fuel reprocessing, vis à vis Iran and other hostile Muslim states, in energy and other vital areas—will balance competition. This prediction is qualified by the expectation that both sides can maintain some degree of maturity in each other's management of public relations challenges that must be dealt with on a continuing basis. The recent imbroglio over missile placement in Europe gives one pause on this score. We did not consult the Russians in advance (after our *fait accompli,* we are in our traditional mode of exclaiming "they have no veto over our policy"), and they overreacted.
- This will continue to be an American century, but in a more multipolar world with Europe, China, Japan, and India, but not Latin America or Africa, playing increasingly important roles (each with its own national interests to promote).
- The traditional negativity of Russia's intellectuals will abate as the more positive and robust younger generation proves that

democracy and the free market can work for the best interests of Russians, too.

- The influx of Muslim immigrants into Russia will be managed in a culturally acceptable manner (this is its greatest cultural challenge).

- Our greatest mutual/collective challenge will be to contain Islamist hostility, led by the oil-rich Islamic Republic of Arabia.

- Russia will sport world-class movie, biotech, aerospace, nuclear, and IT industries.

- Russia-based businesses will join the ranks of the leading global firms. Intellectual capital (IT, biotech, aerospace) and financial strength will dominate not services, but commodities will continue unabated. Russian businessmen and women will be counted not only among the world's top billionaires, but as innovators and leaders.

- With the current election cycle in Russia over, assuming Vladimir Putin follows through on his willingness to be Prime Minister, with Dmitry Medvedev as the new President, political uncertainty is minimal and the current professional, effective management of the Russian economy should continue, which appears to be the foremost concern of Russia's voters (as well as foreign investors). As described in this book, Medvedev's main focus has been domestic social and economic programs so, in choosing him, Putin showed a clear commitment to continuing reform and improvement in these areas. Also highlighted was his interest in improving Russia's image abroad since the other front-runner, Sergei Ivanov—a capable, English-speaking deputy prime minister—was a former KGB head too. Pragmatism reigns and, even where the State re-asserts a central role in steering targeted companies, the Putin/ Medvedev team will eventually launch these ships back into the stream of private business.

- So, what will the future bring for the Russian economy and its investible companies? Such a question must always be approached with caution in the timeframe of publishing a book. (Here, the heading "Predictions" must be supplanted by a heading for this bullet of "Speculation" and further qualified by the admonition that past results are never an indication of future performance. TMRFX has averaged gains of over 40 percent a year for the past five years, or more than 500 percent for the period.) Even though the US economy is currently weakening, the Russian economy appears set for continued expansion given the domestic investment boom and continuing Asian domestic demand for commodities. The rising cost of oil extraction and greenfield development dampen prospects for oil, but, given lower taxes and tariff increases for domestic prices, gas looks stronger. As Anatoly Chubais predicted, the completion of utility reform portends continued expansion in that sector and, assuming a secular growth in demand, construction, real estate, autos, financial and consumer products all look promising. The UN predicts that Russia in 2008 will enjoy a GDP increase in excess of 8 percent. Whether or not the Government can get on top of the ugly rise in inflation given a new emphasis on social programs remains the main open question.

- Fresh water will become one of the world's scarcest resources, and Russia's got it.

Summary

This book was meant to give the reader some insight into the remarkable recent transformation of Russia from a centrally planned communist state into a leading free-market economy. We thought it important to begin with a discussion of this transformation and how Russia had to learn the lessons of capitalism the hard way (the 1998 crisis), and how this shaped the economic and political policies to this day. The discussions of risk and reward were designed to give the reader some sense as to what can be expected when investing in Russia.

The discussion on the development of business in Russia and the sectors and companies that have emerged in capitalist Russia was designed to go beyond the type of business news that is generally available about Russia—which is usually negative. We hope that the reader benefits from learning about the growth in Russia's economy away from oil and natural gas into a modern, diversified economy.

The book finished with discussions about the negative image that Russia is given in the Western media, as well as an outlook for the future. Hopefully, the reader was able to put the negative press surrounding Russia in context, so as to better make an informed judgment about what is happening in that country. As outlined in this chapter, we believe that the future of Russia remains bright. If Russia's government can continue the fiscal discipline it has shown, the country will grow and diversify its economy in its drive to come closer to Western European economies.

Notes

Chapter 1

1. Russian Trading System Stock Exchange, September 20, 2007.
2. Volodymyr G. Butkevych, *Who Has a Right to Crimea,* www.infoukes.com/history/crimea/page-03.html (accessed September 10, 2007).
3. Pauline J., Luong and Erika Weinthal, "Contra Coercion: Russian Tax Reform, Exogenous Shocks, and Negotiated Institutional Change,"*American Political Science Review* 98, no. 1 (February 2004).
4. Vincent Koen and Steven Phillips, "Price Liberalization in Russia: The Early Record,"*International Monetary Fund* (November 1, 1992).
5. Deutsche UFG Research: Russian Banking Sector, July 25, 2007.
6. Abbigail J. Chiodo and Michael T. Owyang, "A Case Study of a Currency Crisis: The Russian Default of 1998," The Federal Reserve Bank of St. Louis (November/December 2002).
7. Russian Trading System Stock Exchange, September 20, 2007.
8. Andrew Meier, "The Crash: The Russian Market—From Start to Crash," *Frontline* (June 29, 1999).
9. Chiodo and Owyang.
10. Meier.
11. Chiodo and Owyang.
12. Ibid.
13. Ibid.
14. Central Bank of the Russian Federation, September 20, 2007.
15. Meier.
16. Chiodo and Owyang.

17. Meier.

18. Ibid.

19. UBS Investment Research, "Equity Guide 2006–07" (August 2006).

20. Office of the President of the Russian Federation. www.kremlin.ru/eng/ (accessed September 20, 2007).

21. U.S. Department of State Bureau of European and Eurasian Affairs, *Russia Profile* (February 2007).

22. Vladimir Putin, Speech at the Meeting with Cabinet Members, the Heads of the Federal Assembly, and State Council Members, September 5, 2005.

23. Office of the President of the Russian Federation, www.kremlin.ru/eng/ (accessed September 20, 2007).

24. Ibid.

25. Vladimir Putin, Annual Address to the Federal Assembly of the Russian Federation, May 10, 2006.

26. U.S. Department of State Bureau of European and Eurasian Affairs.

27. "Bringing the Internet to Schools," *Moscow News* 23 (June 14, 2007).

28. Vladimir Putin, Annual Address to the Federal Assembly of the Russian Federation, May 10, 2006.

29. Ibid.

30. Vladimir Putin, Annual Address to the Federal Assembly of the Russian Federation, May 26, 2004.

31. Vladimir Putin, Annual Address to the Federal Assembly of the Russian Federation, April 26, 2007.

32. Vladimir Putin, Speech at the Meeting with the Cabinet Members, the Heads of the Federal Assembly, and State Council Members, September 5, 2005

33. Putin, Annual Address to the Federal Assembly of the Russian Federation, May 10, 2006.

34. Vladimir Putin, Opening Address at the Council for Implementing Priority National Projects, November 29, 2005.

35. Vladimir Putin, Annual Address to the Federal Assembly of the Russian Federation, April 26, 2007.

36. Putin, Annual Address to the Federal Assembly of the Russian Federation, May 10, 2006.

37. Ibid.

38. Putin, Annual Address to the Federal Assembly of the Russian Federation, April 26, 2007.

39. "Dmitry Anatolievich Medvedev," biography from www.gazprom.com/eng/articles/article8822.shtml (accessed September 15, 2007).

40. Dmitry Medvedev: profile by Renaissance Capital Research.

41. OAO Gazprom from www.gazprom.com/eng/articles/article8511.shtml (accessed September 15, 2007)

42. Henry Meyer, "Putin tightens Internet Controls Before Presidential Election," *Bloomberg News* (April 9, 2007).

43. Andrew E. Kramer, "50% Good News Is the Bad News in Russian Radio," *New York Times* (April 22, 2007).

44. Meyer.

45. "More Moscow Crackdowns," *The Other Russia*. www.theotherrussia.org/2007/04/24/more-moscow-crackdowns/(accessed September 20, 2007).

46. Andrei Smirnov, "North Caucasus-Tested Strategies Used to Counter March of the Discontented," *Eurasia Daily Monitor* 4, no. 78, The Jamestown Foundation (April 20, 2007).

47. Yevgeny Volk, "Russia's NGO Law: An Attack on Freedom and Civil Society," *Russia and Eurasia Issues WebMemo #1090.* The Heritage Foundation (May 24, 2006).

48. Peter Finn, "Russian Probe Shuts Media Foundation," *Washington Post Foreign Service* (June 29, 2007).

Chapter 2

1. The Central Bank of the Russian Federation, www.cbr.ru/eng/statistics/credit_statistics/(accessed September 20, 2007).

2. Dmitry Dmitriev and Mikhail Shlemov. (2007). Russian Banking Sector, Deutsche UFG Investment Research, July 25, 2007.

3. UBS Investment Research, "Equity Guide 2006–07" (August 2006).

4. The Central Bank of the Russian Federation, www.cbr.ru/eng/statistics/credit_statistics/(accessed September 20, 2007).

5. Vladimir Osakovsky, Ph.D. (2007). Putin Nominates Zubkov PM, Waiting Game Continues. Politics Flashnote. Aton Investment Research. September 13, 2007.

6. Roland Nash (2007). "Viktor Zubkov—A Holding Prime Minister." Renaissance Capital Research. September 12, 2007.

7. Ibid.

8. Ibid.

9. *Transition: The First Ten Years—Analysis and Lessons for Eastern Europe and the Former Soviet Union* (Washington, D.C.: World Bank, 2002).

10. UBS Investment Research.

11. Clemens Grafe, "EMEA Economic Monitor: Russia," UBS Investment Research (January 9, 2007).

12. Russian Trading System Stock Exchange, September 20, 2007.

13. UBS Investment Research.

14. Yaroslav Lissovolik, "Russia: Escaping the Inequality Trap," Deutsche UFG Research (May 4, 2007).

15. Grafe.

16. U.S. Department of State, *2006 Investment Climate Statement—Russia* (Washington, D.C.: U.S. Government Printing Office, 2006).

Chapter 3

1. G. Thomas Sims, "Former Siemens Executives Convicted of Bribery," *International Herald Tribune* (May 14, 2007).

2. Clemens Grafe, "EMEA Economic Monitor: Russia," UBS Investment Research (January 9, 2007).

3. The Central Bank of the Russian Federation, September 20, 2007.

4. Ministry of Finance of the Russian Federation, September 1, 2007.

5. Peter Westin and Irina Plevako, "Charting Russia," MDM Bank Strategy & Economics Research (May 8, 2007).

6. Pauline J. Luong and Erika Weinthal, "Contra Coercion: Russian Tax Reform, Exogenous Shocks, and Negotiated Institutional Change," *American Political Science Review* 98, no. 1 (February 2004).

7. Dmitry Gololobov, *The Yukos Money Laundering Case: A Never-ending Story*.

8. UBS Investment Research, "Equity Guide 2006–07" (August 2006).

Chapter 4

1. UBS Investment Research, "Equity Guide 2006–07" (August 2006).

2. UBS Investment Research.

3. Ian Blanchard, "Russia and International Iron Markets, ca. 1740-1850," The University of Glamorgan (April 2001).

4. Ibid.

5. *Library of Congress Country Studies: Russia* (Washington, D.C.: U.S. Government Printing Office, 1996).

6. *Josef Stalin Biography* (n.d.). *Red Files.* Public Broadcasting Company. www.pbs
   .org/redfiles/bios/all_bio_joseph_stalin.htm (accessed June 25, 2007).

7. "Josef Stalin," *Encyclopedia Britannica* (2007).

8. Stalin I.V. (n.d.). Russia the Great russia.rin.ru/guides_e/4140.html
   (accessed June 25, 2007).

9. *Library of Congress Country Studies: Russia.*

10. Ibid.

11. Geoff Crocker, *Can Russian Steel Compete?* ALT Research & Consulting
    Company (n.d.).

12. UBS Investment Research.

13. L. Iperti, "Do Russian Steel Producers Really Have a Competitive
    Advantage?" *Atti Notizie* (October 2005).

14. Severstal Company History. www.severstal.com/eng/company_profile/
    history/(accessed September 15, 2007)

15. Alexei Morozov, Andrew Snowdowne, and Alexander Trofimov, "Severstal,"
    UBS Investment Research (January 23, 2007).

16. Ibid.

17. Ibid.

18. Guy Chazan and Paul Glader, "East-West Alloy Scrappy Russian Steel
    Executive Builds an Empire with Castoffs," *Wall Street Journal* (June 9, 2004).

19. Ibid.

20. UBS Investment Research.

21. Ibid.

22. Ibid.

23. Ibid.

24. Valery Virkunen, "The Battle for Russia's Aluminum Comes to a Head,"
    Prism 6, no. 1, The Jamestown Foundation (January 21, 2000).

25. Andrew Meier, "The Crash: The Russian Market—From Start to Crash,"
    Frontline (June 29, 1999).

26. Yuriy Humber, "RUSAL Wins Russian Approval to Merge with SUAL,"
    International Herald Tribune (January 18, 2007).

27. Oleg V. Deripaska, National Council on Corporate Governance Member
    Biography. www.corp-gov-russia.com/en/site.xp/050049050124.html
    (accessed July 20, 2007).

28. Ibid.

29. Patrizia Kokot, "RPT Hochtief in Talks to Cooperate with Russian
    Billionaire Deripaska," *Forbes* (May 4, 2007).

30. Deripaska.

31. "Oleg Deripaska Stripped of U.S. Visa," *Kommersant* (April 20, 2007).

32. UBS Investment Research.

33. Brett Foley, "Norilsk Bids C$5.3 Billion for Lionore, Balks Xstrata," *Bloomberg News* (May 3, 2007).

34. Norilsk Nickel Company Presentation from www.nornik.ru/en/investor/presentations/(accessed June 30, 2007).

35. Ibid.

36. Norilsk Nickel Company History from Interros, www.interros.ru/eng/assets/nornikel/(accessed June 25, 2007).

37. Ibid.

38. Vladimir Potanin Biography from Interros, www.interros.ru/eng/about/direction/Potanin/(accessed June 30, 2007).

39. Company Information from Interros. www.interros.ru (accessed June 30, 2007).

40. Vladimir Potanin Biography from Mosnews MN-Files, www.mosnews.com (September 23, 2005).

41. Information from Vladimir Potanin Foundation, www.eng.fund.potanin.ru (accessed June 30, 2007).

42. Vladimir Potanin Biography.

43. UBS Investment Research.

44. Roydel Stewart, "Uralkaliy: A Growing Stake in the Potash Industry," Alfa-Bank Investment Research (June 13, 2007).

Chapter 5

1. UBS Investment Research, "Equity Guide 2006–07" (August 2006).

2. Ibid.

3. Ibid.

4. Ibid.

5. Ibid.

6. Lucian Kim and Torrey Clark, "Shell Cedes Sakhalin Stake, Strengthening Putin Grip," *Bloomberg News* (December 21, 2006).

7. UBS Investment Research.

8. Ibid.

9. Company Information from www.lukoil.com (accessed August 13, 2007).

10. Ibid.

11. Ibid.

12. Ibid.

13. Vagit Y. Alekperov, "International Directory of Business Biographies. eNotes.com," *Inc.* (2007).

14. Ibid.

15. Ibid.

16. Company Information from www.lukoil.com. (accessed August 13, 2007).

17. UBS Investment Research.

18. Ibid.

19. Ibid.

20. Nadia Kazakova and Andrey Gromadin, "Switch on the Gas," MDM Bank Investment Research (February 5, 2007).

21. Ibid.

22. Alexander Burgansky and Irina Elinevskaya, "Building New Power," Renaissance Capital Research (September 4, 2006).

23. Kazakova and Gromadin.

24. Burgansky and Elinevskaya.

25. UBS Investment Research.

26. Kazakova and Gromadin.

27. Ibid.

28. Ibid.

29. UBS Investment Research.

30. Ibid.

31. Kazakova and Gromadin.

32. "Expert: Ukraine vs. Gazprom: The Price of the Problem," *Regnum News Agency* (January 10, 2006).

33. Kazakova and Gromadin.

Chapter 6

1. UBS Investment Research, "Equity Guide 2006–07" (August 2006).

2. Alexei Yakovitsky and Anastasia Obukhova, "VimpelCom ADR Valuation Upgraded as Visibility on Stronger Earnings Improves," Deutsche UFG Investment Research (August 31, 2007).

3. Ibid.

4. UBS Investment Research.

5. Ibid.

6. Ibid.

7. Ibid.

8. Ibid.

9. Ibid.

10. Ibid.

11. Yakovitsky and Obukhova.

12. UBS Investment Research.

13. Ibid.

14. Ibid.

15. Ibid.

16. Ibid.

17. Ibid.

18. Ibid.

19. Ibid.

20. Ibid.

Chapter 7

1. Peter Westin and Irina Plevako, "Charting Russia," MDM Bank Strategy & Economics Research (May 8, 2007).

2. UBS Investment Research, *Equity Guide 2006–07* (August 2006).

3. Natasha Zagvozdina and Ivan Nikolaev, "X5 Retail Group 2Q07 Results Preview and Upgrade," Renaissance Capital Investment Research (August 1, 2007).

4. UBS Investment Research.

5. Natasha Zagvozdina, Alexei Yazykov, and Ivan Nikolaev, "Consumer Outlook 2007: Take Your Pick," Renaissance Capital Investment Research (January 9, 2007).

6. Zagvozdina, Yazykov, and Nikolaev.

7. UBS Investment Research.

8. Ibid.

9. Zagvozdina and Nikolaev.

10. Maksim Isaev, "Pharmacy Chain 36.6: Large Rewards for Aggressive Expansion," RMG Investment Research (August 13, 2007).

11. Svetlana Sukhanova. (2007). "Pharmstandard Setting the Russian Pharma Standard" UBS Investment Research (June 22, 2007)

12. Information from company Web site, www.eng.phstd.ru (accessed September 15, 2007).

13. "Roman Abramovich, Stealth Oligarch: How to Make a Billion Dollars," *Frontline* (2003).

14. Ibid.

15. Chris Stephen, "Roman Abramovich," *Prospect* 94 (January 2004).

16. Ibid.

17. Ibid.

18. Yuri Govorushko, "Money Is No Object for Roman Abramovich," *Alexander's Gas & Oil Connections* 8, no. 15 (August 8, 2003).

19. Tom Cahill and Eduard Gismatullin, "Chelsea Owner Abramovich Gains $13 Billion; Rival Sits in Jail," *Bloomberg News* (September 29, 2005).

20. UBS Investment Research.

21. Elena Rogovina, "Russian Real Estate," UBS Investment Research (March 19, 2007).

22. Ibid.

23. Ibid.

24. Ibid.

25. Ibid.

26. Ibid.

27. Nikolay Saperov, "Sberbank and the Russian Banking Sector," Sovlink Investment Research (February 2, 2007).

28. Dmitry Dmitriev and Mikhail Shlemov, "Russian Banking Sector Still the Story of Growth," Deutsche UFG Investment Research (July 25, 2007).

29. Ibid.

30. Ibid.

31. Saperov.

32. UBS Investment Research.

33. Saperov.

34. Bob Kommers and Yulia Rusanova, "VTB The Runner-Up," UBS Investment Research (May 31, 2007).

35. Denis Sokolov, "Severstal-Auto: Great Plans," CIT Finance Investment Research (June 21, 2007).

36. UBS Investment Research.

37. Boris Berezovsky Biography from Mosnews MN-Files, www.mosnews .com (October 31, 2006).

38. Ibid.

39. Ibid.

40. Ibid.

41. Ian Cobain, Matthew Taylor, and Luke Harding, "I Am Plotting a New Russian Revolution," *The Guardian* (April 13, 2007).

42. UBS Investment Research.

43. Ibid.

44. Denis Sokolov.

Chapter 8

1. Alexander Burgansky and Irina Elinevskaya, "Building New Power," Renaissance Capital Research (September 4, 2006).

2. Information from RAO UES, www.rao-ees.ru/en/reforming/laws/show. cgi?flaws.htm (accessed June 20, 2007).

3. Burgansky and Elinevskaya.

4. Igor Goncharov, "Russian Electricity Generation From Buying Assets to Buying Growth," UBS Investment Research (March 12, 2007).

5. Information from RAO UES.

6. Burgansky and Elinevskaya.

7. Ibid.

8. Ibid.

9. UBS Investment Research, "Equity Guide 2006–07" (August 2006).

10. Ibid.

11. Ibid.

12. Burgansky and Elinevskaya.

13. Ibid.

14. Ibid.

15. *Commanding Heights: Anatoly Chubais.* Public Broadcasting System (2000).

16. Anatoly Chubais Biography from National Council on Corporate Governance, www.nccg.ru/en/site.xp/050050057124.html (accessed July 20, 2007).

17. Vladimir Putin, Annual Address to the Federal Assembly of the Russian Federation, April 26, 2007.

18. Georgy Ivaning, "Russian Cement Industry High Price and Robust Outlook," Antana Capital Investment Research (June 24, 2006).

19. Ibid.

20. Ibid.

21. Andrei Rozhkov, "Mostotrest Update," CentreInvest Group Investment Research (August 1, 2007).

22. UBS Investment Research.

Chapter 9

1. Clemens Grafe, "EMEA Economic Monitor: Ukraine," UBS Investment Research (January 9, 2007).

2. Ibid.

3. First Securities Trading System (PFTS), www.pfts.com (accessed September 20, 2007).

4. Clemens Grafe.

5. First Securities Trading System (PFTS).

6. UBS Investment Research, "Equity Guide 2006–07" (August 2006).

7. Ibid.

8. Ibid.

9. Ibid.

10. Andriy Gostik and Alexander Romanov, "TMM Real Estate Development Sizing Up XXL," Concorde Capital Investment Research (August 9, 2007).

11. UBS Investment Research.

12. Ibid.

13. Clemens Grafe.

14. Ibid.

15. UBS Investment Research.

16. Ibid.

17. Bob Kommers and Yulia Rusanova, "Kazkommertsbank Faster Growth at Lower Cost," UBS Investment Research (May 23, 2007).

18. Maria Radina and Alex Fak, "KazMunaiGas EP Upgrading to Buy on Underperformance," UBS Investment Research (September 12, 2007).

19. Lucian Kim, "Eni Group Cedes Greater Stake to Kazakhs in Kashagan," *Bloomberg News* (January 13, 2008).

Chapter 10

1. "How to Fight Back: Planning the West's Counter-Attack Against Russia," The Economist Online, www.economist.com/world/europe/displaystory. cfm?story_id=9253825, May 31, 2007.

2. Information from Freedom House, www.freedomhouse.org (accessed June 6, 2007).

3. Freedom House Information from Media Transparency, www.mediatrans parency.org (accessed June 12, 2007)

4. Information from Freedom House.

5. Ibid.

6. The Heritage Foundation Information from Media Transparency, www. mediatransparency.org (accessed June 12, 2007).

7. Information from The Heritage Foundation, www.heritage.org (accessed June 11, 2007).

8. Information from The Jamestown Foundation, www.jamestown.org (accessed June 11, 2007).

9. The Jamestown Foundation from Media Transparency, www.mediatrans parency.org (accessed June 12, 2007).

10. Information from The Jamestown Foundation.

11. The Hudson Institute Information from Media Transparency, www.medi atransparency.org (accessed June 12, 2007).

12. Information from The Hudson Institute, www.hudson.org. (accessed April 16, 2007).

13. American Enterprise Institute Information from Media Transparency, www.mediatransparency.org. (accessed June 12, 2007).

14. Leon Aron, "Democracy in Russia," American Enterprise Institute (September 20, 2005).

15. The Foreign Policy Research Institute Information from Media Transparency, www.mediatransparency.org (accessed June 12, 2007).

16. Information from the Foreign Policy Research Institute, www.fpri.org (accessed June 12, 2007).

17. William H. Cooper, "Permanent Normal Trade Relations (PNTR) Status for Russia and U.S.-Russian Economic Ties," Congressional Research Service (January 4, 2007).

18. Ibid.

19. "Israel Says Jackson-Vanik Amendment has to be Scrapped," *ITAR-TASS* (April 16, 2007).

20. William H. Cooper.

21. Sergei Stroken, "Insufferable Strategies: US Lays Out Strategic Goals for Next Five Years, Slams Russia in Report," *Kommersant* (April 17, 2007).

22. Roy Walmsley, "World Prison Population List (Fifth Edition)," Research, Development and Statistics Directorate of Great Britain (2003).

23. Stroken.

24. Ibid.

25. Ibid.

26. "More Moscow Crackdowns," The Other Russia. www.theotherrussia .org/2007/04/24/more-moscow-crackdowns/(accessed September 20, 2007).

27. Clifford J Levy, "Russia's Knockoff Democracy," *New York Times*. December 16, 2007.

Chapter 11

1. Kareem Fahim, "George Washington Letter Found in Scrapbook," *New York Times* (April 26, 2007).

About the Authors

John T. Connor Jr. is the founder and portfolio manager of the Third Millennium Russia Fund, a U.S. SEC-registered mutual fund specializing in the equities of Russian public companies. Since its inception in October 1998, the Fund has had an annual compound growth of 36 percent a year. In August 2003, and again in August 2006, he was ranked number one portfolio manager in the United States by the annual *Barron's/Value Line* survey. The *Wall Street Journal* cited him as the "Five Year Winner" (October 4, 2004, p. R4) and in its December 23, 2004 issue (p. D1), it ranked him as the fifth best "Overall Fund Manager" in the United States. He also has been the Featured Guest on *Louis Rukeyser's Wall Street* (CNBC, October 22, 2004). He has appeared frequently on CNBC and other business programs.

Mr. Connor is a member of the board of directors of Teton Energy Corporation (listed on the American Stock Exchange), based in Denver, Colorado, and acts as chairman of its audit committee. For 10 years earlier, he served on the board of directors and as chairman of the audit committee of Micros Systems, Inc. (NASD listed).

During its start-up year, Mr. Connor was the president of mail.ru, Russia's leading Internet portal with millions of registered users. Earlier, he headed the Moscow, Russia, office of the U.S.–USSR Trade & Economic Council (ASTEC), having been deputy director of the U.S. Commerce Department's Bureau of East–West Trade. He continues as a director of CTEC, chaired by Arkady Volsky.

Trained as a lawyer at Cravath, Swaine & Moore in New York City, he was a partner in leading law firms in New York, Washington, and New Jersey. In the 1980s he was a member of the management committee and general counsel of New York Stock Exchange–listed PHH Corporation.

Mr. Connor is a member of the Council on Foreign Relations and was a member of the American Law Institute from 1984 to 2004. He graduated from Williams College, Phi Beta Kappa, with highest honors (after which he taught on a Fulbright grant at Fergusson College in Pune, India) and from Harvard Law School.

Lawrence P. Milford currently works as the Equity Analyst for Third Millennium Russia Fund. Mr. Milford has worked in the financial field for the past seven years. He has received his bachelor's degree in business management from the University of Phoenix in 2003, as well as his master of business administration (MBA) from Regis University in 2005.

Index

The sacred game

========

The sacred game

Provincialism and frontier consciousness
in American literature,
1630–1860

ALBERT J. VON FRANK

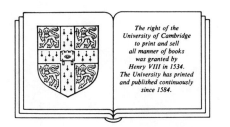

The right of the
University of Cambridge
to print and sell
all manner of books
was granted by
Henry VIII in 1534.
The University has printed
and published continuously
since 1584.

CAMBRIDGE UNIVERSITY PRESS

Cambridge

London   New York   New Rochelle

Melbourne   Sydney

Published by the Press Syndicate of the University of Cambridge
The Pitt Building, Trumpington Street, Cambridge CB2 1RP
32 East 57th Street, New York, NY 10022, USA
10 Stamford Road, Oakleigh, Melbourne 3166, Australia

First published 1985

Printed in the United States of America

Library of Congress Cataloging in Publication Data
von Frank, Albert J.
The sacred game.
(Cambridge studies in American literature and
culture)
Bibliography: p.
Includes index.
1. American literature – History and criticism.
2. Frontier and pioneer life in literature.
3. Regionalism in literature. 4. National
characteristics, American, in literature. 5. United
States – Civilization. I. Title. II. Series.
PS169.F7V66   1985   810'.9'355   84-21381
ISBN 0 521 30159 9

Contents

Whilst the tradition is every day assailed, in their sorrow at the loss of the objects of the sentiment, men go back to the old books, reprint them, repair the old monuments, celebrate ancient anniversaries, praise that which is old though it was never good, and in new buildings copy the elder architecture and in modern poetry and fiction reproduce the antique or the middle age...

This dilettantism is a certain sign that a revolution is on foot. This holding back betrays the fact that the general movement is forward. The retreat on the old literature is a sort of truce and sacred game, in which eminent persons of both parties take a part, as nations delight to mitigate the horrors of war by celebrating in weeds of peace, friends mixed with foes, a religious festival. The analysts take part in this movement. They see in the life of these splendid periods new argument to convict the degeneracy of the age, and even the ablest reformer has relentings of common sympathy which make him glad to find a sort of expiation for the shock he occasions in his admiration for the genius of the Past.

– Ralph Waldo Emerson

The fault of our New England custom is that it is memorial.

– Henry David Thoreau

No man also having drunk old wine straightway desireth new: for he saith, The old is better.

– Luke 5:39

Preface

To open up a subject that was before thought unrewarding, the writer must at the outset convince the reader that a misunderstanding exists. For example, to announce that one's subject is provincialism in American literature is probably to raise an expectation that the discussion to follow will occupy itself only with a small and rejected corner of the national literary culture. So long as provincialism is understood mainly as the disabling liability of backwoods regionalists or self-taught writers of the second rank, such an expectation would indeed be warranted. But the argument of this book is at once broader in scope and, I hope, much less patronizing than such ordinary conceptions of the provincial would allow.

The argument, in brief, is that provincial conditions were not the special case in America before the Civil War but, in fact, quite the ordinary context for artistic expression; as a consequence, they seem largely to account for what appears characteristic or nationally distinctive in the literature. The argument is, further, that these conditions, historically associated with frontier patterns of settlement and cultural transmission, could at times be enriching challenges to American artists, who met them with differing ideals, differing temperaments, and differing strategies.

A number of colleagues at several institutions shared their wisdom with me, which makes this book that much better. I would especially like to thank J. Donald Crowley and Richard A. Hocks, true mentors and good friends, for aid and encouragement; indeed, as often happens with the best of teachers, their influence has been as much or more on the writer as on the written. Whether I profited sufficiently from John R. Lankford's love of good prose and responsible historiography is not for me to say, although I am grateful to him for models of both. Andrew Delbanco, Alan Heimert, David W. Hill, Joel Myerson, and Joel Porte read the manuscript in whole or in part and offered valuable suggestions. If errors or eccentricities remain, they are, of course, my responsibility.

Finally, I must acknowledge how important to me have been the cheerful encouragement and solid editorial helpfulness of my wife, Jane, who caused me at last to say right many things I had said wrong, and whose tolerance for the umpteenth draft of a passage has been a blessing beyond reward.

Introduction: provincialism
and the frontier

The frontier is the line of most rapid and effective Americanization. The wilderness masters the colonist. It finds him a European in dress, industries, tools, modes of travel, and thought. . . . It strips off the garments of civilization. . . . It puts him in the log cabin . . . and runs an Indian palisade around him. Little by little he transforms the wilderness, but the outcome is not the old Europe, not simply the development of Germanic germs. . . . The fact is that here is a new product that is American. . . . Thus the advance of the frontier has meant a steady movement away from the influence of Europe, a steady growth of independence on American lines.

– F. J. Turner[1]

The early history of American culture is overwhelmingly the story of civilization moving westward, and hardly at all the story of its springing up spontaneously on the frontier. The more or less contrary position – that the frontier was an agent of abrupt cultural change, or a "gate of escape from the bondage of the past"[2]–was advanced with intentional exaggeration by Frederick Jackson Turner in 1893 and has since achieved an almost mythic hold on popular conceptions of American history. Even though this view continues to be influential, historians since Turner have demonstrated its shortcomings, pointing out that a significant number of those who settled the frontier, including especially the educated and socially prominent classes, were desperately intent on maintaining the old ways and were, in fact, fearful not only of lapsing into barbarism, but of making the apparently most innocuous adjustments to their surroundings as well.[3] The frontier was certainly a formidable antagonist to the natural conservatism of these pioneers, but it was not the impenetrable barrier to the transmission of culture that Turner, in his more emphatic moments, could make it out to be. To allege, as he did, that "complex European life was sharply precipitated by the wilderness into the simplicity of primitive conditions"[4] is to overlook an important, highly functional desire for continuity on the settlers' part in favor of

1

the national myth that America does somehow represent a new order of the ages. Recent historians have found it necessary in light of the continued vitality of Turner's hypothesis to report what are after all some rather self-evident conclusions – for example, that the culture of American pioneers was "Western European rather than aboriginal"[5] and that "they had an almost grim determination to reproduce modes of life which they had respected and honored in the old country."[6]

The historical record is full of indications of a lively western interest in cultural matters. Alexis de Tocqueville and other foreign travelers were regularly astonished that in the remotest places and in the rudest conditions, Americans contrived to have books: "There is hardly a pioneer's hut," Tocqueville wrote, "which does not contain a few odd volumes of Shakespeare. I remember that I read the feudal drama of Henry V for the first time in a log-house."[7] Writing in 1818, an English traveler named Elias Fordham observed about the West that a "universal spirit of enquiry [existed] among all classes of people. In the state of Indiana, in which there is but one town of six years standing, there are several book-clubs. Newspapers and Reviews from Philadelphia, Baltimore, Kentucky, and St. Louis, are received weekly."[8] Altogether, the typical pattern of early commentary on the West involves a contrast between a sophisticated, rather condescending expectation of barbarism and a finding of cultivation. The tone is either humorous or surprised, for very early in America's history the stereotype of the Westerner had been established as a rough-and-ready brawler, an antisocial figure whose interests were largely confined to the pursuit of necessities. Speaking of Lexington, Kentucky, in 1814, a writer for *Niles' Register* remarked with astonishment that "society is polished and polite, and their balls and assemblies are conducted with as much grace and ease as they are anywhere else, and the dresses at the parties are as tasty and elegant. Strange things these in the 'backwoods!' "[9]

But not so strange after all. The men and women who actually settled the West – as distinct from those who, merely blazing trails or trapping furs, had little lasting impact on western society – were generally people who had a stake in society and its progress.[10] Little insight is required to see that the Westerners' hunger for culture had unusual psychological and emotional dimensions, or that their motive for so remarkably pursuing cultural interests under such adverse circumstances was a desire, finally, to keep up contact with a world they had left behind yet never meant to abandon. "I have read in books," said a nineteenth-century Kansas homesteader, "that the people of the frontier kept moving ever westward to escape civilization. But if my experience counts for anything, such people were the exceptions. So eager were we to keep in touch with civilization that even when we could not afford a shotgun and ammunition to kill rabbits, we subscribed to newspapers and periodicals and bought books.""[11] This pioneer and many thousands of others in comparable situations doggedly insisted that whatever difficulties their environment might present, certain standards of civilization would be observed. They recognized that the struggle for survival was a matter of the spirit as well as the flesh and that they could be as thoroughly defeated by isolation and cultural regression as by hunger. It was for this reason, of course, that frontier settlers would so often, and at such expense of effort, take with them pianos, fine furniture, and other preposterously bulky heirlooms as ballast for suddenly unanchored identities.[12]

To a significant and influential portion of the frontier population, culture in its various forms meant community. Whether this community was the one established through news in local periodicals or the community of literary societies, theatricals, and lyceum meetings, Westerners relied on such contacts as much to assure themselves of who they were as simply to engage in recreation. The presence in out-of-the-way western places of vital and often rather ostentatious centers of high culture was, in effect, a declaration on the settlers' part that they had not been defeated or changed by their arduous environment but remained as before, civilized beings with specific cultural ties to older communities.

Without consciously intending anything more than the provision in a new setting of a comfortable and familiar life, Westerners were actually accomplishing two other things as well: they were conserving their personal identities through the trauma of relocation (with all its attendant invitations to change), *and* they were transmitting the culture of Europe or of the eastern parts of America to the West. Success in the first of these matters depended to a great extent on success in the second. The relation between them – between the individual and internal issue of continuing to know oneself and the communal issue of retaining shared and sharable values – was intimate, complex, and largely decisive in shaping American cultural attitudes. Historically, in America, the feeling *for* culture has been bound up with a sense of the difficulty of transmitting it, with a sense of the attritional failures, the dilutions, the memorial lapses, associated with all attempts to reestablish older cultures in a new land. The irony is that, while culture degenerated in specific and intriguing ways as it traveled (or was carried) westward, the interest that Westerners took in it (their psychic investment, as it were) deepened proportionately. Ray A. Billington expresses all of this with his usual succinctness and clarity:

> The pioneers were cultural transplants who had moved to new homes not to escape the old, but only to achieve greater economic and personal self-realization. They went west in hope rather than

despair, and so they looked back upon the value system of the East with nostalgia instead of bitterness. To expect them to shed cultural baggage under these circumstances would be to deny the force of habit in human nature. Alexis de Tocqueville spoke truly when he characterized the frontiersman as "a highly civilized being, who consents for a time to inhabit the backwoods, and who penetrates into the wilds of the New World with the Bible, an axe, and some newspapers." As they moved, the culture that the pioneers carried with them was diluted, but their loyalty to it was strengthened. Forced to shed some elements of their civilization, they clung so tenaciously to the remainder that it assumed a new importance in their lives. Morality, education, and learning bulked larger in the consciences of the "better sort" in the West than among their counterparts in the East. [13]

Away from the community, away from a culturally reinforcing environment and the presence of "correct" models, there was a progressive deterioration in the way that traditional ideas – such ideas as had in the past held communities together – were understood and formulated. This western deterioration, too natural, too inevitable to be seriously deprecated, is to be seen in virtually all aspects of the nation's cultural life, from the expression of artists to the various forms of popular culture and the work of craftsmen; and it came about in large part from conservative attempts to reproduce older forms without adequate materials or without an appreciation of the originals sufficient to preserve their integrity. The tendency of the process was, of course, toward greater simplicity, toward a filtering out of nuance and the accommodation of a pragmatic, materialist world view. Ironically, this degeneration of culture was primarily the responsibility of those who cared most about its survival; in fact, the peculiarly intense and almost desperate quality of Westerners' attachment to culture has had, as we shall see, its own distorting effect on transmission. In any event, this particular sort of intense regard for a diluted culture is just what we recognize as "provincialism."

Provincialism, and the American variety perhaps especially, ought not to be thought of simply as a condition of cultural inferiority with respect to some acknowledged center. Apart from the difficulty of knowing just what we might mean in this case by "inferiority," it should be evident that provincial cultures in all parts of the world, and again particularly those bearing some relation to European societies, have produced works of art of lasting, worldwide significance. Unless we merely wish to preserve the word as a pejorative term with little genuine descriptive value, we could, instead, think of provincial cultures as those with an absence or scarcity of cultural artifacts together with a marked desire for them. It follows from this definition that provincials will be acutely conscious of their own cultural conditions and will look elsewhere, either to another region or into the past, for specific guidance, and that in either case the past or that other region will assume special importance as a supplier of "standards." It follows, too, that a provincial culture will be imitative, though one of the innumerable dilemmas faced by such societies is the need to balance imitation or the observance of extrinsic standards with a self-respecting nativist independence.

The American case is clearly special by virtue of the important role played by the frontier as an antagonist to the continuity of culture, that is to say, in creating and enforcing provincial conditions. Furthermore, the exceptional nature of America's cultural experience allows one to speak of the modes of thought and apprehension that arose in response to this experience, modes in themselves special and, indeed, characteristically American. It allows us, in short, to speak in terms of an enduring provincial mentality in America and thus to move beyond the broadest historical generalities into a consideration of provincialism in its bearing on American literature.

The provincial mind is formed under conditions of cultural attenuation and amid a scarcity of cultural artifacts. It is the mind formed at and by the end of a long and necessarily faulty transmission of culture. Among several natural responses to this kind of deprivation would be heightened curiosity and inquisitiveness – traits regularly reported by European travelers in America. Charles Dickens tells of his exasperation at being questioned on a Mississippi steamboat first about his rather elegant fur coat and then about his watch; he was "asked what *that* cost, and whether it was a French watch, and where I got it, and whether I bought it or had it given me, and how it went, and where the keyhole was, and when I wound it, every night or every morning, and whether I ever forgot to wind it at all, and if I did, what then?"[14] The question of what provincials may or may not know is less interesting than the question of how they live with what they know, how they think, how they imagine, what status they accord to culture. To read, for example, Nathaniel Hawthorne's private comments on the compelling appeal of a painter's studio is to penetrate some distance into that writer's provincial mentality:

I love the odor of paint in an artist's room; his palette and all his other tools have a mysterious charm for me. The pursuit has always interested my imagination more than any other; and I remember, before having my first portrait taken, there was a great bewitchery in the idea, as if it were a magic process. Even now, it is not without interest for me.[15]

The provincial, in short, is the farthest thing from a jaded personality; lack of familiarity with cultural artifacts or with the processes of art creates in the provincial a rare liveliness of interest that would be ill served by being called simply naive. One might cite comparable examples of a provincially awe-struck response to poetry, or to prose fiction; but for the moment the point is merely that the provincial mind has, after all, certain traits beyond ignorance and simplicity, traits such as wonder, curiosity, and an imaginative freedom that might be supposed to stand a poet or writer of fiction in good stead.

Beyond this the American provincial mind respects learning and cultural accomplishment in others, though it is not a rigorously critical mind. It proves too omnivorously receptive to be discriminating, a fact that further accounts for its astonishingly eclectic character. Nothing, as it were, comes amiss to provincials, and it is therefore often true that their mental as well as their physical equipment consists of the most surprising conjunctions of odds and ends and bastardized forms. Casting about for a typical frontier figure to serve in a tale, the popular western writer James Hall settled in one instance on a Mr. Edgarton, head of an English family emigrating to Ohio:

> He wore cambric ruffles, a diamond breast-pin, a dandy waist-coat, and a store of jewelry appended to a watch-chain; but his nether limbs were clad in long splatter-dashes, reaching to the knee, a farmer's coarse frock covered his shoulders, and a great fur cap was on his head. He was equipped, moreover, with a powder-horn, shot-pouch and bird-bag, and held in his hand an elegant double-barrelled gun. We mention these things to show how difficult it is for men to throw off their accustomed habits, and to assume those which are suitable to a change of country or condition. Mr. Edgarton, when at home, was a modest, and a well dressed man; but in attempting to assume the guise of a farmer, and the equipment of a hunter, had jumbled together a grotesque assortment of costume, which gave him the appearance of a stage-player dressed for exhibition, more than that of a plain man of business, which was his real character.[16]

Lack of coherence is generally as evident in provincial thought as it is here in Mr. Edgarton's dress, and for much the same reason. Away from the community, the provincial mind is not only susceptible to influence from every conceivable direction, but it generally lacks the means and incentive to maintain the sort of strong, traditional ideology that might encourage coherence. Miscellaneous influences turn out to be acceptable that are directly inconsistent with inherited beliefs, and go, together with the remnants of these beliefs, to make up provincial minds that are often

impressively eccentric. It may be, for example, that the frontier prolif-
eration of "new" religions has less to do with the sheer inventiveness of
Americans than with a provincial inability to refuse influence.

The traits of the provincial mind indicated thus far reflect the isolation
and the relative scarcity of cultural artifacts associated with a western or
frontier environment. Another important condition, already referred to,
must now be reintroduced to round out and in some measure qualify
the portrait as it stands.

A large and influential portion of the population – including but not
limited to the "better sort" of pioneer – observed this provincializing
process and mounted a strong conservative reaction to it. Recognizing
the threat to inherited religious, social, and aesthetic values, they understood that frontier conditions had to be consciously opposed, their attenuating effects alertly guarded against. The Puritan settlers of
Massachusetts, for example, were at first greatly concerned that their
new surroundings might prove unmanageably hostile in a spiritual as
well as a physical sense, foisting influence on them where they had
particularly sought freedom from influence; they were anxious that their
best conservative efforts might fail to prevent a general falling away of
culture and a corresponding forfeiture of community – in short, they
were afraid that they might come to live like Indians. Surviving in the
wilderness therefore meant resisting conditions, not adjusting to them,
and the result was that these embattled conservatives became as fully
conscious of their traditions in a defensive, protective way as they were
suspiciously alert to the circumstances that threatened them.[17]

Although we are entitled to speak of a provincial mind, we have at
the same time to acknowledge the existence of something like an antiprovincial mind, one whose processes are largely governed by a reaction
to the prospect of becoming provincial through the loss of inherited
values. The term "antiprovincial," however, is inconvenient and finally
misleading because, in fact, the conservatives ordinarily failed to conserve
adequately and, despite their protest, became increasingly provincial
themselves. The irony of their cultural holding actions – especially in a
frontier setting – lay in the fact that as soon as one becomes self-conscious
and defensive about one's culture, one's relation to it is irreversibly altered; it tends then to become artificial and petrified, and the very thing
the individual had sought to preserve has suddenly become something
quite different. Frontier conditions, in other words, promoted cultural
conservatism but at the same time required its defeat. Hawthorne was
characteristically sensitive to the tragic and destructive irony of this situation – undoubtedly out of a feeling for the history of his own family.
Explaining why, as he felt, the "sons and grandchildren of the first settlers
were a race of lower and narrower souls than their progenitors had been,"

he pointed to the inevitability of distortion and collapse in the transmission of vital cultural values: "One generation," he wrote, "had bequeathed its religious gloom, and the counterfeit of its religious ardor,
to the next; for these characteristics, as was inevitable, assumed the form
both of hypocrisy and exaggeration, by being inherited from the example
and precept of other human beings, and not from an original and spiritual
source."[18]

In its terms and tone, Hawthorne's explanation is rather that of a poet
than that of a cultural historian. It reflects the influential if not universally
shared American beliefs that history is a tragic thing in general and that
in its naturally degenerative course it continually disestablishes the community of past and present. This was the hard lesson taught to conservatives by their frontier experience, and as the lesson was taught over and
over again the disappointment of defeated conservatives became a fixture
of the antiprovincial mentality – or, as I should prefer to call it, of
"frontier consciousness." The process hinted at in Hawthorne's explanation is clearly being made to serve a mythic view of history, but it
ought not for that reason to be dismissed as a fiction. R. W. B. Lewis
outlines a substantially similar process while accounting for the failure
in America of the doctrine of original sin, a failure he lays at the door
of the "party of Memory" rather than of liberal Unitarianism:

> If all the force and meaning of the old idea of original sin had
> disappeared from the religious consciousness of the day, it was
> largely the fault of orthodoxy, the religious element in the party
> of Memory. For that party... argued the case in almost exclusively
> historical terms, affirming the enslavement of the present by the
> past as heatedly as the hopeful insisted on its freedom. But the
> orthodox showed little awareness of the organic vitality of history,
> of the way in which the past can enliven the present: the past was
> simply the place where the issues had been decided, and the decision
> was all that mattered. The orthodox habit of presenting the end-
> product of religious belief drained of all the spiritual impulses which
> had gone into the historical shaping of it led to a frozen but fragile
> structure, and one not likely to hold very long against the assaults
> of the opposition.[19]

One could hardly improve on this statement except perhaps to suggest
that the tendency of the orthodox to present the "end-product" as something finished and decided had only a coincidental relation to their belief
in original sin; it was much more directly a consequence of their being
forced by circumstances, by their American situation, into a defensive
posture in respect to their traditions and beliefs. What Lewis says here
about original sin might as aptly be said of the conservatives' behavior

in regard to language, education, literary style, or table manners. Given that America was a transplanted culture, it was also, necessarily, a culture of end products, of forms detached from the societies and environments that had given them birth and nourishment. Americans who chose to resist the attritional destruction of these "liberated" forms had, therefore, to operate at a unique and ultimately decisive disadvantage. Incapable of redeeming a culture of displaced end products by an infusion of under-standing, adaptation or imagination, the conservatives simply retrenched and made the forms themselves, apart from any vital present context, an unalterable standard. But these forms, relayed time and again through the isolation of the American environment, decayed, and the individual identities that had been invested in them altered as well. The results were new, provincial variations of the originals, though not necessarily – as the conservatives invariably supposed – inferior, vulgar, or disfunctional versions. They were, however, American. As Hamlin Garland puts it, "the 'provincialism' which the conservative deplores is not provincialism, but the beginning of an indigenous literature."[20]

Having said all this, I am aware that I may have raised in the reader an expectation that – with apologies beforehand – I do not mean to meet in the ensuing chapters. It is important for all that follows that the connection between the presence of a frontier and the resultant provin-cialism of America's early culture be stated at the outset, and more will be said on the subject presently; but in fact it forms no part of my intention in this work to present a rigorous historical tracing of the connection and its consequences. The subject, as I view it, is not one that will submit to relentless pursuit or an attempt at "definitive" treatment; I believe it is best handled, if it is to be handled at all, in a way that may serve to organize and make sense of what an intelligent student of American literature already knows. The figures I have chosen to consider illustrate, in their different historical settings, different aspects of American literary provincialism; and although the chapters are arranged chronologically, they cannot, I think, taken together, be said to constitute a history in the larger, most legitimate sense of that term. What I have tried to do instead is to make literary history serve the ends of literary criticism, since, finally, my own main interest is in the qualities of mind and imagination that distinguish the work of American writers, a matter that is never more than partly a question of history.

This disclaimer notwithstanding, the reader may still wonder about my choice of writers. Why, after all, Anne Bradstreet, Royall Tyler, Timothy Dwight, Washington Irving, Nathaniel Hawthorne, Ralph Waldo Emerson, and Margaret Fuller and not Edward Taylor, Jonathan Edwards, James Fenimore Cooper, and Walt Whitman? One answer is that a much longer book might well include these figures, though it may be that an advantage still attaches to having one's say with the fewest points of reference. In general, I have tried to draw attention to the important elegiac note supplied in American literature by the frontier consciousness of defeated conservatives; and if I have skewed the selection at all, it is in the direction of these unfashionable writers. In more particular terms, the colonial and early national writers included here (unlike Taylor and Edwards) have not received the sort of recognition they deserve or may yet receive if their situations are better understood. Anne Bradstreet, in particular, has not been thought of as the frontier writer she preeminently was. The chapters on Irving and Hawthorne form a contrasting pair that would make the introduction of Cooper seem artificial and to a certain extent superfluous, much as the chapters on Fuller and Emerson necessarily leave Whitman out of account. On these matters, however, readers will surely judge for themselves. If in the end one sees how the omitted writers might have been treated, I (preferring always the opening to the closing word) will be entirely satisfied that I have done my job.

Chapter 1

"But enmity this amity did break"

*What could now sustaine them but the spirite of God and his grace?
May not and ought not the children of these fathers rightly say:* Our
fathers were English men which came over this great ocean,
and were ready to perish in this wildernes, but they cried unto
the Lord, and he heard their voyce, and looked on their
adversitie.

– William Bradford[1]

Permanent voluntary removal from a civilized to an uncivilized country
has not been an experience of common occurrence in human history,
yet it was one that Anne Bradstreet shared with all her neighbors. For
her, though, even more than for most of the emigrants, it had been an
especially traumatic experience, partly because as a woman she did not
participate in the public achievements that sustained the men but also,
and more decisively, because in England, at the earl of Lincoln's estate,
she had grown up from girlhood accustomed to a life of intellectual
activity and physical comfort such as she was unlikely ever to recover
in her new surroundings. As the daughter of Thomas Dudley, the earl's
highly regarded steward, she had lived well, had access to the library of
Sempringham, heard music, engaged in stimulating conversation, attended church, seen the "riches of some famous Fair"[2] – in short, she
had lived the sort of pleasant and civilized life that, in later years in rude
New England, would provide a fund of ideal memories. She married
Simon Bradstreet in 1628 and within two years was a housewife on the
Massachusetts frontier.

Bred for one world, she was to live in another so entirely different
that the fact of disruption and the dream of continuity became almost
inevitably the central concerns of her recorded expressions, even as they
were the terms of her evolving frontier consciousness. Anne Bradstreet's
emigration to a new world necessarily forced upon her attention the
value of the one she had left behind, a world associated in her mind with

11

ease and security and her own familiar childhood. She knew, and the more intelligent and sensitive of her neighbors also knew, that adaptation to this novel transatlantic environment was in all important respects out of the question, even if it would alleviate the burden of disruption or overcome one's sense of being constantly out of place. Not only would such an accommodation seem to involve a rejection of everything that had been habitually congenial, but it would also appear to threaten the very identity of these settlers as civilized men and women, English subjects, and Puritans. They believed that their "howling wilderness," like chaos and old night, was to be molded and made useful by an infusion of order and meaning. They expected to mold the environment into a tool serviceable in their errand and, at the same time, not to allow themselves to be altered by it.

The sermon Anne Bradstreet heard aboard the *Arbella* on the way to the New World – John Winthrop's celebrated "Model of Christian Charity" – shows that even before arriving the emigrants were more concerned about the psychic and social threats posed by the environment than about physical dangers. In his sermon Winthrop reminded his fellow passengers of the great work they had to do, pointed out the crucial importance of the continued integrity of the group, and warned against lapsing into chaotic individualism. Something of Anne Bradstreet's initial expectations may perhaps be gleaned from the sermon, which shows that Winthrop at least assumed that the new land would be fertile and inviting; hardship appears to have been less thought of than a wealth too easily won. He explained:

> Thus stands the cause between God and us: we are entered into covenant with Him for this work; we have taken out a commission, the Lord hath given us leave to draw our own articles. We have professed to enterprise these actions upon these and these ends; we have hereupon besought Him of favour and blessing.... But if we shall neglect the observation of these articles which are the ends we have propounded, and dissembling with our God, shall fall to embrace this present world and prosecute our carnal intentions, seeking great things for ourselves and our posterity, the Lord will surely break out in wrath against us, be revenged of such a perjured people, and make us know the price of the breach of such a covenant.[3]

The new and "present world," it was feared, would be full of centrifugal forces tending to disrupt the community. "To avoid this shipwreck," Winthrop suggested, they "must be knit together in this work as one man."[4] And so a countervailing impulse toward unity, coherence, and continuity, based on the covenant, came to be viewed as a political and spiritual necessity.

On arriving, the Winthrop party discovered to their dismay that the community at Salem, established two years earlier under John Endecott, had failed to make provision for their coming. In a letter to the countess of Lincoln, Dudley reported that the town was "in a sad and unexpected condition, above eighty of [the settlers] being dead the winter before; and many of those alive weak and sick; all the corn and bread amongst them... hardly sufficient to feed them a fortnight."[5] Also disturbing as an indication that not everyone was willing to be "knit together in this work as one man" was the fact that Salem's minister, Samuel Skelton, peremptorily refused communion to Winthrop, Dudley, and several others who could not show that they belonged to one of the few congregationally organized churches in England. Repelled as they were by the physical and spiritual condition of the Salemites, Winthrop's group determined to alter their plans and settle elsewhere, despite the advice of those who feared a scattering of the population. The women, fatigued by the long voyage, were lodged in the overcrowded houses at Salem, while the men, having transferred the group's belongings into smaller craft, headed south toward Charlestown and Boston.

Years later, Anne Bradstreet recalled her arrival: "I . . . came into this Country," she said, "where I found a new world and new manners, at which my heart rose. But after I was convinced it was the way of God, I submitted to it and joined to the church at Boston."[6] She signed the covenant of this church probably on August 3 or 4, 1630, having spent nearly two months in Salem apart from her husband and her father. During that time, as the earl of Lincoln's sister, Lady Arbella Johnson, sickened and died, Bradstreet struggled to see the way of God in the new manners that so appalled her. The difficulty of this struggle, together with the deliberation implied in her statement ("after I was convinced it was the way of God"), suggests that for a while she may have longed to be among those who were then returning to England.[7] Significantly, her greatest misgiving involved the behavior of the people rather than any physical dangers; so far as she was concerned, the problem of living in Massachusetts was a cultural one, and the solution lay in a personal and institutional resistance to the environment.

The manners of the stricken residents of Salem were to be seen not only in their shabby conduct toward the Winthrop party but also in the fact of their being compelled to spend much of their time foraging for food and attending to their own and others' ills. Bradstreet was never so fatuous as to object, under such circumstances, to mere lapses in social formalities; but she could see plainly that by failing to extend the hand of fellowship and in general by slighting the ideal of cooperative endeavor, Endecott's people were succumbing to the environment.

Inevitably the manners of a people struggling for survival are respon-

sive to the demands of necessity. Such a life must nevertheless have struck
Bradstreet as a sort of exile of the exiled: being in the New World was
bad enough in itself; but to submit to circumstances, to attend incessantly
to physical requirements, is after all to be forced out of one's specific
calling and away from God. The afflicted of Salem perhaps remembered
William Perkins's observation that "to wander up and down from year
to year ... to seek and procure bodily maintenance, is no calling, but
the life of a beast, and consequently flat against the rule that everyone
must have a particular calling."[8] To behave in this manner while maintaining a Puritan conscience is to feel in New England more than in old
England like history's first frontiersman, the exiled Adam portrayed in
Bradstreet's poem:

> Who like a miscreant's driven from that place,
> To get his bread with pain, and sweat of face:
> A penalty impos'd on his backsliding Race.[9]

For the men and women who followed Winthrop, to whom it seemed
that God ordered all things, there could be no doubt that the suffering
in Salem was a special "penalty impos'd" as well as a warning to themselves that if they failed to be "knit together" they must surely be absorbed by the natural chaos and spiritual entropy of their environment.

   Anne Bradstreet could only have been confirmed in an intellectual and
social conservatism by the crucial experiences of 1630. The personal
upheaval of the emigration itself, Winthrop's closely reasoned and yet
impassioned plea for group solidarity, and the negative example of Salem
combined to impress upon her both as a social being and as an artist the
need to conserve civilized traditions against the attritional force of present
circumstance. Not surprisingly, then, Bradstreet's earliest poems are highly
conventional in form and substance, and on occasion even deliberately
imitative. These early poems, including what appears to be the very first,
"Upon a Fit of Sickness, Anno 1632, Aetatis Suae, 19," contain little
that a postromantic sensibility would call "personal," yet as poems they
succeed in nothing so well as in fixing and affirming the writer's identity.
Here, for example, is "Upon a Fit of Sickness":

> Twice ten years old, not fully told
>   Since nature gave me breath,
> My race is run, my thread is spun,
>   lo here is fatal Death.
> All men must dye, and so must I
>   this cannot be revok'd
> For Adams sake, this word God spake
>   when he so high provok'd.

Yet live I shall, this life's but small,
   in place of highest bliss,
Where I shall have all I can crave,
   no life is like to this.
For what's this life, but care and strife?
   since first we came from womb,
Our strength doth waste, our time doth hast,
   and then we go to th' Tomb.
O Bubble blast, how long can'st last?
   that always art a breaking,
No sooner blown, but dead and gone,
   ev'n as a word that's speaking.
O whil'st I live, this grace me give,
   I doing good may be,
Then deaths arrest I shall count best,
   because it's thy decree;
Bestow much cost there's nothing lost,
   to make Salvation sure,
O great's the gain, though got with pain,
   comes by profession pure.
The race is run, the field is won,
   the victory's mine I see,
For ever know, thou envious foe,
   the foyle belongs to thee.[10]

To be sure, the sense of self that such poems create arises from conformity to convention and tradition and is, therefore, quite the reverse of the typically self-centered or "eccentric" identity created when, as with the "new manners" of Salem, personality is divorced from culture. Bradstreet rarely calls attention to herself in these early poems, but attempts instead to understand the self as part of a larger, more significant unity, and, by locating the part in relation to the whole, to achieve a sense of belonging. The frontier had taught her not the lesson of liberty, not the attractions of the forest freedom, but the truth that cooperation and amity depend on civilized behavior, which in turn depends on honoring past traditions; discord and enmity, on the other hand, were the chief signs of individualism.

Perhaps there is little point in claiming this poem as an American expression simply because it can be read in its conventional qualities as a defense of the writer's identity against conditions that are American. But the frontier character of the poem is evident also in the increments of meaning supplied to convention by the writer's situation: A young woman in England might easily say that "life's but small," though it has a somewhat different import when spoken from the wildest farthest end of the known world. By the same token, to imagine heaven as a place where "I shall have all I can crave" is not simply a naively conventional view of the afterlife but is, additionally, the expression of one who is conscious of having been displaced in this life. What, as suggested by the poem, Anne Bradstreet most longed for, after the great change of emigration and the incessant improvisations that followed, was permanence and escape from further change, so that to compose a conventional statement about the changeless truth of immortal life is in a sense to muster a protest against the very circumstances that were killing her. Another protest was her decision not to cast that statement in "a word that's speaking," which is both the woman's conventional medium and the very image of fleeting life, but instead to entrust it to a written poem that would survive the writer.

Critics and literary historians have expressed less interest in the poems of *The Tenth Muse Lately Sprung Up in America* (1650) than in those of *Several Poems* (1678), partly for the sufficient reason that they are not so good, but also for the simply mistaken reason that, because they do not address personal and local issues, they cannot genuinely reflect the poet's American experience. This fallacy (which seems frequently to interfere with the appreciation and discussion of colonial literature) is particularly troublesome in regard to Bradstreet's quaternions, her thematically interlocking poems on "the Four Elements, Constitutions, Ages of Man [and] Seasons of the Year." Of these poems it is often said that, worldly as they so surprisingly are, they portray nature in terms appropriate to England, and that as a result the American note is entirely missing.[11] Such an argument makes the most of the difference between Bradstreet's early and late poetry, but in fact the early quaternions are neither so worldly nor so English as they have been made out.

The selection of subject and treatment in these poems was most directly influenced by two earlier works: One, by her father, on the four parts of the world evidently provided a method of organization and a model of style;[12] the other was Joshua Sylvester's translation of Guillaume Salluste du Bartas, which supplied innumerable ideas and rhetorical hints. The first two of the poet's "fours" – "The Four Elements" and "Of the Four Humours" – were completed and presented to her father with a prefatory poem on March 20, 1642.[13]

> Dear Sir of late delighted with the sight
> Of your four Sisters cloth'd in black and white,
> Of fairer Dames the Sun ne'r saw the face;
> Though made a pedestal for *Adams* Race;
> Their worth so shines in these rich lines you show

> Their paralels to finde I scarcely know
> To climbe the Climes, I have nor strength nor skill
> To mount so high requires an Eagles quill;
> Yet view thereof did cause my thoughts to soar;
> My lowly pen might wait upon these four.[14]

To Bradstreet's perception, the excellence of her father's verse seemed attributable to his superior relation to his material. To see and describe the four parts of the world requires a position, a point of view, intellectually above and abstracted from the world's material existence. The conventional imagery of ascent expresses the conservative's knowledge that no one can have a lively sense of wholeness who is entrapped in an earthly tangle of immediate circumstance. In this way, art becomes an ally of the frontier Puritan who fears being too much "of this world."

The dedicatory epistle goes on to define the relationship between Bradstreet's poems and her father's:

> I bring my four times four, now meanly clad
> To do their homage, unto yours, full glad:
> Who for their Age, their worth and quality
> Might seem of yours to claim precedency:
> But my humble hand, thus rudely pen'd
> They are, your bounden handmaids to attend
> These same are they, from whom we being have
> These are all, the Life, the Nurse, the Grave,
> These are the hot, the cold, the moist, the dry,
> That sink, that swim, that fill, that upwards fly,
> Of these consists our bodies, Cloathes and Food,
> The World, the useful, hurtful, and the good.

Her subject, like Dudley's, requires a lofty, abstracted perspective. She is not drawn to delineating particular details, but instead is most interested in and compelled by the very act of subsuming all physical existence, which explains why her representations are finally neither American nor English. The poems are an effort to subordinate the apparent reality of outward circumstance to the actual reality of an intellectually discernible order; yet, comprehending the audacity of the attempt, she implies that the necessary perspective is only to be attained through the vehicle of a fine, polished and elevated style which she cannot claim for herself. For the want of such a style, because her lines are "rudely pen'd" and her subject "meanly clad," the whole effect is compromised, and the poem, relatively speaking, a failure. Style or "manner" – the very thing that deteriorates fastest on the frontier – is most intensely cherished for the escape it seems to provide by elevating the stylist above the particular and into the sublime, by permitting the sort of expansive view that Bradstreet admired in her father's poem.

The stance adopted in dedicatory poems is usually conventional, as it surely is here, but Bradstreet's conviction about the crudity of her own style emerges so often and with such evident feeling – most notably in "The Author to Her Book"[15] – that we are warranted in believing such expressions a genuine self-appraisal. They would also seem to represent something of her sense of the limiting nature of her crude environment. The association of her often ragged and jolting style with the primitive conditions in which she worked would be a natural one for her to have made.[16] As we shall see in the chapters that follow, a debasement of style was endemic to the frontier, the first effect of living far from cultural centers. A conscious acknowledgment of that debasement, a sense of one's own cultural deterioration, is often the second effect, which in turn is the fundamental element in the evolution of a frontier consciousness.

For Anne Bradstreet the conviction of possessing a rude style seems to have dictated, in some measure, the sorts of experiences she would be most aware of. The dedicatory poem, referring now to the elements and the humors, continues:

> Sweet harmony they keep, yet jar oft times
> Their discord doth appear, by these harsh rimes.

Dudley's style and perspective are sublime because they embrace all things equally; Bradstreet's "blemished Muse" – her rougher style and lower perspective – best accommodates instances of disharmony. She seems to have sensed in her own poetry as well as in her father's a certain fitness of style to content, but because Dudley's mind and imagination work on a level so far superior to her own, her perception is ironic. It is difficult to tell whether Bradstreet's couplet means that her poetry has been sabotaged by the inherent anarchy of material existence (a phenomenon she might have related to original sin), or whether it means that her lines *show* disharmony by mimetic act. Just possibly the ambiguity is intended. Whatever form of perception underlies the statement, the couplet is an acute piece of self-criticism, for if we turn to the first of the quaternions, "The Four Elements," we find striking images of disorder competing for attention with relatively flat and prosaic descriptions of order. In fact, so frequently and so vividly is disorder portrayed in her work that she may justly be said to have possessed what Henry James called an "imagination of disaster."

The opening of "The Four Elements" is highly suggestive of the dissension even then appearing in the closed community of Massachusetts and actually anticipates some elements of the jeremiad:

> The Fire, Air, Earth and water did contest
> Which was the strongest, noblest and the best,
> Who was of greatest use and might'est force;
> In placide Terms they thought now to discourse,
> That in due order each her turn should speak;
> But enmity this amity did break.
> All would be chief, and all scorn'd to be under
> Whence issu'd winds & rains, lightning & thunder
> The quaking earth did groan, the Sky lookt black
> The Fire, the forced Air, in sunder crack;
> The sea did threat the heav'ns, the heav'ns the earth,
> All looked like a Chaos or new birth.[17]

The evidence is insufficient to show that the poem is a deliberate allegory on the decay of New England's social and spiritual order, so recently and spectacularly indicated by the Antinomian crisis; still, it is worth recalling in this regard that the poem was written expressly for Thomas Dudley, who, as governor and deputy governor, was responsible for enforcing the civil and spiritual order of the colony. The unity that served as the recurrent subject of Bradstreet's poetry was for Dudley a political ideal of paramount importance. As the chief prosecutor in the heresy trial of Anne Hutchinson, and as the sworn enemy of the radical separatist Roger Williams, he had well earned his reputation for zealous intolerance of heterodoxy. To his daughter he seemed "To Truth a shield, to right a Wall, / To Sectaryes a whip and Maul."[18] It was the poet's father, in other words, who day in and day out confronted the worst of the colony's discord and felt the centrifugal pressure of a community in decay. His daughter, who was never very far away, could hardly have escaped the profound influence of his alertness to disruption or of his countervailing dedication to unity.

The poet's response to the strange particularity of her New World environment was to deny its claim to her attention and to subsume it all in a vision of consolidation of which the immediate intellectual model was the covenant. If the quaternions are not explicitly theological in the terms of their argument, they are in no sense antagonistic to or incompatible with her religion. The notion of the four elements – and the other "fours" that depend schematically on them – derived ultimately from Empedocles, was still an acceptably scientific concept in Bradstreet's day, and its association with the medieval scholastic tradition posed no difficulties for her Protestant contemporaries. Francis Higginson's *New Englands Plantation*, a description of the colony on which Winthrop relied in coming to the New World, was organized in terms of the four elements. The scheme was in fact so much a part of the imported English

consciousness that it naturally organized the most casual of observations
about the territory, as may be seen, for example, in this passage from a
letter sent by Winthrop in 1630 to his son in England:

> For the country itself I can discern little difference between it and
> our own. We have had only two days which I have observed more
> hot than in England. Here is as good land as I have seen there, but
> none so bad as there. Here is sweet air, fair rivers and plenty of
> springs, and the water better than in England. Here can be no want
> of anything to those who bring means to raise out of earth and
> sea.[19]

Bradstreet's use of the four elements in the first of her quaternions,
however, is essentially different from either Higginson's or Winthrop's.
Unlike them, she had no official duties to keep her in contact with
England, nor did she write anything to encourage emigration to America.
Her effort was not to make her surroundings appear attractive, and there
is reason to believe that she did not always *feel* them as attractive. Thus,
unlike Winthrop and Higginson, she made no attempt to relate the four
elements to her immediate surroundings, but used them instead as a
means of abrogating the objective world in order to make way for a
tradition – that of du Bartas and Dudley – that affirmed order and continuity, as she saw it, through an inseparably coordinated style and
perception.

The end of the second quaternion represents the culmination of this
vision of order, for it is here that the model of Christian charity, the
essence of the covenanted community, prevails over faction and division.
After listening to the vaunting claims and slanderous malignity of Choler,
Blood, and Melancholy, Phlegm proposes a truce and a covenant:

> Let's now be friends; its time our spight were spent,
> Lest we too late this rashness do repent,
> Such premises will force a sad conclusion,
> Unless we agree, all falls into confusion.
> Let Sangine with her hot hand Choler hold,
> To take her moist my moisture will be bold:
> My cold, cold melancholy hand shall clasp;
> Her dry, dry Choler other hand shall grasp.
> Two hot, two moist, two cold, two dry here be,
> A golden Ring, the Poesy UNITY.
> Nor jarrs nor scoffs, let none hereafter see,
> But all admire our perfect Amity
> Nor be discern'd here's water, earth, air, fire,
> But here a compact body, whole intire.[20]

This passage, echoing the language of the chaos passage at the opening of the first quaternion, is identical in spirit to Winthrop's call to subordinate individual claims to the claims of the community as a whole.

Each of the four elements, each of the four humors, had sought to establish its own separate importance by explaining the things of which it was uniquely capable; yet each in its partiality and vanity failed to see the interlocking plan that alone related them to God and life and made them meaningful. Just as Winthrop's sermon was a plan to protect the larger communal identity, so these poems, by denying ontological value to the individual particular in isolation, constitute a defense of meaning against the power of the physical environment to dissolve and dissipate the transcendental point of view. It is not easy to forget, when reading Bradstreet's poems, that her Massachusetts environment, very much unlike that of England, presented to her consciousness, as things not to be ignored, physical threats from wolves, Indians, and illness, while simultaneously absorbing her time and effort in nearly incessant labor, much of it directed toward the most basic requirements of food, shelter, clothing, and physical well-being. Circumstances called out and emphasized her physical self, but she clung to the knowledge that her new home challenged: that she was, first and last, a civilized being and an immortal soul. Her poetry is evidence of a determination to set her mind on what she knew and not on what she saw, for only in that direction lay the clew that would lead her out of isolation. The irony of Bradstreet's situation was simply that the more obstinately dedicated she became to a conservative unity and a remembrance of England, the more acutely attuned she became to the disharmony, the disorder, and the inadequacy of her present world. In other words, her "imagination of disaster" was born of her rage for order and kept pace with it.

Bradstreet was not, in all this, so much withholding herself from her surroundings as she was bringing her culture and intelligence to bear in the creation of a substitute environment, one that she could regard as congenial and habitable. In this manner and for these motives is culture transmitted at all. The immense contradiction between the "real" environment and the one she had formed artistically could not, however, be tolerated indefinitely, and it is in the nature of this sustained difficulty that one finds the reasons for the remarkable change that occurs in the quality of her poetry after *The Tenth Muse* was published, apparently without her knowledge or consent, in London in 1650. Thereafter, her poetry was far less abstract; her attention came finally to rest on herself and on the members of the smaller community of her family, their illnesses, their deaths, the travels of her husband and son, the burning of their house at Andover.

The "Verses upon the Burning of Our House, July 10th 1666," are as fully realized an example of Bradstreet's later poetry as the quaternions are of her earlier, apprentice work. The unmistakable advance in quality has much to do with the felt decay of that conservative effort which the early work represented. Here is the poem:

> In silent night when rest I took,
> For sorrow neer I did not look,
> I waken'd was with thundring nois
> And Piteous shreiks of dreadfull voice.
> That fearful sound of fire and fire,
> Let no man know is my Desire.
>
> I, starting up, the light did spye,
> And to my God my heart did cry
> To strengthen me in my Distresse
> And not to leave me succourlesse.
> Then coming out beheld a space,
> The flame consume my dwelling place.
>
> And, when I could no longer look,
> I blest his Name that gave and took,
> That layd my good now in the dust:
> Yea so it was, and so 'twas just.
> It was his own: it was not mine;
> Far be it that I should repine.
>
> He might of All justly bereft,
> But yet sufficient for us left.
> When by the Ruines oft I past,
> My sorrowing eyes aside did cast,
> And here and there the places spye
> Where oft I sate, and long did lye.
>
> Here stood that Trunk, and there that chest;
> There lay that store I counted best:
> My pleasant things in ashes lye,
> And them behold no more shall I.
> Under thy roof no guest shall sitt,
> Nor at thy Table eat a bitt.
>
> No pleasant tale shall 'ere be told,
> Nor things recounted done of old.
> No Candle 'ere shall shine in Thee,
> Nor bridegroom's voice ere heard shall bee.
> In silence ever shalt thou lye;
> Adieu, Adieu; All's vanity.

Then streight I 'gin my heart to chide,
And did thy wealth on earth abide?
Didst fix thy hope on mouldring dust,
The arm of flesh didst make thy trust?
Raise up thy thoughts above the skye
That dunghill mists away may flie.

Thou hast an house on high erect,
Fram'd by that mighty Architect,
With glory richly furnished
Stands permanent though this bee fled.
It's purchased, and paid for too
By him who hath enough to doe.

A prise so vast as is unknown,
Yet, but his Gift, is made thine own.
Ther's wealth enough, I need no more;
Farewell my Pelf, farewell my Store.
The world no longer let me Love,
My hope and Treasure lyes Above.[21]

"No more Ages of Man," as Adrienne Rich has observed; "no more Assyrian monarchies; but poems in response to the simple events in a woman's life."[22] The change in content is evident to anyone who compares the early and late work, but there is a corresponding and authorizing change in style and consciousness that can with confidence be laid to the attritional effect of the frontier on the poet's conservative resistance.

The diction of the later poems is simpler, tighter, more subdued. The effect is aided by the octosyllabic couplets which are appropriate in the later work to the reduced scale of the poet's foreground. But there are also more words of one syllable, a greater proportion of Anglo-Saxon terms, and on balance fewer literary allusions. Compared with the elevated idiom of the quaternions, the later poetry in general and this poem in particular are written in a lean, stripped style aptly suited to the expression of loss. The nouns, which are in most instances attachable to concrete, even individual realities, show most clearly the changed consciousness of the writer. The word "fire," to choose first the most obvious example, is no longer the sign of a scientific abstraction or the name of a personified element but is instead an emotionally complex designation for a blaze that existed uniquely on July 10, 1666. Specific items, each with its freight of sentiment – trunk, chest, roof, table, and candle – pass in ghostly review, their reality sensed most keenly in their disappearance. This purgation of the familiar from the poet's life is a sort of reenactment of her initial emigration to the frontier, but thirty-six years of coping with circumstances have had their effect. Those individual constituents of her physical environment that her earlier poetry had sought to deny by uniting in ideal abstraction return in her age to haunt her, and her heart is evidently with them. As her surroundings became progressively less natural, less foreign, more civilized and more comfortable, she found she had, after all, made the arm of flesh her trust. She owed much to the art and culture that had transformed her surroundings, but the disruption and cleansing of a fire taught her the limit of her obligation. The poem dramatizes a profound alteration in the way her consciousness registers both concrete and abstract "thingness." Her qualitative apprehension of nouns has changed appreciably since the writing of the quaternions.

One way to understand how the frontier can effect such a change is to consider that the cultural disruption of emigration to a wilderness is inevitably accompanied by a revolution of indeterminate extent in language. When the Puritans, a highly civilized and cultured people, came to occupy the emptiness of New England, a large part of their customary vocabulary became, under the circumstances, immediately obsolete. Certain words and meanings of words common in England often had no referents on the frontier – the word "inn," for example – so they simply ceased for a time to be part of the normal lexical equipment of individual settlers. Other words less often employed in the New World than in the Old, especially in oral communication, became rarer but did not pass out of the vocabulary altogether. A few words were added to refer to items that did not exist in England; these of course came mostly from the various Indian languages and pertained mainly to items of food and clothing. The decrease in effective vocabulary, however, together with the influx of words from the heathen culture of the Indians, must have disturbed many people consciously or unconsciously. When Endecott and his people came to Salem, they first adopted the Indian place name *Naumkeag*, but discovering that the term meant "place of peace," they translated it into Hebrew, which resulted in the culturally more congenial "Salem." Throughout New England Indian names, especially of towns, gave way to familiar English place names: *Shawmut* became "Boston," for example, and *Aggawam* was christened "Ipswich," reflecting the natural conservatism of displaced persons.

But the effect of the frontier on language was also subtler than this, affecting not only the quantity but the quality of words. In a generally comfortable environment such as Anne Bradstreet had known in England – an environment, that is, in which one feels particularly at home and at ease – one does not typically take special notice of its various components; much is taken for granted. The pleasure of being accustomed to a place is a generalized state of mind, in the sense that irritation is a specific and particular condition. "Fire" means one thing to a person who lives in a stone castle such as Sempringham, and quite another to one who lives in a wooden house with a chimney of wattle and daub. Examples could be multiplied indefinitely of things – nouns – that had been inconspicuous in England because they were either culturally neutral or simply pleasant, but that, on the frontier, became obtrusive realities, insistent and threatening.[23] An English field or meadow would likely have evoked an aesthetic response from such a person as the young Anne Dudley seems to have been; in the environs of Ipswich or Andover, on the other hand, the field she saw most often was the one her husband and his servants labored in, the field that produced their food and from time to time concealed a wolf or two. One way to express in general terms this frontier-altered sense of words is to suggest that the portion of the immigrant's idiolect composed of signifiers like "field" and "fire" – that is to say, the portion made up of culturally neutral words used in casual reference to the environment – became depleted. The words themselves remain, but they begin to comprise a class of emotionally significant and concretely meaningful terms. Such heightened awareness of the concrete is a sort of linguistically enforced recognition of the power of the physical, which is precisely what Bradstreet had rather heroically held out against in her early conservative work.

In England, where the poet received an education of unusual quality for a woman at that time, her engagement with the world of abstractions had been strong, especially in the realms of science and history. The words and ideas of this portion of her idiolect comprised the material from which she spun her early poetry in an attempt to get "home" psychically, back to pleasant Sempringham, or, in any event, away from the appalling "new world and new manners." On the other hand, if one judges from her autobiographical statement and from her first poem, religion clearly did not figure in her youthful, English consciousness as an abstraction at all; religion and all that pertained to it were quite real, quite incapable of being manipulated intellectually.

The frontier seems to have greatly affected the polar realms of concrete and abstract "thingness." After a period of conservative objection to the intimidating physicality of the local environment, she seems to have sensed that her style, limited by the frontier, was inadequate to sustain the refined high culture that she associated with her youth, with her father, and with England. The abstractions of history and science in which these early objections were couched depended for their vitality on a style she could not match, as she repeatedly tells us, and so, as abstractions, they passed generally from her consciousness. What had been most real to her in her youth, her religion, became itself increasingly abstract, increasingly subject to the manipulations of speculative thought, as the physical became more emotionally real. This is the sort of reversal of consciousness that Tocqueville observed when he said of Americans that they "put the real in the place of the ideal."[24] In Bradstreet's later poems God appears often, but is with increasing frequency presented metaphorically rather than in the direct, nonmetaphorical manner of her first poem. In the "Verses upon the Burning of Our House" God is "that mighty Architect"; in "On My Dear Grand-child, Simon Bradstreet," God is a monarch, or, like the poet's father, a magistrate. In "Contemplations," Bradstreet wonders aloud about the strange transformation occurring in her consciousness; she only half understands what is happening to her, but writes, nevertheless, a fine and moving poem out of the decay of her conservative imagination.

If this transformation is an Americanizing process, it is so because it reflects the fundamental dialectic between New World circumstances and traditional Old World identities. The English Puritan consciousness had a continuous range of thought from the largely intellectual abstractions of high culture down through a neutral consciousness of place to a rich concept of the real, which was religious. American immigrants in their earliest stages are deliberately conservative, since they feel, with much justification, that their identities depend on retaining this old configuration. The community helps in this conservative resistance, but as the effort is almost exclusively nostalgic, time and circumstance wear it down – first in the realm of public style, then in the private consciousness where the ideals are preserved. Finally, the neutral consciousness of environment – where the sense of being "at home" really originates – is vacated, leaving an enormous void between the physical world (the material for the Puritans' "homely images") and the abstract (the religious). The metaphorical style of the American Puritans, their fondness for "domesticating the infinite" or for expressing the grandest by the meanest, is an effort to fill the void where home was and is no more.

Chapter 2

Brother Jonathan

==========

Yet I had planted thee a noble vine, wholly a right seed: how then art thou turned into the degenerate plant of a strange vine unto me?
– Jeremiah 2:21

Adam. *And so, Mr. Jonathen, you say that your country is better than ours.*
Jonathen. *Aye, that it is, I swear for it – much finer, more abundant, larger and more like a world than yours – and what's better, the people ayn't half so wicked, or given to Belzebub, as you are.*
– Joseph Atkinson[1]

The first New England settlers genuinely feared that in their unaccustomed surroundings they would begin to degenerate, to lose not only their sense of mission but their culture in general. John Cotton addressed the departing Winthrop fleet in a sermon urging them to "have a care that you look well to the plants that spring from you, that is, your children, that they do not degenerate." Citing his text from Jeremiah 2:21, he continued: "Your ancestors were of a noble divine spirit, but if [you] suffer [your] children to degenerate, to take loose courses, then God will surely pluck you up."[2]

The same fear pervades William Bradford's history *Of Plymouth Plantation*, in which the novelty of the environment is seen mainly in its capacity to generate crime and wealth, Cotton's "loose courses," and Winthrop's "great things for ourselves." By 1644 the lure of better land elsewhere had so depleted the first settlement that, as Bradford poignantly noted,

this poore church [was] left, like an anciente mother, growne olde, and forsaken of her children, (though not in their affections,) yett in regarde of their bodily presence and personall helpfulness. Her anciente members being most of them worne away by death; and these of later time being like children translated into other families,

27

and she like a widow left only to trust in God. Thus she that had
made so many rich became her selfe poore.[3]

Bradford's distrust of the environment was even more dramatically in
evidence two years earlier in the case of young Thomas Granger. In the
official investigation following Granger's confession to the crime of so-
domy, the magistrates, including Bradford, were eager to establish that
the practice was imported and not, as they very much feared, a result of
conditions at Plymouth.[4] These two incidents neatly illustrate the predicament that later generations were to approach mainly through the
jeremiad: the dissolution by wealth of the leader class, and, simultaneously, the moral corruption of those who ought to have been led – both
perceived as failures of the center to hold against the force of frontier
circumstance.

Beginning about the middle of the seventeenth century, the New England clergy increasingly turned its attention to this problem, to the
religious apathy of the people, and to their apparent rejection of the ideals
of the passing generation. In other words, for the first time conservatives
were attempting to identify and protect an essentially American tradition.
By holding up the earliest settlers as a standard of piety, probity, and
sacrifice, the ministers in their jeremiads created a mythic American past
which threw into the boldest relief the degeneracy of the real American
present. While they denounced wordly ambition, hardheartedness, idleness, dancing, gaming, sumptuous dress, and the secular orientation
generally, the ministers impressed the people with the excellence of a
tradition by which they could no longer live. The sermons, in effect,
compounded the parishioners' sense of guilt over the attenuation of their
culture without materially affecting the quality of public behavior – which
failure contributed further to the decline of ministerial authority.[5] Still,
the issue was kept alive and burning in a century of sermons, while the
ironic disparity between popular conduct and professed values became
inescapably evident. The people had not given up their traditional beliefs
and ideals, and for that very reason their increasingly secular and "modern" behavior came to seem a terrible problem.

The ministers identified the abuses of prosperity as the immediate
cultural threats – not the limited and modest prosperity of the past, but
the new ease of upward mobility that seemed everywhere to unsettle
social and business relations and to encourage new and alarming forms
of personal ambition. As the ministers pointed out, the result of all this
was fraud, bankruptcy, indebtedness, and in general a loss of a sense of
community obligation. But in the long run the most serious problem
was neither religious nor economic, but psychic. The divergence between
real and ideal behavior was not being glossed over or hidden, but re-

lentlessly exposed and challenged; ironic contradiction became the hall-mark of contemporary life, and the guilt that many people felt over their failure to acquit themselves by the austere standards of the past was being confirmed throughout the early eighteenth century in the words of in-dignant sermons addressed to an "Evil and Adulterous Generation."[6]

The model of American identity promulgated by these Puritan jere-miads was not quite compatible with the nationalism of the revolutionary generation, though by the 1770s and 1780s the ministers' hypothesis had become so firmly established in the popular mind that benign alternatives were not easily arrived at. This very difficulty, however, was turned to literary account because it demanded a genuine tough-mindedness of postrevolutionary Federalist writers in their attempts to compose an adequate portrait of the national character. What makes their work in-teresting and readable even today is the provincial awareness of atten-uation that informed the Federalist mind. Like the ministers, but unlike Benjamin Franklin in the *Autobiography*, they were unusually sensitive to disruptions and failures in social and cultural traditions and were prepared, in arguing for the ideal over the real, to conduct their argument in a historical context.[7] Unlike such liberals as Philip Freneau, St. Jean de Crèvecoeur or the Joel Barlow of *The Columbiad*, Royall Tyler, Joseph Dennie, Timothy Dwight, even the Jeffersonian Hugh Henry Brack-enridge, made a habit of looking upon a lapsed reality in the moral, ethical, and spiritual context of an ideal past, and although they typically expressed their idealism with a semblance of the ministers' old authority, they also typically engaged in a counterpointing, self-parodying realism.

The most obvious instance of this conservative realism is the fact that their ideal heroes (Tyler's Colonel Manly, Brackenridge's Captain Far-ago, Cooper's Judge Temple) always appear in tandem with a reductively clownish alter ego (Tyler's Jonathan, Brackenridge's Teague O'Regan, Cooper's Richard Jones), as though to remind us of what has already happened and what might yet happen to traditional cultural values in a frontier society. These constantly recurring pairs of "ideal" and "real" characters are signs of the conservative's bifurcated approach to the task of producing a national self-portrait; they also reflect the artists' percep-tion, derived as much from the ministers as from their own sense of things, that current real behavior too often contravened generally agreed upon and traditionally affirmed values, especially those of the Puritan founders.

Although Tyler, in *The Contrast* (1787), graphically depicted the at-tenuated idealism of his increasingly secular world, his attack was partly diffused by the liabilities of his own provincial artistic consciousness. The poignant historical irony, repeated over and over again, is that con-servatives proved to be ineffectual reformers because they suffered from the very problems they meant to set right. Hampered by the conventions of current British writing, and only imperfectly understanding them, Tyler and many of his contemporaries tended to see the deeper problems of their own society as "foibles" to be exposed with the decorous forbearance of a London gentleman. The virile indignation of the earlier Puritans, effective so long as ministerial authority held out, was now old-fashioned and had, in any event, no place in the mannered, civilized world of Sheridan and Goldsmith. Timothy Dwight, wishing to affirm the values of Winthrop's generation, yet determined not to appear provincial, ironically confined himself to the style and language, as he believed, of *Cooper's Hill* and *Windsor Forest*. Even the acid voice of Pope's *Dunciad*, adopted by the Connecticut Wits in their *Anarchiad*, could never convey the direct simplicity, the morally emphatic forthrightness of the Puritan plain style, apart from which the substance of Puritan values is scarcely conceivable. Trying valiantly, then, to conserve two distinct and contradictory cultures, seeking to preserve the substance of seventeenth-century Massachusetts in the style of eighteenth-century England, these postrevolutionary conservatives were bound to cut a figure not unlike Judge Hall's Mr. Edgarton: that is to say, they were bound to fail magnificently.

Tyler's *Contrast* is one such failure, and not the least splendid. The peculiar cultural compromise that it represents is startlingly in evidence at the very outset, when the moral standards of the stage-hating Puritans are invoked in the Prologue:

> Who travels now to ape the rich or great,
> To deck an equipage and roll in state;
> To court the graces, or to dance with ease,
> Or by hyprocrisy to strive to please?
> Our free-born ancestors such arts despis'd;
> Genuine sincerity alone they priz'd;
> Their minds, with honest emulation fir'd,
> To solid good – not ornament – aspir'd;
> Or, if ambition rous'd a bolder flame,
> Stern virtue throve, where indolence was shame.[8]

Another difficulty arises when we are told in the Prologue to this native comedy modeled closely on Sheridan's *School for Scandal* that American imitation of European arts is becoming a major social problem.

> But modern youth, with imitative sense,
> Deem taste in dress the proof of excellence;
> And spurn the meanness of your homespun arts,
> Since homespun habits would obscure their parts;

Whilst all, which aims at splendour and parade,
Must come from Europe, *and be ready made.*
Strange! we should thus our native worth disclaim,
And check the progress of our rising fame.
Yet *one*, whilst imitation bears the sway,
Aspires to nobler heights, and points the way.
Be rous'd, my friends! his bold example view;
Let your own Bards be proud to copy you!

Although the Prologue seems at first to repudiate the imitation of foreign models, it argues in fact that certain things – even, presumably, certain *English* things – are worthy of being copied. The mistake of the "modern youth" is not that they imitate (compare the Puritans' "honest emulation"), but that in a manner altogether un-American they honor style above and apart from substance. In Tyler's conservative but provincial consciousness, Puritan idealism has become the substance ("solid good") and is valuable because it is indigenous; on the other hand, and opposed to it, is style ("ornament"), which comes to be understood as foreign and frivolous, of no importance except as it helps to conserve the substance. Thus Tyler is in much the same position as the modern youths who find little difficulty in divorcing style and content; he opposes them only on the issue of which is the more important. Tyler hopes to convince his audience that the man of "homespun habits" who refuses to dissemble is actually less objectionably provincial than he seems, or than the modern youths who appropriate a foreign style without the corresponding substance that alone could justify it. Native simplicity, because it preserves the Puritan heritage, is better and more "manly" than an exotic and insubstantial stylishness, of which the only real effect is a deficit in the financial and cultural balance of trade. So, just as Tyler takes pains to contrast good and bad imitation, he discriminates with equal care in presenting their respective consequences: good and bad provincialism. And of course he claims for himself and his hero the moral advantages of the former.

The "contrast" of the title is generally taken to refer to that between the upright Colonel Manly and the foppishly Europeanized Billy Dimple, whose morality derives immediately from Chesterfield's *Letters*. But the play has as many contrasts of character as of ideas, and that between Manly and Dimple may not, after all, be the most interesting. The behavior of this pair is highlighted and to an extent defined by the behavior of their respective servants, Jonathan and Jessamy. Significantly, the contrast between Dimple and his retainer is slight indeed. They differ only in the scope of their action, Jessamy being limited by his lack of money and by his acquiescence in a class system that defines him as a servant; on the whole he is as unctuously accomplished and as fashionably amoral as his master. Like Dimple, Jessamy is a manipulator of circumstances, an intriguer, making a show of a style of which he has not the substantial virtues, and is thus, as Fielding defined the term in the preface to *Joseph Andrews*, "Ridiculous." On the other hand, the contrast between Manly and *his* servant is considerable, suggesting that Tyler felt the need to make further distinctions within the moral area of "good provincialism." Because Jonathan is in many respects a culturally attenuated Colonel Manly, it will be best to examine the master's character before turning to the servant's.

Colonel Manly represents the ultimate American values, those of the Puritan past.[9] He is an educated and thoroughly upright rural gentleman whose manners, if they err at all err on the side of the strictest honesty. His sister, Charlotte, a fashionable young lady of New York, finds him stiff and grimly moralistic, a wet blanket in a world that had begun to feel comfortable with laughter and lightness: "He read me such lectures, out of pure brotherly affection, against the extremes of fashion, dress, flirting, and coquetry, and all the other dear things which he knows I doat upon, that, I protest, his conversation made me as melancholy as if I had been at church."[10] Her brother's themes are those of the Congregationalists, and his effect on sinners is the same as the ministers'; failing to alter behavior, he creates guilt and melancholy. Unlike the wordly city characters, Manly honors his parents, rejects the dictates of fashion, approves things American on the score of their Americanness, and speaks, unremittingly, the language of sentiment. Where his companions are gay and frivolous, he is serious, even somber; he neither drinks nor gambles and is therefore frugal. His patriotism, which is active (he is a soldier) and philosophical (he is a student of history), is squarely in the tradition of Winthrop's "Model of Christian Charity" because it leads him to prefer the welfare of the larger community to his own. When Charlotte asks her brother to sell the notes with which he had been paid for his military services, he replies carefully and at length:

I shall be ever willing to contribute as far as it is in my power, to adorn, or in any way to please my sister; yet, I hope, I shall never be obliged for this, to sell my notes. I may be romantic, but I preserve them as a sacred deposit. Their full amount is justly owing to me, but as embarrassments, the natural consequences of a long war, disable my country from supporting its credit, I shall wait with patience until it is rich enough to discharge them. If that is not in my day, they shall be transmitted as an honorable certificate to posterity, that I have humbly imitated our illustrious *WASH-INGTON*, in having exposed my health and life in the service of my country, without reaping any other reward than the glory of conquering in so arduous a contest.[11]

After another such speech, one of his auditors breathlessly exclaims, "What noble sentiments!" – and surely the modern reader must agree. Manly's speech is deliberately "sentimental" because, as the inheritor and guardian of the Puritan past, he declines to hide his beliefs where an elevated morality is unfashionable – this is, in New York. While putting the special honor of his own century in escrow, he is in effect disbursing much older notes: those "transmitted as an honorable certificate" to him from the generation of John Winthrop.

In a culture that is accommodating itself to the declension (and taking some pleasure in doing so), Manly, as the conservative man of action, opposes the tyranny of the majority as courageously as he had recently opposed the king's own troops. It is hard not to notice, however, that Manly's Puritan idealism, unlike that of Winthrop, is unselfish in a way that strongly calls attention to himself. He *is* the model of Christian charity. What had been abstract or ideal in Winthrop's sermon and had remained so in the sermons of his spiritual descendants is now really formulated, made vivid and personified, in order to serve the formal interests of a society deteriorating for lack of present models. But, as regularly happens, the "realization" of old abstract values and traditions involves the provincial American artist in a virtually insurmountable stylistic dilemma. Manly, in all his brittleness, is being offered as an "end-product," a provincialized version of a once-living ideal.

Not only does the conservative American encounter the difficulty of expressing old values in a new style, but he is frequently, for lack of present models, no master of the modern style he so incongruously admires. Often he will make up for a deficiency of technical knowledge with sheer gusto, as Tyler seems to have done in *The Contrast*. He wrote the play within a month of seeing for the first time a live dramatic performance – of *The School for Scandal* – in New York where he had come on business. At the time there was not a single playhouse in all of his native New England, nor would there be for another seven years.[12] His amateur standing (or rather the peculiar disability of the provincial artist) was neatly turned from a seeming liability to a distinct advantage in the "Advertisement" to the published play: "It is the first essay of American genius in a difficult species of composition; it was written by one who never critically studied the rules of the drama, and, indeed, had seen but few of the exhibitions of the stage; it was undertaken and finished in the course of three weeks."[13] That the concept of a natural, untutored genius should flourish in a frontier society is hardly surprising, but the effect of such a concept, which is the explicit disparagement of style, is worth noting because it bears directly on the process by which cultural attenuation takes place and is rationalized.

The speed with which Tyler wrote testifies to the impact that seeing *The School for Scandal* had on him. His great delight with this "new" art form must have been nearly inseparable from the particular modes of the few plays he had seen. In other words, anything he might be inclined to "say" as a dramatist would naturally fall into the style of Sheridan in particular, whether that style – as he could reproduce it – was appropriate or not to the subject at hand. Much of the interest of *The Contrast* as a work of art results directly from this characteristic limitation in Tyler's knowledge. The style of the play is in fact quite at odds with its subject. It is not just that there is an incongruity of form and content, but there is a confirmed antagonism between them. In the character of Manly, for example, Puritan ideals are made to venture forth as "sentiment," an error that is at once artistic and philosophical, and that proceeds from Tyler's failure to recognize that such a modernizing transformation simply stripped Puritanism of its integrity. The result is an unintentional comedy behind the intentional one. There is no reason why Manly has to be ponderous and sententious except that Tyler regarded his hero's ideas as seriously valuable and therefore was at pains to contrast them sharply with the light and witty repartee of the other characters.

By thus displacing the central virtue of the British comedy of manners, subordinating and virtually condemning the wit of his own play, Tyler provincializes his model and at the same time creates stupendous artistic difficulties for himself. Charlotte's funny lines mocking her brother's seriousness reveal among other things the uneasiness that Tyler must have felt with his decision that truth is, after all, a weighty matter, and that in light and frivolous times right behavior must appear unwelcome. Thus the artist's difficulty: the wit of Charlotte's speeches and the low comedy of Jonathan's scenes are two of the most attractive elements of the play, while at the same time the hero exists for no other purpose than to repudiate them both. The dilemma can only be resolved by implying just what the "Advertisement" implied: that style does not matter. We are permitted to respond to Charlotte's fashionable cynicism and to Jonathan's earthy vernacular only until Manly reminds us that they are both merely stylists. The argument, though compelling, overlooks the fact that the success of Charlotte and Jonathan is as necessary to the comedy at the level of style as their exposure and defeat are at the level of meaning. Charlotte's last speech is, significantly, a contrite admission of the emptiness of style: "I now find, that . . . the finest assemblage of features, the greatest taste in dress, the genteelest address, or the most brilliant wit, cannot eventually secure a coquette from contempt and ridicule."[14] Tyler seems most American in his readiness to use substance by example and precept as a brick to throw at style.

As so often happens in provincial American literature, however, the aim is slightly off and the intended mark is missed. *The Contrast*, as an attack on style, founders on the impossibility of presenting in Manly a perfectly styleless hero. The attempt is made, certainly, to suggest that he represents a pure and unadorned virtue; he is presented, in fact, as a natural gentleman in the same sense that one who writes plays without studying the rules is a natural playwright. The operative assumption is Tyler's belief that character in its republican simplicity is a kind of primordial moral substance, prior to and therefore distinct from style. Substantial character naturally expresses itself in deeds rather than in words, which is why Manly is a soldier and the others are primarily talkers. On the other hand, by corrupting the natural sequence of character and action, style becomes virtually a denial of life, as even Charlotte realizes when she broadly hints at the sexual impotence of the men about town: "I will say this to the credit of our city beaux ... that, even had I no reliance upon the honour of the dear Adonises, I would trust myself in any possible situation with them, without the least apprehension of rudeness."[15] Manly is a product of the conviction that, where most style is foreign and all style deceives and perverts, the only honest manner is no manner at all.

Despite himself, and despite the author's attempt to convince us otherwise, Manly indeed has a style, that is to say, a particular manner of presenting to others the Puritan values that make up his character. Aware of being a right-minded person in a confused society, Manly finds frequent occasion to consider and to articulate his ideals. His verbal sentiments become at once rebukes, which distance him from the morally hostile city, and appealing models, which tie him to it by acknowledgments of responsibility. Even the villain, Billy Dimple, has to admit that "he awes me by the superiority of his sentiments."[16] Manly's willingness to stand a moral pattern for decadent New Yorkers, to be to them what Washington is to him, argues well for his benevolence, but is stylistically problematical. This deliberate setting up of oneself as a model would have seemed impossibly arrogant and pretentious to Winthrop, who would moreover have seen, as no one could in 1787, that such behavior was a concession to individualism, to the very cause of the difficulties it sought to remove. Manly's style, then, is in accord not with the more unified consciousness of 1640, but with the late-eighteenth-century awareness of competing ideals – with, for instance, Franklin's composing his memoirs in hopes that his son and others would find his "conducing Means" to a useful life "fit to be imitated."[17]

In *The Contrast* Manly opposes what one colonial minister called that "narrow, contracted and selfish Spirit" which is "pernicious to the *State*."[18] In so doing, he resembles Winthrop who construed liberty as subjection to goodness and who sought the welfare of the state or community. But his style is in its way as decadent as are the evils against which that style is ostensibly directed. In act 3 Manly delivers a monologue on the historic evils of luxury:

> The kings of Greece devoted their lives to the service of their country, and her senators knew no other superiority over their fellow-citizens than a glorious preeminence in danger and virtue. They exhibited to the world a noble spectacle, – a number of independent states united by a similarity of language, sentiment, manners, common interest, and common consent, in one grand mutual league of protection. – And, thus united, long might they have continued the cherishers of arts and sciences, the protectors of the oppressed, the scourge of tyrants, and the safe asylum of liberty: But when foreign gold, and still more pernicious, foreign luxury, had crept among them, they sapped the vitals of their virtue. The virtues of their ancestors were only found in their writings. Envy and suspicion, the vices of little minds, possessed them. The various states engendered jealousies of each other; and, more unfortunately, growing jealous of their great federal council, the Amphictyons, they forgot that their common safety had existed, and would exist, in giving them an honorable and extensive prerogative. The common good was lost in the pursuit of private interest; and that people, who, by uniting, might have stood against the world in arms, by dividing, crumbled into ruin.... Oh! that America! Oh! that my country, would in this her day, learn the things which belong to her peace![19]

Longing for unanimity, Tyler echoes the pleas of Winthrop's conservative model, but of course without reference to any commission from God; feeling that virtue has passed tragically from life into the literature of history, he tries to oppose the noble ideals of "our free-born ancestors" against the personal sins of hypocrisy, jealousy, and pride (now, however, called "vices," as in Franklin they are called "errata").[20] Just as Manly regrets the loss of the glory that was Greece in the period of its unification, so Tyler tries to revive a unified Puritan past as a bulwark against the decadence and worldliness of the present. But in the general declension Tyler's own memory fails; the history of Greece obscures that of New England (typology sinking into mere analogy), and the past dissolves steadily away in the incongruities of a modern provincial consciousness. In the typical pattern of the frontier dialectic, Manly and Tyler admire unity very much, but like Anne Bradstreet are aware of it primarily through its absence. Their attempts to foster it are entirely ethical and pragmatically rational, and so, ironically, they share in the general tendency of their culture toward a more worldly orientation. By betraying the essential source of Puritan unity in a mistaken anxiety to see the substance of its values preserved, Tyler misconstrues and compromises its style, believing, as he does, that style is unimportant.

With all his unconscious faults, Manly is still the type of the educated New England gentleman, a virtual collection of the manners and virtues of the Puritan past. Even stripped of their informing spirit, Puritan manners remain distinctly admirable, as Tyler shows, because Manly's rational devotion to his country's welfare is an almost convincing substitute for religious conviction. Yet his servant, Jonathan, is present to remind us of the fragility of a character such as Manly's. The frontier environment in which Jonathan matured is obviously antipathetic to the tradition of Puritan high-mindedness; and the two characters together demonstrate that if any tradition is to survive on the frontier, it must be preserved by deliberate, self-conscious, and conservative acts of resistance to circumstance. For those unwilling or unable to make such an effort, the Puritan ideal will surely degenerate into the low-minded materialist strain one sees in Jonathan and which, in the play, serves both as contrast to Manly's better maintained idealism and as parodic commentary on the naturally degenerative course of culture. ("Yet I had planted thee a noble vine, wholly a right seed.") Manly's whole crusade, as it forms the plot of *The Contrast*, is to keep idealism from lapsing into materialism, and Jonathan is a reminder of the consequences of failure. The clownish servant, in whom the old idealism is more than a bit seedy, is in a curious way an illustration of Emerson's observation that "a fact is the end or last issue of spirit."[21]

It is as fact to spirit that Jonathan contrasts with Manly, and in the quality of this relationship lies the wry humor and the realistic self-parody that have always marked the true conservative imagination in America. Jonathan's importance in this respect usually goes unnoticed because he is not often seen in ideological relation to Manly and to the New England past; myth criticism has made him a progenitor rather than a descendant, the first in a line of stereotyped Yankees rather than the wayward child of a degenerating Puritanism. "Astute and simple, gross and rambling, rural to the core, he talked 'nat'r'l,' " as Constance Rourke observed, "talked his way through scenes, and became the presiding genius."[22]

But Jonathan is the "presiding genius" of *The Contrast* only in being the most comic and the most memorably original character in this comic play, and not, certainly, for any effect he had on the development of the plot. Actually, the subplot to which his activities are confined is never

allowed to impinge on the main story line, nor is it even resolved on its
own terms. What is in fact being portrayed in the figure of Jonathan is
not the free soul of the mythic Yankee, but the confusion and ignorance
of a victim. Even before he appears on stage, he has been identified and
named as one who can be taken advantage of. Dimple's vain and pompous
servant, Jessamy, "display[ing] his person to advantage" on the Mall,
observes at a distance an object of fun: "Ah! who comes here? This, by
his aukwardness, must be the Yankee colonel's servant. I'll accost him."[23]
As Hemingway said of himself, so it is with Jonathan: his awkwardness
is his style and by his style is he known.

Jonathan's gross ignorance of manners, serving naturally to constrain
and limit his action, is of course deliberately contrasted with Manly's
principled indifference to style and his consequent freedom to act. Tyler's
attitude toward Jonathan is evident in the care with which he shows that
his character's fiercely proclaimed "independence" and "self-reliance"
are not only unlike Manly's, but are in fact a dangerous illusion. When
Jessamy asks whether he is indeed the servant of Colonel Manly, Jonathan
bristles at the implication:

> *Jonathan.* Servant! Sir, do you take me for a neger, – I am Colonel
>   Manly's waiter.
> *Jessamy.* A true Yankee distinction, egad, without a difference.
>   Why, Sir, do you not perform all the offices of a servant? Do
>   you not even blacken his boots?
> *Jonathan.* Yes; I do grease them a bit sometimes; but I am a true
>   blue son of liberty, for all that. Father said I should come as
>   Colonel Manly's waiter to see the world, and all that; but no
>   man shall master me: my father has as good a farm as the
>   colonel.[24]

Compared with Jessamy's willingness to consider himself a servant,
Jonathan's repudiation of inferiority is compelling, but the New England
conservative's distrust of democracy, apparent in the contrast between
Jonathan and Manly, ironically undercuts the waiter's bravado. Jonathan's decision to be masterless is intellectually absolute and forecloses
even the "honest emulation" that Manly practices in relation to Washington. Committed to freedom (he *is* "a true blue son of liberty"), the
masterless servant has no sense of the use or end of freedom, and would
simply have stood gaping had he heard Winthrop argue that genuine
liberty "is maintained in a way of subjection to authority: it is of the
same kind of liberty wherewith Christ has made us free."[25]

The political implications of Jonathan's extreme democracy come in
for their share of sly condemnation when we learn that he has all along

secretly approved of Shays' Rebellion, which Manly had recently helped to quell.

> *Jonathan.* Why, I swear we don't make any great matter of dis-
> tinction in our state, between quality and other folk.
>
> *Jessamy.* This is, indeed, a levelling principle. I hope, Mr. Jonathan,
> you have not taken part with the insurgents.
>
> *Jonathan.* Why, since General Shays has sneaked off, and given us
> the bag to hold, I don't care to give my opinion; but you'll
> promise not to tell – put your ear this way – you won't tell?
> – I vow, I did think the sturgeons were right.[26]

Whereas Manly places the welfare of the community above his own immediate ends, Jonathan thoughtlessly reverses these priorities – partly because abstractions have lost their meaning for him, but also because he is deeply confused about his relationship to the sorts of people who might, in the more cohesive Puritan past, have guided him. The mere anarchy that Jonathan stands for is precisely revealed in his categorical refusal to distinguish "between quality and other folk" – a neat paradox in which language fights a Shays' Rebellion of its own against the weakness of the speaker's thought.

Distortion of meaning and language is directly symptomatic of Jonathan's cultural pathology, and here Tyler is at his most realistic. Innocent of instruction, provincially ignorant, Jonathan nevertheless knows that niceness of language is a sign of culture. In his insistence on the distinction between "servant" and "waiter" we see the dilemma of the frontiersman whose respect for culture so frequently outran his knowledge. In the difference between "insurgents" and "sturgeons" Tyler conveys something of the psychology of frontier degeneracy, and hints how culture loses integrity by attrition despite the willingness, even the eagerness, of provincials to learn. Respect for culture, "style," and the power of language finally motivates Jonathan, a professedly masterless man, to submit to instruction and imitate a model. His attitude toward Jessamy's apparently polished style is remarkably like Charlotte's breathless admiration of things European. Both Jonathan and Charlotte are provincials, both are materialists, both sense something missing from their lives that exotic culture can supply, and both receive instruction in a way calculated to promote distortion. By stressing the fallibility of cultural transmission, the susceptibility of a style to degenerate under essentially frontier conditions, Tyler characterizes the dilemma of an entire society, which stands in relation to the cultural ideal of Britain as Jonathan stands in relation to Jessamy (and, one might add, as *The Contrast* stands in relation to *The School for Scandal*).

The satire of Jonathan's provincial mentality and of the peculiar quality of his ignorance reaches its comic zenith when Jonathan tries to act on Jessamy's advice in the matter of wooing Jenny, a maid servant, or, as Jonathan prefers, a "wait'ress": "Then you must press and kiss her hand," Jessamy instructs him, "then press and kiss, and so on to her lips and cheeks; then talk as much as you can about hearts, darts, flames, nectar and ambrosia – the more incoherent the better."[27] When Jonathan later attempts to act on this advice, he is at several removes from a tradition whose pertinence is questionable to begin with. Notice that Jessamy's formulation is arrived at by a process of abstraction. He has given the Petrarchan convention *as* a convention in the worst sense, as "end-product knowledge," and placed it therefore where Jonathan is least able to recover it. As a result, the rustic Yankee's attempt to reconstitute the abstract principle in the real world (that is, in his address to Jenny), inevitably proceeds by misunderstanding. Confronting her, he stammers: "Burning rivers! cooling flames! red hot roses! pig–nuts! hasty–pudding and ambrosia!"[28] Jenny's outraged reply ("What means this freedom!") is thus perfectly apt. The courtly tradition has attenuated into thinnest air and the inheritor of it is suddenly awash in its disappearance. Jonathan is meant to prejudice us against nihilistic individualism and vulgar traditionlessness, just as Manly is meant to win us to the belief that conformity to a worthy model is admirable and dignified. Freedom, Tyler insists, lies where Winthrop said it did: in conformity to a received authority.

If we can imagine *The Contrast* without Jonathan – which is not difficult to do – we would see that Tyler had presented his audience with a straightforward choice between "natural" behavior, portrayed in Manly, and artificial behavior, portrayed in the New York characters. The play without Jonathan would have been a wholehearted denunciation of European influence, and would have resulted in no greater irony than the spectacle of a playwright, an artist, pronouncing art a vagrant. But of course Jonathan *is* there, and the effect of his presence is to discredit radically natural behavior and to remind us that if the ideals of the past are to be preserved, then natural conservatives such as Jonathan must not be allowed to go uneducated. They must at least be civilized. They must be intelligently aware of a world larger than the self, that is to say, they must be refined by exposure to a culture essentially British rather than American. In 1787 there were few American differentiae to set a New England education apart from a British one. European rather than American standards ultimately define the characters of *The Contrast*: Charlotte and the New Yorkers err in being too European, stylish but lacking substance; Jonathan, by allowing his style to deteriorate beneath the European level, is greatly in danger of losing the last vestige of his attenuated Puritan substance.

The fall from an ideal Puritan culture into a semblance of London dissipation is at the heart of the play's ostensible satire, as it had been the subject of the Puritan jeremiads, but Tyler adds a new note to the controversy. All the while he is conducting his attack on Americans who ape British manners he is conscious of America's cultural and stylistic provincialism, its *failure* to resemble London. This failure, of course, is not Jonathan's alone but Tyler's as well. The very act of writing the play is a recognition of British literary traditions and an affirmation of them, whatever the quality of the result. It is implicitly an attempt to reduce the cultural disparity that defines provincialism and at the same time an attempt to show, as the "Advertisement" all but explicitly states, that Americans can produce culture as well as anyone. But attenuation – or degeneracy, to use a harsher word – is both the subject of the play and the problem of its style. It is almost as if Tyler had meant to say "hearts and darts," only to have it come out as "burning rivers and cooling flames."

The Contrast is another instance of the fact that when culture was brought across the Atlantic to the relative emptiness of America it suffered distortion and attenuation, not in spite of but largely because of the ardent respect in which the parent civilization was held. Culture was changed, not destroyed; it became nonstandard by the only standards then fully accredited; it became, simply, American. In the experience of reading Tyler's play, the frequent clashes between the often unmet formal requirements of a European literary tradition and the homespun American subject matter rarely quite defeat our willingness to appreciate; the lapses are likely to strike a modern reader as charming in much the same way that the "mistakes" of American folk painters seem charming, and for the same reasons. Looking for tradition, early American artists fell, all unpremeditatedly, into individual talent.

Chapter 3

"A musy in the thicket"

It would seem to me, that a philosopher ought to know how to write, or at least to read.

— H. H. Brackenridge[1]

The frontier often had a prismatic effect on British culture. We have already seen how the frontier struggle to reproduce culture could set style against content; but content itself was never wholly unitary, and so it too was frequently broken up into culturally more manageable elements. The idea of the gentleman in *The Contrast* is a case in point: Edwin H. Cady has described the dramatic tension in Tyler's play in terms of a nearly schematic opposition of two contradictory English traditions – the fine gentleman, represented by the Chesterfieldian Billy Dimple, and the natural or Christian gentleman, represented by Colonel Manly, whose character, Cady argues, owes much to Sir Charles Grandison.[2] Seen from this perspective, the play sets forth in relatively unequivocal terms the dilemma of a habitually imitative people who find themselves faced with a choice between two contradictory British modes or models.

Although Americans were willing, even eager, to affirm the cultural standards of England, they were not always certain what those standards were. Colonials who viewed English ideas with an eye to modifying their own behavior found ambiguity naturally distressing. As a frontier people and as colonials, they did not have the complacent security in their cultural values that the native English enjoyed; they did not, in other words, have the ability of the more settled English population to rest content with a variety of conflicting ideas on a given topic, a kind of "negative capability" in cultural matters that allowed the two traditions of gentlemanliness to coexist in England in intimate compromise with each other. As these notions were transmitted to America, frontier conditions emphasized their inherently contradictory relationship, and like

42

a prism separated the discrete elements, finally presenting them as moral alternatives. The thinness of American culture made the tradition of the fine gentleman seem far more ridiculous in New York or Boston than it ever did in London, and simultaneously made the natural gentleman, whose appeal did not rely on the wealth and plenitude of an opulent high culture, seem correspondingly more attractive. The nationalism of *The Contrast* consists of its expressed preference for what is culturally more appropriate to American circumstances, but the Americanness of the play is distinct from its nationalism and consists in the way it reduces ambiguous polarities in British culture to simple antitheses and so facilitates imitation.

But of course it was not the strict imitation of Britain that made American culture distinctive. The peculiar way that frontier conservatives tried and failed to imitate and the distortions into which they were led by seeking to make the parent culture unambiguously available had the effect of altering the European germs as well as the American minds that received them. For example, well into the nineteenth century militant conservatives typically thought of themselves, and were thought of by others, as gentlemen, and so they opposed the frontier tendency to divest gentility of its time-honored political dimensions. (The careers of Fenimore Cooper in the North and of Gilmore Simms and Edgar Allan Poe in the South would be the most obvious examples of this pattern among writers.) The motives of such conservatives were not, however, altogether selfish. They sincerely believed that in choosing men to run the government everyone's best interest would be served if men of learning, men with some knowledge of the world, were preferred above others. The arrangement moreover suited their notion of civilized behavior since both the arrangement and their notion of civilized behavior were based (sometimes rather remotely) on English precedents which were important to them precisely because they *were* English. The failure of these gentlemen to retain political power (most dramatically in the so-called revolution of 1800) was thus an attenuation of British culture, and indicated a decay in the integrity of the gentlemanly style under the dissociative impact of frontier circumstances. One historian of the frontier expressed this process in a way that suggests the conservative's understandable resentment:

Upper-class settlers intended besides profiting themselves in the wilderness to plant a culture expressive of the best part of their Old World legacy, and for a time they appeared to labor effectually. . . . Their ambitions were finally frustrated by their own misconceptions but rather more by irrational forces embodied in the ignorant generality of emigrants, who had the sense of moving out of a circumscribed life dominated by magistrate and priest into a largely unrestrained condition. Although it is incorrect to assert that license and ignorance triumphed altogether, the emigrants seldom listened to wise and educated counsel in vital matters.[3]

The gentlemanly tradition in America, as Cady has argued, is responsible for much that Americans currently value in their civilization,[4] but the cultural successes of the conservative gentleman were not often apparent to him. His were Pyrrhic victories, and the very fact that he went down fighting and resentful has left an enduring impression not only on the shape of American culture, but on the attitudes Americans characteristically hold toward culture in general. The historic labors of these conservatives created no sense of obligation or gratitude in those who came after. The genteel tradition remains an embarrassment because, although Americans are alive to its excesses, they are nearly unconscious of its occult motives, forgetful that anything important ever seemed at stake. In America the pursuit of culture still retains (as it does not in European societies) the stigma of elitism first given it in the struggle for culture in the wilderness.

Hugh Henry Brackenridge was one of those frontier gentlemen whose lives illustrate the importance to the evolving character of American culture of the repeated frustration of conservative hopes. Born in Scotland, Brackenridge emigrated with his family at the age of five to the Pennsylvania wilderness. His father, an impoverished farmer, provided Hugh with as good an education as the vicinity could offer, sending him first to a school in "a log building at the confluence of Scott's Run and Muddy Creek," and later to a newly opened Latin school in Peach Bottom Township.[5] Here Brackenridge formed a warm attachment to literature and the classics, as we may deduce from his habit of neglecting farm chores to read the Latin authors on the shady banks of the Susquehanna. This particular dereliction of duty was for a time halted when the family cow ate his beloved copy of Horace. Day-to-day life on the Pennsylvania frontier in the mid-eighteenth century was in many respects antipathetic to the life of the mind, but young Hugh may not have been so forcibly struck by the contrast between his rude environment and the quality of his literary preoccupations as he certainly was when, years later, he recalled this period of his life in a fine dialect poem which deserves to be better known:

> Soon after this I gaed to Latin:
> And read a buke, I kenna what in,
> That talk'd o' things that whir in bushes,
> Dryads, Hamadryads, Muses,
> On tops o' hills wad sing like Mavies,

And in the shady woods, and cavies,
Thought I, it maun be this vile clearing,
And grubbing up the trees, and bleering,
And burning brush and making fences,
That scares these things out o' their senses;
And drives them frae our fields and patches;
For who sees any, now, or catches,
A moor-land deity or Nymphy,
That roosts in trees, or wades in lymphy?
Or hears a musy in the thicket,
Just as you wad hear a cricket?
May be in places farther back,
The vestige may na be sae slack;
Where woods are green and country new,
The breed may yet remain, a few,
May sing to mak' our spirits glow.[6]

Given his frontier upbringing, Brackenridge could never associate the West with a flourishing and respectable culture; yet when he went to Princeton to finish his education, he brought with him a mind still inclined to parallel Parnassus with the Alleghenies.

Princeton, under the presidency of John Witherspoon, was a notably cosmopolitan school, drawing students from all over the East and South and from a number of foreign countries. In this atmosphere, so different from anything he had previously known, Brackenridge continued his literary studies and took part in the fitful debates that forecast the coming Revolution. He joined the undergraduate Whig society and participated with Philip Freneau and James Madison in its literary war with their Tory counterparts, finding both politics and satire to his liking. In his junior year he collaborated with Freneau in writing *The Rising Glory of America* (1772), a prophecy of cultural fulfillment in the New World. Princeton, in short, gave him the values, manners, attitudes, and learning necessary to the American scholar–gentleman.

After graduation, Brackenridge tried out careers in the ministry and journalism, turning finally to the practice of law, but the momentous decision in his life, and the foundation of his literary career, was his selection of the remote village of Pittsburgh as the site of his law practice. A professional man, his education complete, he could expect to serve others as a model of civilized attainments, or, if not as a model, then as a source of guidance in political and cultural matters, since, as ever, the function of the gentleman is to allow himself to be emulated. Nowhere was such a model more needed than on the frontier; yet, as Brackenridge discovered, nowhere was it less likely to find acceptance. Secure now in his cultural values, he looked on the old frontier with new eyes and perhaps for the first time was acutely aware of an omnipresent western provincialism. If in observing these signs he was examining his own past, then the quality of his responses was an indication of just how far he had come. This change of perspective was surely an indispensable catalyst to his satire.

Brackenridge saw the effects of frontier life on the minds of provincials even before reaching Pittsburgh. Stopping for the night at the isolated wayside home of Hermon Husbands, he was regaled with a startling new interpretation of Ezekiel:

> It was the vision of the temple; the walls, the gates, the sea of glass, &c. Logger-head divines, heretofore, had interpreted it of the New Jerusalem; but he conceived it to apply to the western country; and the walls were the mountains, the gates, the gaps in them, by which the roads came, and the sea of glass, the lake on the west of us. I had no hesitation in saying, that the commentary was analogous to the vision. He was pleased; and said, I was the only person, except his wife, that he ever got to believe it. Thought I, your church is composed, like many others, of the ignorant and the dissembling.[7]

To Brackenridge such eccentricity was at best comic and harmless; at worst it was a sign of decay, evidence at once of the lapse of traditional learning and of the need for the mental culture that schools could provide. The many instances of such thinking that Brackenridge encountered impressed him always as aberrations, as the sort of intellectual eccentricity that children evince, and which are mainly attributable to immaturity. He scarcely suspected that such eccentricity might be fundamental to an evolving western mind, one independent of traditions, literal and innovative, that would yet have time to establish itself and resist vigorously the elite culture that eastern gentlemen insisted upon. As an eastern gentleman, Brackenridge was not interested in the etiology of west-Pennsylvania thought patterns, and gave them no more attention than was necessary to discount and discourage them. Still, the point must be made that he always noticed them. His eastern education and western environment gave him an extraordinary sensitivity to substandard usage and to cultural aberrations of all sorts, which he pilloried in his satires. But in the end he underestimated his opponents. The eccentricity of the frontier interpretation of Ezekiel was not, as Brackenridge thought, an isolated and unpredictable instance of the forest freedom, but part of a large and coherent pattern that he simply failed to discern. Because Hermon Husbands was himself physically isolated in the frontier and had lost contact with prevailing modes of thought, it did not necessarily follow that his own thinking would be purely idiosyncratic. Such apparently bizarre interpretations might naturally occur – and frequently did occur – to unsophisticated persons, convinced of the vital importance and reality of religious truth, who yet have no other standard or measure of reality than the environment immediately surrounding. Hermon Husbands's provincial mentality is akin to that of the Kentucky Baptist preacher who strained to give his audience a lively sense of the joys of heaven: "O my dear honeys," he told a meeting at Paint Lick in 1818, "heaven is a Kentucky of a place."[8] That Brackenridge himself had assimilated something of this mentality is evidenced in his dialect poem; his own youthful expectation of finding a "musy in the thicket" – that is, of locating a distinctly cultural solace in his immediate environment – bears more than a coincidental relation to patterns of thought that in others he found ridiculous.

Bound by the cultural assumptions of an eastern gentleman, Brackenridge seriously underestimated the weedlike persistence and characteristic integrity of western thought. He seems also to have underestimated the broad appeal of its intrinsically democratic implications. Like Hermon Husbands, however, Brackenridge was determined not to lose the conviction he had of the reality of *his* culture. Instead of relinquishing standards that were so painfully besieged, he found them, as time passed, more and more personally important. He became, as Cooper would later become, the embattled conservative par excellence, the professional gentleman, virtually a caricature of the culture he so assiduously defended.

The descent into caricature is a wholly typical element in the frontier attenuation of culture.[9] The adjustments that a defender of culture must make in the face of opposition, the exaggerations induced by forever being challenged, the compromises that subtly insinuate themselves – these were the conservative's worst and most dangerous enemies. From them arose the misconceptions that defeated Brackenridge more certainly than the ignorance and antipathy of those whom he sought to win over. The triumph of the conservative's designs can only be complete if he himself resists change. But in the adverse circumstances of a frontier environment even retrenchment involves change; he necessarily becomes a publicist, alternately combative and defensive, perpetually in motion, perpetually expending energy in an effort to stand still. His perceptions are necessarily altered, occasionally to the enrichment of our literature, but always to the detriment of the conservative's own cause.

Because he lived on the frontier in an area of cultural attenuation, Brackenridge felt, as he would not otherwise have felt, the intense reality and importance of intellectual culture. Religion and morality, on the other hand, as distinct from intellectual culture, seemed utterly natural to him, neither important nor unimportant, but rather neutrally present to his consciousness because they were not under constant siege. His son, Henry Marie, wrote of the consequences that such perceptions had on his own education:

> My religious and moral principles were left to spring up sponta-
> neously, the cultivation of the intellect being erroneously consid-
> ered all-sufficient. . . . Vice and impiety may be regarded as follies
> in the eye of reason, and the mind rightly trained may be supposed
> to view them in that light; and such was the philosophy of my
> father, who was a perfectly honest man, – so much so that he
> scarcely allowed more than a negative merit to mere honesty, but
> thundered terrific denunciations against the opposite quality.[10]

Although the philosophy of the elder Brackenridge had evidently been influenced by French rationalism, he was certainly helped to his appre-ciation of reason by the irrational and eccentric behavior that he observed on the frontier. His European culture was at least in that sense domes-ticated. He knew from local experience and not from the philosophes that civilization, as opposed to mere goodness or piety, constituted, in a special sense, the exceptional being. More than anything else, the fron-tier had confirmed his respect for culture. The simple virtues seemed to flourish unattended, but the determination to avoid being brutalized or made ridiculous involved anyone living away from the centers of culture in a painfully self-conscious and laborious effort. The frontier also had shown Brackenridge how precarious an affair civilization really was, how tenuous its hold on people, how liable to degenerate, as though it might dissolve into nothing if even for a moment one's attention were withdrawn.

For all its roughness and incivility, the frontier still appealed to Brack-enridge. Not only did it remind him of his boyhood home, but it offered him unparalleled opportunities for professional recognition and even po-litical power, which he regarded, in the spirit of Franklin, as opportunities to "do good" where service was needed. He shows, if proof were re-quired, that cultural conservatism is not incompatible with political lib-eralism. A follower of Jefferson, Brackenridge had a genuine faith in the possibilities of democracy, and found that he could excuse much in the behavior of his frontier neighbors on the grounds of a political faith in the common man. He was himself, of course, a "common man." He has been described accurately as an "aristocratic democrat,"[11] one who, like Jefferson, believed that the task of democracy was to discover the aristoi, the "natural gentlemen," and make use of their capacity for wise, judicious leadership. Although his frontier constituents were not always appreciative, turning him out of office once in favor of an illiterate weaver (as he characterized his opponent in Modern Chivalry), his political lib-eralism allowed him to take a generally humorous view of what his cultural conservatism might otherwise have led him to condemn with bitter sarcasm. One supposes that, were it not for his political philosophy, he would have found the frontier a nearly intolerable environment. In that respect he was fortunate.

Other cultural conservatives did not have the political liberalism that might have helped them see past the crudity of the West, nor the humor that might have enabled them to tolerate it. Such a one was the Reverend Timothy Dwight, the Federalist "Pope of Connecticut," a dogged opponent of Jeffersonian democracy and an interesting contrast to Brackenridge. Like most responsible, educated, conservative New Englanders of his generation, Dwight despised the frontier and all that it was taken to stand for. Accustomed to a well-regulated society that kept man's fallen nature carefully in check, Dwight time and again denounced the irreligious wantonness and the dissoluteness of manners that characterized the disestablished life of the West. The best that he could ever say of the frontier was that by draining off malcontents from his native Connecticut, it helped to confirm the state's social and cultural solidarity.

The reasons for Dwight's disgust with the frontier were as complex as his animosity was strong. During the Revolution his father and a few of his brothers had gone west rather than stay and commit themselves to either side of the conflict at home.[12] Their plan had been to establish a New England–style settlement on the Mississippi, but the project was hardly begun before Dwight's father (who was also Jonathan Edwards's son-in-law) succumbed to fever and died in Natchez in 1778. His sons, harassed by Indians and robbed repeatedly, ultimately gave up in defeat. All this sad news arrived in Connecticut where Timothy Dwight, recently married and recently ordained, was serving as a chaplain in the Continental Army. He realized at once the necessity of going back to the family home in Northampton, and there, for the next five years, he worked to support his mother and twelve siblings. Thus the frontier may be a hardship for some who never stir from the Connecticut Valley.

His attitude toward the frontier was only hardened by his direct observations in later years. There sin and sickness seemed to him endemic. With no institutions to regulate behavior, men grew coarse, materialistic, democratic, and, worst of all, indifferent to religion; they became at last little better than the Indians, and in some respects, as Dwight pointed out, far worse. The tours he took through New England for the sake of his health brought him up short before the Vermont log cabin, a symbol to Dwight of perfect shiftlessness: "If a poor man builds a poor house," he wrote, "without any design or hope of possessing a better, he will either originally, or within a short time, conform his expectations to the style of his house."[13]

Like Brackenridge, Dwight understood that the future of America lay

in the uncleared forests of the West, and was therefore concerned to see
that frontier lawlessness and cultural retrogression neither destroyed nor
tainted the careful balance of eastern society; whatever transregional influence was to occur should instead be all in the other direction. The
great work that Dwight thus set about to accomplish seems like a magnificent metaphor of his father's failed hopes; he proposed, in the words
of a recent biographer, to "Connecticutize the world."[14]

For Dwight, as for Tyler, the worst effect of the frontier was that it
was too "nat'r'l"; that is, it gave too much freedom to fallen human
nature; yet neither he nor Tyler seems to have grasped fully that their
ideal society was not so much a Puritan construct as a secular and cultural
one. In Dwight's frontier consciousness, human happiness depended less
on such traditional concepts as saving grace than on owning property,
maintaining a satisfactory degree of cultural sophistication, and having
the public institutions and private habits that would preserve the souls
of men from a frontier degradation.

Dwight's own "frontier thesis," unlike Turner's, stressed the emergence of culture; the first settlers, the "foresters,"

> cannot live in regular society. They are too idle; too talkative; too
> passionate; too prodigal; and too shiftless; to acquire either property
> or character. They are impatient of the restraints of law, religion,
> and morality; grumble about taxes, by which Rulers, Ministers,
> and Schoolmasters, are supported; and complain incessantly, as well
> as bitterly, of the extortions of mechanics, farmers, merchants, and
> physicians; to whom they are always indebted. At the same time,
> they are usually possessed, in their own view, of uncommon wis-
> dom; understand medical science, politics, and religion, better than
> those, who have studied them through life; and although they man-
> age their own concerns worse than any other men, feel perfectly
> satisfied, that they could manage those of the nation far better than
> the agents, to whom they are committed by the public...they
> become at length discouraged: and under the pressure of poverty,
> the fear of gaol, and the consciousness of public contempt, leave
> their native places, and betake themselves to the wilderness.[15]

These off-scourings of civilized society leave no lasting impression on
anything; they merely clear the wilderness and temporarily occupy it,
sinking still further into barbarism. They build log houses and partially
improve the land, but they ultimately sell out to more responsible and
industrious emigrants. "The proprietor," Dwight tells us, "is always
ready to sell: he loves this irregular, adventurous, half-working, half-
lounging life; and hates the sober industry, and prudent economy, by
which his bush pasture might be changed into a farm."[16] The energetic

farmer attracts neighbors, and the rudiments of a social order begin to take shape. By his thrift and industry he prospers and is soon able to build a respectable frame house:

> Among the pleasures, furnished by the melioration of [these farm-ers'] circumstances, the exchange of their log-huts for decent houses must not be forgotten.... This is a change, always bringing with it a train of advantages. The comfort, the spirit, the manners, nay even the morals, of his family, if not of himself, are almost of course improved. The transition from a good house is, by the association of ideas natural to the human mind, a very easy one to good furniture; a handsome dress; a handsome mode of living; better manners; and everything else connected with a higher reputation.[17]

In Dwight's view, as Kenneth Silverman has pointed out, "the settler refines and civilizes what in turn refines and civilizes him. He does not aim at grabbing land but at founding a community."[18] This is, Dwight argued, "the New England way of settling," and as a concept it reflects his assumption that people need a stake in society to prod them along in the essentially unnatural direction of refinement and civilization. His concern with property, in other words, was ultimately subordinate to his concern with the idea of community and with the kind of social order that could be fixed and perpetuated by traditional institutions. This prog-ress in turn would have the effect of fixing and perpetuating those in-stitutions – the church, the schools, the legal system – that Dwight was all along hoping to preserve. "The New England way of settling" would keep the values of Connecticut flourishing in Ohio when the last solitary forester had ended his brutish and alienated life.

The western threat of the overly natural life was balanced by an even more insidious threat from the East, one that Dwight's concept of set-tlement would seem at first glance to encourage. The effete overrefine-ment of the eastern cities was finally no more acceptable to Dwight than to Royall Tyler. Between these two forms of decadence there was little to choose; each in its peculiar way declared the irrelevance of the old institutions and undermined the delicate balance of the Connecticut model. On the frontier, itinerant preachers, each a law unto himself, were busily misrepresenting the word of God to ignorant audiences; in Boston, in John Cotton's old church, the sophisticated and very modern Charles Chauncy was making the way smooth for the Universalist heresy. Dwight spoke sharply of the "Boston style" and maintained that the term was universally understood "to denote a florid, pompous manner of writ-ing."[19] That such an objection could come from the author of *The Con-quest of Canaan* illustrates the confusions that were inescapably a part of provincial life. For Dwight, as for other American writers, the attraction of high-culture models was intense, but it was also continually being undermined by a suspicion that such models were dangerously out of place in American society.[20]

By condemning as a fault a leading characteristic of his own verse, Dwight also suggests that the threat from the East was harder to guard against and less easily articulated than the threat from the West. In his conception of the progress of culture Americans were, and ought to be, moving in the direction of improvement and refinement, but only so that they could at some point stop. Tyler shared this assumption: Jonathan ought to be educated to Manly's standard, but ought somehow to have the moral sense to resist the overrefinement of Charlotte or Dimple. Paradoxically, the advocates of a perfect social and cultural stability recognized the need for change; to stand still requires considerable movement. The implications of this paradox were clear enough to Dwight. Between culture and anarchy, between East and West, between freedom and restraint, between wealth and poverty, between extremes of all sorts, lay an attractive and stable middle ground, a golden mean toward which all movement ideally tended. There he would settle in his hyperconscious New England way and preach the virtues of a calculated mediocrity.

Provincial Connecticut, of course, rather than the frontier, was for Dwight that middle landscape. Here all the valuable pleasures of a well-ordered life were secured by a "Competence" that permitted no soul-destroying luxury. This argument forms the attractive center of his finest work in verse, the poem *Greenfield Hill*:

> But chief, Connecticut! on thy fair breast
> These splendours glow. A rich improvement smiles
> Around thy lovely borders; in thy fields
> And all that in thy fields delighted dwell.
> Here that pure, golden mean, so oft of yore
> By sages wished, and prais'd, by Augur's voice
> Implored, while God th'approving sanction gave
> Of wisdom infinite; that golden mean,
> Shines unalloy'd; and here the extended good,
> That mean alone secures, is ceaseless found.[21]

The only thing that set Connecticut apart from Utopia in Dwight's mind was that Connecticut had the blessed fortune to exist as a physical fact; its virtues and felicities were not merely theoretical but were there to be seen, the end product of an actual historical process.

In his social commentary Dwight carefully avoided all appearance of theory, and indeed often went out of his way to impugn theoretical perspectives, insisting that the country could do no better than to take an actual Connecticut rather than some visionary democracy for its model. His own gloss on the passage quoted above illustrates his intense disapproval of human tinkering with all that providence and the common sense of his Puritan ancestors had established as successful:

> The happiness of the inhabitants of Connecticut appears, like their manners, morals, and government, to exceed any thing, of which the Eastern continent could ever boast. A thorough and impartial development of the state of society, in Connecticut, and a complete investigation of the sources of its happiness, would probably throw more light on the true methods of promoting the interests of mankind, than all the volumes of philosophy, which have ever been written. The causes, which have already produced happiness, will ever produce it. To facts alone, therefore, ought we to resort, if we would obtain this important knowledge. Theories are usually mere dreams; fitted to amuse, not to instruct; and Philosophers, at least political ones, are usually mere Theorists. The common sense of the early Colonists of New England saw further into political subjects, those at least, which are of great importance to human happiness, than all the Philosophers, who have written since the World began. [22]

Although this passage was probably written several years after the lines of verse to which it refers – most likely in 1793 or 1794, when the lessons of the French Revolution had been well learned – Dwight's wholesale rejection of philosophy in favor of common sense and immediate observation is characteristic of frontier provincialism; it is to politics what folk painting is to academic art, and corresponds in his poetry to his preference for self-evident statement in place of interpretive analysis or figurative expression. Extend that preference far enough and one arrives at an American poetry of the Real. But any such extension would have been inconsistent with Dwight's contempt for extremes and would certainly have seemed to him a capitulation to a gross and circumstantial view of reality.

Greenfield Hill (written in 1787 and published in 1794) is Dwight's great paean to mediocrity, "Competence," and the golden mean. The texture of the poem is consistent with its thematic concerns and might be aptly described in the phrase a "rough smoothness." If Dwight's idea of cultural progress is to have "the howling forest polish'd as the plain," [23] then his idea of poetic achievement is implicitly to have the circumstantial consciousness softened and refined by a technical accommodation with literary tradition, or, in other words, to serve up New England's humble yet wholesome hasty-pudding in the approved metric and generic traditions of English poetry. The same impulse that led Tyler to find in

Sheridan a showcase for Manly and Jonathan led Dwight to attempt to imitate the standard poets of England in the various parts of his poem.

This design of Dwight's – of imitating James Thomson's *Seasons* in the first part, Oliver Goldsmith's *Deserted Village* in the second, James Beattie's *Minstrel* in the fourth, of echoing at various other points Virgil, Pope, Milton, John Dyer, and John Gay, of employing the distinctive metrics of Spenser and Edward Moore, of imitating in verse the prose of Franklin's *Way to Wealth* in the sixth part – produced, of course, no unified impression, an error hardly excusable in a poem ostensibly describing a harmonious society. For this failure Dwight could only apologize in his introduction, and thereby add his mite to the growing American tradition of the shamefaced author which had begun with Anne Bradstreet:

> Originally the writer designed to imitate, in the several parts, the manner of as many British Poets; but finding himself too much occupied, when he projected the publication, to pursue that design, he relinquished it. The little appearance of such a design, still remaining, was the result of distant and general recollection. Much, of that nature, he has rejected, had not even that rejection demanded more time than he could afford for such a purpose. These facts will, he hopes, apologize to the reader, for the mixed manner which he may, at times, observe in the performance.[24]

One might suspect a ruse in Dwight's protestation that he could not "afford" the time to polish and refine his work. On the other hand, he was, in all probability, deeply uncertain about the value or the "moral importance" of style. The implication that "such a purpose" is unworthy obscures the likelihood that the job exceeded his talents or patience. In any event, the poem *said* what he wanted it to say, and the additional increment of amusement that a more nearly perfect style could offer must have seemed frivolous when Dwight considered the significance of its didactic intent. If in this connection one thinks back to Richard Mather's famous defense of literary awkwardness in his preface to *The Bay Psalm Book* – "God's Altar needs not our polishings" – one senses something more than a mere rejection of unworthy concerns about style. It becomes evident that both writers are constrained by a fear that style is in itself an impediment to the transmission of important ideas, that it is, in itself, a source of corruption. So, in *Greenfield Hill* style and content are again at odds and the author himself is aware of it; if, however, the "manner" seems "mixed" the poem's obsessive allusiveness (with notes giving sources) is sufficient proof that the poet is no rube. Dwight noticed style and admired it tremendously. Evidence of his intense regard for elegant artistic expression is clear in his frequent remarks on poetry and especially on architecture, though when he himself wrote verse his style, as he understood it, always turned out cracked and compromised. *Greenfield Hill* remained, for all the halfhearted patching he did, a sampler of the culture of the mother country. Its provincial quality is quite unmistakable.

What coherence the poem achieves is likewise a product of imitation. The few critics who have been concerned to demonstrate some principle of unity in it have pointed out that the conventional device of the topographical poem – having the narrator survey a local scene from the top of some eminence – serves, if rather mechanically, to unite the many disparate observations. But the eclectic style that Dwight hit upon has obscured the poem's true generic allegiance. The accident of Dwight's strong attachment to his home region has led readers to the unprofitable conclusion that *Greenfield Hill* is a landscape poem; in fact it is squarely within a tradition that originated with Virgil's *Georgics* and includes Pope's *Windsor Forest* and Sir John Denham's *Cooper's Hill*. *Greenfield Hill* is a georgic, and, for all its problems, the most successful example of the genre in American literature.

The georgic tradition differs from the later topographical tradition in concerning itself with political rather than aesthetic issues. Virgil's *Georgics* presumes to instruct in matters political and to that end subordinates the farming theme, symbolically and emblematically, to the more significant theme of imperial government. The purely topographical poem, such as Dyer's *Grongar Hill*, merely exploits the aesthetic qualities of a ruggedly handsome terrain, and is to poetry what the works of Salvator Rosa and Claude Lorrain are to painting. In the Virgilian scheme, the georgic falls between the extremes of the humble pastoral (the *Eclogues*) and the heroic epic (the *Aeneid*), so that Dwight's decision to adopt this tradition was again consistent with his instinctive avoidance of extremes.

Like Tyler, Dwight had to convert a European tradition to the American scene. Some of this adaptation, as in Tyler's case, was done for him by his provincial understanding of the form. These adaptations may perhaps best be seen by comparing *Greenfield Hill* to *Cooper's Hill*. To read the two poems side by side is to be impressed by the relative "flatness" of Dwight's mind, a flatness that is strikingly analogous to that pictorially represented by the untutored portrait painters of early America. In poetry, flatness is achieved by an inexorably linear development of thought and image. Dwight rarely writes a line of poetry that illuminates or even recalls a previous one. Conceptions are not built up, and thereby given a third dimension of depth, but are simply laid end to end, one image succeeding or superannuating its predecessor. This approach would seem to be the mental habit of one for whom, whatever his protestations to the contrary, the present is important and the past functionally unreal.

Such a mind is, for example, prone to exploit set pieces. The moral or political didacticism of Dwight's poem is often, in fact, concentrated and marked off in exemplary tales, which nineteenth-century anthologists found easily detachable. One such occurs in the sixth part, the "Farmer's Advice to the Villagers," in which the narrator warns of the eccentricities of fortune typical of an ill-regulated society. The first generation, "firm, busy, plodding, poor, / Earns, saves, and daily swells, his store;"[25] finally prosperous, the successful man is prompted by a love that is really no better than indulgence to be overly generous with his son:

> Ambitious then t'adorn with knowledge
> His son, he places him at college;
> And sends, in smart attire, and neat,
> To travel, thro' each neighbouring state;
> Builds him a handsome house, or buys,
> Sees him a gentleman, and dies.[26]

The son, bred to wealth, ease, and luxury, has of course no starch in him, and so declines into debauchery, sloth, and final ruin. *His* son, therefore, finds himself in his grandfather's position and the cycle is begun again. The specific point of the story is not, really, that morals ought to be reformed (a desirable goal, but too visionary); rather, Dwight is arguing that extremes of wealth and poverty ought to be regulated into mediocrity. Here the poet sounds more than a little like Robinson Crusoe's father with his admiration for "the middle way." But Dwight had something other than Christian virtue on his mind; he felt that the finest and most hopeful aspect of democracy was its suggestion that change itself could be overcome, that the accidental vagaries of circumstance might be submerged in a broad equality of condition. The wild fluctuations of society, its cycles of rise and decline, might, like the "howling forest," be tamed into uniformity. The vision that lay behind the scheme was an ultimate freedom from circumstance, a final decisive defeat for the enemy of tradition and culture in America.[27]

Logically the set piece applies a principle that pervades *Greenfield Hill*. Its function in the larger fabric of the poem is as *one more* application intended for an audience to whom the principle itself is of little or no metaphysical interest. Even Dwight's concern with the principle is limited to its ability to generate examples; and in this restricted intellectual curiosity, this delight in cultivating the periphery and ignoring the centers of questions, Dwight's consciousness shows its affinities with his American frontier audience rather than with anything distinctively English.[28] The difference here between an English and a frontier American consciousness may be illustrated or clarified by reference to Denham's handling of a similar idea in *Cooper's Hill*. That Denham's mind is especially reflexive rather than linear is evident in the first lines of the poem; his fascination with the relations of source and issue is intellectual and witty, and deliberately nonlinear:

> Sure there are Poets which did never dream
> Upon Parnassus, nor did taste the stream
> Of Helicon, we therefore may suppose
> Those made not Poets, but the Poets those,
> And as Courts make no Kings, but Kings the Court,
> So where the Muses and their train resort,
> Parnassus stands; if I can be to thee
> A Poet, thou Parnassus art to me.[29]

A few lines later, surveying London's commercial activity from the distant prospect of Cooper's Hill, Denham points with a languid superiority to that place

> Where, with...haste, through several ways, they run
> Some to undo, and some to be undone;
> While luxury, and wealth, like war and peace,
> Are each the others ruin, and increase.[30]

In treating the idea by analysis rather than dramatic example, and by maintaining the terms of discourse at a relatively high order of abstraction, Denham keeps the reader's attention at the level of the principle itself, where all the pleasure of the poetry resides in the disengaged and intellectual quality of its play. Luxury and wealth, we are surprised and delighted to learn, are opposites whose antagonism is expressible by another pair of opposites, ruin and increase. We have, as readers, the distinct impression that Denham has conveyed more in these four lines than Dwight had in all the eighty-five lines of his exemplum. The difference is not merely that Dwight is accommodating a different audience; he *shares* the provincial incapacities of his American audience, and finally writes to a great extent as he can, not as he would. His awareness of the flat, patched quality of his poem, and of the fact that he did *not* write "as he would" is there to be judged in the apology of his introduction.

This difference of consciousness between Denham and Dwight goes much deeper. Because Denham is genuinely interested in the principle, that principle is constantly available to him to help organize and unify his poem. This sort of unity adds immeasurably to the comparative richness of *Cooper's Hill*. On the other hand, the accidental and disconnected quality of *Greenfield Hill* is the natural result of Dwight's relative indifference to the informing idea as idea, and of his frontier preference for the example. One notices the same thing in Dwight's prose, partic-

ularly in the *Travels*, a work that absolutely teems with statistics, anec-
dotes, curiosities, biographical sketches and innumerable other digressions,
but has little besides a casual observance of geographical boundaries to
unify the parts. Even more than the poem, the *Travels* is, in a very
American way, a stew of experience.

Although it is certainly true to say that Dwight's mind was empirical,
the term itself explains nothing of the peculiarly successful failure that
Dwight achieved in *Greenfield Hill*. Any real explanation, so far as there
can be one, must recognize that this particular empirical intelligence,
with its acute sense of the rural environment, tried to express itself in a
mode that had always in the past been highly intellectualized and symbolic, and related only in a deceptively tentative way to the facts of rural
life. In the georgic tradition, the "facts" were symbols of the informing
ideas; Dwight's facts, however, *were* the idea. Life in Connecticut, in
other words, was not a symbol for the perfect state, it *was* perfect –
except that here and there, for the sake of pointing a moral, someone
might be struggling to achieve the ideal Connecticut reality, or else might
have passed beyond it into decadence. In these meaningful deviations lies
the key to the Americanness of Dwight's empiricism. His attention was
constantly coming to focus on the essentially restless evidence of a fractured culture, on those poignant details that ever marred his Utopian
picture.

As Dwight surveyed the noble prospect, his eye was always, annoy-
ingly, drawn to the ignoble log hut. Here then was a detail that de-
monstrably did have symbolic meaning even if its more pleasant context
did not. It annoyed and preoccupied him, in one sense, for the very
reason that it *was* symbolic, that is, because its significance was excessive
and therefore disruptive of that "neutral consciousness" identified with
ideal home feeling. Dwight's objections to the log house, as we have
seen, were primarily social and pertained to what it signified about social
and cultural regression (i.e., about the abandonment of home), but he
as often, almost interchangeably, couched his remarks in aesthetic terms.
Concerning the houses, Dwight wrote that "although they are often
absolutely necessary to the planter, when he first adventures into the
forest, yet they are certainly no ornaments to the landscape."[31] But it
was not, or not merely, the inherent ugliness of the details that gave
them their power to dismay; they testified, for Dwight, to the subju-
gation of the human spirit to necessity and circumstance. The fact that
the eye could not well take in a view that had a log house in it shows
the power of these overwhelmingly petty details to divide and scatter
one's consciousness; against such details the poet would struggle in vain
for unity. Instances of disharmony in a fundamentally harmonious society
are naturally discrete experiences to the observer, and Dwight failed to

overcome that enforced sense of discreteness in his poem. He failed to unify his "examples" for the same reasons that Brackenridge was drawn to the picaresque mode, and, indeed, for the same reasons that prevented American writers before the emergence of a romantic aesthetic from achieving a satisfactory artistic coherence in their productions.

A series of examples can only be unified by reference to the principle exemplified, and if the poet is functionally unconscious of that principle, it is clear that he must forgo the advantages of unity. Late in *Cooper's Hill*, Denham echoes his earlier treatment of the interdependence of opposites, but this time in the specifically imperial context of the georgic form:

> Thus Kings, by grasping more than they could hold,
> First made their Subjects by oppression bold:
> And popular sway, by forcing Kings to give
> More than was fit for Subjects to receive,
> Ran to the same extreams; and one excess
> Made both, by striving to be greater, less.[32]

The way in which this passage recalls the other is no mere technical trick, nor is the echo merely rhetorical. By treating the same principle, laying out the relationship of opposites (power and obedience), and thereby revealing the nature of their mutual dependency, Denham achieves three separate, or at least separable, artistic triumphs at once. First, he impresses the reader with a sense of novelty by allowing one to see the same principle of self-regulating compensation at work in a new and different context; second, he impresses the reader with something very nearly the opposite of novelty by eliciting a recognition that this principle pervades all of nature; and third, by keeping the principle so clearly before the reader, Denham assures the integrity of his poem.

Yet what makes a satisfactory poem from this standpoint is precisely what Dwight would likely object to in it, and which he did object to in European culture generally. What, in other words, strikes us now as denseness and richness, Dwight tended to dismiss as hyperrefinement. Although he admired Pope and Denham to the point of imitating them, their poetry stood convicted of a frivolous toying with ideas for no good or worthy purpose, and of being what Dwight chiefly opposed: abstract, morally disengaged, concerned more with their own internal integrity than with any practical benefit to man. Herein lies the historical irony that throughout American literary history up to the Civil War would haunt and dismay creative writers. Dwight assumed a style that he simply could not support. In a gesture of pure sentiment, a gesture of purely abstract regard for European culture, he embraced a style that he could neither grasp intellectually nor approve morally, and that the involuntary workings of his frontier consciousness distorted and simplified, and, in a word, made American. Can we be surprised, therefore, that he apologized for the result?

In the face of this perennial difficulty, Dwight took a rationalizing comfort in the mediocrity of his environment, pointing out that, unlike the frontier and unlike the cities, Connecticut was by and large free of disturbingly substandard or suprastandard cultural elements. He is in effect saying that here is a place where, whatever problems it may pose for the artist, one can happily live. If circumstances limited the artistic mind in America and made provincialism inevitable, the only course left open to the self-respecting American conservative was to defend provincialism itself, as Dwight did, for example, in this passage, written in 1813:

> *The mediocrity of our circumstances* has often been an object of ridicule, as well as of contempt, with *Englishmen*. Here, however, it is believed to be a source of no small happiness to the inhabitants. There is, it must be acknowledged, much less splendour; much less to admire; much less to boast of. There are fewer palaces; fewer stupendous public buildings; fewer magnificent public works. But, Sir, one rich man is always surrounded by many who are poor; and one great man, by many who are little. Wretchedness always follows in the train of pomp, and rags and beggary haunt the mansions, as well as the walks, of pride and grandeur. If we have not many opulent inhabitants; we have few, that are indigent. If we have not palaces; we have few cottages. One would think, that a benevolent man would feel some satisfaction in looking around him, and seeing competence and enjoyment diffused universally.... To me, no prospect, confined to this world, has been so delightful, as that, which I am always sure to find, when travelling in this country; the great body of the inhabitants enjoying all the pleasure, *furnished by these very circumstances*. Surely, Sir, even you must be willing, that there should be one country of which these things may be said with truth.[33]

Dwight's theory, however, is a transparent attempt to make the best of a bad cultural situation, as evidenced by the enthusiasm he invariably registered in the *Travels* and elsewhere when noting improvement in the direction of English taste and sumptuousness. But the statement is significant as an early indication of a line of argument that a later generation, more secure in its cultural values, could adopt with greater conviction and less ambiguity.

Chapter 4

Geoffrey Crayon and the gigantic race

My brain is filled, therefore, with all kinds of odds and ends.
                                                    – Geoffrey Crayon[1]

The conservative struggle of American artists against provincialism was the complementary reverse side of the liberal campaign for a national literature. These two strong motives, with their respective psychological and political implications, relate to each other as the positive and negative prints of a photograph; that is to say, from opposite grounds they project the same image: the prospective fulfillment (even to "perfection") of the postponed cultural significance of America. This intimate relation through all the wide and fundamental differences is most apparent in the seeming contradictions and inconsistencies in the cultural pronouncements of American artists. Given the coincidence of the projected image, it is often difficult to distinguish between the literary nationalist, with his grudge against history, and the provincial Anglophile who wants nothing more than to have history reassert itself.

One finds a bona fide conservative such as Washington Irving, for example, a man temperamentally disposed to admire the traditions of Europe, intermittently attracted to the antihistorical myth of the new beginning. One finds, for another example, a man of liberal outlook, such as James Russell Lowell, typically contemptuous of European influence in America, speaking nostalgically of "...that Old World so strangely beautiful / To us the disinherited of eld."[2] Yet allowing that the conservative Irving may sometimes sound like the liberal Lowell and vice versa, there remains a fundamental difference, one that may for some make Irving the more interesting and compelling figure. These two men illustrate, positively and negatively, the fact that the artist who links the fate of beauty with the resuscitation of the past must, at least in America, live with the knowledge that he and it are losing. The point about Irving is not (as it really *is* with the critics who dismiss him) that he lives superfluously in the past, but rather that he lives, in ways important to his imagination, with loss, and that, perhaps, ought to commend him to our age. Lowell, on the other hand, rarely invests the past with a similar personal significance and so rarely, if ever, feels its loss as significant. Even in the lines quoted above from "The Cathedral," Lowell's imagination barely warms to the idea of disinheritance, which is merely, after all, a setting for hopeful statements about a democratic culture ungrounded in the past.

The campaigns of the literary nationalists were open and public, whereas the native artists' depressing consciousness of American provincialism was, by contrast, a quietly personal and private affliction. Embarrassed and discouraged by the immaturity of their cultural environment, these artists were for the most part reluctant to discuss the problem candidly and instead resorted to indirection and implication. Unlike the fully documented public sentiment in favor of a national literature, the private consciousness of provincialism remains obscure and almost unexplored, though it is finally a matter of greater historical importance, not only because it had to precede the campaign for a national literature as a motive for its expressions, but also because it was the source of the characteristic anxiety and insecurity that early American writers clearly felt – the source of a self-doubt that radically shaped their art. Of all these observations, Washington Irving's *Sketch-Book* may stand as an especially revealing illustration.

The essential issue addressed in *The Sketch-Book* is that of the relationship of American to English or Old World culture, whereas the unifying drama is supplied by Irving's indecision as to where in that relationship to place himself as an artist and as a man. The various sketches and essays contribute incrementally to some rather sharply realized summary conceptions of what America means in European terms and of what Europe means in American terms, but as Irving clarifies this relationship and explores the meaning of its polar configuration, he discovers that he has not at all settled the question of where he will make his home, nor, indeed, the question of just what "home" means to a provincial American artist. He discovers that the pursuit of art is very nearly related to the pursuit of older, traditional values, or at least of an artistic environment, associated with Europe but not with the United States, in which social, moral, and aesthetic values exist in a close, mutually dependent harmony, protected and virtually sanctified by the force of tradition. The anxious possibility with which Irving is recurrently concerned is that his commitment to art may take him out of sympathy with, or may ultimately debar him from, his American background. Not only had artistic accomplishment been long associated in the provincial mind with England, but art in America had typically been pursued as a means of liberating both artist and audience from the matrix of their ordinary associations. The result was a frontier consciousness of art as dangerously incompatible with home feeling, a perception that is at once a cause and a consequence of the frequent portrayals of failed and endangered homes, as well as of American artists' marked preference for the romance, an essentially provincial genre, over the novel.

The American Anglophile and the literary nationalist both recognized this problem and each sought ways to make "home" and "art" more compatible. The conservative solution was, as Dwight had said, to have "the forest polish'd as the plain," that is, to refine and give artistic significance to the environment itself rather than to reconsider the idea of art and so give up on tradition. Political and aesthetic motives merged behind this desire for an environment more conducive to the florescence of culture. Learning and the arts were then presumed to thrive when governments were stable and society at large content; conversely, the upheavals in revolutionary France together with the attendant weakening of traditional institutions were frequently held responsible for what seemed to some conservatives in the first years of the new century a recent and alarming decay of culture.[3] But the connection between culture and social and political stability had always been asserted more frequently and strenuously in America than in most other places because the presence of a frontier constantly stirred the imagination with visions of cultural and social disaster. "Where Schools are not vigorously and Honorably Encouraged," Cotton Mather had written, "whole *Colonies* will sink apace, into a Degenerate and Contemptible Condition, and at last become horribly Barbarous."[4]

The conservative dream from the seventeenth to the nineteenth century was that as civic and cultural values flourished and cross-fertilized, the country would more nearly approach the condition of a genuine community ("a more perfect Union"), and that by exertions on behalf of civilized values Americans would finally cease to be a frontier people and rediscover, on a new and better basis, their identity with Europe. The strength of this desire for a wider kinship, for a broader sense of cultural identity, has often been underestimated in light of the country's fascination with the unaffiliated American Adam; its artists, however, have affirmed it time and again, most vitally, perhaps, in the purely conservative myth of the English ancestral home. Irving, Hawthorne, James, and Twain all explored the meaning of this myth, but in fact it proved attractive to many lesser American writers during the century and to ordinary citizens as well.[5] As this myth helps to show, the effort to defeat provincialism was ultimately an effort to recover America's nearly lost history and to reaffirm its connection with a larger Atlantic community of which the United States was really but a fragment.

The special homage that Irving paid to English culture in *The Sketch-Book* needs to be understood as the natural consequence of a provincial education, one that identifies all that is most gracious and accomplished with an exotic foreign land which is nevertheless specially tied to one's own. Irving was aware of this quality of deference in himself and because it often made him uneasy he turned it frequently to humorous ends. "There is nothing so baleful to a small man as the shade of a great one, particularly the great man of a city," says Irving in his "Account of Himself":

> But I was anxious to see the great men of Europe; for I had read in the works of various philosophers, that all animals degenerated in America, and man among the number. A great man of Europe, thought I, must therefore be as superior to a great man of America as a peak of the Alps to a highland of the Hudson; and in this idea I was confirmed by observing the comparative importance and swelling magnitude of many English travellers among us, who, I was assured, were very little people in their own country. I will visit this land of wonders, thought I, and see the gigantic race from which I am degenerated.[6]

At times, Irving's attitude toward "the gigantic race" consisted in unaffected veneration; more often, as here, he chose to be gently satirical; but the absolute unintermitted necessity of *having* an attitude was the stamp of Irving's provincialism. In *The Sketch-Book* he is, in fact, constantly measuring himself against the stature of Europeans.

Anglo-American literary relations are the explicit subject of only one of the essays in *The Sketch-Book* – "English Writers on America" – which attempts to solve the problem of American provincialism by pretending that it is no problem at all. Sensing that the concept of the provincial is at bottom nothing but a means of making invidious and unprofitable distinctions, Irving tries to forestall condescension by insisting that a close national kinship with Britain makes all such slighting comparisons meaningless, arguing in effect that Americans, no less than their English cousins, are the legitimate inheritors of an identical cultural legacy. He notes that between the two nations there exists a "golden band of kindred sympathies" which places the culture of his homeland squarely within the continuing British tradition.

Irving is here engaged in a conscious act of appropriation. In an almost lawyer-like way, he hoped to vindicate American claims on English literary history, to domesticate that history, and in his own modest manner to extend it. But he went still further in the argument of "English Writers on America." Not satisfied simply to indicate the unity of Anglo-American culture, Irving proceeded to castigate those English critics who by constantly drawing attention to national differences acted out of the most parochial of motives. Disclaiming the narrow view and neatly turning the tables, he intimates that of the two nations America is the more cosmopolitan:

> What have we to do with national prejudices? They are the inveterate diseases of old countries, contracted in rude and ignorant ages, when nations knew but little of each other, and looked beyond their own boundaries with distrust and hostility. We, on the contrary, have sprung into national existence in an enlightened and philosophical age...and we forego the advantages of our birth if we do not shake off the national prejudices, as we would the local superstitions, of the old world.[7]

This may seem surprising doctrine coming from the American writer who more than any other perpetuated the "local superstitions of the old world" in the New; but the contradiction serves to emphasize the primary advantage that American circumstances, otherwise so limiting, offered to the conservative artist. The very absence of a proper history seemed to allow Americans the freedom to pick and choose the traditions they might wish to assimilate. In old countries, Irving felt, history simply denied people the capacity to choose and change; for Americans, however, history was a library of choices, ever yielding and usable. In fact, Irving ends his essay by rather grandly reducing the traditions of British culture to the practical benefits they offer to the free citizens of the new Republic: "We may thus place England before us as a perpetual volume of reference, wherein are recorded sound deductions from ages of experience; and while we avoid the errors and absurdities which may have crept into the page, we may draw thence golden maxims of practical wisdom, wherewith to strengthen and to embellish our national character."[8] Insofar as Irving can bring himself to regard the Old World as merely tributary to the New, Europe becomes the provincial edge, and America assumes the role of the new center.

This idea draws heavily on the old providential view of American destiny, but its more immediate source lies in the popular understanding of what the framers of the Constitution had done in 1787 in making a new government out of the odds and ends of old European systems. Examining the governments of Europe, ancient and modern, they had found elements worthy of imitation and had constructed from them a coherent system far better and more efficient than any of its predecessors. This masterful, pragmatic, eclectic relationship between the United States and Old World cultures, dramatized in the work of the founding fathers, was so enormously flattering to American national feeling that it continued for a long while after Irving gave it expression to engage the public imagination. In the nineteenth century much the most popular statement of the idea was Henry Wadsworth Longfellow's patriotic parable, "The Building of the Ship" (1849), in which a venerable shipwright, having mastered his art, is commissioned by a merchant–patron to build a perfect ship:

> ...as he labored, his mind ran o'er
> The various ships that were built of yore,
> And above them all, and strangest of all,
> Towered the Great Harry, crank and tall,
> Whose picture was hanging on the wall,
> With bows and stern raised high in air,
> And balconies hanging here and there,
> And signal lanterns and flags afloat,
> And eight round towers, like those that frown
> From some old castle, looking down
> Upon the drawbridge and the moat.
> And he said with a smile, "Our ship, I wis,
> Shall be of another form than this!"[9]

Being able literally to profit from the mistakes of the past, the American is still not bound by history. In Irving's essay as in Longfellow's poem, there is an emphasis on the American's freedom of choice that discloses a rather arrogantly judicial attitude toward old cultures as well as an indifference to historical circumstance that we should today call "presentism." Each is a "national prejudice" that stems from the detaching isolation of America's frontier experience and that typically finds expression in the reductive metaphor of the Old World as a Baedeker for America's tour of the future. The conservative who abhors cultural rootlessness and who suspects anxiously that Americans, to use Philip Rahv's phrase, "are afloat in history without moorings in prehistory,"[10] has here made up for the deficiency by advancing the mythic doctrine that *not* having a history gives Americans a valuable objectivity in regard to the history and cultures of other people less free, less happy, than themselves. The art envisioned in this doctrine is innovative without being original, dependent on tradition yet free and independent; it is an art that gathers odds and ends and adds the quickening fire. Irving, however, more certainly than Longfellow, knows that no matter how one counts the debits and credits in the American scene, the artist stands beyond the pale of history and tradition.

This large misgiving is much in evidence in "English Writers on America," which is not, after all, the work of some cocky Jonathan thumbing his nose at the English. The tone of the essay is actually quite conciliatory since a pragmatic, go-ahead approach to culture is not at all what Irving wants. He points out that for all America's freedom to choose the models it would imitate and to discard the mistakes of the past, England is in actual possession of "the fountain-head whence the literature of the language flows."[11] England *has* the traditions; Americans, on the other hand, "are a young people, necessarily an imitative one, and must take our examples and models, in a great degree, from the existing nations of Europe."[12] Although this line of reasoning appears to contradict the concurrent argument for the unity of Anglo-American culture, in fact it does not. From the time when permanent settlements were first established, America had been overwhelmingly English; yet, having lived for two hundred years on the remote rim of the British colonial empire, Americans found themselves in the ironic position of having to imitate their "own" culture.

Irving's contention that Americans are a "young people" refers ostensibly to the recent creation of the state by revolution, but in reality the context is cultural rather than political; the assertion of youth as an explanation of the need to imitate is an admission that the country's national experience with the frontier had deprived Americans of an original relation to their Old World background. Irving sees that, paradoxically, America was not born young, but evolved slowly into something like adolescence as British colonial culture lost the integrity of its style and thereby its capacity to connect Americans with Europe. His nostalgic dismay at the degenerative loss of origins (expressed complexly in "Rip Van Winkle") was not to be altogether placated by the thought of somehow creating an efficient patchwork culture from the odds and ends of observed European life; nothing of that sort could finally compensate for the loss of an orderly, organic transmission of past values. The solution was to struggle to reclaim America's own cultural history in all its restored continuity and fullness. Irving felt that, in such a task of clarification and recovery, imitation would inevitably be a primary tool, though he seems also to have believed that the need to imitate was circumstantial and temporary and would gradually disappear as America matured along more settled and conventional lines. By selecting and imitating "worthy" models, Americans simply affirmed those broad "kindred sympathies" which, obscured for a time by their frontier experience, naturally bound them to their Old World origins. In due time, their ties to Europe would again become organic and they would cease to be "a young people." Until then, however, the requirement of a frontier society for culture and a sense of origins would greatly outweigh the need to be original.[13]

Such convictions largely determined Irving's notion of what as an artist he should ideally be and do. His own imitativeness, for example, was both temperamental and functional. It not only placed him in the security of those traditions he sought to preserve (and so legitimized his art to himself), but it also served to promote the idea of tradition in all its attractiveness among his American audience.

The important though much neglected essay on "Roscoe" in the first installment of *The Sketch-Book* demonstrates Irving's belief that what was immediately called for in the United States were promoters and disseminators rather than propagators of culture. Especially needed were men such as William Roscoe, "the elegant historian of the Medici," who could rise above the most disadvantageous circumstances and, combining the roles of patron and artist, transmit the riches of the past in a scholarly, graceful manner to the present. Roscoe becomes the appropriate Old World model for the American scholar because he does *not* remove himself to some more congenial environment (as Irving had done), but instead strikes root "even in the clefts of the rock" of commercial, provincial Liverpool, and through his writings and his support of such local public institutions as the Athenaeum, turns his "sterile birthplace" into a center of culture and learning. Reviving the Roman and Florentine traits of civic consciousness, Roscoe avoids the irresponsibility of decadent European scholarship and so qualifies himself to stand as a model to Americans: "He has shut himself up in no garden of thought, nor elysium of fancy," Irving points out, "but has planted bowers by the wayside, for the refreshment of the pilgrim and the sojourner, and has opened pure fountains, where the laboring man may turn aside from the dust and heat of the day, and drink of the living streams of knowledge."[4] The special task of provincial artists, in other words, is not selfishly to save themselves but democratically to redeem the provincial environment.

Implicit in Irving's sketch is the belief that Americans, but not the jaded, worldly-wise English, know how to appreciate such a man as Roscoe, whose art, appropriately enough, consists not in romantic originality but in bringing things together. When financial misfortune puts an end to his public career, he is regarded by his neighbors simply as a politician whose time has come, or as yet another banker who has failed. There is the suggestion that Roscoe's benevolence and liberality have failed to root out the suppressed but stubborn and self-defeating class jealousy of his Liverpool neighbors, which, at the forced sale of his personal library, rears up in comic malignity. Here Irving stops to imagine those who "thronged like wreckers" to the auction, "rummaging the armory of a giant, and contending for the possession of weapons which they could not wield"; he pictures "the air of intense but baffled sagacity with which some successful purchaser attempted to dive into the black-letter bargain he had secured."[5] What had been concentrated and quickened through force of character is now dispersed through lack of character, and it is the American, not the Englishman, who sees in this brief and otherwise unremarkable spectacle the lesson of the essential uninterchangeability of money and culture. It is the American who comprehends the full value of "that amiable and unostentatious simplicity of character, which gives the nameless grace to real excellence."[16] So, also, in Longfellow's poem, it is not the merchant's money, but the character of the old shipwright, "whose heart was in his work," that endows the disparate elements of a synthetic art with life: "and the heart / Giveth grace unto every Art."[17] In the expanding mythology of frontier consciousness, provincial innocence is being more and more clearly identified as a sure foundation for cultural perfection.

There are obvious links between the American desire for a "perfect" culture purified of European "error" and the conviction of millenarian religionists. Perhaps it is only to be expected that these two ideals should so often come together in an unsettled nation where religion and civilization were being simultaneously and deliberately promoted. Perhaps it is more inevitable still that the confusion should arise in a mind so marginally religious as Irving's. However that may be, it is indicative of the provincial temper that Irving managed to find in Roscoe a mythic reminiscence of Christ. Not only is he, as we have seen, the redemptive prophet who "opened pure fountains where the laboring men may. . . drink of the living streams of knowledge," but he is also that prophet who is tragically without honor in his own land. The sale of the books is a pathetic crucifixion, and Roscoe a nobly sacrificial figure who, asking little or nothing for himself, benefits others in ways they cannot comprehend. He stands for spiritual as opposed to commercial values, and presents "a picture of active, yet simple and imitable virtues, which are within every man's reach, but which, unfortunately, are not exercised by many, or this world would be a paradise."[18]

This messianic language may, from one point of view, be regarded as mere rhetorical investment, as a way of registering a provincially heightened admiration for the idea of culture and for those martyred heroes who sacrifice all in its name. But to do so would be to miss the genuine dramatic tension in the sketch, for what had begun as an apparently unequivocal recommendation to an American audience of a "worthy model," a successful, instructive instance of provincialism overcome, deepens under the pressure of Irving's typological impulse into a lesson about the inevitable cost to the artist of any attempt to redeem the provincial environment. Roscoe's penalty goes significantly beyond the loss of his books to include the loss of his "favorite residence," a "spacious mansion of freestone, built in the Grecian style."[19] Although we have Roscoe's valedictory address to his books to show his stoic acceptance on that point, we are told nothing of his subsequent life, and so are left to imagine him in the end as either dead or wandering. The individual who would have both art and a home must finally have neither, Irving seems to be saying, and the appropriate type of such a figure is Christ the dispossessed of Heaven, the Christ of Matthew 8:20.

Throughout *The Sketch-Book* Irving is concerned with the mythic penalty of separation from home. What gives this theme its unifying vitality is not so much the fact that Irving himself was away from home when the book was written, but rather that he could see his own artistic exodus to Europe in these mythic and national terms. His letters of this period are replete with longing references to home interspersed with justifications for staying abroad. On March 3, 1819, he writes to his brother Ebenezer that "it is important for me to remain a little longer in Europe, where there is so much food for observation, and objects of taste on which to meditate and improve."[20] A year and a half later, still in England, *The Sketch-Book* now finished, he is sounding like his own Rip Van Winkle:

What would I not give for a few days among the Highlands of the Hudson, with the little knot that was once assembled there! But I shall return home, and find all changed, and shall be made sensible how much I have changed myself. It is this idea which continually comes across my mind, when I think of home; and I am continually picturing to myself the dreary state of a poor devil like myself, who, after wandering about the world among strangers, returns to find himself a still greater stranger in his native place.[21]

Irving's slightly antiquated commitment to the psychology of "sensibility" facilitates the emotional drama of setting solid domestic values, and especially those of childhood, against the values of culture: the "Kaatskills" in conflict with "objects of taste." Neurotic and self-destructive as this may now seem, it is after all a rather typical expression of the predicament faced by American artists before the Civil War. They tended to believe that, although the local environment possessed important moral and personal associations, it was otherwise so devoid of distinction, so "unpolished," as to be positively a threat to art, or, conversely, that art was a threat to the values of hearth and home. The discrepancy that provincial Americans so often felt between style and content, between home and art, between Europe and America (each distinction coinciding and merging with the others), came to seem so radically decisive that one began naturally to think in terms of choice rather than synthesis, and at last to indulge the tragic emotions in contemplating the loss that either choice entailed. The American's freedom to choose became in this way the subject of public boasting and private misgiving. Irving was among the first to consider this issue seriously, and though his treatment forms a major part of his achievement, he merely penetrates the surface. Hawthorne, in *The Scarlet Letter*, searches the subject to its depths.

Home, as image or as ideal, figures so largely in American literature because of the troublesome relation it often bore to the writers' sense of art. The sentimental image of home, especially of the childhood home, was a popular nineteenth-century motif that provided endless opportunities for the writing of third-rate verse on both sides of the Atlantic. But the childhood home often figures in more substantial works of American literature less as a warm familiar scene than as an eccentric cultural environment, reflecting the writers' acknowledgment that they grew up in a provincial setting where art and tradition were fragmented. Just as John Greenleaf Whittier's imagination was forever affected by the avidity with which he read the few books available to him as a boy,[22] so Irving's imagination bears the stamp of his early environment, a provocative but miscellaneous assortment of disconnected traditions and superstitions, many of them Dutch. We read in "The Author's Account of Himself" that as

> a mere child I began my travels, and made many tours of discovery into foreign parts and unknown regions of my native city, to the frequent alarm of my parents, and the emolument of the town-crier. As I grew into boyhood, I extended the range of my observations. My holiday afternoons were spent in rambles about the surrounding country. I made myself familiar with all its places famous in history or fable. I knew every spot where a murder or robbery had been committed, or a ghost seen. I visited the neighboring villages, and added greatly to my stock of knowledge by noting their habits and customs, and conversing with their sages and great men.[23]

If, as so many of our writers have complained, life in America is circumscribed, experience contracted, and the materials of existence mundane or dreary, the deficiencies might still be rectified by an imagination sufficiently active (a "grasping imagination" in the Jamesian phrase) and by recourse to the purely local if the individual's need for culture is sufficiently strong. There is a befitting and thoroughly American innocence in Irving's notion of "add[ing] greatly to my stock of knowledge," and yet, of course, there is irony, too. He knows that this knowledge is on one level spurious, as undistinguished in its way as the contents of Tom Sawyer's pockets. This is the miscellaneous and fractured knowledge that one accumulates who is thrown on his or her own resources; it is "American knowledge," an intrinsically humorous counterpart to the superior knowledge of the "great man of Europe." Irving's own situation is much like that described by the Boston artist, John

Singleton Copley, who felt the poignant limits of his American condition: "I think myself peculiarly unlucky," he wrote to Benjamin West, then in England, "in liveing in a place into which there has not been one portrait brought that is worthy to be call'd a Picture within my memory, which leaves me at a great loss to gess the stil that You, Mr. Reynolds, and other Artists Pracktice."[24] Provincialism contributes to the vigor of the artists' work by requiring that they find for themselves new answers to the old questions of their craft, and often by intensifying through restriction the scope of their vision; but these benefits have their corresponding cost: artists are condemned to wonder whether their work has any value, whether their answers are not perhaps ridiculous. They must always doubt the value of their American knowledge.

Irving seems to have been particularly successful in balancing this doubt with confidence, much to the enrichment of *The Sketch-Book*. In the passage above, as in so much of his writing, Irving manages to imply that despite the standards of a senescent Europe, an American knowledge of odds and ends is essentially and fundamentally true. On this point he seems almost to have anticipated Thoreau, whose "travell[ing] a good deal in Concord" is a joyous acceptance of the limits that Irving felt in New York and that Copley resented so bitterly in Boston. There is something especially valid in the knowledge available close to home, with its unstylish tinge of earthiness, that makes the scholars of the British Museum fair game for the satirical treatment they receive in another *Sketch-Book* essay, "The Art of Bookmaking."

Irving suspected that the primitive was ultimately the source of the vitality of literature and that civilization provided its shape – a conception that Henry James (who paid more attention to Irving than did most of his contemporaries) would later explore and develop more fully. Like other American artists, Irving consciously conceived of his art in terms of a dissonance between form and substance. The form, he felt, was to be as highly civilized, as stylishly impeccable, and as classically chaste as it was in his power to make it, whereas the most suitable subject matter was legendary, touched by folk wisdom, dependent on locality rather than universality, and limited or provincial in scope. Thus, while getting his *Tales of a Traveller* together, he directed the following characteristic note to his brother, Peter:

I have been thinking over the German subjects. . . . There are such quantities of these legendary and romantic tales now littering from the press both in England and Germany, that one must take care not to fall into the commonplace of the day. Scott's manner must likewise be widely avoided. In short, I must strike out some way of my own, suited to my own way of thinking and writing. I wish, in everything I do, to write in such a manner that my productions may have something more than the mere interest of narrative to recommend them, which is very evanescent; something, if I dare to use the phrase, of classic merit, *i.e.*, depending upon style, &c., which gives a production some chance for duration beyond the mere whim and fashion of the day. I have my mind tolerably well supplied with German localities, manners, characters, &c., and . . . I trust I shall be able to spin them out very fluently.[25]

In making a smooth, fluent style rather than the rugged appeal of folk materials the final determinant of literary value and durability, Irving places himself in the traditional, conservative camp. The predicament in which he also placed himself – that of resorting to provincial material for the vital strength of his art while at the same time having to overcome it with style and culture – is among the most persistent of the problems confronted by American artists in the nineteenth century (and, one might add, a main source of the inappropriately fine rhetoric that Tocqueville objected to in American writing generally).[26]

The tendency to counter localizing content with universalizing style frequently left Irving bewildered and diffident; it contributed significantly to his sense of not quite belonging anywhere, and in the end made his treatment of the theme of homelessness all the more compelling.[27] Feeling the need to remain in touch with the primitive springs of life (which he associated with the "young giant," America), he nevertheless also felt that the primitive was, in a pejorative sense, childlike. In a nation that was everywhere growing up and civilizing itself, the defense of primitivism seemed increasingly irrelevant; nor could he, as an artist uncertain of the value of his art, afford to make a mockery of high culture. Intrigued by frontier values – as *Astoria, A Tour on the Prairies*, and *Captain Bonneville* show – he was in the latter half of his career more comfortable and less apologetic when, seeming to follow Roscoe, he turned his sights as historian and biographer on such established culture-heroes as Columbus, Goldsmith, Mahomet, and, finally, Washington. Irving was perhaps the first American writer to understand rather than merely reveal the artistic difficulties, the divisions, and antagonisms that a frontier consciousness entailed, and his scholarly treatment of this pantheon of representative men was the fruit of a personal resolution of just these issues. In *The Sketch-Book*, however, written while the problems seemed most lively and immediate, he explored them in the wholly appropriate context of the search for a satisfactory home. Would he be psychically more comfortable in an atmosphere of vitiated strength but of superior form and finish? In a nascent chaos or a decadent orderliness?

Geoffrey Crayon, the narrative persona of Irving's most celebrated

work, was a notoriously miscellaneous man, a dilettante genuinely accomplished in nothing at all though interested, apparently, in everything.
Responsible also for *The Crayon Miscellany*, he never claimed to be unduly
concerned about the formal unity of his productions. Irving was the first
to suggest that whatever coherence *The Sketch-Book* possessed lay in the
variety of its elements, in the stubbornness of their refusal to become a
connected narrative. Perry Miller captured the nuance of this contradiction when he said that we "must peruse the whole as a unit, observing
the conscious alternation of moods – for example, the jolt intended by
the shift from 'The Wife' to 'Rip' – in order to comprehend that Irving
had every right to call the result a *book* and not a collection of random
'sketches.' "[28] But the pattern of alternation in *The Sketch-Book* involves
more than mood; distinct themes run throughout the work and unify
the sketches. One device contributing to the structural unity is, of course,
the concept of the voyage itself; another is the alternation of attention
(often within essays) from England to America and back again, the way
a person might glance back and forth between two houses before choosing one for a home – once again in recognition that Americans are both
blessed and cursed with the freedom to make such choices. This motif
is introduced with utter explicitness in the epigraph from John Lyly that
heads the first essay:

> I am of this mind with Homer, that as the snaile that crept out of
> her shel was turned eftsoons into a toad, and thereby was forced
> to make a stoole to sit on; so the traveller that straggleth from his
> owne country is in a short time transformed into so monstrous a
> shape that he is faine to alter his mansion with his manners, and
> to live where he can, not where he would.[29]

The book organizes and presents the attractions (and some of the
problems) of living in England for a man of Irving's personal and artistic
sensibilities. "Rural Life in England" most ostensibly performs this function on the personal level, as does the picture of genial social life in the
five essays on Christmas. The lure of tradition and history is variously
presented in "The Country Church," "Rural Funerals," and "London
Antiques." The home that England affords to a literary man is examined
in "English Writers on America," "The Art of Bookmaking" (together
with its companion piece, "A Royal Poet," with its variations on the
themes in "Roscoe"), and especially in "Stratford on Avon."
    The ending of *The Sketch-Book* is particularly revealing. Relatively few
of the earlier selections had dealt primarily with Irving's native country,
but to conclude the work, he set four of the last six sketches in America.
Of these, the first two – "Traits of Indian Character" and "Philip of
Pokanoket" – constitute a statement of quintessential Americanness, and

are juxtaposed to "John Bull," Irving's playful summary of English traits.[30] The contrast that emerges is again that between power without form and form without power. Philip of Pokanoket, the Wampanoag sachem who led the revolt of 1675, is the subject of an explicit study in primitivism. Irving's introduction reveals much of his own personal concerns:

> In civilized life, where the happiness, and indeed almost the existence, of man depends so much upon the opinion of his fellow-men, he is constantly acting a studied part. The bold and peculiar traits of native character are refined away, or softened down by the levelling influence of what is termed good breeding; and he practices so many petty deceptions, and affects so many generous sentiments, for the purposes of popularity, that it is difficult to distinguish his real from his artificial character. The Indian, on the contrary, free from the restraints and refinements of polished life, and, in a great degree, a solitary and independent being, obeys the impulses of his inclination or the dictates of his judgment; and thus the attributes of his nature, being freely indulged, grow singly great and striking. Society is like a lawn, where every roughness is smoothed, every bramble eradicated, and where the eye is delighted by the smiling verdure of a velvet surface; he, however, who would study nature in its wildness and variety, must plunge into the forest, must explore the glen, must stem the torrent, and dare the precipice.[31]

We have come round again to Dwight's "forest polish'd as the plain," only to find that it is no longer so attractive as it once was. The difficulty of being civilized in America, of holding on to Old World values, made the conservative's task so thoroughly self-conscious and so laborious that culture ceased after a while to seem the perfect complement to nature that Dwight felt it was; instead, art and learning, gracious manners and old aesthetic values were being looked upon more and more frequently in terms of affectation, deception, and unreality. In America, a man who had to win his culture from a hostile environment was obviously "acting a studied part"; he was repudiating nature, or escaping from it, in favor of artifice. For the same reason style began to seem much like a way of eradicating substance, of polishing, refining, and smoothing away reality itself. The presence of frontier conditions, in other words, was conducive to the illusion that one had to choose between style on the one hand and substance, or "life," on the other. Not only is the inevitability of such a choice strongly implied in Irving's "own way of thinking and writing," as we have seen, but it is an especially American illusion, as Lionel Trilling argued so convincingly in "Reality in America."

The passage from "Philip of Pokanoket" quoted above suggests that style and culture had lost some of their value for Irving, but in spite of his misgivings (which seem here to verge on self-criticism) he remained committed to a search for "classic merit" in style and for the perennial beauty of the velvet surface, hoping in these to find some final shelter from raw circumstance and the degenerative mutations of time. He felt that the cultivation of a superior style provided the only victory possible to a provincial writer, and his reception in England undoubtedly confirmed him in this view. William Godwin spoke for many English readers when he said that he found everywhere in *The Sketch-Book* "the marks of a mind of the utmost elegance and refinement, a thing . . . that I was not exactly prepared to look for in an American."[32] The value of a smooth, graceful style, then, was just that it overcame the time and space that pejoratively defined American provincialism. But to resolve the dilemma in this manner laid Irving open to an objection specifically anticipated in "Philip" and later expressed by Herman Melville, who faulted him precisely for exchanging "life" for style:

> . . . that graceful writer, who perhaps of all Americans has received the most plaudits from his own country for his productions, – that very popular and amiable writer, however good and self-reliant in many things, perhaps owes his chief reputation to the self-acknowledged imitation of a foreign model, and to the studied avoidance of all topics but smooth ones.[33]

A critic who understood the source and nature of Irving's provincial difficulties might come to appreciate such faults as being, at least, native American faults. But we can do Irving no more justice than Melville does in this somewhat intolerant analysis until we understand that beneath the polish of his Augustan prose, Irving was wrestling with an artistic and personal problem of considerable significance, bringing it to one temporary solution after another and finding always that he had not solved it.

The ending of "Philip of Pokanoket" provides one such instance: here Philip is made to appear as a kind of "Outcast of the Universe," strongly tied to a definite home, yet tragically wandering:

> He was a patriot attached to his native soil. . . . Proud of heart, and with an untamable love of natural liberty, he preferred to enjoy it among the beasts of the forest or in the dismal and famished recesses of swamps and morasses, rather than bow his haughty spirit to submission, and live dependent and despised in the ease and luxury of the settlements. With heroic qualities and bold achievements that would have graced a civilized warrior, and have rendered him the theme of the poet and the historian, he lived a wanderer and a

fugitive in his native land, and went down, like a lonely bark foundering amid darkness and tempest – without a pitying eye to weep his fall, or a friendly hand to record his struggle.[34]

The assumption is that a civilized man is simply a defeated Indian, a being who has lost his real home and the "natural liberty" that flows from possessing it, and has won nothing in compensation but an artistic and historical perspective on its disappearance. Like Philip, Irving had a home and no home; unlike Philip, he was clearly attracted to living dependently, "artistically," close to the hub of the culture that mattered. Ironically, if Irving is to supply that "friendly hand to record his struggle," he must deny himself the sort of home he extols through Philip's story.

There is a complementary ambivalence in Irving's treatment of the English home toward which the exercise of his art – the impowering of the friendly, recording hand – seemed to be drawing him. In the essay that follows, "John Bull," the strong, brooding, tragic tone of "Philip" is joltingly dispelled, and replaced by a caricature of English society, genial to be sure, but reductive and comic. Significantly, England is represented by John Bull's "old castellated manor house," a comic version of Roscoe's classic mansion, the site at which *The Sketch-Book* had really begun. Here Irving's conservative frontier consciousness is allowed to confront his rationalizing tendency to speak slightingly about the history and traditions that England has and America has not:

> There is something...in the appearance of this old family mansion that is extremely poetical and picturesque; and, as long as it can be rendered comfortably habitable, I should almost tremble to see it meddled with, during the present conflict of taste and opinions. Some of [John Bull's] advisors are no doubt good architects, that might be of service; but many, I fear, are mere levellers, who, when they had once got to work with their mattocks on this venerable edifice, would never stop until they had brought it to the ground, and perhaps buried themselves among the ruins.[35]

The generally irreverent and comic tone of this sketch qualifies Irving as one of those "levellers" whom he claims to fear. The consequence is that, insofar as he also defends the house and grounds, he can be seen as engaging himself in argument, fending off, as it were, the hand of power with the hand that writes, the American with the English hand. Perhaps the greatest attraction of the manor house, for Irving, consists in the opportunity it presents to resist the temptation to renovate. It is still habitable. Its clipped lawn makes it pretty, and its antique associations make it picturesque. He knows, however, that he is not the rightful resident and never will be. The real Irving, the natural man, belongs in wild America, and England must remain for him a distant fascination, a myth and inspiration in whose continuance he must always be intensely interested. England can offer him form and discipline, but Lyly's caution – that the traveler might be transformed into a monstrous shape – is constantly in his mind. The form that a refining European style might give to Irving's American substance could, in time, come to resemble his own outlandish caricature of John Bull. Some might argue that this is just what *did* happen to Irving, and they would seem to have Melville on their side. But if Irving never altogether transcended his cultural conservatism, *The Sketch-Book* serves to remind us that some rich and excellent writing had been generated from the conflict he felt between his love of art and his love of home.

The volume ends with an apology that is rather different from those of Bradstreet and Dwight. It brings us very near the difficulty of the provincial conflict as Irving felt it:

> The author is conscious of the numerous faults and imperfections of his work; and well aware of how little he is disciplined and accomplished in the arts of authorship. His deficiencies are also increased by a diffidence arising from his peculiar situation. He finds himself writing in a strange land, and appearing before a public which he has been accustomed, from childhood, to regard with the highest feelings of awe and reverence. He is full of solicitude to deserve their approbation, yet finds that very solicitude continually embarrassing his powers, and depriving him of that ease and confidence which are necessary to successful exertion. Still the kindness with which he is treated encourages him to go on, hoping that in time he may acquire a steadier footing; and thus he proceeds, half venturing, half shrinking, surprised at his own good fortune, and wondering at his own temerity.[36]

Chapter 5

Hawthorne's provincial imagination

*Voices of people talking on the other side of the river; the tones being
so distinguishable, in all their variations, that it seemed as if what
was being said might be understood; but it was not so.*

*A dream, the other night, that the world had become dissatisfied with
the inaccurate manner in which facts are reported, and had employed
me, with a salary of a thousand dollars, to relate things of public
importance exactly as they happen.*

– Nathaniel Hawthorne[1]

If it is true in general that American cultural life has been provincial and
that it was made so by the attenuation of eastern or European culture
transmitted and retransmitted under frontier conditions, it follows that
this provincialism would eventually be diffused thoroughly and that signs
of it would not, for example, be confined to statements about European
culture, on the one hand, or about the frontier, on the other. If, as has
been argued here, a "frontier consciousness" is at the center of what we
recognize as nationally distinctive in the character of earlier American
literature, it ought to be discernible in the works of major artists who
have had little or nothing to do with obviously "western" experience.
After all, a consciousness of any sort is not exclusively, or even primarily,
a bundle of typical concerns or ideas, although for the sake of discussion
it is often treated as if it were. It is, in itself, no more substantial than a
habit of attention or a prejudice about experience that causes certain things
to be noticed in certain ways and with certain intensities. Clearly it would
be more difficult to proceed from this point of view than from the point
of view of the ideas that frontier consciousness results in (as by and large
we have been doing), but the important fact remains that such a consciousness has more immediately to do with patterns and tendencies of
perception than with deliberate and purposeful expression.

There is little point in trying to explore "discrepancies" between per-

ception and expression ("What *really* happened to Melville in the Mar-
quesas?") because they are radically incomparable in the first place. Our
own experience tells us that no expression has ever been like a perception,
however intimate the connection between them may have been, conceived even as stimulus and response. Our experience further suggests
that perceptions are in any event private to the perceiver and cannot
confidently be reconstructed by a second party. What *would* be worth
knowing, given a set of expressions (the body of Hawthorne's writings,
for example), is whether an eccentric pattern of implied valuation (what
seems unusually or characteristically important to the writer) can be
explained by supposing that a corresponding pattern of perception underlies it.

Take, for example, the two passages from Hawthorne's American
notebooks that serve as epigraphs for this chapter. That a pattern of some
sort inheres in them is evident from the fact that readers familiar with
Hawthorne's work would have no difficulty in pronouncing them his,
or at least as having been written by someone trying hard to sound like
Hawthorne. This is also, of course, to say that the pattern is characteristic
in that it points to one author out of all possible authors. But in addition
to being idiosyncratic, these passages are in a special sense "eccentric"
as well. They are representative of the kind of notebook entries that most
puzzled Henry James, who wondered in print what purposes Hawthorne
could have had in recording events so trivial.[2] Whether we begin with
James's sense of puzzlement or with our own, we are immediately forced
to infer that some pattern of valuation operative in Hawthorne's writing
has become inoperative for subsequent readers, testifying, in short, to a
difference in consciousness sufficiently dramatic as to deflect the course
of meaning. Needless to say, these eccentricities are ports of entry for
the literary historian. They are where one begins to penetrate the distinctive consciousness of a writer.

The character of Hawthorne's frontier consciousness alerted him to
certain kinds of faulty communication; it conferred importance (in the
first of the two passages) on the ironic contrast between the expectation
that human intelligence is communicable and the finding that something
in the nature of the world stands ready to block it. The perceptions of
a provincial American artist are literally "distinguished" by the continually attenuating process whereby the artist's culture is itself provincialized. There is no reason, of course, why this effect should pertain
only to writers and artists, but they are obliged above all others to concern
themselves with the trustworthiness of expression and the likelihood of
"getting one's message across" in a society where the decay of meaning
seems especially problematical. This concern figures as a professional
issue in the more complex second passage. The endemic fact of faulty

communication naturally invested accuracy, or an adequate transmission of intelligence, with the significance of a Platonic ideal, even as it gave special point to the comparison so often rehearsed in the literature of the period between newswriting (which in Hawthorne's society was both powerful and audible) and more permanent forms of expression (which by and large were neither). When Tocqueville identified journalists as "the only authors whom I acknowledge as American," observing that "they speak the language of their country and make themselves heard,"[3] he was closer to the ordinary perception than Emerson had come in his optative definition of the poet as "the only teller of news,"[4] which presumed the poet's own restatement of "things of public importance." The significance of Hawthorne's dream is just that he is caught, as in a dream, between these points of view, wanting to open an intercourse with the world, wanting (perhaps even more ardently) to be useful in the world's employ, but knowing at the same time that because he cannot share his employer's values he will not "speak the language" that will cause him to be heard.

More than most writers, Hawthorne conceived of his work as a mediatorial effort and behaved as if the perfection of his craft consisted wholly in the establishment of efficient relations between himself at the center and his materials and his audience on either side. Knowing, in his protesting, conservative frontier consciousness, that his audience was provincial, he regularly complains of the consequent lack of sympathy between them and him and of the complications to which it led in his efforts to manage these relations. Such complaining is Hawthorne's habitual practice in his prefaces, but it is the hallmark, too, of his celebrated letter to Longfellow following the publication of the *Twice-Told Tales* in 1837:

> As to my literary efforts, I do not think much of them – neither [is it] worth while to be ashamed of them. They would have been better, I trust, if written under more favorable circumstances. I have had no external excitement – no consciousness that the public would like what I wrote, nor much hope nor a very passionate desire that they should do so. Nevertheless, having nothing else to be ambitious of, I have felt considerably interested in literature; and if my writings had made any decided impression, I should probably have been stimulated to greater exertions; but there has been no warmth of approbation, so that I have always written with benumbed fingers. I have another great difficulty, in the lack of materials; for I have nothing but thin air to concoct my stories of, and it is not easy to give a lifelike semblance to such shadowy stuff. Sometimes, through a peep-hole, I have caught a glimpse of the

real world; and the two or three articles, in which I have portrayed such glimpses, please me better than the others.[5]

Apart from Hawthorne's self-deprecating acknowledgment of the provincial conditions of his art, the most striking revelation is the chilling isolation he depicts, an isolation altogether different from the sort generally made out, and that consists of an author's alienation from audience and materials alike. The meaning of the complaint becomes a little clearer when we realize that in constructing, autobiographically, his own literary self through all the stages from anonymity to personality, Hawthorne had available to him no convincing model of a writer as a man fully participating in the world of ordinary relations. (In this regard, James may have been right in thinking that Hawthorne would have benefited from the society of other writers.)[6] What notions he *did* have about "literary personages" were to a great extent mere inferences and impressions from his vividly crucial experience as a young, intensely sympathetic provincial reader of English literature. Referring to his childhood in Salem and in Raymond, Maine, Hawthorne observed:

> It is only a solitary child – left to such wild modes of culture as he chooses for himself while yet ignorant what culture means, standing tiptoe to pull down books from no very lofty shelf, and then shutting himself up, as it were, between the leaves, going astray through the volume at his own pleasure, and comprehending it rather by his sensibilities and affections than his intellect – that child is the only student that ever gets the sort of intimacy which I am now thinking of, with a literary personage.[7]

This wilderness experience (for so it is in the description) points to the figure of the author as a distant, olympian, rather magical presence conceived as occupying no space but who, for the reader, mediates between the realms of ordinary and extraordinary experience. So in the letter to Longfellow Hawthorne saw himself in a similar position, in a region largely undefined and unpopulated, between an uncaptivated audience, associated in his mind with the numbing coldness of the "real world," and his materials, which partake of the thinness and shadowiness of the imagination. Even as he seeks, however, to mediate between these realms of the obdurate and the impalpable he feels isolated from each in turn, and the projected effect is one of struggle and alienation, of distance and kinship or attraction combined. This sense of struggle was all the more on Hawthorne's mind because it was inconsistent with what he imagined were European conditions of authorship as well as with the European ideal of the *sprezzatura* performance. The burden of the provincial in this respect was the feeling that one had to expend enormous efforts to obtain the kinds of results that were elsewhere almost freely given.[8] The compensatory reward, however, at least in Hawthorne's case, lay in the value to his art of finding his difficulties constantly uppermost, in a position where he could not only deal with them, as with sins dragged into the light, but where, in a strikingly modern and original way, he could be *seen* as dealing with them. Emerson was the first to point this out, though he failed, as he often did in discussing fiction, to be appreciative.[9]

In Hawthorne's complaints about the elusiveness or unavailability of materials one sees the effect of the provincial conviction that all transmission involves loss and distortion, that all reports arriving across time and space are suspect, their images decayed and attenuated. Literary nationalists who were not themselves writers of fiction were in the 1820s and 1830s confidently asserting that serviceable materials were ready to hand in the nation's history, but Hawthorne, who knew that America was a "country that has no Past,"[10] knew better. He had discovered early in his career that history does not *supply* stories, but rather that stories had to be rescued *from* history, and in fact most of his historical tales show him doing just that: "brightening the materials which time has rusted."[11] The evolution of "Alice Doane's Appeal," so far as it can be reconstructed, illustrates this point. Having tried and failed on two occasions to publish the story as a tale of the supernatural set in old Salem, Hawthorne significantly improved it by adding, apparently out of sheer frustration, a narrative frame that turned it into a story, set in the present, in which the original story is told to an unsympathetic and superficial audience. After this involuted, self-referential revision was completed, the story sold quickly. He had thus brought it closer to his central interest, which was not in history at all, but in the awful mystery of how an author does what he does with what he has. The elusiveness itself became, in the light of this interest, Hawthorne's primary material, so that he conveyed events and circumstances in his fiction as conveyance itself was provincially conceived as occurring: in distorting half light, in mirrored reflection, by rumor or faulty report.

The significance, therefore, of Hawthorne's provincial situation is not that his materials were cripplingly insufficient (as a literal reading of his complaints might suggest, or indeed as Hawthorne might actually have felt at times), but rather that their insufficiency assumed for him the look of an epistemological mystery – one so intriguing as to impel him to an enormously fruitful examination of the nature of materials and their relation to fiction and fictionality. This motive is especially evident in the group of tales he had meant to publish serially under the title "The Story Teller," but which the newspaper editor Park Benjamin disastrously broke up in 1835.[12]

The collection began with the telling of "Mr. Higginbotham's Catastrophe," which centers on a traveling tobacco peddler named Dominicus Pike, a man as eager for gossip "as a city shopkeeper to read the morning paper."[3] Pike is told by the first man he meets on the road that a certain Mr. Higginbotham of Kimballton had been murdered the preceding night and that his body was hung on the branch of a St. Michael's pear tree. Delighted with this piquant bit of news, Pike retells the story as he continues his rounds, finding to his immense satisfaction that he is everywhere "the first bearer of the intelligence."[4] It is not long, however, before Pike's story is contradicted by a more authoritative statement of the case, supplied by a personal acquaintance of Higginbotham, to the effect that the old gentleman had been seen alive that very morning: " 'Why, then, it can't be a fact' exclaimed Dominicus Pike. 'I guess he'd have mentioned, if it was,' said the old farmer; and he removed his chair back to the corner, leaving Dominicus quite down in the mouth."[5]

Setting off on his rounds once more, he encounters a second traveler who also gives an account of the murder. At Parker's Falls, Pike again spreads the story, though more cautiously this time, no longer professing "to relate it on his own authority, or that of any one person; but mention[ing] it as a report generally diffused."[6] The effect is even more exciting than before: the story "ran through the town like fire among girdled trees," and the Parker's Falls *Gazette*, supplying details as necessary, rushed into print to announce to its little world the "HORRID MURDER OF MR. HIGGINBOTHAM!"[7] When, however, the story is once again refuted, Pike determines to visit Kimballton in person to learn the truth. He arrives, as fate would have it, just in time to prevent the murder from actually taking place – at which point the Story Teller himself intervenes:

> If the riddle be not already guessed, a few words will explain the simple machinery by which this "coming event" was made to "cast its shadow before." Three men had plotted the robbery and murder of Mr. Higginbotham; two of them, successively, lost courage and fled, each delaying the crime one night by their disappearance; the third was in the act of perpetration, when a champion, blindly obeying the call of fate, like the heroes of old romance, appeared in the person of Dominicus Pike.[18]

Since the story comically illustrates, among other things, the importance to meaning of having the whole context of a story, there is considerable irony in the fact that Benjamin destroyed the context of "The Story Teller," and that Hawthorne, to salvage this tale, had to print it out of context in *Twice-Told Tales*. Apart from its original setting, the story seems merely farcical, a happy if isolated experiment in New England regional humor. But as the introductory tale in "The Story Teller," it demands to be seen as an experiment of somewhat more serious pretensions, since in it Hawthorne is clearly concerned with the curiously deforming relationships that link materials to stories and stories to storytellers.

Pike at the inn and Pike at Parker's Falls are two different kinds of narrators, illustrating in the first instance some of the primitive motives for wanting to repeat stories, and, in the second, some of the effects of suppressing the agency of the narrator. The editor of the *Gazette* is another storyteller, turning an oral tale into "hard news" and corrupting it as he does so. The two conspirators are the real authors of the story in the sense that by giving up on their initial role as "characters" or "actors" in favor of that of "narrators," they transform what could have been tragic news into mere comic fiction. Pike, on the other hand, abandons the role of "narrator" as an altogether too hazardous occupation (having nearly been tarred and feathered at Parker's Falls), and becomes his own story's hero, a transformation that legitimately entitles him to marry Higginbotham's pretty niece and to settle into a prosperous, and stationary, occupation in Kimballton. That Pike chooses to go out of his way to concern himself in the tale he has not only heard but been telling – a sort of freewill baptism in fiction – is the true source of the comic mystery of the story, and it remains mysterious and effective even when the "simple machinery" is revealed. Like the ideal provincial reader whom Hawthorne was to imagine as "shutting himself up, as it were, between the leaves," Pike has escaped a world hostile to fiction and become a citizen of romance.[19]

The burlesque quality of "Mr. Higginbotham's Catastrophe" reminds us that difficulties of communication have always served the purposes of humor, yet before the twentieth century it was the provincial artist almost exclusively who looked upon such problems as the determining conditions under which he worked. Hawthorne's awareness of the literal absurdity of his position as a writer of fiction is the essential element in his various quite genial self-portraits, but it is also a fixture in his portrayal of artists in the tales (Owen Warland of "The Artist of the Beautiful" is the best example) whose difficult and thankless task it is to bring excessively trivial materials to life for an obtuse audience. Believing, however, that "no fountain [is] so small, but that Heaven may be imaged in its bosom,"[20] Hawthorne indulged rather than resisted his own perceptual habit of submitting the most mundane materials to an intense and imaginative scrutiny. The result of this indulgence was an American provincial comic mode, a decorous kin to the frontier humor of Augustus Baldwin Longstreet's *Georgia Scenes* or Joseph Glover Baldwin's *Flush Times*, in which a sophisticated point of view is brought to bear on preposterously subliterary materials. Expressions in this mode are eccentric or hyperimaginative; they verge toward the "extravagant" in Thoreau's sense.

Here, for example, is an entry from Hawthorne's notebook that is perhaps all the more startling for having been composed in the month preceding the writer's thirty-eighth birthday and his marriage:

> One of my chief amusements is to see the boys sail their miniature vessels on the Frog Pond [in Boston]. There is a great variety of shipping owned among the young people; and they appear to have a considerable knowledge of the art of managing vessels. There is a full-rigged man of war, with, I believe, every spar, rope, and sail, that sometimes makes its appearance; and when on a voyage across the pond, it so identically resembles a great ship, except in size, that it has the effect of a picture. All its motions – its tossing up and down on the mimic waves, and its sinking and rising in a calm swell, its heeling to the breeze – the whole effect, in short, is that of a real ship at sea; while, moreover, there is something that kindles the imagination more than the reality would. If we see a real, great ship, the mind grasps and possesses, within its real clutch, all that there is of it; while here, the mimic ship is the representative of an ideal one, and so gives us a more imaginative pleasure.[21]

This is not a passage that in any simple sense "turns serious," though the contrast between its beginning and end is important. The significance of its conclusion carries with it, necessarily, the savor of its origin in the Frog Pond, just as Owen Warland's artistic triumph is kept in perspective by what R. H. Fogle has called the "slightness of the archetype."[22] The fact is that Hawthorne's comic sense often involves his delight at being able to rescue his materials from triviality by an almost athletic exercise of the imagination, as well as in being seen as having daringly done so. It is the delight of *making* something of the town pump or an old apple dealer – a newspaper account of a man's leaving his wife, or, at last, a scarlet letter "A."

Horatio Bridge, perhaps Hawthorne's closest friend, remarked that the author's "mental sight was *both* panoramic and microscopic; . . . he looked at persons and things with a discerning and discriminating eye, whether the object of his attention were a friend or a stranger – a tree or a flower – a hill or a pebble."[23] The materials that occupy Hawthorne's field of vision bear satirically on all that he is able to do with them in the sense that the minuteness of the butterfly and the common occurrence of butterflies in nature constitute a satire on Warland's efforts without, however, making them wholly ridiculous to a sympathetic audience. "The Artist of the Beautiful," then, is a parable of the situation of the *provincial* artist specifically, who, if he is to do anything at all, must magnify. The important tension in Hawthorne's work which this requirement serves to establish is that between the author's knowledge, on the one hand, of the triviality of his materials, and, on the other, of the great things he can elaborate from them.

The tension between these two areas of consciousness is not unique to Hawthorne but *is* characteristic of the provincial mind and the provincial style. Irving's fine little story of "The Stout Gentleman," for example, is humorous in proportion to the contrast between the narrator's initially trivial observation and the grandiose imaginings that follow for him simply because he is bored and wants intellectual stimulation. Carefully, even laboriously, Irving indicates the cultural deprivation from which the narrator suffers, and so makes plausible the peculiar hypersensitivity he shares with all provincial artists:

> I was dreadfully hipped. The hours seemed as if they would never creep by. The very ticking of the clock became irksome. At length the stillness of the house was interrupted by the ringing of a bell. Shortly after I heard the voice of a waiter at the bar: "The stout gentleman in No. 13 wants his breakfast. Tea and bread and butter, with ham and eggs not to be too much done."
>
> In such a situation as mine, every incident is of importance. Here was a subject of speculation presented to my mind, and ample exercise for my imagination.... "The stout gentleman!" – the very name had something in it of the picturesque. It at once gave the size; it embodied the personage to my mind's eye, and my fancy did the rest.[24]

"Wakefield" among Hawthorne's better-known short works, and *The Scarlet Letter* (together with "The Custom-House") among the romances, are structured in just this way. First comes the meager detail, too slight to attract the notice of anyone but an idle gentleman or a man bored with his job – too trifling, certainly, to divert the attention of a busy, commercial American. The detail is then filled out with more or less of plausibility, the whole depending for a certain measure of its effect on the preponderance of significant elaboration over insignificant hard fact. Many of the notebook entries, like the Frog Pond meditation, follow this pattern, and taken all in all, suggest a sort of secular version of the Puritans' typological perception – *their* habit of finding "no fountain so small, but that Heaven may be imaged in its bosom." Yet Hawthorne's purpose is very different from that of the Puritans, who would typically subordinate the fountain to its image of Heaven. Hawthorne's dual perception, his panoramic and microscopic vision, was a tool he used to confront and revalue the reduced circumstances of his thin, provincial

New England, and was fashioned of his need as an artist to have something worth writing about.

What he does with the newspaper account of Wakefield or with the scarlet letter is to restore to them the "life," or more precisely the capacity for meaning, of which a constantly attenuating process of transmission has deprived them. Wakefield survives "without a proper distinction of circumstances"[25] in an old, half-forgotten newspaper article; the scarlet letter is at first as trivial and unmeaning an artifact as the frizzled wig of Surveyor Pue. Hawthorne does with these obscurely descended materials what Alice Vane does with the time-blackened portrait of Edward Randolph,[26] that is to say, he creates or restores meaning by opposing momentarily a process he knows to be inexorable, one that tends everywhere toward the simplification and ultimately the obliteration of life and meaning. This overwhelming sense of the necessary failure of transmission – which he could present humorously or seriously as the mood took him – applied equally to all forms, from biological inheritance to literary translation to the importation of fashions from Europe,[27] and carried with it two implications of crucial importance to his art. The first was that, because everything of which one can be aware is in the process of transmission and has behind it a longer or shorter history of transmission, it is positively a moral error ever to pretend that one sees the thing itself rather than some temporary *version* of the thing. The second was that art as representation must acknowledge this fact by relying on indirection, "suggestiveness," and symbolism as the means of most adequately indicating the subject's status as version.

These insights determined the character of Hawthorne's relationship to his materials and account for what Henry James took to be a "curious paleness of colour and paucity of detail" in the notebooks, as well as the impression he had in reading through them of "a general vacancy in the field of vision."[28] Consider, for instance, the way in which the following scene – more colorful and detailed than most in the notebooks – is deliberately unrealized in Hawthorne's characteristic manner of seeing it:

But now, the surface of the sea was not at all commoved with billows; there was only roughness enough to take off the gleam, and give it the aspect of iron, after cooling. The clouds above added to the black appearance. A few sea birds flitting over the surface, only visible at moments, when they turned their white under parts towards me; as if they were then just created. The sunshine had a singular effect. The clouds would interpose in such a manner, that some objects were shaded from it, while others were strongly illuminated. Some of the islands lay in the shade, dark and gloomy; while others seemed like sunny and favored spots, on the dark sea and beneath the dark sky. The white lighthouses sometimes very cheerfully marked. There was a schooner about a mile from the shore, at anchor, laden with lumber apparently. The sea all about her had the black iron aspect which I have described; but the vessel herself was brightly illuminated. Hull, masts, spars, were all gilded; and the rigging was made of golden threads. A small white streak of foam breaking around her bows, which were towards the wind. The shadowiness of the clouds over head made the effect of the sunlight strange where it fell.[29]

The most notable quality of this passage is surely not its representational vividness, but its commitment to making the ordinary object struggle with its own "singular" or extraordinary version. In the first sentence, the careful attention paid to texture seems to serve no end but the curiosity of having rendered color in terms of mass, as if to imply by the conceit some riddling relation of water and metal. The water fowl are as much unseen as seen, with the effect of their finally becoming messengers of the idea of spontaneous creation. Hawthorne's interest throughout the passage, as Irving's in "The Stout Gentleman," lies in what is to be gained by *not* seeing directly or steadily, by *not* giving in to the imaginative inadequacy of a commonplace environment. More especially he is intrigued by the possibility that the natural disintegration of the transmitted and received image can seem at times analogous to the constructive re-creation of the object by the imagination, that, in other words, imagination may be a principle operative in nature, coinciding with the circumstantially imperfect grasp of that provincial reader who receives the literary work "rather by his sensibilities and affections than his intellect." The effect in such a passage as this is produced by the fully deliberate way in which Hawthorne suppresses his knowledge of what a thing is in cold and simple fact. The schooner is "laden with lumber apparently," but as a *transmitted* object it becomes a vessel of romance, whose "hull, masts, and spars, were all gilded; and the rigging ... made of golden threads." In the drama that Hawthorne's enlivening vision creates, this golden ship, riding at anchor, makes headway through an iron sea. (All this is, as readers will parenthetically note, no image out of *The Faerie Queene*, but a derived form of the Massachusetts lumber industry!)

For Hawthorne, as for other romantic artists, the function of the imagination was to unsettle meanings, to break up the false and easy clarities of life and introduce the mysteriously organic complexities that in normal perception things ought to have but do not.[30] In "My Kinsman, Major Molineux," the "imaginative power" produces "a beautiful strangeness in familiar objects" that subverts Robin's thoroughly provincial readiness to settle points "shrewdly, rationally, and satisfactorily."[31] Ironically, he sees nothing, learns nothing, so long as his vision remains distinct; in moonlight, however, and in dream-vision – in the very distortion of the transmitted image – mysteries convey their secret meanings. In the tale, then, Robin is shown as discovering precisely the sort of vision that in the notebook passage Hawthorne is consciously exercising. The discovery, as Robin makes it, is nothing less than an American revolution in consciousness, in which one sort of provincial vision is deposed and another, better one installed. Hawthorne's "shrewd youth" is at first presented as a sort of Jonathan character, unintimidated by the strange, yet at the same time defying strangeness by innocently taking everything for what it seems. His frontier culture, like Jonathan's, has settled into an attenuated simplicity undisturbed by foreign competition, in which meanings are as fixed and assured as they conceivably can be in a still-functioning society. This is of course the attraction the old home has for Robin in his mounting discomfort: the attraction that all homes always have. But the same distress that prompts a longing for the gentle certainties of childhood creates simultaneously the conditions for a more imaginative, more venturesome kind of vision – that which Hawthorne identified in the ideal reader (also a child) who eagerly turns from the ordinary fact to the extraordinary version as soon as he becomes aware of the difference.

In Robin's revolution of consciousness the safe but stultifying belief in the ordinary as the *only* possibility is presented as generally analogous to colonial or "provincial" dependence on extrinsic authority. Hawthorne (as will be argued at greater length in a moment) regarded both as in general analogous to the stiff, reductive operations of allegory. Robin's educated vision, on the other hand, is operationally defined as open to literally untold possibilities of meaning, and thus of personal growth as well. It is a liberated and "open" vision because it is born of dislocation and the sudden acknowledgment of a larger "world elsewhere" that is to the giddy entrant what the book pulled "from no very lofty shelf" is to the ideal reader. Linked explicitly to the "imaginative power," this better vision is associated in Hawthorne's writings with the freedom and indeterminacy of the symbolic mode, and, not arbitrarily, with the capacity for evil.

Readers have generally agreed that Robin's earned consciousness is indeed the "better" one, though the character's movement toward a vision that can be credited to Hawthorne himself is by no means presented in the story as an unalloyed improvement; we are allowed to see, for example, that it is consistent with cruelty to Major Molineux and that it has a certain friendly relation to anarchy. The immediate point, however, is not to reaffirm the celebrated ambiguity of the tale, nor even to commend the work as an adroit display of the deeper psychology, but rather to isolate Hawthorne's interest in defining the nature – the dangers as well as the virtues – of each of these opposed kinds of provincial vision in their respective, characterizing relationship to allegory and symbolism.

These relationships, complexly interwoven in "Molineux," are somewhat easier to see in two simpler tales, "The Hollow of the Three Hills" and "The Snow-Image," in which, in a manner of speaking, Robin's "allegorical" prerevolutionary vision and his "symbolic" postrevolutionary vision are separately arraigned. A brief examination of these stories will help us to estimate, in turn, the extent to which Hawthorne's masterpiece, *The Scarlet Letter*, owes its great strengths to an imagination richly provoked and sternly disciplined by a lifetime's experience with a provincial environment.

One of Hawthorne's earliest short stories, "The Hollow of the Three Hills" concerns a woman, married and a mother, who has been led by imaginings of a freer life to abandon her own family in favor of an adulterous affair. All this suffering and decision has taken place before the beginning of the story, which, like *The Scarlet Letter*, has less to do with original acts than with what might be thought of as "transmitted acts" or consequences. She appears, at the beginning of the tale, at a meeting with a witch who provides her with a succession of three supernatural revelations: first of her grief-stricken parents, then of her husband screaming in a madhouse, and finally of her child's funeral. These revelations may be accurate; they may, on the other hand, have been falsely conjured up for the purpose of tormenting the woman (who has, after all, made a compact with a witch to procure them); or, they may be projections of a guilty conscience, in which case the accuracy of their reference is immaterial. Hawthorne tempts us to choose among these rather simple alternatives, but the ambiguity is in fact real and irreducible. It is also, however, a dramatically functional ambiguity, important for its suggestion that the protagonist, by rejecting relationships that had increasingly come to define and stultify her, has succeeded in unsettling *all* meaning, especially but not exclusively the meaning that her position as daughter, wife, and mother ought to confer on others, as parent, husband, and child. It is, in her case, just as if the hollow to which she has come were somehow to secede from the three surrounding hills that define it. The story makes much of what in "Wakefield" (a male version of the parable) is a relatively minor consideration: that freedom is a function of the imagination that keeps the world's meanings fluid and alive – what the truly redemptive conservative wants to see prevail – whereas restriction, as its opposite, is a function of assigned meanings and "concluded" relationships, which are in turn, of course, the essence of the allegorical mode.

"The Snow-Image," one of Hawthorne's last short stories, illustrates the triumph of assigned meaning over the creative imagination, and so nearly reverses the terms of "The Hollow of the Three Hills," though the net effect is arguably very similar indeed. Two children, in the course of some unsupervised outdoor play, fashion a little girl out of snow. Their childish faith in the esemplastic power, applied (as Hawthorne makes clear) to heavenly materials, brings the image fully to life. Arriving home from work, the father – "a certain Mr. Lindsey, ... an excellent but matter-of-fact sort of man," and, ominously, "a dealer in hardware"[32] – insists that this tertium quid must of course be a stray urchin from the neighborhood, and so, ignoring the protests of his own children, he brings her into the overheated parlor to warm up. The father's well-meaning but nevertheless lethal style is essentially allegorical in that it forcibly imposes, from a position of assumed authority, a simple single meaning, uncontextual because it is arbitrary, arbitrary because it is uncontextual.

These two stories of parents who kill children, written twenty years apart and bracketing Hawthorne's whole career as a teller of tales, neatly indicate the dangers that lie in the opposed modes of allegory and symbolism when they are not sufficiently tempered each by the other. Hawthorne associated allegory with the death-in-life stiffness of intolerance and bigotry, and with the closed and finished version of the living thing; but he would also, and often at the same time, associate it with the endurance of meaningful forms, and with the tough, courageous acceptance of unpleasant truths. Symbolism he associated with precisely opposite qualities: with warmth and vitality, with the living and unfixed version of the thing, but also with sentimentality and moral escapism. ("The May-Pole of Merry Mount," though not Hawthorne's best story, manages to illustrate all of these qualities and their major interrelationships.) Between these opposites with their complementary virtues and defects, Hawthorne sought a middle ground, a compromise of which, on the evidence of the stories, the appropriate sign would be a kind of successful cultural transmission: the preservation of children in a satisfactory home. In "The Custom-House" this middle ground takes the form, notoriously, of the "neutral territory" between "the Actual and the Imaginary," which, insofar as it is "Actual" is the writer's own parlor in his home in Mall Street, Salem, in the year 1849, littered with the toys and tokens of his two small children, and which, insofar as it is "Imaginary," is a projection into the public realm of art of the writer's private, symbolic sense of the generative center of life. Proceeding from this point to *The Scarlet Letter*, one sees just why the central dramatic issue must be Pearl's legitimacy and the creation for her of a proper. home. One also sees that the issue will have to be determined in the context of two competing and incompatible world views, each fundamentally provincial as the author derives them: the "allegorical" and the "symbolic."

The Puritan establishment naturally adopts the allegorical mode, and for two reasons: first, because it is the basis for the language of authority, in which the privilege of stipulating meanings is implicit, and, second, because it is an instrument of public policy, an efficient and powerful means of securing order in the midst of change. Both aspects of Hawthorne's Puritan allegory are evident in the condemnation of Hester by the authorities. Not only have they settled the nature of her act through legal process, but in an effort as much to curb her wildness as to punish it, they actually attempt to stipulate *her* meaning, to fix it once and for all. Chillingworth fully understands the dehumanizing effect of their sentence and vindictively approves, calling it "wise" and observing that "she will be a living sermon against sin, until the ignominious letter be engraved upon her tombstone."[33]

In a single burst of official heat, in the "living sermon" of the Reverend Mr. Wilson, the meaning of the letter, and thereby of Hester Prynne, is publicly determined: "So forcibly did he dwell upon this symbol, for the hour or more during which his periods were rolling over the people's heads, that it assumed new terrors in their imagination, and seemed to derive its scarlet hue from the flames of the infernal pit."[34] Hawthorne depicts this performance as an act of brutal aggression against a spirit helpless to resist, a spirit that "could only shelter itself beneath a stony crust of insensibility, while the faculties of animal life remained entire."[35] Thus, in its mechanism, in its appeal to force, in its dehumanizing effect as well as in its perversely benevolent motive, the act parallels that of Mr. Lindsey in "The Snow-Image," a character whom in other respects Wilson much resembles. Above all there is about both of these men a flatness and simplicity of response that make them intruders in any scene of life. In carefully appropriate language, Hawthorne asserts their affinity to bad art (bad partly because twice transmitted) when he says that Wilson "looked like the darkly engraved portraits that we see prefixed to old volumes of sermons; and had no more right than one of those portraits would have, to step forth, as he now did, and meddle with a question of human guilt, passion, and anguish."[36]

If the Puritan establishment takes to itself the high fierce ground of allegory, Hester occupies a symbolic realm of mysteriously shifting, fluid meanings. Like the nameless protagonist of "The Hollow of the Three Hills," she has in the commission of her sin subverted her own defining network of relations to the community. Her relations in particular to her husband and her minister have been complexly disestablished, but she also, suddenly and bewilderingly, finds herself on a new footing with everyone else. Soon after the public humiliation of Wilson's sermon,

Hester discovers that she has a "new sense" which, without conveying to her the meaning of the fact, imparts involuntarily "a sympathetic knowledge of the hidden sin in other hearts."[37] Such dissolution of the psychosocial landmarks is an external counterpart to the erosion of the old metes and bounds of her ego, a process of which we see the consequences in the self-sacrificing and loving work that she – like Apollo toiling for Admetus – performs in the community.

Hawthorne discusses the difficulty of Hester's situation in the well-known passage that begins Chapter 18. Read properly, it contains the whole of her story:

> But Hester Prynne, with a mind of native courage and activity, and for so long a period not merely estranged, but outlawed, from society, had habituated herself to such latitude of speculation as was altogether foreign to the clergyman. She had wandered, without rule or guidance, in a moral wilderness; as vast, as intricate and shadowy, as the untamed forest, amid the gloom of which they were now holding a colloquy that was to decide their fate. Her intellect and heart had their home, as it were, in desert places, where she roamed as freely as the wild Indian in his woods. For years past she had looked from this estranged point of view at human institutions, and whatever priests or legislators had established; criticizing all with hardly more reverence than the Indian would feel for the clerical band, the judicial robe, the pillory, the gallows, the fireside, or the church. The tendency of her fate and fortunes had been to set her free. The scarlet letter was her passport into regions where other women dared not tread. Shame, Despair, Solitude! These had been her teachers, – stern and wild ones, – and they had made her strong, but taught her much amiss.[38]

The appearance of Hester's teachers as allegorical figures (Shame, Despair, Solitude) aptly indicates the manner in which she has been victimized, whereas the connection that Hawthorne draws between her lack of a home and her lack of fixed and certifiable values (or more specifically her lack of "reverence" for them) falls directly into the tradition of frontier conservatives – such as Dwight – who fear the consequences when men and women have in effect to construct themselves apart from history and the agreement of communities. The utter independence of Hester's inner life is of course the product of her reaction against the allegory that condemns her, and *as* its opposite is not more healthy or more tenable.

It thus falls to Dimmesdale to discover the "neutral territory" between these fatal opposites and make it prevail. He alone is in a position to experience both alternatives and to observe experimentally how each fails. He is at first captive of a peculiarly rigid system of laws which are meant to apply equally to public and private behavior. It is the essence of the theocracy as Hawthorne depicts it to keep these realms in alignment, but Dimmesdale's secret sin has introduced him, privately, to the passion and energy of the symbolic imagination. For seven years he struggles to subdue this internal freedom beneath the constraints of public form without ever fully acknowledging that this procedure is simply and precisely hypocritical. Then, under the influence of Hester's sentimental and ill-advised plan of escape, a plan that consists altogether in evading the external constraints and accusations that pain him, Dimmesdale concludes that if there is no place for passion in religion, he will try to subsume religion in passion. Calling Hester his "better angel," he now declares that he is "risen up all made anew, and with new powers to glorify Him that hath been merciful!"[39] But this vision of release and redemption (the chapter is called "A Flood of Sunshine") is not the revolution he takes it for. The intoxicating freedom of the ungoverned symbolic imagination proves incompatible not only with established dogma but, as it turns out, with a concern for the community as well. Returning to town after his meeting with Hester, and taking "an impression of change from the series of familiar objects that presented themselves,"[40] Dimmesdale gives way to all manner of frantic and perverse impulses, gleefully alienating his parishioners with blasphemies and wanton cruelties.

The final scaffold scene, in which all this anguish and moral error are as far resolved as humanly possible, represents not merely the symbolic marriage of Hester and the minister, but the too long delayed creation of that neutral territory in which life will at last be allowed to the child. This creation has required that Dimmesdale see and reject the inherent selfishness of the Puritan allegorical mode with its reliance on force and its fundamental lack of reverence for the human soul, and likewise, the selfishness of the symbolic mode with its commitment to individual salvation through escape. He is redeemed and can redeem others (notably Pearl) only when, leaving such selfishness behind, he acknowledges his family in the context of all his proper relationships. In thus reaching out to include others, he is suddenly transformed from a dependent, ineffectual, and boyish figure into a man, a husband, and a father – one who, mounting the steps of the scaffold, can for the first time dispense with the assistance of Bellingham and Wilson.

In *The Scarlet Letter* Hawthorne was able to imagine the profoundest moral issues in terms that throughout his career most centrally occupied his imagination as a provincial. When one recognizes that the grand conflict the novel depicts is resolvable into the two great and equally tragic possibilities that American frontier consciousness was forever imagining – on the one hand, the acquisition of a meaningless freedom through the attritional loss of values and, on the other, the hardening of values into a tyranny of sheer historical force – then one begins to approach the sources of the power and the relevance of Hawthorne's masterpiece.

Chapter 6

Working in Eden

I have heard, that from the beginning of her life, Margaret Fuller idealized herself as a sovereign. She told ——— she early saw herself to be intellectually superior to those around her, and that for years she dwelt upon the idea, until she believed that she was not her parents' child, but an European princess confided to their care. She remembered that, while a little girl, she was walking one day under the apple trees with such an air and step, that her father pointed her out to her sister, saying, Incedit regina.

– Ralph Waldo Emerson[1]

One of the most obvious psychological burdens that artists in a frontier nation have to bear is the knowledge that the artifacts of culture, as well as a generous public concern for them, are primarily to be found elsewhere. Provincialism, in this sense, is the perception that real culture is exterior or foreign to one's place, and involves the corollary proposition that if one is to "have" culture at all, one must earn it personally and laboriously. Culture must, in the abstract, matter a great deal before serious effort will be expended to secure it. This may seem a truism today, but it has been an especially American truism with important, sometimes obscure implications for the artistic mind in America.

When T. S. Eliot asserts that tradition "cannot be inherited," Americans know immediately what he means and are prepared, somewhat sadly perhaps, to give assent because the conclusion is deeply a part of the American lesson. "If you want it," as Eliot said, "you must obtain it by great labour."[2] Ever since the first colonial planter realized he would have to send his son to England for schooling, a sense of the sheer labor of education has been a decisive element in the consciousness of most Americans who in an anticultural environment have managed to assert the value of a cultivated life. From time to time some have rebelled against the difficulty of this work, and in a variety of colorful ways (most memorably, perhaps, by "lighting out for the territory"); others have taken it up, either humorously as dilettantes, or grimly with a sense of its vital importance. But nearly all have felt the difficulty of transmitting culture, that is, of maintaining or consolidating traditional standards of civilization in a frontier society. In particular, many American artists have felt this condition as a distinctly national hardship and have registered their resentment by drawing up lists of cultural facilities absent from American life.[3] The American Eden bore fruit in abundance, but the tableware, the napkins, and the fingerbowls were all missing.

Before the twentieth century, American resentment at the extravagant difficulty of being cultured was deeply colored by the belief that Europeans, for their part, did not have to work nearly so hard at it. To the American mind it seemed that Europeans absorbed their culture directly, without conscious effort, from their surroundings. The artificial, as it were, came naturally to Europeans and perhaps for that very reason seemed to suit them well. Their case inevitably suggested to Americans that tradition *could* be inherited – Eliot notwithstanding – if one happened to live in Europe or, it might be, in one of those isolated, unassimilated Old World settlements in the New. The thoroughly Dutch Rip Van Winkle, without work (indeed, while playing), absorbed all the lore, learning, and values that his little Dutch community had to offer. For Irving, the real appeal of these besieged outposts of European culture was the completely organic, unself-conscious quality of a cultural life not modeled on the work ethic, and the correspondingly vulnerable, effortless, and humane style that went with it – one that could not, as things turned out, muster enough working energy even to save itself.[4]

Toward the other end of the century, William Dean Howells made the same point even more explicitly in Bromfield Corey's observation to his son in *The Rise of Silas Lapham*: "All civilization comes through literature now, especially in our country. A Greek got his civilization by talking and looking, and in some measure a Parisian may still do it. But we, who live remote from history and monuments, we must read or we must barbarise."[5] The remark is at best but a half truth; it certainly expresses a more severely conservative view than Howells held or than *The Rise of Silas Lapham* finally conveys. But Howells took note of the idea because it was a nearly standard view of culture in America, and also because it expressed the importance of that American middle-class struggle for culture the difficulty of which the Laphams intermittently but intensely felt. Upwardly mobile nineteenth-century Americans such as Silas Lapham and his family met the challenge of "self-improvement" largely unprepared, but often with the same gritty determination to make good that they brought to work of more accustomed sorts. The Coreys, a Brahmin family grown markedly European with age, were, of course, exempt from such struggle; but for the rest, for the culturally hungry who knew that they could not be "refined" by osmosis, *labor vincit omnia* was the hopeful motto. They would have to pry culture loose from their new books, discover it by many an embarrassed glance at plaster statues, win it from long hours at the lyceum, or try to see it through a stereopticon – all in an effort to supply the real or imagined defects of American knowledge.

At the bottom of this insatiable thirst for culture was a sense that civilization had lapsed in this country relative to conditions in England. For years, Americans had been assuring themselves that the home-grown had a particular virtue; they had declared time and time again that imitation was suicide and that the imitation of England in particular was suicide on a grand scale. These arguments had flattered a certain self-sufficiency in the American character, but they were not entirely compelling, as shown most obviously by the reluctance of publishers and public alike to patronize American writers. Emerson, who encouraged a radical originality in all things and decried imitation wherever he discovered it, found the most representative and characteristic American monuments to be, almost by a circumstantial necessity, cheap failures compared with their historically organic European counterparts. "Very coarse, very abhorrent to the imagination is the American White House," he wrote in 1837, "[b]ecause it has no historic lustre & natural growth out of feudalism &c like theirs, & is not on the other hand a new creation out of the soul, out of virtue & truth, outshining theirs but is an imitation of their gaudiness like a negro gay with cast off epaulettes & gold laced hat of his master."[6]

Culture in the United States seemed so obviously a hobbled attempt to extend European traditions that the American failure to be naturally an unself-consciously conservative (as Europeans always were) called into question for Emerson the ultimate value of tradition itself, as if tradition were fated by an inner necessity to degenerate into a mechanical imitation of form. If the situation were such that Americans could make no vital and continuous extension of a culture that was organic in Europe, then perhaps they ought to start again, from the beginning, forgetting what was proper to Europe. Emerson's frontier consciousness consisted largely in the perception that the transmission of culture from Europe to the United States was insurmountably difficult, and that it simply ought not to be attempted on a national scale because of the tendency to cultural caricature that circumstances induced. Americans might look at and admire Versailles, but they produced the White House, much as Jonathan, trying to say "hearts and darts," could come no closer than "burning rivers and cooling flames."

Few Americans had got so far in their thinking about their cultural situation as to find solace in Emerson's conclusion that a culture of art was a petty and insignificant thing compared with the cultivation of the spirit. "Culture" never meant to Emerson merely an easy familiarity with art products. Like others of his countrymen before and since, Emerson was prompted, partly by his country's apparent incapacity to sustain a traditional culture, to redefine the idea,[7] to give it some very new and some very old dimensions that suited the grandest possibilities that he saw around him:

> Culture, the height of Culture, highest behaviour consist in the identification of the Ego with the universe, so that when a man says, I think, I hope, I find, – he might properly say, the human race thinks, hopes, & finds – he states a fact which commands the understandings & affections of all the company, and yet, at the same time, he shall be able continually to keep sight of his biographical *ego*, – I had an ague, I had a fortune; my father had black hair; &c. as rhetoric, fun, or footman, to his grand & public *ego*, without impertinence or ever confounding them.[8]

The various definitions of culture scattered throughout Emerson's journals are often, if not always, thinly veiled attempts to state the essential difference between the cultural tendencies of England and America as Emerson perceived them, and, simultaneously, to define and make respectable the sort of culture that Americans could possibly have and be at home with. Here, for example, is one definition that implicitly levels at England the most conventional American imputation, that the "standard" notion of culture (that is, the English notion) involves a superficial concern with smoothness and prettiness:

> Culture in the highest sense does not consist in polishing or varnishing but in so presenting the attractions of Nature that the slumbering attributes of man may burst their iron sleep & rush, full grown, into day. Culture is not the trimming & turfing of gardens, but the showing the true harmony of the unshorn landscape with horrid thickets & bald mountains & the balance of the land & sea.[9]

Although this definition is couched mainly in negative terms, its significance resides in the wholly positive hint that the very idea of culture might be made to conform to American circumstances. We shall not have foreigners settling our frontier, Emerson seems to be saying: let the frontier settle our foreigners instead. Consistently his strategy is to encourage that American renaissance, or "revolution," which, he said, "is to be wrought by the gradual domestication of the idea of Culture."[10]

All of Emerson's definitions converge on at least one point: that an ideal culture has to be radically organic. He was quick to recognize the profound pathos of America's conservative provincial commitment to culture à la mode, as he understood that, whatever naive idealism lay behind such a commitment, it involved in practice an inorganic, me- chanical appropriation of the externals of European culture (that is to say, its "end-products") by imitation. What he singled out for praise in European art invariably evidenced some sort of organic principle, no matter how apparently "unnatural" the object. Thus, for instance, he could commend a palace for being "a natural growth out of feudalism," as in the passage on the White House, without implying an approval of feudalism. We have seen, too, that Irving was inclined to praise the organic quality of a European culture that promoted contentment and play rather than ambition and work. This view of European civilization was widely shared by Americans, not excepting many prominent literary nationalists such as James Russell Lowell, George Bancroft, and N. P. Willis. They acknowledged that Europe was mannered and artificial, but added that it was beautifully and appropriately so.

The Old World had, always, its exotic forms and social codes, so often repugnant to democratic principles, yet historically proper to a European people, expressive of their distinctive genius, and so not without a certain fitness and attraction. Their culture was, like any other, a means of stylizing, abstracting, abridging, and even denying natural experience; but, significantly, the artificiality seemed, to Amer- icans who concerned themselves with it, somehow natural, evolved, grown, in a way that was impossible to imitate. The quality in Eu- ropean civilization most attractive to Americans – the appearance of unpremeditated, unforced evolution, the implication of age – was pre- cisely the quality that defeated every attempt to transmit it. Emerson's poem "Each and All" taught a lesson that was as true of the artificial European environment as it was of the natural American landscape. Abstract and carry off a single favored element, reerect it on a new foundation, and the accomplishment, for all the work involved, is at last less than nothing – as the London Bridge, now in Arizona, testifies in our own day. How a thing fits is surely a part of the thing itself. This fact, so easy to overlook in Americans' frontier eagerness to be done with provincialism, has kept them continually dissatisfied with imported European culture, and with the European artifacts they la- boriously brought home to enshrine.

The infusion of the New World with the culture of the Old proceeded compulsively, notwithstanding the haunting sense of unfitness that it so frequently evoked, as though this cultural transmission were always ahead of or behind some obscure, unpublished schedule. One of the most directly revealing portrayals of this cultural malaise in all of American literature is Cooper's description of the fitting out of Judge Temple's frontier mansion in *The Pioneers*:

The walls were hung with a dark, lead-colored English paper that represented Britannia weeping over the tomb of Wolfe. The hero himself stood at a little distance from the mourning goddess, and at the edge of the paper. Each width contained the figure, with the slight exception of one arm of the General, which ran over on the next piece, so that when Richard essayed, with his own hands, to put together this delicate outline, some difficulties occurred that prevented a nice conjunction; and Britannia had reason to lament, in addition to the loss of her favorite's life, numberless cruel amputations of his right arm.[11]

The most admired European artifacts, with their delicate integrity, their requirement of "nice conjunctions," could rarely withstand the roughness of the Procrustean American environment, and in being forcibly transferred were doomed to be cracked, patched, and amputated, rendering, as it were, the paint and pasteboard of their composition but too painfully discernible.

So long as Americans had a consciousness of their native culture as a sadly imperfect rendition of an ideal European original, they continued to be self-conscious and sensitive, particularly to aspersions cast on the quality of their culture by the authoritative voice of England. The English were notoriously ready to find fault, and the Americans were equally notorious for their provincial defensiveness. Both of these attitudes may be observed in Hawthorne's record of his 1855 visit to Smithell's Hall, the country estate of Peter Ainsworth, a retired member of Parliament. In his *Notebook*, Hawthorne transcribed the "characteristic" anecdote with which Mrs. Ainsworth, entirely without success, attempted to amuse him:

Mr. [George] Bancroft, while Minister here, was telling somebody about the effect of the London atmosphere on his wife's health. "She is now very delicate," said he; "whereas, when we lived in New York, she was one of the most *indelicate* women in the city!" And Mrs. Ainsworth had the face to tell this foolish story for truth, and as indicating the mistakes into which Americans are liable to fall, in the use of the English language.... It is very queer, this resolute quizzing of our manners.[12]

It is easy enough to believe the story true; that Bancroft had meant it as a deliberate witticism; that his British listeners, with their assumptions about what an American is apt to say, misunderstood the joke, and that Hawthorne, on hearing it, was too provincially sensitive to detect the humor. The incident illustrates the sub rosa war of nerves that was likely to be engaged at any time during the nineteenth century when Americans and Britons met and spoke together.

The story illustrates another point as well. At least since Jonathan first appeared on the stage, language and usage had been the primary signs of American provincialism; these were the foundation of the English view of American speakers and writers, and the most frequently cited of all the cultural differentiae. American sensitivity to the norms of English usage fell at times little short of paranoia. In a compensatory way, this provincial fear of violating the proprieties contributed to the rigor of grammar school instruction with its insistence on hard and fast criteria of "correctness." The immense importance attached by nineteenth-century American educators to a punctilious exactitude in grammar and diction may well seem incredible today, but one senses that it was then cultivated not only for the benefit of rising Silas Laphams but in part also to prevent the kind of ridicule that may or may not have been directed at Bancroft.

In 1845 an American educator named Pardon Davis, staggering under the gravity of his cultural mission, wrote in defense of an early schooling in rhetoric, adducing "the case of some of the most eminent scholars, whose unguarded diction betrays provincialisms and undignified modes of expression haunting their whole lives, to their unbounded mortification."

> In order to avoid this humiliating and debasing dilemma [he continued] it is only necessary to eradicate *in early life* those improprieties and vulgarisms contracted during the imbecility of youth, and substitute that purity of expression easily attainable at an early age. In this manner are acquired that confidence and self-respect which not infrequently elevate their possessor to intercourse with a grade of society much superior to the circle in which he would otherwise be found.[13]

In the dire and frantic tone – the "humiliating and debasing dilemma," the "unbounded mortification" – we observe American culture *in extremis*. The conservative tactic, of which this may serve as an example, was to paint in the most horrific colors the social consequences of cultural backwardness, or of provincialism, especially in speech, and to insist on the hard, exacting work of being civilized to standard. For Americans culture rapidly took on the aspect of work or of duty (contrasting with the European linking of culture and play or leisure), and as a result attitudes toward art and education began to show the pressure of the burden.

New England was particularly inventive in overcoming the cultural disadvantages of its frontier origins, and indeed took up the work of self-improvement with a greater sense of mission than did other regions, perhaps because Puritan attitudes toward work and duty were still vital enough to make the task appear congenial. It is easy now to take a humorous view of the situation of New England as it awoke more and more fully to a sense of its provincial limitations. Inevitably there was much that was ludicrous both in the situation itself and in many of the expedients devised to meet it, but when the best minds of the time confronted the same dilemma, as unavoidably they did, the results were permanent contributions to American culture. Hawthorne's historical narratives, for instance, have in common with Emerson's approval of the lyceum system and Horace Mann's advocacy of free schools a complex desire to fix region and nation alike in a genuinely rooted temporal context, one that at the same time would provide aesthetic values capable of spiritually elevating and refining a people who, it seemed, were becoming increasingly trapped in and defined by their local circumstances, and who could therefore only fail, in Emerson's words, to "resist the vulgar prosperity that retrogrades ever to barbarism."[4]

It became the characteristic task of American art to oppose the reductive, isolating presentism of the farmers, the tradesmen, the mechanics, who were the spiritual victims of an attenuated culture. The New England transcendentalists most of all feared that if this condition were to continue, Americans would lose through disuse an otherwise innate capacity to detect and respond to the spiritual and ideal. "Most men," said Thoreau, "even in this comparatively free country, through mere ignorance and mistake, are so occupied with the factitious cares and superfluously coarse labors of life that its finer fruits cannot be plucked by them."[5] One of the most important remedies offered by New England artists was simply a reminder to their countrymen that the world was larger than their farms and older than themselves. But in a new country the remembrance of things past brought one immediately to the doorstep of Europe, admittance to be gained by serious study alone.

Such studious application was remarkably popular in New England, where to an unusual degree it was organized. William Emerson's founding of *The Monthly Anthology* and of the Boston Athenaeum in what his son called "that early ignorant and transitional *Month-of-March* in our New England culture,"[16] is representative of similar occurrences throughout the region. Mechanics' institutes, lyceums, informal as well as formal gatherings to discuss current science and literature, subscription libraries and Sunday schools proliferated steadily throughout the nineteenth century and helped to satisfy the need of a culture-starved population for a view of things wider than the merely personal. The first free public library in the world is said to have been established in 1833 in the small farming community of Peterborough, New Hampshire.[17]

In Victorian America, from the establishment of the Massachusetts Board of Education in 1837 to the decline of the Chautauqua movement toward the end of the century, culture was a panacea.

Yet this same period, or at least the greater part of it, was marked by an upsurge of nativist and exclusionary sentiment, a demand for a national literature and a desire to repudiate cultural subservience to Europe. In the *New York Mirror*, N. P. Willis asserted that "the Country is tired of being *be-Britished*,"[18] though in his own poetry he could not seem to break the mold of the sentimental Mrs. Hemans of Wales. Emerson, speaking at the beginning of this period, argued that American scholars "have listened too long to the courtly muses of Europe,"[19] and have become timid and imitative. Just when culture came to be in large demand among a rising middle class, Europe, the acknowledged possessor of culture, was being contemptuously dismissed as a decadent, depleted civilization where art was the province of the leisured dilettante and cultivation the mark of the amoral aristocrat.

In addition to the obvious motives of politics and simple envy, there was yet another, perhaps even more profound, motive than these for America's condemnation of Old World decadence. In the midst of their own cultural insecurities the belief persisted that Europeans had not come by their cultural treasure honestly (that is to say, they had inherited it). If inheritance, conceived of as an easy, passive transmission of culture, was in itself the source of the taint, then the Puritan work ethic might well supply the necessary rationale for an *earned* American culture, and happily prevent it from ever being regarded as decadent. Long before Henry James lamented that there were "no great Universities nor public schools – no Oxford, nor Eton, nor Harrow" to help make the United States a less provincial nation,[20] Americans had evolved a way of arguing defensively the irrelevance of such institutions. One writer observed in 1826 that "there are none of those splendid establishments in America such as Oxford and Cambridge in which immense salaries maintain the professors of literature in monastic idleness. . . . The People of this country have not yet been inclined to make much literary display – They have rather aimed at works of general utility."[21]

So completely was culture identified with Europe, and Europe with an idle and irresponsible aristocracy, that attitudes proper to one might virtually be transferred to the other. It was entirely too easy for the provincial American who despised and perhaps feared British social ideas to dismiss that great body of English literature that he had not read by pretending to regard it as "display." Opposition to Europe – even such opposition as was mainly political – thus often involved suspicion of culture itself, and the result looked very much like a Know-Nothing anti-intellectualism.[22] Other evidence points to the conclusion that to the

American provincial consciousness culture was primarily valuable as it disclosed a capacity for work or, conversely, was decadent in proportion as it hinted at idleness. The stylistic ideal of "repose" was for a time, because of English influence, associated with the "idle man" persona, as in Irving and, more complexly, in Hawthorne; both, to the extent that they serve the purposes of the American artist, may be understood as the products of conservative longing for European conditions of authorship or, conversely, of a calculated rebellion against the native view of art as a form of labor like any other. American culture heroes, as distinct from their personae, were almost invariably presented in their biographies (accurately enough in most instances) as having overcome enormous circumstantial difficulties by perseverance and hard work. The formula for the life of an artist in America was, in other words, precisely that of the successful man of business and stressed the same qualities of character. Perhaps the prototype in this respect was Benjamin West, whose luck and pluck as a boy were part of an inspirational legend long before Hawthorne rehearsed the tale in his *Biographical Stories for Children*. Elsewhere, and certainly with more candor, Hawthorne admitted that he had always found West's work "chilling."[23]

New England's Puritan background steeled it for the "great labour" that Eliot would later identify; its contacts with Europe, together with the provincial disadvantages that the frontier had bequeathed, brought the imperative psychological need to perform that labor into full consciousness in the light of a duty. It is no coincidence that Massachusetts of all the states pioneered in educational reform, gave the greatest encouragement to lyceums, became, by midcentury, the publishing capital of the nation, and was the *fons et origo* of the American Renaissance. The stultifying horror of provincial isolation together with the felt need to "master" culture prompted New Englanders to educate themselves through a variety of progressively more sophisticated expedients.

So certain was New England of its civilizing mission – its new "errand into the wilderness" – that it embarked on a program of evangelizing not only the Northeast but the West as well, a region generally recognized by educated New Englanders as the locus of America's future strength, and, in cultural terms, of its present embarrassment. The term "evangelizing" is appropriate, not only in regard to the fervor and dedication with which the mission was carried forth but also in respect to the religious motives which from the very first operated strongly in the desire of the East to "save" the West. The problem of frontier indifference to religion, which had bothered Timothy Dwight in the 1790s, was becoming crucially important to eastern conservatives as the population of the West expanded. To Lyman Beecher in 1835 it was perfectly plain that the religious and political destiny of our nation is to be decided in the west.... What will become of the West if her prosperity rushes up to such a majesty of power, while those great [eastern] institutions ["which discipline the mind and arm the conscience and the heart"] linger ... ? It must not be permitted.... Let no man at the East quiet himself and dream of liberty, whatever may become of the West.... Her destiny is our destiny.[24]

Although Dwight had in a measure anticipated this line of reasoning, the outright identification of "our destiny" with that of the West was nevertheless a crucial change of emphasis in America's self-image, implying as it did that the nation would stand or fall not on the accomplishments of an independent eastern seaboard, but on its ability to civilize an emergent West. This vastly larger idea of America's future – an idea that would shortly culminate in the political concept of "manifest destiny" – implied a much more restrained and tolerant attitude than Dwight ever had of the social and cultural failings of western society. The tolerance arose from the discovery by men like Beecher that the West was after all an accurate if somewhat outsized representation of the nation as a whole, displaying the full complement of its problems and virtues, and not, as had been thought, a natural selection of America's worst traits only.[25] The West was being brought into the ambit of civilization simultaneously as an idea and as a region.

Not the least of the several reasons for this change in attitudes was the election of 1828 in which Andrew Jackson, "who can fight," beat John Quincy Adams, "who can write." The election not only made Jackson president, it also, to popular perception, made him a Representative Man as well. To Melville and other "Young Americans" this rough frontier hero was an impressive symbol of the "Spirit of Equality."[26] Even Emerson, who despised Jackson's vulgarity and spoke of his "rank rabble party" as being "heedless of English & of all literature,"[27] nevertheless recognized the frontier as the wellspring of American democracy and urged the nation's poets to sing "the western clearing, Oregon, and Texas."[28] The election, then, dramatically confirmed a tendency already under way in eastern attitudes toward seeing the West as indispensably representative of the cherished spirit of equality, even as the East continued to represent the similarly cherished value of achievement.[29]

The West was, in short, too American, too representative of essential national values, to be allowed to go its crazy way unguided by the shaping hand of eastern institutions. New Englanders, whose view this primarily was, prepared themselves to supply the required aid, partly (and only partly) because they knew that Europe would continue to judge them according to the depressed cultural standards of the West – this being one of the most evident consequences of an identity of destinies. The West, in all its frontier crudity, always seemed to give the lie to the cultural pretensions of the nation as a whole, and more especially to raise doubts about whether, at last, a democracy *can* be civilized. European visitors, not unnaturally, took special note of the most outrageous and extravagant behavior, filling their travel accounts with horrified descriptions of tobacco-chewing, spitting, swearing, drinking, brawling, in short, with the widest variety of dishonest and barbarous western conduct. Many of these descriptions were willfully malicious and belonged to the "resolute quizzing of our manners" that Hawthorne found so "queer." But the accuracy or exaggeration of such reports is less important than the fact that from them the European idea of America was to a surprising extent actually formed, and formed in a way that made little distinction between settled East and frontier West. Even among educated Europeans, Americans were often supposed to be aboriginal if not aborigines per se. When Emerson went abroad, the English were pleased to believe that he looked rather like an Indian.[30] Hawthorne had a similar experience. A certain Englishman, surprised that the urbane gentleman with whom he had been speaking was an American, asked whether he had not been some considerable time in England: "He meant (finding me not absolutely a savage) that I must have been caught a good while ago."[31] We need search no further for the explanation of Hawthorne's well-known antipathy to Indian stories than the general inclination of civilized Europe to regard America as a barbarous country.

Needless to say, few Americans were prepared to accept such a judgment, and those who considered themselves artists and scholars were especially resentful that they should be characterized by frontier (even Indian) standards, or that such characterizations should in the least be sustained by the quality of their actual environment. These resentments, however, and the cultural conservatism they insensibly called forth, proved to be the source of considerable artistic energy and were finally as important to the shape and texture of American art as the cultural thinness that had, in the first place, provoked so much of this British ridicule. America was a rough place, certainly, but its crudity had less detectable effect on artistic theory and practice than did the artists' often deliberate resistance to it.[32] Thoreau's love of Indian stories was implicitly a criticism of just this fact. With an eccentricity both characteristic and admirable, he, unlike Hawthorne, loved that genuine wildness of which the country was just then profoundly ashamed and which it was fighting with all of its resources. Whatever else the Indians may from time to time have meant to white America, they always served to figure for it the end point of the provincializing process: a perfect adaptation to circumstance, a perfect indifference to all recognizable tradition and to all of what white Americans called culture. Presented, then, with Europe's intolerable sense of American barbarism, touching closely as it did on the most secret of America's cultural fears, two modes of provincial response seemed open. Some, ignoring the historical logic of Beecher's essentially missionary argument, simply dissociated themselves from the West and devoted the energy of their resentment to forging a temperamental and cultural alliance with Europe; others, such as Emerson in his frontier lecture tours or Beecher himself at the Lane Seminary, worked to remove the blot from the cultural reputation of the country. Rather like the English Puritans of the 1630s and 1640s, conscientious Americans two centuries later had a choice to make: whether to stay and try to meliorate conditions at home or escape across the Atlantic to a better world.

Probably none who chose the latter course understood these issues and their importance more thoroughly than Henry James, who was prompted to make the "international theme" his own by the clear-eyed perception that American identity was inescapably bound up in European attitudes. His third novel, *The American*, embodies this perception by provocatively dramatizing Old World condescension in the Bellegardes much as the New World provincial might *expect* to see it – as outsized, melodramatic, feminine, depleted, and, of course, as deeply corrupt. The western American hero, Christopher Newman, who sees them this way, is in turn seen by them as the awkward, culturally rootless, sexually aggressive provincial of the light-comedy stereotype. In the course of the novel, Newman develops out of his assigned role by seeming to drive the Bellegardes ever more deeply into theirs, while the imperfectly serious question to which all this movement is an answer is whether Newman is finally to be regarded as a civilized man or as an enemy and attacker of civilization. This theme is announced early, in the interview between the hero, newly arrived in Europe, and Mrs. Tristram, a Europeanized American resident in Paris:

> "Bravo!" said Mrs. Tristram, "that is very fine. You are the great Western Barbarian, stepping forth in his innocence and might, gazing a while at this poor effete Old World, and then swooping down on it."
>
> "Oh, come," said Newman. "I am not a barbarian, by a good deal. I am very much the reverse. I have seen barbarians; I know what they are."
>
> "I don't mean that you are a Comanche chief, or that you wear a blanket and feathers. There are different shades."
>
> "I am a highly civilized man," said Newman. "I stick to that."[33]

Yet Newman's motive for being in Europe at all is precisely the dissatisfaction he has felt with his purely commercial prosperity, with the barbarism, in other words, that the Bellegardes most hold against him. Newman *is* an innocent, as Mrs. Tristram says, but an innocent with awareness enough to respond actively to the deficiencies in his old life and to be hungry for the kinds of new experience that he imagines will remold him; he is a man of substance in search of form, and he is prepared to work to achieve it. His most immediate concern, apart from responsibly touring all the museums, is to gain the "best" wife, by which he means the most cultivated, the most *stylish*. He wishes, on his part, to "do the thing in handsome style," since for an American so clearly "indelicate" as Newman, securing such a wife is, as he says, "the greatest victory over circumstances."[34]

Like many of his contemporaries, James was ambivalent in his attitudes toward the western American ethos from which Newman had come. The provincial thinness of its culture, the narrowness of the experience it could support, were much like that which James found in Hawthorne's New England. These (especially from the perspective of Europe) were American and not merely western traits; they were not in themselves to be defended, but neither were they to be apologized for. However, as *The American* sought to show in 1877, and as James's study of Hawthorne would suggest again in 1879, the creatively independent, morally egalitarian spirit so central to Americans' national sense of self was arguably dependent on the lack of an artificial or "given" cultivation, a provincial absence that, for all the limitations it really imposed, encouraged in their responses as human beings to situations, or as artists to materials, a moral spontaneity and freshness of vision that would, naturally, bear more the impress of immediate life than of life stored and sorted by tradition. The style that Newman had created for himself by the end of the novel was quite obviously not artificial; it was not that of the dilettantish tourist whom Emerson had objected to in "The American Scholar," but was instead very much an earned style. Newman is at the conclusion of the novel (and in a way that he was not at the beginning) a "highly civilized man," one no longer looking for perpetual victories over circumstance, but instead learning how to behave in a world where some things cannot be helped. His culture, as experience develops it and draws it out, differs from the passive, inherited culture of the Bellegardes in proportion as he has earned it both by the experience of his personal defeats and by the difficult labor of conscious moral choices. The potential for this sort of development is what James found appealing in the provincialism of his western hero.

By 1877 the Westerner was fairly well established as the prototypical American (Beecher's prescience having been confirmed to that extent),

but in the 1830s and 1840s Easterners were only beginning to explore
the idea. During the period of the steady rapprochement between the
Northeast and West which culminated in an alliance of mutual interest
against the South by the time of the Civil War, New Englanders were
increasingly inclined to speak of the West in ways that seemed self-
consciously to rehearse their own cultural dilemmas. Margaret Fuller's
firsthand assessment of frontier Wisconsin, written in 1843, is typical of
the New England intellectual's revised sense of the West, and suggests,
too, the sort of illumination that was now more and more to be shed
by this region on the whole problem of American civilization:

> I come to the West prepared for the distaste I must experience at
> its mushroom growth. I know that where "go ahead" is the only
> motto, the village cannot grow in the gentle proportions that suc-
> cessive lives and the gradations of experience involuntarily give. In
> older countries the house of the son grew from that of the father,
> as naturally as new joints on a bough, and the cathedral crowned
> the whole as naturally as the leafy summit the tree. This cannot be
> here.[35]

Culture, in other words, cannot be organic in America, because it is
in the nature of the frontier to prevent Americans, perhaps for all time,
from being a settled people. Nor is there any hopeful Edenic myth of
western renewal to compensate; nothing of the youthful American Adam
for whom culture is gloriously irrelevant; in fact, the immediate implication of Fuller's observation is that if anyone is in an Edenic condition,
it is the European whose houses and villages "grow" naturally, and
whose cultural wants are supplied without voluntary effort.

The image of the cathedral in Fuller's statement has important symbolic
value in this respect because on the one hand it recalls the habit of Irving
and of William Cullen Bryant, among earlier writers, of seeing "cathe-
drals" in stands of native American trees,[36] and because on the other
hand it anticipates Henry Adams's brilliant evocation of the organic
fitness of Chartres and Mont-St.-Michel to the culture they represent –
a rendering that only an American frontier consciousness could have
managed quite so appreciatively. Only an American who had worked
as hard and as self-consciously at his education as Adams had done could
possibly feel so deeply and poignantly the fact that these religious monuments had been created (not here and now, but so exclusively there and
then) without a sense of work or sacrifice, much as, to bring the point
round to Henry James again, the civilization of the Bellegardes was the
organic accretion of eight hundred years rather than the self-conscious
labor of an acquisitive and receptive pilgrim, however passionate. Newman himself, having, like Fuller, the provincial West for contrast, had

been impressed, if not entirely won over, by the Edenic quality in Madame de Bellegarde's culture:

> "She is a woman of conventions and proprieties," he said to himself as he looked at her; "her world is the world of things immutably decreed. But how she is at home in it, and what a paradise she finds it! She walks about in it as if it were a blooming park, a Garden of Eden; and when she sees 'This is genteel,' or 'This is improper,' written on a mile-stone she stops ecstatically, as if she were listening to a nightingale or smelling a rose."[37]

All three of these American ambassadors to the cultural Eden of Europe – Fuller, Christopher Newman, Adams – were drawn there roughly in proportion to the frictional resistance offered by circumstances at home to the life of the mind and spirit, in proportion, that is, to the difficulty of being civilized in America, which, for the conservative, is finally equivalent to the difficulty of being at home in America. Margaret Fuller and Henry Adams felt that it was an unfair burden and a distinctly American one. Henry James agreed. In a notebook entry dated November 25, 1881, James declared:

> My work lies there [i.e., in Europe] – and with this vast new world, *je n'ai que faire*. One can't do both – one must choose. No European writer is called upon to assume that terrible burden, and it seems hard that I should be. The burden is necessarily greater for an American – for he *must* deal, more or less, even if only by implication, with Europe.[38]

The conservative solution to the problem of provincialism is to attach oneself to the mind of Europe, as Eliot would later suggest, a solution that Adams, Fuller, and Henry James all strove to implement. Speaking of the difficulty of that solution, Henry Adams described the plight of Augustus St. Gaudens as a parallel to his own, and in a way that Margaret Fuller would have understood and approved:

> In mere time [St. Gaudens] was a lost soul that had strayed by chance into the twentieth century, and forgotten where it came from. He writhed and cursed his ignorance, much as Adams did at his own, but in the opposite sense. St. Gaudens was a child of Benvenuto Cellini, smothered in an American cradle. Adams was a quintessence of Boston, devoured by curiosity to think like Benvenuto. St. Gaudens's art was starved from birth, and Adams's instinct was blighted from babyhood. Each had but half a nature, and when they came together before the Virgin of Amiens they ought to have felt in her the force that made them one; but it was

not so. To Adams she became more than ever a channel of force; to St. Gaudens she remained as before a channel of taste.[39]

Adams's "but it was not so" and James's "one can't do both" and Fuller's "this cannot be here" are the laments of conservatives who have recognized that the thin, unsettled, frontier quality of American life poses the greatest possible threat to cultural continuity and thus to the chance to be civilized. All three saw that such a radical alienation from the sources of culture requires in an American a vast compensatory dedication, a laborious conservative effort, a lifelong perseverance with no guarantee of final "success." A sense of this difficulty, as James implied in his notebook entry, is apparent in much of America's best literature and largely characterizes it *as* American.

Two solutions to this cultural dilemma are evident in American thought in the 1830s and 1840s. One is a liberal solution, associated with Emerson and Thoreau; the other is the conservative solution just referred to, which may be exemplified in the career and thought of Margaret Fuller, a woman who with the utmost deliberation assumed the task of educating herself, of learning the culture that seemed always to beckon her home to a European and aristocratic identity. The person she strove always to be was one "who, recognizing the immense advantage of being born to a new world and on virgin soil, yet does not wish one seed from the past to be lost," and is instead determined to "gather and carry back" from Europe "every plant that will bear a new climate and new culture."[40]

Chapter 7

Life as art in America

<hr>

We lead a life of glimpses & glances. We see nothing good steadily or long, and though love-sick with Ideas they hide their faces alway.
– Emerson to Margaret Fuller, October 20, 1836[1]

Of all the circumstances that contributed to the shaping of Margaret Fuller's mind and career, perhaps none was more fatally decisive than the provinciality of her environment. For most of her life, lacking the perspective of foreign travel, she could scarcely gauge the meaning of the handicap she labored under; but she nevertheless felt its constraints from an early age. Only on arriving in Italy in 1846 could she acknowledge that for once her surroundings were adequate; and by then, the mental irritant of provincial conditions removed, her major work was over. As Henry James seems to have understood, Fuller was, and remains, the best example of the American scholar-artist of the antebellum period, the one figure of her time from whom the clearest insights may be had concerning the effects of cultural attenuation on the ardent, aspiring mind.

These effects, peculiar as they were to the American scene, are for the most part so far from being regrettable that one insists on her provincialism just as James insisted on Hawthorne's – "not in the least in condemnation, but, on the contrary, in support of an appreciative view."[2] If she was temperamentally and intellectually provincial, she was so most obviously in the passionate attachment she formed with ideas, in her devotion to the idea, in particular, of salvation through art, in the sense she always had of seeing partially and of expecting in the future to see more fully, in her habitual, almost programmatic independence from her surroundings, and in her fondness, generally, for the abstract. The cultural paucity of her environment made her a hard-working if undisciplined student and, within certain bounds, a daring, unsatisfied thinker. So much of the shape of her career and the quality of her mind can be referred to the provincial cast of her circumstances that she threatens to become a sort of "representative person," a fact of cultural history by which others, such as Emerson and Hawthorne, might be gauged and understood. Recognizing this archetypal quality in her, James explained a digression in *Hawthorne* by saying, "I mention Margaret Fuller here because a glimpse of her state of mind – her vivacity of desire and poverty of knowledge – helps to define the situation."[3] So, indeed, it does.

The Cambridge-Cambridgeport area where Margaret Fuller spent the first twenty-three years of her life had but four discernible centers of culture, and the salient fact about them is that they had absolutely nothing to do with one another. First, in point of popularity, was the barbershop that doubled as a museum. Run by a genial antiquarian Dutchman, the museum offered an impressively jumbled display of live Java sparrows, scrimshaw, Dutch prints, and decorated canoe paddles from New Zealand, among many other odds and ends. The barber himself was not the least interesting exhibit, the town being "so purely indigenous," as James Russell Lowell recalled, that the proprietor had "a certain exotic charm, a kind of game flavor, by being a Dutchman."[4] Barbershops were, of course, patronized by men only, but young Margaret could not have escaped acquaintance with this breathtaking assortment, nor with the colorful and miscellaneous idea of the world that it must have suggested.

The second center of culture in the narrow universe of Margaret Fuller's youth was of an altogether different order. In a modest Cambridgeport house not two miles from her own, Washington Allston lived and worked. A displaced South Carolina gentleman of impeccable manners and appearance, Allston had seen the wider world, had been to England and spoken with Wordsworth, Coleridge, and Southey. The fact that this quiet, industrious, and thoughtful man was the most significant painter of his generation in America was largely lost on Cambridgeport, where, indeed, he seemed more foreign than the barber's Hall of Fantasy. Fuller, at the age of twenty, knew of the artist only from the scanty gossip of the town crier; she would first see him and speak to him early in January 1839, and even then, for all her study of the arts at the Boston Athenaeum, she felt compelled to reserve judgment on his work.[5]

The third and, of course, the most personally significant source of learning and culture was Timothy Fuller, Margaret's father. The educational regimen that he established for his daughter was almost brutally strict and certainly eccentric. By the age of six she was reading the Latin authors daily and studying late each night. The unremitting intellectual labors and the evident pressure under which she worked resulted in a chronic tendency to nightmare; they also, in her words, "prevented the harmonious development of my bodily powers and checked my growth, while, later, they induced continual head-ache."[6] Needless to say, such a program succeeded first of all in alienating her socially and intellectually from people her own age. The personal associations she valued most were with people much older than herself, especially with her tutors – Uncle Elisha, for example, who taught her Greek when she was ten, and Dr. Park, with whom she was a particular favorite. Intellectually competitive, Margaret had worked hard for her knowledge and was proud of it in a way that drew attention from her parents' generation and antagonism from her own. At the age of eleven she impressed two of her classmates, Oliver Wendell Holmes and Richard Henry Dana, as being "smart," but for a girl rather "queer."[7]

As a fourth source of culture in her home town, Harvard was important as it kept present to her consciousness an ideal of education and intellectual community. She heard some of the best speakers of the day on public occasions at the college, and could share in the general enthusiasm for the European polish of Edward Everett and George Ticknor. But by default Fuller's attention was more often drawn to the other, eccentric side of New England's college town, to the turbaned widow, for example, who lived in Washington's headquarters, "studious only of Spinoza, and refusing to molest the canker-worms that annually disleaved her elms, because we were all vermicular alike."[8]

To look back on Fuller's early environment is to be struck by its comic incongruities, and to notice that the sublime and the ridiculous were constantly being brought into contact by the subtle pressure of provincial circumstance. In the commercial town of Cambridgeport, Allston's work bore lightly on the public consciousness, whereas the arrival of the sloop *Harvard* with firewood from Maine was an event to stir the imagination. In Cambridge, when the undergraduate militia came to muster drunk, President Kirkland left his study to investigate personally the flip at Porter's Inn. Margaret Fuller would be prevented from going to school to Ma'am Betty because that worthy drank water from the nose of her teakettle; instead, the little scholar somehow found, and read through, Léonarde Simonde de Sismondi's *Literature of the South of Europe*, and then, in the evening, sang "Bounding Billows" at Mrs. McTheague's cotillion.[9]

The colorful eccentricities of such a place as Cambridge in the early nineteenth century have been amply reported in published reminiscences, and they are more than merely amusing: they are valuable indices to the cultural stresses that typically underlie and define provincial societies. During Margaret Fuller's childhood, the old, relatively stable social order was rapidly dissolving into a broader, more fluid democracy. The old guard, much less concerned with public opinion than the rising classes would be, were notably eccentric in their behavior. Lowell recalled that "when social distinctions were more marked in Cambridge . . . men felt that their personalities were their castles, in which they could intrench themselves against the world. . . . Formerly they used to insist upon your giving the wall to their peculiarities, and you still find examples of it in the parson or doctor of retired villages."¹⁰ These "peculiarities" seem to have been especially characteristic of the educated and influential portions of society, and were to a degree simply imitated by upwardly mobile provincials along with more conventional manners. But, as Lowell pointed out, public opinion to all appearances was responsible for the decadence of eccentricity and for the conformity that superseded it. His attribution of a unique personal freedom to the older, more class-conscious social order is an explanation of patrician behavior evidently drawn on the model of European nobility, and in any event fails to account for the *kinds* of eccentricity that distinguished the provincial Cambridge of Fuller's youth.

The clue to a broader interpretation than Lowell offers is implicit in his association of eccentricity with "retired villages," and Cambridge in 1820 was still, essentially, such a village. One way to begin to understand these curious phenomena would be to note that Fuller's situation was more like that of her frontier countrymen than we generally assume, and that the eccentricity of the gentleman Lowell recalled who "used to sit at the open window during thunder-storms, and had a Grecian feeling about death by lightning,"¹¹ is in precisely the same key as Hermon Husbands's interpretation of Ezekiel. Both instances of eccentricity are attempts, without regard to fitness, to assimilate a vaguely attractive yet essentially foreign cultural idea into private behavior. In either case, to quote James, a certain "vivacity of desire and poverty of knowledge . . . helps to define the situation."

Perhaps this context will reveal some aspects of Fuller's achievement more clearly than conventional approaches have done, which, by always seeming to apologize for her eccentricities, miss much of the essentially American quality of a flamboyant and rough-hewn career. Fuller's "style" has always posed a problem for those who propose to talk seriously about her. Most appear to agree that the greatest damage to her reputation as an artist was done by three of her closest friends, Emerson, James Freeman Clarke, and William Henry Channing, who, in their 1852 *Memoirs*, are supposed to have concocted the so-called Margaret Myth. This "myth" emphasizes her many awkwardnesses, including her most notorious departures from the ideal of self-effacing womanhood: her feminism, her political activism, her pedantry, her intellectual snobbishness, the curiosity of her late marriage and early death, even the awkwardness of her prose style. Some of these eccentricities and extravagances she no doubt cultivated with intense deliberation for their dramatic effect; they have all, in any event, been summed up and typified in her legendary gesture of accepting the universe, and are certainly responsible for whatever limited place she now occupies in the popular imagination.

Since 1940, however, and the appearance of Mason Wade's biography, a steady revaluation aggressively opposed to the "myth" has sought to find the artist beneath the character, and has attempted to establish her "real" contribution to American culture. Centering on her neglected critical writings, commentators have discovered in Fuller a critic second in her generation only to Poe, as well as an important cultural link between Europe and the New England transcendentalists. If Fuller's style made her a spectacle in her own day, contemporary examination of her substantive achievement has had nearly the reverse effect, as though criticism had to choose whether to see the eccentric style or the solid substance. Nearly everyone who has written about her has felt her importance, though few, then or now, have suggested any vital connection between *what* she did and the *way* she did it.

Fuller's eccentricities share a basic principle with those of her less famous Cambridge neighbors: a deeply rooted, and perhaps preconscious conviction that one's circumstances are distressingly undistinguished. The more deeply one holds such a conviction, the more one is willing to regard art – both in the high-culture sense and in the sense of artifice or artificial behavior – as actually preferable to "life"; just as the distinction between art and life comes to seem wholly natural and unavoidable. This conviction might well be held preconsciously by one who would reject it out of hand were it ever explicitly formulated. Probably Fuller never put the issue to herself in precisely this way, however convinced she was that the life around her failed to approach her own artistic expectations. She nevertheless could and did say that "the fine arts were one compensation for the necessary prose of life,"[12] and could so far act on this perception as to offer in the winter of 1839 a series of "Conversations" for women on Greek mythology, "in a city which, with great pretensions to mental refinement, boasts, at present, nothing of the kind."[13] Such life as she was willing to repudiate, such life as she had known in provincial, materialistic New England, was not what *she* had ever meant by "life."

Shortly before the first of her Conversations, she confessed some of her dissatisfactions and longings in a discussion of Alfred de Vigny which she sent to Emerson: "So materialistic is the course of common life," she wrote, "that we *ask daily* new Messiahs from literature and art, to turn us from the Pharisaic observance of the law, to the baptism of the spirit."[14] The sentiment itself is hardly unique, and the phrasing surely owes something to Thomas Carlyle; the desire to be rid of the cruel world and to escape to a heaven of beauty, truth, and goodness was generally conventional among romantic poets, British and American.

But her emphasis is not conventional. Her statement is not that of an artist kicking against mortal limitations, but rather that of a reader, a patron of the arts, annoyed that life as it is lived should be so less valuable than the life available in art. Her expression is important for the reflection it gives of a provincial frontier consciousness, of the antagonism between American circumstances and the sort of intellectual refinement that she had always been given to understand was ideal. Hers was the view, the consciousness, of one who had grown up with the unfulfilled ideal held out by the imperious Timothy Fuller and no less by the teasing, ambiguous image of Harvard. The horror of education was not that it was so demanding, but that it always, at every turn, took her out of sympathy with the place where she lived; that it so demonstrated the excellent charms of the past as to make the present hardly bearable; that it made Europe so brightly exciting, so high-minded and ideal, as to convince her that her own country could offer nothing to match; that it required her, in a word, to view her own home and her own mentality as wholly discontinuous and even contradictory phenomena.

Fuller's sense of dislocation evolved slowly, helped along by recognizing time and again that her finest pleasures in life were all acts of art and imagination, and equally by repeated discoveries that her sharpest disappointments came from the failure of her environment to aid and support these acts. But if the attitude took form slowly, it burst in full upon her consciousness on Thanksgiving Day, 1831, in what seems much like a religious epiphany:

> I saw how long it must be before the soul can learn to act under these limitations of time and space, and human nature; but I saw also, that it MUST do it, – that it must make all this false true, – and sow new and immortal plants in the garden of God, before it could return again. I saw there was no self; that selfishness was all folly, and the result of circumstance; that it was only because I thought self real that I suffered; that I had only to live in the idea of the ALL, and all was mine. This truth came to me, and I received it unhesitatingly; so that I was for that hour taken up into God. In that true ray most of the relations of earth seemed mere films, phenomena.[15]

This ambiguous resisting and accepting the limitations of time, space, and circumstance Fuller shared not only with the transcendentalists, but with the generality of frontier Americans who knew these three fates for genuine enemies, Lords of Life whose function it was to enforce a spiritually intolerable isolation. But she went well beyond most other Americans when she realized that what makes for the psychic pain of isolation is the consciousness of selfhood; and if self is a function of circumstance, then the pain of isolation could be alleviated by doing away with one's circumstances or by rendering them innocuous.[16] Education, and specifically an acquaintance with philosophy and the arts, was one way (and for Fuller it was *the way*) of denying circumstance, first by declaring its components unreal, and second by affirming the supremacy of the imagination over the senses. In this way she was at war with her surroundings, and in that war the first casualties were the temporal and spatial attachments that would otherwise have supplied her with a conventional sense of home.

Often she would speak of being "a pilgrim and sojourner on earth" and suggest that "the birds and foxes would be surer of a place to lay the head than I."[17] She would long for the day when she might "feel no more that sometimes despairing, sometimes insolently contemptuous, feeling of incongeniality with my time and place."[18] Occasionally even art would fail to give shelter against the oppression of circumstance. She refused, for example, to read the eighteenth-century English novelists because, she said, they "deal too broadly with the coarse actualities of life."[19] From the age of twelve when disease disfigured her complexion, she seems to have felt repeatedly betrayed by the physical, and always her refuge and compensation was the mind. Speaking later of the consequences of that early disease, she observed, "My own vanity was for a time severely wounded; but I recovered, and made up my mind to be bright and ugly."[20] Few physical or natural objects ever quite satisfied Fuller, who once referred to Niagara Falls as "the one object in the world that would not disappoint."[21] Environments challenged her and invited her resistance, even as they resisted and threatened to overwhelm her soul. Cambridge and Cambridgeport might dissolve before the action of the mind, but only for so long as she applied the whole strength of her will to the task. To an extraordinary degree, she was bent on *not* accepting the universe, choosing instead to create and sustain one of her own making. The battle was thus to be waged on behalf of the spirit and in the domain of art; her triumph, should it come, would be at once an exile and a coming home.

By 1832 Fuller was beginning to feel some success. She had established contact with a number of young Cambridge intellectuals and for a time enjoyed what must have seemed a heady and sophisticated life of the mind. Indeed, the avidity of Fuller's enthusiasm seems markedly to have invigorated the others. They all were stirred, but none so deeply as she, by Carlyle's essays on Goethe, with their compelling indications of the value of German literature and their promise of a writer who would at last "speak to the whole soul," and "in these hard, unbelieving, utilitarian days, reveal to us glimpses of the unseen but not unreal World, so that the Actual and the Ideal may again meet together, and clear knowledge be again wedded to religion, in the life and business of men."[22] Nothing could have spoken more directly to Fuller's needs at this critical moment, and she responded with a typically voracious enthusiasm by learning German with the help of Frederic Henry Hedge. In 1833 she read all that Goethe had written and much of Körner, Novalis, Richter, and Schiller.[23] "The thought and the beauty of this rich literature," James Freeman Clarke later wrote, "equally filled her mind and fascinated her imagination."[24]

It was important that she should have made this discovery when she did, since in the spring of 1833, with her imagination at fever pitch and her intellectual ambition whetted as it never had been before, her father retired from politics and chose for himself, and perforce for Margaret as well, the rural isolation of a Groton farm. Margaret's eclectic education, governed so entirely by her enthusiasms (and so hardly governed at all) was now suddenly and severely curtailed. Her enforced rustication was to be a discovery of limits. So it later seemed to Emerson who described her situation at this time: "Cut off from access to the scholars, libraries, lectures, galleries of art, museums of science, antiquities, and historic scenes of Europe, Margaret bent her powers to use such opportunities as she could command in her solitary country-home."[25]

She continued her reading in German, allowing herself three nights a week – all that she could spare from household duties – but complained of a lack of progress, her work being now, by force of circumstance, "necessarily broken up."[26] Again she blamed the immediate surroundings, linking her predicament to the very contours of her environment: "The Peterborough hills and the Wachusetts are associated in my mind with many hours of anguish, as great I think as I am capable of feeling. I used to look at them, towering to the sky, and feel that I, too, from my birth had longed to rise, but I felt crushed to earth, yet again a nobler spirit said *that* could never be."[27] Cambridge and Boston, with their eastern cultural advantages, such as they were, represented aspiration, the ascendancy of the spirit, the freeing of the soul from the earth; Groton, which brought circumstances and a sense of the pressing physical environment to the fore, was by contrast a crushing defeat. It was at Groton that her father sickened and died; she and her brother Arthur were also dangerously ill, and their mother was all the while overworked and worried.

This "Groton exile," much like Anne Bradstreet's rustication in the New World, was radically a frontier experience, involving a shutting down of cultural, aesthetic, and spiritual horizons. For both women the effect for consciousness was an inward turning, a strained determination

to meet circumstantial threats to the spirit with whatever cultural resources came to hand. Like Hester Prynne, Fuller found some compensation in her trials:

> There ... in solitude the mind acquired more power of concen-
> tration and discerned the beauty of a stricter method. There the
> heart was awakened to sympathize with the ignorant, to pity the
> vulgar, and hope for the seemingly worthless, for a need was felt
> of realizing the only reality, the divine soul of this visible creation,
> which cannot err and will not sleep, which cannot permit evil to
> be permanent or its aim of beauty to be eventually frustrated in the
> smallest particular.[28]

The more stubbornly the environment resisted her inner compulsion to
rise clear of it, the harder she applied herself to her education; the harder,
in short, she worked.

The Groton years were but two and a half, ending with the death of
Margaret's father in October 1835; it had been a short but crucial interlude
of which the most immediately obvious effect was to deepen her resolve
to study on a more regular basis. For a time she thought of going to
Europe to meet the writers who meant the most to her, but her father's
death and the sad reduction of his once prosperous estate required still
more years of sacrifice. Briefly she taught German and Italian at Alcott's
underfinanced Temple School where her talent for conversation made
her a valuable teacher, and afterward at a school in Rhode Island where,
if the work was less congenial, she was at least able to complete her
translation of Johann Eckermann's *Conversations with Goethe* and see to
its publication in Boston in 1839.

If Fuller had a home anywhere during these years it was Boston. There
she found, as she thought, all that Groton and her Rhode Island exile
had denied her. With Emerson, whom she had first met in 1835, she
truly made the most of the city's cultural institutions, and showed her
older, mellower, and Harvard-educated companion an enthusiasm of
response that he seems to have found bracing. Her excitement in the face
of a cultural artifact is a notorious part of the "Margaret Myth," but in
this, as Henry James so acutely observed,[29] she was simply an epitome
of the New England mind of the 1830s and 1840s. She could enjoy – in
a way that seems all but closed to modern Americans – an afternoon
ramble among the dozen or so plaster casts of Greek and Roman statuary
that a Boston merchant fifteen years earlier had imported from Italy and
placed in the Athenaeum gallery.

Paltry as this collection may now seem, no observers were then so
jaded as to scorn it. The gallery and its adjacent gardens were in fact
fashionable resorts which conveyed an impression of lavish display only

because sculpture was in general so scarce in America. The deprivation which the gallery was intended to alleviate was a frontier legacy, of course, just as the gallery itself was a consequence and an expression of New England's isolation from all that its people called "culture." Yet the deprivation and the isolation, which at the time seemed such unmitigated evils, were ironically the root cause of an appreciation so markedly intense and vital as, for that very reason, to appear eccentric, original, and American.

To view the sculpture gallery of the Boston Athenaeum as Fuller did in 1839 would be to experience a shock of recognition, and to sense, as Emerson himself recorded, that "here was old Greece and old Italy brought bodily to New England, and a verification given to all our dreams and readings."[30] It is not easy now to grasp the full measure of surprise in Emerson's statement. The rhetorical device of representing the plaster masses *as* old Greece and Italy ought not to be taken too lightly: it conveys a feeling as of encountering an idea that for once has not hidden its face. The old struggle of trying to place oneself in ancient Greece (and so beyond the frontiers of one's encircling environment) by the laborious American way of culture seems finally at an end, and to have it end this way is like the surprise of finding that one has, without intending it, escaped the penalties of original sin.

Perhaps behind the surprise and contributing to it is Emerson's appreciation of the irony that this bodily bringing was the very American work of one Augustus Thorndike, who, with an application of cash, succeeded where other, less commercial people had failed in bringing to bay those twin enemies of culture in America, time and space. By making the past present, and by bringing Greece to New England, Thorndike had struck a real blow at the root of America's cultural predicament; and Emerson, by phrasing his response as he did, acknowledged the true terms by which provincialism was present to the minds of thoughtful Americans.

Efforts like Thorndike's were so well received by a culture-hungry population that few were inclined to cavil at the quality of what was brought in. Often it was sufficient merely to know that the material was "from Europe," but fundamentally the uncritical acceptance of foreign culture was an effect of the absence of qualified, critical observers who had seen the originals in place and could judge the copies. Having always to deal with imitations and transplanted copies discouraged, of course, certain kinds of critical response and promoted others. "Margaret's love of art," said Emerson, "like that of most cultivated persons in this country, was not at all technical, but truly a sympathy with the artist, in the protest which his work pronounced on the deformity of our daily manners; her co-perception with him of the eloquence of form; her aspiration with him to a fairer life."[31] Emerson's remark about the eloquence of form is especially pertinent to the sort of frontier consciousness that Fuller evinced, since the transmission of culture to America typically preserved the form or body at the expense of style and relation. The process of bodily bringing that seemed most effectual in supplying America with culture turned out to be by its very nature a process that stripped style from form and transmitted the latter. One of the clearest examples is the New England vogue for the work of John Flaxman, in which Fuller heartily participated. "I have been studying Flaxman and Retzsch," she wrote. "How pure, how immortal, the language of Form! Fools cannot fancy that they fathom its meaning; witless *dillettanti* cannot degrade it by hackneyed usage; none but genius can create or reproduce it. Unlike the colorist, he who expresses his thought in form is secure as a man can be against the ravages of time."[32]

Henry James is again helpful in interpreting this deeply revealing preference for form. In his biography of Hawthorne, James notes that the first evening Hawthorne spent with the Peabody sisters was given over to a study of "Flaxman's designs for Dante, just received from Professor Felton, of Harvard." The spectacle, James suggests, reveals "the lonely frigidity which characterized most attempts at social recreation in the New England world some forty years ago":

> There was at that time a great desire for culture, a great interest in knowledge, in art, in aesthetics, together with a very scanty supply of the materials for such pursuits. Small things were made to do large service; and there is something even touching in the solemnity of consideration that was bestowed by the emancipated New England conscience upon little wandering books and prints, little echoes and rumors of observation and experience.... The initiated mind, as I have ventured to call it, has a vision of a little unadorned parlour, with the snow-drifts of a Massachusetts winter piled up about its windows, and a group of sensitive and serious people, modest votaries of opportunity, fixing their eyes upon a bookful of Flaxman's attenuated outlines.[33]

By a necessity of its frontier character America knew European culture largely if not exclusively by the tokens, the "little echoes and rumors of observation and experience," that were brought bodily to it. Fuller accepted these tokens gratefully and like most Americans tended to overvalue them; but what is even more important in terms of consciousness is that, like other Americans, she adjusted more than slightly her conception of culture (which was for the most part synonymous with the culture of Europe) to accommodate what the decisively selective process of transatlantic communication might give her. She had, of necessity, little experience with the "colorist," whom she found so inferior an artist to the worker in "form." It is safe to say that her experience was limited to hand-colored and often cheap engravings, to the paintings of a few American artists, Allston in particular, and to a few probably inferior imported paintings.[34] The fact that Flaxman's drawings could penetrate New England's isolation seemed to recommend them; perhaps to Fuller's mind the security of the worker in form against the ravages of time was actually demonstrated by the success of the copies arriving in America. In other words, those aspects of a work of art were deemed timeless (and therefore more to be valued) that could be transmitted to a nation so otherwise cut off by time and space. On the other hand, those subtler aspects of style, such as color, that could not easily be reproduced and transmitted were conversely discounted, because they were dependent on, or mixed up with, environment, that is, with time and space.[35]

At the heart of Margaret Fuller's response to art, shaping and dictating it, was always a fear of time and space, the direct consequence of an early frontier-like isolation. This fear, this rejection, was in its way as profound as that which motivated the one great national campaign against spatial and temporal limits, the building of the railroads. The effect of the antagonism in both the public and the private instance was an acute psychic dislocation, a loss of attachment to place. More than most Americans, Fuller consciously recognized the problem, and the recognition itself became for her an additional source of sorrow and regret. It was at best a mixed blessing that this prime irony of her life was always present to her consciousness. The more successful she was in evading an oppressively circumstantial real world in favor of a timeless, spaceless realm of culture and tradition, the greater was her actual conviction of having failed as a person in a world of persons, a world governed and made meaningful by time and relationships. Her wanderings, as though in acknowledgment of a crisis, were more frequently in the "real world" after 1843 when she left New England for a tour of the frontier. In the winter of 1844 she left New England for good to take a position with Horace Greeley's *New-York Daily Tribune*, and finally, in 1846, she satisfied her life's desire and sailed to Europe.

In all these outward wanderings Fuller sought remedies for the imbalances and distortions of consciousness that her early provincial experience had bequeathed her. In the last decade of her life, her sense of the peculiar shortcomings of her mind was becoming more distinct, their penalties more obvious. The intensely inward and self-concentrating quality of her education, so deep and yet so narrow, so intense yet, at last, so superficial (as she herself came to acknowledge) had to an agonizing degree reduced her intercourse with other human beings to the stylized interchange of the Conversations. Even her informal talk was formal, or at least stiffly ethereal; one's response to having spoken with her was typically to observe that she had "risen perceptibly to a higher state" since one's last meeting.[36] Increasingly she came to feel that, although her escape into art might indeed remove her from "the deformity of our daily manners," it also, to quote Emerson's censure of idealism, "baulks the affections in denying substantive being to men and women."[37]

Her experience had effectually schooled her to deny such substantive being precisely because of the vulgar, spirit-killing way that Americans had of insisting on it. Her appreciation of "form" in art may in this context be a sort of troubled and even desperate compromise between, on the one hand, a dislocating response to art as a phenomenon wholly spiritual, and, on the other, an earthy and earthbound acknowledgment of actual being. Her provincial circumstances made such a compromise virtually inevitable, since the art in which she sought refuge had been winnowed and distorted by a process that gave to form almost exclusively the place that, in European minds, would be occupied by a whole range of subtler aspects of style, from color to historical and even spatial context. Yet what most concerned her in the early years of the 1840s was the personal anguish entailed by her own lack of context, by a "feeling of incongeniality" with her time and place. All that was disagreeable and utilitarian had from the beginning been associated in her mind with the engrossing tendency of American life, and with that it was difficult to compromise. The real world seemed most real to her when it was most disagreeable, as when, at Niagara Falls in 1843, she observed a man who, "after looking at [the Falls] for a moment, with an air as if thinking how he could best appropriate it to his own use, . . . spat into it."[38] Such details were the making of transcendentalists.

Fuller understood that the issue or context to which all these personal dilemmas pointed was love, and that a crisis at this meeting point of the physical and spiritual could not be avoided. The experience of love might be a trial of her ideas or a resolution to her life, a freeing or a bonding. It would be more than "interesting"; it would be decisive. Her conception of love seems to have been in all respects parallel to, and as provincially eccentric as, her conception of culture: love was to be as spiritual, as pure, as much like that which existed between the angels, as possible,[39] for the alternative she conceived to be submission and slavery, limitation once more in time and space. This was the recurrent theme of her 1845 *Woman in the Nineteenth Century*, which advocated the liberation of women by the attainment of a transcendental oneness of consciousness that absorbs and denies particularity. "When the same community of life and consciousness of mind begin among men [as is portrayed in the Greek gods], humanity will have, positively and finally, subjugated its brute elements and Titanic childhood; criticism will have perished; arbitrary

limits and ignorant censure be impossible; all will have entered upon the
liberty of law, and the harmony of common growth."[40] Fuller's extreme
idealism culminates in a final statement of the rejection of "substantive
being": "It is a vulgar error that love, *a* love to woman is her whole
existence; she also is born for Truth and Love in their universal energy.
Would she but assume her inheritance, Mary would not be the only
virgin mother."[41]

The personal consequences of holding these views seem shortly to
have proved less than satisfactory. In New York in 1845 she formed an
intense attachment to James Nathan, a German Jew, who allowed the
romance to go only so far and then, to Fuller's great disillusionment,
sailed to Europe, "fleeing," as Perry Miller has said, "for his life."[42] The
surviving letters from Fuller show a curious indecision about the competing claims of the physical and the spiritual:

> With you [she wrote] all seems to assume such palpable reality,
> though you do not forget its inner sense either. I love to hear you
> read off the secret, and yet you sometimes make me tremble too.
> I confide in you, as this bird, now warbling without, confides in
> me. You will understand my song, but you will not translate it
> into language too human. I wish, I long to be human, but divinely
> human. Let the soul invest every act of its abode with somewhat
> of its own lightness and subtlety. Are you my guardian to do-
> mesticate me in the body, and attach it more firmly to the earth?
> ... I hung lightly as an air-plant. Am I to be rooted on earth, ah!
> choose for me a good soil and a sunny place, that I may be a green
> shelter to the weary and bear fruit enough to pay for staying.[43]

Another letter to Nathan, written on August 31, 1845, after he had been
two months in Germany, suggests an advance in self-knowledge: "But
I should have been so much more happy in the real than in the ideal
intercourse! Why! Why? Yes I must fret, must, must grieve."[44] The
penalties of her frontier consciousness, of her ideological opposition to
time and space, were brought home to her as they had never been before.

This late discovery might have been the great tragedy of her tragic
life were it not for the fact that she managed with considerable success
to change and adapt. Whether consciously or not, she pursued a grand
personal synthesis during the latter part of her life, in which the conservative frontier consciousness with all its characteristic intensity and
its high regard for art and self-improvement, confronted its own shortcomings, the detachment from life that it enforced, the damage it did to
personal relationships, the distortions and eccentricities it led to. The
synthesis was of course a gradual process and its commencement cannot
be dated precisely. The motives to prompt it had always been there, just

as the problems it might solve had also been there. But in the last part of her life, beginning about 1843, the kinds of ideas that would conduce to a genuine synthesis of the material and spiritual rather than aggravate the opposition, ideas that for years had been available to her, began to assume a new and vital place in her consciousness.

Among the ideas that sprang to life under this late synthetic urge was one she had originally encountered in two sources in 1836. Her reading in Emerson's *Nature* and in various works by Johann Gottfried Herder revealed to her that the true critical approach, whether to things in nature or to art objects, was first to possess the indwelling law that dictated the object's formal being. As Emerson had observed in *Nature*, " 'Every scripture is to be interpreted by the same spirit which gave it forth,' – is the fundamental law of criticism."[45] Fuller employed this idea in her provocative first essay in the *Dial* for July 1840 to define the "apprehensive" and the "comprehensive" critics and to set them apart from the prevailing sort, the "subjective" critic who judges all things from a wholly personal, solipsistic perspective. The dicta of this latter sort of critic "are often, in fact, mere records of impressions":

> To judge of their value you must know where the man was brought up, under what influences, – his nation, his church, his family even. He himself has never attempted to estimate the value of these circumstances, and find a law or raise a standard above all circumstances, permanent against all influence. He is content to be the creature of his place, and to represent it by his spoken and written word. He takes the same ground with the savage, who does not hesitate to say of the product of a civilization on which he could not stand, "It is bad," or "It is good."[46]

The subjective critic, in other words, is just what Fuller had all her life a fear of being: the provincial American of savage selfishness, the merest end product of an all too inadequate time and place, a circumstantial and unself-determined being. In this essay she offers two essentially contradictory remedies to the problem of subjectivity. The first is to erect or embrace standards external both to the object and subject of perception; the second is to seek the inherent standard of the object itself. The first approach seems a residual effect of her classical education, a remnant still strongly in evidence five years later when she wrote in justification of learning the metrics of classical poetry.[47] In her 1840 *Dial* essay she wrote that "there is not yet deliberate recognition of a standard of criticism" and expressed the hope that "the always strengthening league of the republic of letters must ere long settle laws on which its Amphictyonic council may act."[48]

The first approach, with its emphasis on the externality of standards, is also a remnant of her conception of education as the painful work of achieving objectivity – or, to put these two observations together, a remnant of her having had a classical education under essentially frontier circumstances.[49] The subjective critics "are not," she writes, "driven to consider, nor forced upon investigation by the fact, that they are deliberately giving their thoughts an independent existence, and that it [sic] may live to others when dead to them. They know no agonies of conscientious research, no timidities of self-respect."[50] The first approach to the problem of subjectivity in criticism is conformable with Fuller's frontier conception of culture as work, though her advocacy of external standards in lieu of a purely personal authority is also understandable in historical terms when we consider the current state of the critical art in America – the shameless puffery, the incredible invective, that often made the reputation of the critic at the expense of the artist. Little wonder, then, that she claimed to "feel the need of a criterion, a standard."[51]

But this "standard" in Fuller's first approach to the problem has only the virtue of being external to the work criticized. Feeling the need for standards, she nevertheless reserves her highest praise for the apprehensive and comprehensive critics, whose distinction is *not* that they have the hard, objective knowledge to support a technical appreciation, but rather, as Emerson said of Fuller, that they enjoy a direct and intuitive sympathy with the artist.

> We will go to the critic [she declares] who trusts Genius and trusts us, who knows that all good writing must be spontaneous, and who will write out the bill of fare for the public as he read it for himself, –
>
>> "Forgetting vulgar rules, with spirit free
>> To judge each author by his own intent,
>> Nor think one standard for all minds is meant."[52]

The second approach, though it logically contradicts the first, is nevertheless compatible with Fuller's frontier jealousy of the effortless way Europeans had of relating, organically, with their culture.

In this essay, then, Fuller has established the contradiction in her own mind between what one might call the classical and romantic approaches to criticism, or, more broadly, to perception itself. The essay gives no reliable indication that she had embraced either course, nor that she had satisfactorily resolved the inherent conflict between them. But her western experiences three years later showed her, by presenting her with a *reductio ad absurdum* of her own situation, the fallacy of believing that an American *had* to take an external approach to culture – had, that is, to work to maintain a priori cultural standards – and, as a result, she began to question her old belief that culture was valuable in proportion as it was foreign and external to one's place. She learned in Illinois that culture could be a means of accommodating oneself to one's place as well as a means of flying from it.

In Illinois she observed the essential impulse of conservative pioneers: "The wives of the poorer settlers, having more hard work to do than before, very frequently become slatterns; but the ladies, accustomed to a refined neatness, feel that they cannot degrade themselves by its absence, and struggle under every disadvantage to keep up the necessary routine of small arrangements."[53] Such resistance against provincialism, such energy spent in hanging on to old identities, seemed suddenly less heroic than pathetic. Still, the analogy to her own situation as a Cambridge lady conserving a European identity was strong enough to startle. Was she, in her own defiance of a circumstantial degradation, as silly a figure as the Illinois housewife? Her "feeling of incongeniality with [her] time and place" had been a nagging frustration, but must her fretting at it be a source of embarrassment as well? Her education had been designed to lift her free from such circumstances as she now found on the frontier, yet she was enough of a realist to see that no similar education could serve a good purpose here. Indeed, the fault with the little culture that she found in the West was that it was *not* adjusted to circumstance:

> Their culture has too generally been that given to women to make them "the ornaments of society." They can dance, but not draw; talk French, but know nothing of the language of flowers; neither in childhood were allowed to cultivate them, lest they should tan their complexions. Accustomed to the pavement of Broadway, they dare not tread the wildwood paths for fear of rattlesnakes!...
>
> Everywhere the fatal spirit of imitation, of reference to European standards, penetrates, and threatens to blight whatever of original growth might adorn the soil.
>
> If the little girls grow up strong, resolute, able to exert their faculties, their mothers mourn over their want of fashionable delicacy....
>
> Their grand ambition for their children, is to send them to school in some eastern city, the measure most likely to make them useless and unhappy at home. I earnestly hope that, ere long, the existence of good schools near themselves, planned by persons of sufficient thought to meet the wants of the place and time, instead of copying New York or Boston, will correct this mania. Instruction the children want to enable them to profit by the great natural advantages of their position; but methods copied from the education of some

English Lady Augusta, are as ill suited to the daughter of an Illinois farmer, as satin shoes to climb the Indian mounds.[54]

One can only guess whether or not she shows here some measure of resentment at the way her own education had unfitted her for a normal life in America; what is more certain, however, is that she now recognizes the need for a new and thoroughly American sort of education, one whose novelty is demanded not by political realities, not by democratic social arrangements, not even by a transcendental theory of childhood, but by the undeniable facts of an American environment. Applying principles that she had first encountered in Herder, she points out the necessity for an education that does not aggravate the antagonism between one's place and one's culture, but is adapted to softening and refining "the coarse actualities of life": "An elegance she would diffuse around her, if her mind were opened to appreciate elegance; it might be of a kind new, original, enchanting, as different from that of the city belle as that of the prairie torch-flower from the shopworn article that touches the cheek of that lady within her bonnet."[55]

The essential fault with all education (including Fuller's) that is imitative and directed toward a remote source is that it never, so to speak, quite understands itself – it is always more or less mechanical and therefore exterior to the student. It is an "inorganic" education, and must remain so regardless of the intensity of the learner. Because the isolation of the frontier and its peculiar physical demands do not permit any fine accuracy or depth in education, the student learns only to be like people she has never seen, or, rather, *approximately* like people she has never seen:

> The piano many carry with them, because it is the fashionable instrument in the eastern cities. Even there, it is so merely from the habit of imitating Europe, for not one in a thousand is willing to give the labor requisite to ensure any valuable use of the instrument....
>
> Add to this, they never know how to tune their own instruments, and as persons seldom visit them who can do so, these pianos are constantly out of tune, and would spoil the ear of one who began by having any.[56]

Fuller never doubted that the soul could be saved through culture or through a dedication to art and beauty; the problem was all in the mode of education, not in what was studied, but in how and under what circumstances it was studied. The external must be made internal. Somehow, the way must be found, as she had said in 1831, to "make all this false true." The synthesis toward which she had been struggling, and which seems really to have been precipitated by her western experiences, assumed a nearly final shape by 1845. In August of that year – the same month in which she wrote the letter to Nathan cited above – she reviewed a volume of poetry by a certain William Thom, an uneducated English factory worker, for the *New-York Tribune*. The subject – poetry composed by an untutored or "primitive" poet – led her to reconsider the topic of her five-year-old *Dial* essay: extrinsic standards versus intrinsic vitality. For all the ponderous weighing she had done in 1840, she had not settled their respective claims; now, having seen the frontier, she could.

Her discussion begins with the same dichotomy. "There are two ways of considering poems," she claims. We may rigorously and critically hold poetry to the standards of formal perfection, "rejecting all that is possible to reject and reserving for toleration only what is capable of standing the severest test," in which case we will "be content only with the Iliads and Odysseys of the mind's endeavor"; *or* we may regard poetry as "the great mutual system of interpretation between all kinds and classes of men," as, in other words, "an epistolary correspondence between brethren of one family."[57] The "two modes of criticism" that spring from these temperamentally opposite conceptions of art "have each their dangers"; the first, in stressing adherence to extrinsic standards, "tends to hypercriticism and pedantry, to a cold restriction on the unstudied action of a large and flowing life," whereas the second, "which believes no impulse to be entirely in vain, which scrutinizes circumstances, motive and object before it condemns, and believes there is a beauty in each natural form, if its law and purpose be understood, . . . shares the usual perils of the genial and affectionate [and] tends to indiscriminate indulgence."

These two modes are true polar opposites as Fuller now conceives them; the fault of one is the virtue of the other. Her synthesis depends on turning the old, simply contradictory dichotomy, in which she had seen only antagonism and frustration, into an organic and therefore impressible polarity. In this 1845 essay the synthesis is, of course, speculative, but because the unity of these opposites has been in a sense revealed to her, the last real difficulty has been removed, and she could now venture to predict an actual fulfillment: "In the golden age to which we are ever looking forward, these two [critical] tendencies will be harmonized. The highest sense of fulfilled excellence will be found to consist with the largest appreciation of every sign of life." "The eye of man," she now concludes, "is fitted to range all around no less than to be lifted on high."

For the transcendentalists of New England, and perhaps for Fuller most of all, the term "golden age" signified the cultural Eden. Although the designation implies a *time*, and although Americans – or at least some of them – spoke hopefully about it as a thing to be looked for in the future, the golden age in fact existed in their imaginations less as a time than as a place; it was an environment in which the difficulties of the present would be no more, and in which the spirit would bring forth fruit in abundance. Circumstances in this golden age would all be conducive rather than antipathetic to the higher human self, and art would flourish as it never had before precisely because the environment would condone and support it. The idea of the golden age as the transcendentalists conceived it was fundamentally a response to their own provincial condition; it consisted, for them, in the defeat of opaque circumstance.

For Fuller and many of her contemporaries, the image of the golden age bore a striking resemblance to their idealized notion of Europe. There, if not yet in America, art and life were wedded, so that life presented no obstacles to art. In proportion as Americans felt the limiting pressure of their own circumstances, they projected an ideal independence, a freedom from constraint, in their conception of European conditions. Fuller implies as much in the conclusion of her essay when she points out that the "greatest efforts of art belong to artistic regions, where boys in the street draw sketches on the wall and torment melodies on rude flutes; shoals of sonneteers follow in the wake of the great poet. The electricity which flashes with the thunderbolts of Jove must first pervade the whole atmosphere."

Nothing remained for Fuller but to go to Europe. All her thinking was converging there, and on the necessity to act, to combine a life, *her* life, with art. "What concerns me now," she had recently written, "is, that my life be a beautiful, powerful, in a word, a complete life of its kind."[58] She sailed from New York on the first of August 1846. Her arrival in Europe was the perfectly logical culmination, the dramatic denouement, of a lifetime of dissatisfied wandering, and it seemed to her, like Moses' view from Pisgah, both an exile and an advent. She noted that "one feels the same joy here that is experienced by the colonist in returning to the parent home."[59] She had arrived finally at the source, had penetrated the golden age, and the letters she sent back are a record of sustained astonishment: "What was but picture to us becomes reality; remote allusions and derivations trouble no more: we see the pattern of the stuff, and understand the whole tapestry. There is a gradual clearing up on many points, and many baseless notions and crude fancies are dropped."[60] The false is made true. The external is now internal. Inconsistencies, once troublesome, are finally resolved. Crudities are refined and the sight restored. In Italy she wrote privately to Emerson about how the place had seemed to take her up, how luxurious it was simply to absorb, involuntarily, what she had earlier learned laboriously or not at all:

> Italy has been glorious to me, and there have been hours in which I received the full benefit of the vision. In Rome, I have known some blessed, quiet days, when I could yield myself to be soothed and instructed by the great thoughts and memories of the place. But those days are swiftly passing. Soon I must begin to exert myself, for there is this incubus of the future, and none to help me, if I am not prudent to face it. So ridiculous, too, this mortal coil, – such small things!
>
> I find how true was the lure that always drew me toward Europe. It was no false instinct that said I might here find an atmosphere to develop me in ways I need. Had I only come ten years earlier! Now my life must be a failure, so much strength has been wasted on abstractions, which only came because I grew not in the right soil. However, it is less a failure than with most others, and not worth thinking twice about.[61]

The synthesis she had arrived at was a means of reconciling the finite, temporal, and local with the cosmic, the absolute, and the timeless – elements that had all her life waged a war in her soul and had sent her on the pilgrimage that was now at an end. The synthesis, as she now realized, could only have been achieved by indulging her love of culture so thoroughly and so intimately that she did not so much learn it as live it. Most obviously and dramatically she lived it in her Roman years when she seemed virtually to *become* Corinne; when she married the marquis Angelo Ossoli and became a countess at last, bending all her energies at the same time to the romantic defense of Garibaldi's and Mazzini's revolution.

But in a subtler and perhaps more interesting sense, she had all along been trying to turn herself into an art object. Few Americans, after all, felt more strongly than Margaret Fuller that the religion of culture needed a hero or heroine to point the way.[62] Emerson recorded the opinion of an anonymous "correspondent" that "she looked upon herself as a living statue, which should always stand on a polished pedestal, with rich accessories, and under the most fitting lights."[63] Emerson's correspondent went on to observe that she "was one of the very few persons who looked upon life as an art, and every person not merely as an artist, but as a work of art."[64] Her early perception of herself as a queen in search of a realm is assuredly the key signature to her whole career, and the one that Hawthorne instinctively seized on in his portrait of Zenobia in *The Blithedale Romance*. Her friends were unanimous in declaring that her artistry was not of the written word, but of the life that she made for herself. That life was, if nothing else, dramatic, outsized, and frequently eccentric. Her life was, indeed, a "complete life of its kind"; but, as these adjectives suggest, that "kind" was the life of a frontier hero.

Chapter 8

Reading God directly:
the morbidity of culture

========================

Man Thinking must not be subdued by his instruments. Books are
for the scholar's idle times. When he can read God directly, the hour
is too precious to be wasted in other men's transcripts of their readings.
But when the intervals of darkness come, as come they must, – when
the soul seeth not, when the sun is hid, and the stars withdraw their
shining, – we repair to the lamps which were kindled by their ray
to guide our steps to the East again, where the dawn is.
– Ralph Waldo Emerson[1]

Nothing that Emerson ever wrote with specific reference to Margaret
Fuller came quite so close to framing a judgment on her European enterprise as a letter that he composed in October 1857, meant for, but
apparently never sent to, Caroline Sturgis Tappan, who was just then
tracing the footsteps of her departed friend through Rome and the
Brownings' Florence. It is a superb letter, full of those surprising phrases
that the mature Emerson so eminently commanded, and suffused, too,
with an autumnal feeling of inner and outer weather. "You will never
write me again, I have been so ungrateful," he begins, "I who value
every line & word from you, or about you. Perhaps 'tis my too much
writing in youth that makes it so repulsive in these old days."[2]

> What to tell you now that I have begun – you that are in the land
> of wine & oil, of us in the land of meal? Italy cannot excel the banks
> of glory which sun & mist paint in these very days on the forest
> by lake & river. But the Muses are as reticent as Nature is flam-
> boyant, & no fireeyed child has yet been born.

Almost like a jealous lover, Emerson imagines how his friend (like an
earlier friend now dead) must be enamored of this exotic new attraction,
and how she, threatened in her turn with seduction, needs somehow to
be warned. He reminds her in a pair of contrasting images that the rich,
appealing beauties of Europe are beauties merely of superaddition, in

136

essence merely accessory, whereas the "land of meal," scorned as it is, still represents a sustaining substance and reality. This contrast affects, poetically, the way one reads the illogically connected next sentence with its preference for American nature over Italian art. The effect of Emerson's ground-setting images is to change the following sentence from a statement of simple preference (as between two competing things) into an evocation of a certain "something missing" from the European feast of the senses. Whatever that "something" is, it redeems the provincial by being older and more radically real than human accomplishment in art. That "something" contains the promise not only of redemption, but of a redeemer as well – that "fireeyed child" who threatens and threatens to come, but who never quite appears.

Just as Emerson understood the meaning of art and culture in ways that set him apart from provincial devotees of the European antique, so he understood differently the American failure of these things. America, he had always felt – somewhat as Edwards before him had felt – was the appointed seat of a great revival, not of the religious spirit narrowly conceived, but of human possibility most broadly conceived. It was to be a revival led by a Poet, by the child whom American nature labored to bring forth:

> But he, the man-child glorious, –
> Where tarries he the while?
> The rainbow shines his harbinger,
> The sunset gleams his smile.
>
> My boreal lights leap upward,
> Forthright my planets roll,
> And still the man-child is not born,
> The summit of the whole.[3]

The American landscape with its more sublime dimensions, its deeper, vibrant colors, and its pristine wildness above all seemed to Emerson to promise that its meanings and uses would be correspondingly greater than those of a subdued European landscape. The sense of newness and of excess was perhaps the "something missing" from the old arts, the hint of powers sensibly latent yet remaining, waiting to be developed by an interpreter who could compass and match it all. In a journal entry of 1838, Emerson had written:

Consider that the perpetual admonition of Nature to us is, The world is new, untried. Do not believe the past. I give you the Universe new & unhandselled every hour. You think in your idle hours that there is literature, history, science, behind you so accumulated as to exhaust thought & prescribe your own future &

the future. In your sane hour you shall see that not a line has yet been written; that for all the poetry that is in the world your first sensation on entering a wood or standing on the shore of a lake has not been chaunted yet. It remains for you, so does all thought, all object, all life remain unwritten yet.[4]

One of the finest meanings of American nature, for Emerson, is that history and tradition, all secondary or vicarious modes of experience, stand repealed, and that future and potential are substituted for them. That the "fireeyed child" is promised, and is perpetually *being* promised, may be a better fate than his arrival.

In his undelivered letter to Mrs. Tappan, Emerson continues:

'Tis strange that the relations of your old friends here remain un- changed to the world of letters & society, I mean, that those who held of the Imagination & believed that the necessities of the New World would presently evoke the mystic Power, & we should not pass away without hearing the Choral Hymns of a new age & adequate to Nature, still find colleges & books as cramp & sterile as ever & our discontent keeps us in the selfsame suspicious relation to beauties & elegant society.

Emerson's sense of the failure of American culture is no less acute than that of the disappointed conservative who sees history lapsing in America. Both are troubled by the conviction that a culture of odds and ends, increasingly distorted and misapplied, has become a national liability. But instead of attacking this "cramp & sterile" provincialism by calling, as Margaret Fuller had done, for a better transmission of cultural values, Emerson insists on a show of faith in American nature. We are to *believe* its constant admonition that the world is new, not only for the sake of honoring the appearance, but because American nature also declares, and just as constantly, that the past is a trap for the imagination. To reerect an Old World culture in the New, to take on the task of extending history, is, for Emerson, to disregard the positive implicit promise of the fact that in America nature has always acted, in William Bradford's words, "as a maine barr and goulfe to seperate [us] from all the civill parts of the world."[5] If, then, America's failed culture of imported end products has been an operation maintained against nature and at the expense of nature, Americans might work a revolution by bringing the soul and its circumstances, the Me and the Not-Me, into harmonious alignment, and thereby usher in a "new age" with a culture "adequate to Nature."

The "new age" comes by faith. It comes by the "unchanged relations" of Mrs. Tappan's friends who once believed, and in their patient Miltonic waiting still believe. As with the Emersonian speaker of the "Ode Inscribed to W. H. Channing," their role is to "hold of the Imagination" and not to give in to the skeptical impatience that drives some good folk desperately to abandon their homes and flee to Europe. They can and do, of course, feel "discontent" at the postponement of expectations; yet the right effect, as Emerson observes, is not to instigate flight but to deepen their prejudice against America's cultural Vanity Fair, taking, as they do, the passing shows of "beauties & elegant society" for the very agents of diversion and postponement. To hold these views is necessarily to see in Caroline Tappan's European travel (or in Margaret Fuller's) a sort of apostasy, and indeed the letter goes on to develop just this point: "We are all the worse that you, & those who are like you, if any such there be, as there are not, – but persons of positive quality, & capacious of beauty – desert us, & abdicate their power at home." Beneath the graceful good manners the judgment is harsh: so much selfish defection, so much postponement.

In the surprising passage that follows, Emerson seems, at least at first, to have in mind the proposition that the artistic temper can be as well cultivated in New England as in Italy, but if so, his examples overwhelm his intention and his meaning quickly moves off in a very different direction:

> Why not a mind as wise & deep & subtle as your Browning, with his trained talent? Why can we not breed a lyric man as exquisite as Tennyson; or such a Burke-like *longanimity* as E. Browning . . . ? Our wild Whitman, with real inspiration but choked by Titanic abdomen, & Delia Bacon, with genius, but mad, & clinging like a tortoise to English soil, are the sole producers that America has yielded in ten years.

Eccentric as this balance-sheet reckoning of the American Renaissance seems, and provincial as it certainly is, one looks past the particular judgments to find a more useful, deeper meaning in the incongruity between the unattractive animal imagery associated with Whitman and Bacon and the vegetative language ("producers," "yielded") by means of which Emerson expresses the nature of the article that is needed. Written in the context of his own failing powers, "in these old days" when he imagines passing away before the advent, the letter hints continually at the limits placed by the animal constitution on the growth of the spirit. And not in Emerson only, or even especially. The trouble with the many geniuses whom he had personally tried to cultivate was that they never had the strength to bear the fruit by which they and America were to be known. "So many promising youths," he had said in "The Transcendentalist," "and never a finished man!"[6] Jones Very,

Ellery Channing, Bronson Alcott – even Fuller and Thoreau – all were failures more or less in Emerson's eyes, where the acuity was ever more for promise than for accomplishment.

"Is all the granite & forest & prairie & superfoetation of millions to no richer result?" he goes on in his letter to ask. "But who cares? As soon as we walk out of doors Nature transcends all poets so far, that a little more or less skill in whistling is of no account. Out of doors we lose the lust of performance, & are content to pass silent, & see others pass silent, into the depths of a Universe so resonant & beaming." It is fitting that this letter in which Emerson trades culture and poetry for nature and silence is itself unfinished and undelivered. The man who in 1838 had understood nature to say that *all* remained to be written, the man who had fed for two decades on promises that were never kept, is here taking stock, balancing "the voice obeyed at prime" against the advancing appeal of surrender, acceptance, and silence. *Who cares?* Not the abdicating tourist, surely. But perhaps not even Emerson himself, whose watching and waiting have been so ill repaid.

What emerges here is a mood that expresses itself in cancellation and the effort to retrieve and undo earlier work. This mood, distinctly funereal, gives rise to the most private of Emerson's personae: the man who has discovered the pleasures of inarticulateness in the truth that nothing but nature itself has ever been consistently "adequate to Nature," and who therefore proposes, in a line canceled from "Terminus," to "hide myself among my thrifty pears."[7] For an aging Emerson whose thoughts have turned to passing silently into the depths of the universe, the only adequate music, the only adequate painting, are the "resonant" tones and "beaming" lights of autumn days in Concord. The mood is that of wishing to be done with disappointment, and this first art, independent of "performance" and incorruptibly original, can never disappoint. As a protest against the mediation of a fallen art between nature and mind, Emerson's formulation is, from one point of view, the most radical of imaginable responses to that magnificent early call for "an original relation to the universe";[8] from another point of view, it is a sad capitulation to solitude, self, and death.

To meet cancellation with cancellation seems rather in than out of the Emerson style, and in reading the letter carefully through, one begins to sense that the devaluation of "skill in whistling" as well as the compensation in nature have been deeply lodged in the subjunctive. In this way Emerson conveys to Mrs. Tappan the circles of effect that her breach of faith have set in motion; he shows that by her personal conduct she kills belief and, in turn, that the negations of skepticism kill her friends, whose faith is precisely that they *do* care. If in this rhetorical sense Emerson's black mood seems provisional or "gotten up" for Mrs. Tappan's sake, it is not therefore inauthentic. Death and skepticism are made in the letter to appear as convertible modes of nonbeing. The American watchers for the "fireeyed child" may or may not lose heart and may or may not go one after another in search of the European simulacrum, but they will all certainly grow old.

The letter, then, for present purposes, may be taken as Emerson's dramatic, unresolved, last speculation on issues quite central to the whole body of his thought: the relation of the new world to the old, the need for a renovated culture based in American nature, faith in the power of a liberated poetic imagination – all of which, in turn, may be understood as belonging to a certain liberal tradition of American response to the problem of provincialism. In order to see in what sense this late expression is truly a culmination of Emerson's career, one has to go back beyond the major texts of the 1830s and 1840s into the still earlier beginnings of the public campaign for a national literature.

One of the best, if not one of the likeliest, places to begin an investigation of this liberal tradition is Longfellow's 1825 Bowdoin oration entitled "Our Native Writers." The value of this address is not that it is a particularly distinguished performance (it is not), nor that Nathaniel Hawthorne was in the audience to hear it (he was), but rather that it discloses more efficiently than some other, similar efforts the theoretical basis for a liberal, nativist response to the difficulties arising from the provincial situation. This response, in general, took the form of attempting to make the most of what Americans could do under the circumstances, and of rejecting as insignificant or even morally dangerous that which Americans found most difficult or inconvenient to do. In other words, instead of maintaining the dogma that culture existed primarily on another continent as a fait accompli to be acquired with the least variation, the literary nationalists affirmed that the individual, as the root cause of culture, ought to be initiating rather than imitating, propagating rather than promoting.

Longfellow's oration reminds us that when citizens of a new nation argue for the creation of a specifically national literature or culture, they cannot have a conception of either culture or literature as evolutionary, as the accrued result of years or centuries of a nation's social life. In fact, Longfellow's suggestions for a new American culture are arrived at by a provincially inappropriate application of logical induction which altogether precludes an evolutionary conception. He has abstracted from a series of past examples, or art objects from foreign cultures, a pattern of what culture appears typically to accomplish. For example, having read Scott and the English topographical poets, Longfellow has concluded that a primary function of literature is to commemorate and lend significance to places. Therefore, in his oration, he asks rhetorically whether "poetry, that hallows every scene, that renders every spot classical," will flourish in America.[9] Yes, he is sure that, with a difference, it will. In the older cultures of Europe, history (or at least the historical event) generates poetry; here in frontier America where there is no history the reverse must be true. Poetry must generate or "make" its own history. The idea thus offers a way of liberating art from time and, in welcome fashion, of displacing culture from its base in tradition. This conception was perhaps not altogether lost on the future author of *The Scarlet Letter* and *The House of the Seven Gables*.

A similar analytical process seems at work when Longfellow observes that another function of culture is the expression of national character. Since English literature expresses the English character, it strikes young Longfellow as eminently reasonable to abstract the character-expressing quality and apply it to the American situation by way of indicating what its native writers ought to keep in mind as they compose. It should be evident that in this mental operation of abstraction and application there is none of what Eliot was to call the "historical sense." Indeed, the argument is not so much ahistorical as it is aggressively antihistorical. For Longfellow, as for many other provincial Americans who looked by habit to the European past for guidance in matters cultural, the history of civilization appeared curiously unidimensional. Because the "pastness of the past," to quote Eliot again, was of no practical concern to them, all art of which they had knowledge seemed equally remote or equally near. The past was laid out for the American as on a single page, from which at any moment any line might be appropriated for service to some present need. Longfellow could hardly have suspected that the mentality that conceived "Our Native Writers," to the extent that it evinces an antihistorical provincial consciousness, would virtually constitute the "national character" of such later poetry as "The Building of the Ship." He could not have suspected it because his conception of national character had nothing to do with the way in which Americans thought; it was, with him, altogether an issue of subject matter, as we may infer from his observation that "as yet we can boast of nothing farther than a first beginning of a national literature; a literature associated and linked in with the grand and beautiful scenery of the country – with our institutions, our manners, our customs, in a word, with all that has helped to form whatever there is peculiar to us and to the land in which we live."

Brackenridge had earlier spoken for many of the cultural conservatives when he expressed the doubt that Americans *had* any perceptible national character or that there was anything seriously "peculiar to us." (In *Modern Chivalry* the Jonathan figure is Irish.) Understanding that the development of a distinctive identity would be simply equivalent to the decay of the nation's English character, traditionalists such as Brackenridge were often, at one level, willfully blind to the significance of cultural change in America, even as, at another level, these changes were the invariable subject of their satire. Supposing always that such change was reversible by intelligent opposition, the satirists were reluctant to conclude that Americans were in any important way distinguishable from the English, and indeed they found these allegations offensive. Even the generation of the Revolution insisted on paying its respects to British culture and assured itself that political independence did not entail an abandonment of the literary and artistic traditions of England. This older, historical view, however, with its deep regard for social order and the continuity of culture, had become so nearly extinct by 1825 that the rising generation could absolutely reverse the ancient values. Nature, the American circumstance, the old antagonist, was now to be the supplier of standards for a renovated culture, whereas the available fund of English tradition, the old supplier of standards, was increasingly to be rejected as a source of limitation and deformity. The influence of romantic thought in America produced no more surprising effect than this wild reversal.

The antitraditional bias of Longfellow's argument emerges early in the address. He struggles to couch his feelings in respectful terms, but the strain is all too evident: "We cannot *yet* throw off our literary allegiance to old England, we cannot *yet* remove from our shelves every book which is not strictly and truly American. English literature is a great and glorious monument, built up by those master-spirits of old time that had no peers, and rising bright and beautiful until its summit is hid in the mists of antiquity" (emphasis added). This obligatory obeisance to England is, even for a schoolboy, awkwardly executed, as evidenced by the dubious metaphor that appears to acquit but in reality convicts. The reference to a "monument" that is "built up" suggests a thing that is massively dead, blockish and impenetrable, while locating its architects in "old time" succeeds wonderfully in evoking the irrelevance of the monument. Placing the "summit . . . in the mists of antiquity" simply defies the logic of the metaphor but hints, nevertheless, at the sort of obscurity with which Americans typically have no patience. By making the literature of England unattractive in this way, Longfellow seems to prepare his audience for that millennial day when Americans *will* be able, with a quiet conscience, to purge their shelves of Chaucer, Spenser, Milton, and Shakespeare.

The remainder of the brief address takes up two topics: the need for a liberal patronage of the arts in America, and the dependence of future American artists on nature. The relationship between these two points is hardly self-evident; indeed, they seem in some ways contradictory. In fact, however, they are related through the crucial issue of culture as work. If the arts are to flourish in the United States, the people (from whom alone patronage is to be expected in a democracy) must be made to understand that a refined art need not be associated with opulence and idle recreation. "We are a plain people," Longfellow declares, "that have nothing to do with the mere pleasures and luxuries of life: and hence there has sprung up within us a quicksightedness to the failings of literary men, and an aversion to everything that is not practical, operative, and thoroughgoing." Whether this passage is ambiguous or simply equivocal would be a nice point to decide. The speaker is evidently uncertain whether to repudiate this typically American distrust of art because it is self-defeating or to affirm the prejudice as native and commonsensical. What Longfellow clearly does recognize, however, is the practical, operative fact that patronage for the arts will not be forthcoming until artistry is generally understood to be work or, as he expresses it, until there is a "deep and thorough conviction of the glory" of the artist's "calling." The mutual dependence of work and patronage is made explicit: "Whatever there may be in letters over which time has no power, must be 'born of great endeavors,' " and those endeavors are the offspring of a liberal patronage. In short, one of the reasons why Americans must renounce their allegiance to English literature and fasten on nature instead is that subservience maintains the popular association, so disheartening to an aggressive democrat such as Longfellow, between art and aristocracy.

But in 1825 Longfellow is not yet prepared (as later he emphatically would be) to accept the conservative demands for scholarly application and an earned culture as a means of forestalling this common prejudice against art. The labor that American artists will in the future give to the job of producing a national culture will be of a kind distinctly different from that which England seems to find so easy and which Americans, precisely because of their frontier isolation, find so inordinately difficult. "In the vanity of scholarship, England has reproached us that we have no finished scholars," Longfellow notes. He then goes on to argue not that Americans *can* have finished scholars (as Margaret Fuller might have argued), but that scholarship, and especially "finished" scholarship, is likely to be a sign of shallowness and sterility; "there is reason for believing that men of mere learning, men of sober research and studied correctness, do not give to a nation its great name." The terms here are close to those of Irving's dilemma in his choice between the rough vitality of America and the smooth and polished culture of the England of his myth; but whereas Irving was always strongly attached by temperament to the ideal of a fine high culture, Longfellow, like Dwight, was more immediately conscious of the frontier difficulties that barred access to such culture.[10] His resolution of the dilemma is for this reason quite different from Irving's and indeed embodies the essential aspects of a

liberal, nativist approach. Referring to the lack of accomplished scholarship in America, Longfellow defiantly asserts that

> our very poverty in this respect will have a tendency to give a
> national character to our literature. Our writers will not be con-
> stantly toiling and panting after classical allusions to the vale of
> Tempe and the Etrurian river, nor to the Roman fountains shall
>
> > The emulous nations of the West repair
> > To kindle their quenched urns, and drink fresh spirit there.

Longfellow not only rejects the need for a learned, allusive style, but
positively makes a virtue of indifference to transmitted convention, and
almost, by implication, to any sort of careful elegance of style. Wishing
to regard the composition of poetry as an honorable occupation for a
democrat, he is nevertheless unwilling to tie that occupation to the sort
of intense work and discipline that conservatives had all along called for.
Thus, rather than hard work, Longfellow demands "great endeavors,"
from which "toiling and panting" have been eliminated along with the
harmful and inappropriate goal of all that struggle: the re-creation, under
frontier circumstances, of a traditional culture. Purging his shelves, Longfellow retains only the abstract function and purpose of literature, declaring that after this denudation, "We are . . . thrown upon ourselves:
and thus shall our native hills become renowned in song, like those of
Greece and Italy. Every rock shall become a chronicle of storied allusions:
and the tomb of the Indian prophet be as hallowed as the sepulchres of
ancient kings, or the damp vault and perpetual lamp of the Saracen
monarch."[11] Longfellow's astonishing proposal, which in a measure anticipates Emerson, is no less than to begin all over again with history
and culture, preserving, somewhat inconsistently, the smuggled-in and
barely noticed seed of structure.

To begin again is the liberal's ultimate dream. Recommencement,
unlike renaissance, avoids the whole vexed issue of transmitting culture
and makes the effort that had been devoted to the conservative ideal seem
not only irrelevant but positively inhibiting. The problem of Europe,
which had been the difficulty of learning its culture, was now that its
culture was being learned at the expense of something morally superior,
nearer at hand, and intellectually liberating. Prompted by a republican
conviction that European civilization was fast sinking into an amoral
aestheticism of clipped lawns and Byronic values, an alternative to a
tradition-based high culture for America was now in the process of
formation, and the emergent duty of the United States as, in a new sense,
a new nation, was more and more clearly to rejuvenate culture by reinventing it.

There seem to have been only two conceptions, and these closely related, of how America might accomplish this reinvention. Longfellow, along with Bryant and many of the pictorial artists of the day,[12] proposed turning to account the very nemesis of the conservatives: that is, place, one's circumstantial environment, nature. Longfellow broaches the idea in "Our Native Writers":

> Men may talk of sitting down in the calm and quiet of their libraries and forgetting, in the eloquent companionship of books, all the vain cares that beset them in the crowded thoroughfares of life: but, after all, there is nothing which so frees us from the turbulent ambition and bustle of the world, nothing which so fills the mind with great and glowing conceptions and at the same time so warms the heart with love and tenderness, as a frequent and close communion with natural scenery.

No one in the nineteenth century seems to have appreciated the irony that the frontier, the prime barrier to the extension of traditional learning and the arts, could be viewed alternatively as the wellspring of a new and more spontaneous culture. If America had, as a consequence of its isolation, no finished scholars, it had, in the isolating circumstance, a superabundance of unspoiled natural beauty, as Longfellow went on to point out. By following nature and surrendering the self to circumstance, the artist paradoxically assures that culture will be timeless:

> Thus shall the mind take color from things around us: from them shall there be a genuine birth of enthusiasm, a rich development of poetic feeling that shall break forth in song. Though . . . works of art must grow old and perish away from the earth, the forms of nature shall keep forever their power over the human mind, and have their influence upon the literature of a people.

In this view nature offers for a sadly mutable world the kind of grand continuity that traditional culture at best only purports to supply. Nature becomes a better mythology, a fund of ready reference for the artist, but held in common by all without distinction. It is the democracy of "Thanatopsis" applied like a balm to the wounds of a provincial culture.

This democratic solution presumed to give to the provincial American what the conservative solution really never could: a standard, a significant reference that was at once whole and present. The appeal of such recommencement is almost too neatly obvious. It makes culture easy, accessible, moral, organic, and, not least of all, American. Then, too, if conservatives were disheartened by the suspicion that their knowledge had been fragmented or distorted by their circumstances, no such doubts could assail those who leaned on nature. Longfellow assumed that nothing could intervene to distort one's perception of nature, which is timeless, indomitable, and soothing – never a source of difficulty, but always of benign influences. Nature is, in short, very much like the old ideal of culture, but actually far superior in its quasi-religious function of softening and refining the commercial mentality and of dispersing the "vain cares that beset" practical and operative men. Once again we can observe in the movement of Longfellow's logic the tendency of the provincial mind to abstract functional patterns from foreign ideas and then to apply them, in extravagant disregard of context, to the local situation. The best evidence that nature might serve as a substitute for the old mode of culture is that both effect a "civilizing" renunciation of worldly preoccupations and both counteract pride and ambition. Once the assumption is made that such are indeed the aims of culture, then anything that appears to accomplish the same result deserves to be considered on pragmatic grounds as an eligible substitute.

Other American romantics shared with Longfellow a broad dissatisfaction with received ideas about culture, as though they had detected a certain unfairness in the suggestion that the rules according to which, as artists, they were expected to perform had been agreed upon elsewhere, at a different time, and in a manner calculated to make their own performance as cruelly difficult as possible. Rebelling, therefore, against the expectation that Americans should, and eventually would, achieve important cultural results by assimilation, they rejected as well the correlative notion that America would be valuable to the extent that it managed to resemble Europe. In neither of these propositions had Americans been consulted; they were both the natural assumption of Europeans, and so became a part of the standard of culture Americans were to accept. Had it not been for the great obstacle to cultural transmission represented by the frontier; had it not been for the fracturing and distorting effects of geographical isolation; had America been, say, a small island off the coast of Spain instead of a large, empty continent vastly different from Europe, these propositions about culture might never have been questioned.

Certainly Emerson shared with Longfellow a deep hostility to the requirement that, despite all difficulties, Americans had to acquire a foreign and traditional culture in order to be accounted civilized. No American was ever quite absolved of that requirement, and scholars and artists were of course the least absolved of any. It was not one of the possible options, as Henry James was to observe, to leave Europe out of the reckoning, however close the literary nationalists would come to regarding it as desirable. The American "*must* deal, more or less, even if only by implication, with Europe."[13] And so Emerson did, but in a way that challenged more radically than Longfellow could have done the old proprietary concepts of tradition. W. C. Brownell, writing in

1909, noticed this hostility in Emerson's response, and, in discussing it, lent support to the persistent though mistaken view that finds in Emerson a species of frontier anti-intellectualism:

> Culture, however, did not enter into Emerson's philosophy. His philosphy, indeed, following his instinct does not so much neglect as positively impeach it. There is no denying the fact, which is vaunted rather than dissembled. He has a hard word for it always. Culture means on the one hand discipline, which irked him, and on the other acquisition, which to him could only have a disciplinary function. In either aspect it involves effort and effort lay quite outside his ideal of surrender to intuition and impulse.[14]

The remarkable blend of astonishment, accusation, and condescension in this passage is in itself sufficient to show that the argument issues from a decidedly conservative and therefore unsympathetic mind. Reading in Emerson that "Civilization is Talent's version of human life,"[15] Brownell responds like the bird in Robert Frost's poem ... "who takes / Everything said as personal to himself." We may doubt whether Emerson was in actual fact irked by discipline but the more important point in getting to the heart of the issue raised in this passage involves seeing that a conservative such as Brownell and a liberal such as Emerson are apt to construe the meaning of "culture" rather differently.

Like Longfellow, Emerson called for a return to the sources of culture in the belief that what was currently regarded as such was not only difficult to obtain by virtue of its extrinsic origin, but was all too often simply not worth having. Emerson is at once more explicit than Longfellow in denominating nature as the ultimate source of culture, and more sophisticated in conceiving of nature as something more than rocks and trees. Emerson's solution to the problem of provincialism is, however, like Longfellow's, a call to his countrymen to rejuvenate culture by reinventing it. The hostility that Brownell remarks in Emerson's attitude is not, finally, directed against culture so much as against prevalent misconceptions, including that superstitious veneration of the foreign and the antique (often, in Emerson's view, amounting to idolatry) which was so prominently a part of frontier consciousness and which for years had been the primary determinant of Americans' debilitating sense of themselves *as* provincial. Longfellow could not imagine, and Brownell would not allow, that culture could be seen as anything but vastly larger than and superior to the individual who is "cultivated." Emerson would not accept such abdication of control and insisted that "I must & will have [the elements of culture] subordinate & not masters, they shall accept & serve my point of view."[16] If Longfellow's vision is explicitly national, Emerson's is just as emphatically personal, and it is precisely this personal quality in Emerson's view of culture that prevented Brownell from seeing anything of what that view affirms.

The fullest expression that Emerson ever gave to his solution of the problem was his 1837 Phi Beta Kappa oration known as "The American Scholar." The first few paragraphs anticipate the opening of "Self-Reliance" in the characteristic citation of the example of the ancient Greeks and in the equally characteristic application of his degenerative theory of history. The occasion of the address, he indicates, is humbler and altogether less remarkable than the gathering of the Athenians, or of the medieval troubadours, or even of the contemporary learned societies in Britain and Europe: "Thus far, our holiday has been simply a friendly sign of the survival of the love of letters amongst a people too busy to give to letters any more."[7] These opening remarks place the instant of Emerson's speaking in the broadest historical context, but in a way that calls attention to the relative insignificance of this present American moment. Unlike Longfellow, Emerson does indeed have a "historical sense," but he regularly insists on showing that its power is most effective in making us uncomfortable with the time in which we live, and therefore is not to be implicitly trusted.

Emerson knew history well enough to understand that those who adopt the past as a guide or reference will sooner or later be overwhelmed by it unless they have some other strength to fortify them. The study of history is of no benefit to a weak or characterless mind. The effect of such study is precisely what frustrated so good a mind as Margaret Fuller's: the induced tendency, in other words, to locate all value, all greatness, in other places and other times, and by extension to be paralyzed in the present. This is not necessarily a false impression, in Emerson's view, but rather one that demanded an active response and not the all too easy resignation and acquiescence he felt it had mainly provoked in his countrymen. Americans *are* a degenerate people, but perhaps only because they concern themselves with a history that tells them so.

> Men are become of no account. Men in history, men in the world of to-day are bugs, are spawn, and are called "the mass" and "the herd." In a century, in a millenium, one or two men; that is to say – one or two approximations to the right state of every man. All the rest behold in the hero or the poet their own green and crude being – ripened; yes, and are content to be less, so *that* may attain to its full stature.[18]

This degenerative view of the history of human consciousness was Emerson's characteristic way of defining the one great philosophical problem that concerned him: the effect of mankind's failure to acknowledge relation or to live in the All. The "American Scholar" address thus begins with Plato's fable of the original dispersion of consciousness when the gods "divided Man into men, that he might be more helpful to himself."[19] Though man's best impulses draw him back to that primal unity, time and circumstances have simply abetted the gods' first division. History is the elaboration of "the *divided* or social state," and the "progress" of mankind is to a great extent a progressive lapse from original relation. Emerson shows by means of this fable that all of mankind is provincial in relation to its center and that the problem is not limited to Americans only.

This strongly marked parallel between Emerson's argument of a general human lapse or a general provincialism of the human spirit in time, and the American frontier consciousness of degeneration in specifically cultural matters is all the more illuminating when one considers how often Emerson reverts to his historical myth when speaking of the morbidity of culture.[20] The similarity between the two phenomena – the one cultural and national, the other spiritual and universal – suggests, perhaps, a deeper reason than is commonly given for the fact that, although there is nothing inherently local or provincial in the nature of Emerson's argument – nothing, for example, that would not be equally pertinent to the situation of the British – he never seriously bothered to trace the implications of his thought for any people but Americans. The temptation is to adopt the thoroughly Emersonian conclusion that one law manifests itself in both instances: that each is a metaphor of the other.

Put another way, what irked Emerson was that frontier America was reenacting the dispersion of consciousness that first occurred in prehistory, and that is variously recorded in Plato's fable and in the biblical account of the Fall – the truth of which is evident to Emerson not as a man of culture, a reader of Plato and the Bible, but as a man thinking and observing in the present. Despite what has so often been said to the contrary, Emerson well knew that the Fall of Man was not a thing that could be made to disappear by argument. Its contemporaneous reenactment suggested to him a repetitive, cyclical concept of history, but it further suggested that Americans were being given a special opportunity to confront fate with fate and thereby break the cycle.[21]

In "The American Scholar," Emerson remarks:

> Historically, there is thought to be a difference in the ideas which predominate over successive epochs, and there are data for marking the genius of the Classic, of the Romantic, and now of the Reflective or Philosophical age. With the views I have intimated of the oneness or the identity of the mind through all individuals, I do not dwell on these differences. In fact, I believe that each individual passes

through all three. The boy is a Greek; the youth, a romantic; the
adult reflective.[22]

Following Wordsworth, Emerson believed that the adult, through "reflection," is capable of understanding his condition as well as the difference between that condition and the unalienated wholeness that was his
as a boy. As Emerson advocated throughout the essays, the adult can
then apply his or her intellect, will, and imagination to achieve the limited
sort of return to original relation that is possible for one who has already
experienced self-consciousness.

The parallel application of this concept to the literary and cultural
situation of the provincial American becomes more apparent when it is
understood that the agency in the dispersion of Consciousness into myr-
iad self-consciousnesses is the intervention of the awareness of circumstance – the capacity (or curse) of knowing the environment is separate
from the self. The perception of nature, on which Longfellow was prepared to base a new American literature, can be as intimidating as a
genuine perception of the vastness of history, if nature is construed as
external and opposed to the individual soul. This frightening perception
of the outer environment as radically discontinuous with the soul is
precisely what, two centuries earlier, had so distressed Anne Bradstreet.
It is significant that Emerson's theory takes a certain perception of circumstance as the primary antagonist to the transcendental perfection of
human consciousness. It is the particular link between Emerson's conception of historic degeneration and the frontier American's conviction
that he or she is leading a contracted life. Speaking for many of his
countrymen, Emerson objects to the absorption of American life and
consciousness by unrelated *things*, dissociated "end-products," and objects sundered from "the universal connexion of nature."[23] This devotion
to the inorganic and the dead merely promotes further degeneration,
further division and "socialization."

Like Anne Bradstreet, Emerson sought to deny the claims that circumstance invariably makes on consciousness, but not, as Bradstreet,
Fuller, or Mrs. Tappan had tried to do, by losing himself in a kind of
culture that his environment was unlikely to support. The conservative
solution was an evasion of fundamental difficulties; as he was shortly to
say, "Travelling is a fool's paradise."[24] He proposed instead to stand his
ground and challenge his environment with the faith that the fatality of
its circumstances was finally no more than an illusion, a function of the
limits of his own perception. "The man must be so much," he wrote in
"Self-Reliance," "that he must make all circumstances indifferent."[25]
Rather than submit to the tyranny of the environment, and rather than
evade such tyranny by acquiring an alienated culture, Emerson advocated

a deliberate recovery of sympathy with the laws of one's own soul. "These laws execute themselves," he said. "They are out of time, out of space, and not subject to circumstance."[26] In advocating, throughout his earlier work, a recovery of original relation, Emerson was writing the prospective biography of the fireeyed child.

Standing aside from the history of Western civilization, Americans were in a unique position to make such a recovery as Emerson spoke of and thereby to precipitate that genuine cultural revolution for which, in his letter of 1857, he was still waiting. Emerson understood that the essential materialism of the old, conservative idea of culture was continually being made evident by the distortions to which culture was subject in its transmission through time and space, and concluded that distortion would continue so long as Americans looked upon culture as something extrinsic to themselves – as the record, indeed the physical record, of what some other, far distant people had once said and done. Only when culture was understood to be radically dependent on spirit rather than matter would distortion and attenuation finally cease, since only then would culture itself be "out of time, out of space." For this sort of culture, Brownell notwithstanding, Emerson never had a hard word.

Neither did he, in a certain sense, for provincialism itself, which, insofar as it points to the failure of traditional culture (that is to say, a culture of traditions), is to be looked upon as an opportunity to return to something better and more fundamental. America's provincialism is its freedom from history and therefore a blessing. Like the ancient Greeks before the dispersion of consciousness (in that Golden Age to which Emerson's generation so often alluded), Americans had, properly speaking, no national history. Unless they chose to forgo this advantage and embrace as their own some imperfectly transmitted version of someone else's culture, they could – if only they might be alerted to the possibility – work a fundamental redemption of culture itself by giving up on tradition and returning to its first source in nature, the symbol of spirit. "The greatness of Greece," Emerson noted, "consists in this, that no Greece preceded it."[27] Preserving a sense of home by accepting their own environment – without, however, yielding the least governance to circumstance – wasting no effort on the vain, delusive wish that they lived in another time or place, Americans might engage nature as the counterpart of themselves and so immediately possess all that culture had ever sought to impart.

By suggesting that the American fall from history might at last be a fortunate fall, Emerson turned the conservatives' position on its head. Whereas they had found culture valuable as an escape from their environment, Emerson could understand the environment in a way to make it the basis for a spiritual and personal culture. Whereas the conservatives dreaded the implications of provincialism, Emerson found in them hope for the limitless development of the individual American. Whereas conservatives were horrified by the freedom implied in the lack of a national history, Emerson gloried in it. And whereas it was important for the conservatives to maintain a traditional identity in defiance of an environment that terribly threatened it, Emerson was relieved by the thought that for once, possibly, the past might not utterly determine the future.

In the letter of 1857, one sees that Emerson had not given up on this vision but one sees also the discouragement and the threat to give up. As Emerson grew older, he had more and more evidence that his vision of a truly organic culture placed the most immense demands on the imagination (which is, of course, why its stewardship was from the first assigned to the poet). As his own imaginative investment in the vision ebbed, certain logical aspects of his youthful sense of possibility seem to have taken on greater and greater prominence: his conviction that culture was a private matter, for example, and his conviction that its value was in its relation to nature and to home. To cultivate one's own garden, and still to feel, in doing so, something of the movements of the currents, is an aged but not impossible way of repeating, in a softer register, what the romantic youth had said.[28]

Postscript: tradition and circumstance

The examples of Margaret Fuller and Ralph Waldo Emerson make for a convenient if not altogether mandatory stopping place. They state, in their respective intellectual lives, two divergent responses to a problem that had dominated the cultural life of America from the beginning. Indeed, they may be said to sum up on the eve of the great changes that came with the Civil War the two positions it was then possible to assume with respect to the issue of provincialism. Furthermore, they illustrate in their contrasting views and contrasting mentalities the range of effects that frontier consciousness might conspire with the environment to elicit.

Frontier consciousness is not, as we have seen, merely or simply a provincial mentality; rather, it is a complex, evolved, and often contradictory consciousness, a rich mix of motives, inclinations, and protests – of protests especially. It is a term, first and last, for a searching and unsatisfied mind. The evolution of frontier consciousness has its origin in the tendency of a wilderness environment to accept immigrants while rejecting the immigrants' culture. Thus it is characterized by a conviction of loss and degradation, by a diminished certitude about personal identity, and by a sense of narrowed horizons in a large and empty land. The antagonism between the American environment and the individual's cultural identity frequently inspired a desperately self-conscious conservatism in those sensitive enough to have felt the threat; it further led them to regard the place where they lived as in a special sense opposed to the meaning of their living. Their resistance to degradation was an affirmation of their own past where identity had been formed and of the ideal of continuity in a place that seemed constantly to demand change and adaptation. The frontier consciousness born of this struggle made past traditions intensely meaningful as an anchor for identity, while at the same time it brought the circumstantial environment into sharp focus as aggressively and distressingly real.

Frontier consciousness tends to polarize the individual's perception of

154

experience according to the terms of this cultural struggle. Circumstance comes to be associated with the present but also with time in its degenerative implications, with decay and mutability; it comes to be associated in the frontier mind with the real, the corporeal, and the solid, with the difficult, the painful, and the intransigent. Circumstance suggests diversity, disunity, particularity. Constant attention to the environment diffuses the unity of the perceiving mind, breaks up impressions, fragments identity, and undermines belief in larger meanings. Circumstances, in short, are both trivial and absorbing. They root the soul firmly in the earth and so prevent it from rising into the heavens above. Against circumstance frontier consciousness deliberately sets tradition, which is associated with the past but also with timelessness, with defiance of mutability. Tradition comes to be associated with the ideal rather than the real, with the intangible qualities of spiritual and aesthetic values, and finally, with meaning in opposition to chaos. In its enhanced function as a standard or guide, tradition signifies ease and grace, as well as release from the hard work of having constantly to invent new responses to new circumstances. It subsumes particularity and ends confusion. It represents consensus and, therefore, unity – a unity of many minds but of the single mind as well. As circumstance promotes isolation, so tradition promotes community. It is as attractive to frontier consciousness as circumstance, its felt opposite, is repellent and frightening.

The maintenance of tradition at such a distance from cultural centers and under such unfavorable circumstances is, however, inordinately difficult. The transmission of Old World culture to America (or of eastern culture to the West) involves a marked attenuation of style; the relative flatness or thinness of the transmitted culture becomes, in turn, a source of vague shame, a hint, often only half perceived, of an encroaching grossness, and a verification, certainly, of the radical separateness of provincial life. To those Americans most thoroughly alert to these issues, artists, the blame for the gradual loss of a cherished standard of civilization rests squarely on the environment and on the weakness of Americans in succumbing to it. The conjunction of an extrinsic ideal culture and an intrinsically resistant environment made America's artists preternaturally sensitive to instances of failure. Precisely because the log hut violated the cultural ideal that Timothy Dwight held dear, he saw that hut with intense clarity and almost to the exclusion of an otherwise beautiful landscape. Because violations of the ideal were present and real while the ideal was distant and abstract, artistic attention came always to focus most vividly on failure. The "negative imagination" resulting from frontier consciousness, however, had less to do with a direct response to the depressing particularity of the artist's environment than with the large and essentially undifferentiated sense he or she has of cultural attenuation on a broad national scale, precisely because it implies the impossibility in America of maintaining stable identities or a traditional culture.

We have seen in Anne Bradstreet the direct confrontation between an identity formed under conditions favorable to learning and an environment intensely hostile to spiritual and aesthetic values. Her response was not the easy, instantaneous adaptation that Turner described in his frontier thesis but, rather, a conservative exercise of art in defiance of circumstance and an affirmation of unity in defense against fragmentation and degeneracy. The decay of these defenses in the face of continuous assault lends a poignant and dramatic force to her poetry. The perceived value of tradition as a counter to degradation often led America's early writers not only to imitate but to regard originality with a greater than usual suspicion. Royall Tyler's *Contrast* shows that imitation had become so important a phenomenon in American culture by 1787 as to require distinctions between acceptable and unacceptable varieties. By advocating the moral discipline implied in the imitation of worthy models, Tyler effectively gauges the extent of provincial attenuation. The clearer one can be about affirmed standards, the easier it becomes to measure (and deplore) the deviation. Such clarity, however, is itself subject to the distortions and misguided compromises that arise from provincial isolation.

The specifically American qualities in the early literature have to be looked for behind the imitative form in the complexly motivated mind of that writer who tries, and yet fails, to imitate adequately. Timothy Dwight is a poet whose most appealing verse is marked by a conflict of aesthetic and didactic aims. Sensing his own failure to appropriate sufficiently well the British styles that he admired, and yet confident that he has carried his point, he pretended on moral grounds to question the value or importance of aesthetic concerns. Both Tyler and Dwight in their frontier consciousness suspected that style is inherently in conflict with substance – as their environment had shown them that substance is in conflict with style – and that Americans, including American artists, have a responsibility to choose moral content or substantial virtue in preference to artistic display. In these writers, representatives of the first postrevolutionary generation, we see the beginnings of a conflict between the desire to affirm native American values, which rely on an austere if not ascetic moralism, and the desire to affirm European culture as older, more expansive, more refined, more civilized, and finally, more beautiful.

This conflict shows its tremendous power in Washington Irving's life and writings. Although Irving is not usually thought of in connection with stress of any sort, he did feel the contrary attractions of the graceful style of European culture and the rough power and undeveloped potential of America. His sympathies as an artist were all with Europe; but America seemed to him far stronger, more virile and vital, in a word, more substantial.

Precisely because Europe had formed the American idea of art, however, provincial writers were led by the very practice of their craft to turn away from home. Hawthorne sensed this, too. His response, like Irving's, took the form of attempting to supply America with a history and a culture of its own – Irving through legend and formal historical writings, Hawthorne through an exploration, brilliantly sustained, of the failure of communal or social values. Yet even as Hawthorne found compelling mythic and psychological uses for the cultural processes that shaped his art, he felt that his constant straining against his materials could only take him farther and farther out of sympathy with the present and the "real," and finally deny him access to the robust vitality that chiefly characterized America. This lack of robustness in Hawthorne is what, in part, Henry James was calling attention to when he remarked on the emptiness in Hawthorne's field of vision. What James failed to understand, however, was that details (or circumstances) were a part of what frontier consciousness sought to overcome; they were not available to America's earlier writers as the richly suggestive material of fiction but all too often as signs only of the failure of culture. Hawthorne struggled all his life against the commonplace of detail, trying always – in his notebooks especially – to make useful contact with the circumstantial world, developing an ironic, transforming imagination as a compromise between the forthright acceptance of particularity that he identified on occasion with Trollope and the tendency of frontier consciousness to use art as an escape from circumstance.

Of the kinds of protests registered by Fuller, the intense expatriate, and Emerson, the man who, at home, dilated and conspired with the morning wind, certainly it was the former and not the latter that would prove the pattern for the time to come. If the issues seemed less momentous to the innocents abroad, or different to the passionate pilgrims, the eagerness of the next generation to explore Venetian life and Tuscan cities might serve to remind us that all the protests of frontier consciousness, Emerson's no less than Fuller's, are invitations to discovery.

The *provincial* mind, as it is usually understood in relation to the American context, is one that has succumbed to environmental pressures and been drawn away from its cultural heritage; *frontier consciousness* is the provincial mind in protest and is, therefore, in its essential genius, conservative. It is a mind that knows the meaning of a loss of heritage; it is a mind that identifies itself in cultural terms and so regards the threat to culture as a threat to personality as well. The fundamental posture of frontier consciousness in America has been defensive and conservative but not negative in its goals or purposes. It has sought always to affirm the individual's connection with the larger civilized community and to protect that community's values from degradation.

Notes

Introduction. *Provincialism and the frontier*

1. F. J. Turner, "The Significance of the Frontier in American History," in *The Frontier in American History* (New York: Henry Holt, 1921), pp. 3–4.
2. Ibid., p. 38.
3. On the conservatism of the western pioneers, see Page Smith, *As a City upon a Hill: The Town in American History* (Cambridge, Mass.: MIT Press, 1966), esp. chap. 3, "The Expansion of New England."
4. Turner, "The Significance of the Frontier," p. 9.
5. Earl Pomeroy, "Toward a Reorientation of Western History: Continuity and Environment," *Mississippi Valley Historical Review*, 41 (March 1955), 582.
6. Louis B. Wright, *Culture on the Moving Frontier* (Bloomington: Indiana University Press, 1955), p. 20.
7. Alexis de Tocqueville, *Democracy in America*, trans. Henry Reeve, ed. Phillips Bradley (New York: Vintage Books, 1945), II, 58.
8. Quoted in Ray Allen Billington, *The Westward Movement in the United States* (Princeton, N.J.: D. Van Nostrand, 1959), p. 120.
9. Quoted in Richard C. Wade, *The Urban Frontier: Pioneer Life in Early Pittsburgh, Cincinnati, Lexington, and St. Louis* (Chicago: University of Chicago Press, 1959), p.105.
10. In the nineteenth century the costs involved in setting up even the most rudimentary pioneer farms were considerable. See Ray A. Billington, *Westward Expansion: A History of the American Frontier*, 4th ed. (New York: Macmillan, 1974), p. 9, and Arthur K. Moore, *The Frontier Mind: A Cultural Analysis of the Kentucky Frontiersman* (Lexington: University of Kentucky Press, 1957), pp. 5–6 and passim.
11. Quoted in Ray A. Billington, *America's Frontier Heritage* (New York: Holt, Rinehart & Winston, 1966), p. 74.
12. This behavior is well documented. Caroline Kirkland, for example, gives several instances in *A New Home – Who'll Follow?* (New York: C. S. Francis, 1839); chapter 19 is a particularly ironic portrait of a self-defeating refusal

160 NOTES TO PAGES 4–13

to adapt to circumstances. See also Ronald L. Davis, "Culture on the Frontier," *Southwest Review*, 53 (1968), 383–403.

13. Billington, *America's Frontier Heritage*, pp. 74–5.

14. Charles Dickens, *American Notes* (London: Chapman & Hall, 1842), II, 55–6.

15. Nathaniel Hawthorne, *The American Notebooks*, ed. Claude M. Simpson (Columbus: Ohio State University Press, 1972), pp. 492–3. The entry is for May 6, 1850.

16. James Hall, "The Emigrants," in *Legends of the West* (Philadelphia: Key & Biddle, 1833), I, 173.

17. Here I am proposing a thesis almost, as I see it, the reverse of that presented by Richard Slotkin in *Regeneration Through Violence* (Middletown, Conn.: Wesleyan University Press, 1973). Slotkin's emphasis on "Indianization" and the sloughing off of European consciousness would seem to ally him with Turner and D. H. Lawrence; although the usefulness of this approach has been amply demonstrated, it is one that historically has made little allowance for the conservative impulse of the pioneers, their attachment not only to older forms but also to the community these forms created. The emergence of an American culture involves more than adaptation to a new environment; it involves the deformation of European elements in a complex, continually changing relationship with the attitudes Americans have adopted *toward* that deformation.

18. Nathaniel Hawthorne, "Main Street," in *The Snow-Image and Uncollected Tales*, ed. J. Donald Crowley (Columbus: Ohio State University Press, 1974), pp. 67–8.

19. R. W. B. Lewis, *The American Adam: Innocence, Tragedy and Tradition in the Nineteenth Century* (Chicago: University of Chicago Press, 1955), p. 31.

20. Hamlin Garland, "Provincialism," in *Crumbling Idols*, ed. Jane Johnson (Cambridge, Mass.: Harvard University Press, 1960), p. 7. Garland's essay, contemporaneous with Turner's on the frontier, shares with it a tendency to discount "eastern" culture and to associate the "indigenous" and the American with western qualities. Garland's better insight is his identification of that process deprecated by conservatives, the attritional failure of an inherited or transmitted culture, with the process of Americanization.

Chapter 1. "But enmity this amity did break"

1. William Bradford, *History of Plymouth Plantation*, ed. Worthington C. Ford (n.p.: Massachusetts Historical Society, 1912), I, 157–8.

2. Anne Bradstreet, "In Honour of Du Bartas," in *The Works of Anne Bradstreet*, ed. John Harvard Ellis (Charlestown, Mass.: Abram E. Cutter, 1867), p. 354. All further citations of the poetry are from this edition. Ellis refers (p. xv) to the passage from which this line is taken as a "very pleasant reminiscence of [the poet's] childhood."

3. *Winthrop Papers*, ed. Stewart Mitchell (n.p.: Massachusetts Historical Society, 1931), II, 294. I have modernized the spelling and punctuation.

4. Ibid.

5. Thomas Dudley, "Dudley's Letter to the Countess of Lincoln," in *Chronicles*

of the First Planters of the Colony of Massachusetts Bay, ed. Alexander Young (Boston: Charles C. Little & James Brown, 1846), p. 259. For a severe contemporary account of the indolence of Endecott's people and their indifference to duty, see *Winthrop Papers*, II, 263, n. 7.

6. Bradstreet, *Works*, p. 5.

7. Upwards of a hundred did return at this time: see Young, *Chronicles*, p. 315, and Charles Edward Banks, *The Winthrop Fleet of 1630* (Boston: Houghton Mifflin, 1930), p. 48.

8. Quoted in *The Puritan Tradition in America*, ed. Alden T. Vaughan (Columbia: University of South Carolina Press, 1972), p. 131.

9. Bradstreet, "Contemplations," in *Works*, p. 373.

10. Bradstreet, "Upon a Fit of Sickness," in ibid., pp. 391–2.

11. See, for example, Adrienne Rich, "Anne Bradstreet and Her Poetry," in *The Works of Anne Bradstreet*, ed. Jeannine Hensley (Cambridge, Mass.: Harvard University Press, 1967), p. xiv. Robert D. Richardson, Jr., in "The Puritan Poetry of Anne Bradstreet," in *The American Puritan Imagination: Essays in Revaluation* (n.p.: Cambridge University Press, 1974), p. 90, says that the quaternions "show a nearly unqualified worldliness."

12. This poem, though possibly published, has disappeared without trace; not even its title survives.

13. Elizabeth Wade White makes a plausible case that this date represents the poet's birthday. The formal presentation of the poem together with the influence of Dudley's verses may indicate that the quaternions were a sort of intellectual "sampler." On the date of the poet's birth, see White, *Anne Bradstreet: "The Tenth Muse"* (New York: Oxford University Press, 1971), pp. 39–40.

14. Bradstreet, *Works*, p. 97.

15. Bradstreet's most extended treatment of the subject occurs in "The Prologue," but she adverts to it in the du Bartas poem, the tributes to Sidney and Queen Elizabeth, and in the ending of the "Four Monarchies."

16. Dudley *did* make the connection in an incidental complaint about New World manners. In his letter to the countess of Lincoln, he remarked that he wrote "rudely, having yet no table, nor other room to write in than by the fireside upon my knee, in this sharp winter; to which my family must have leave to resort, though they break good manners, and make me many times forget what I would say, and say what I would not" in Young, *Chronicles*, p. 305. Edward Taylor's frequent complaints about his own style are in many ways analogous, though he attributes the problem to the effects of sin, as Bradstreet never explicitly does. In Taylor, constraints on literary style rise to consciousness already metaphorized in such a way as to make the American provincial artist an effective symbol of the general human condition. It is a maneuver we will have occasion to observe time and again in the following chapters.

17. Bradstreet, *Works*, p. 103.

18. Bradstreet, "To the Memory of ... Thomas Dudley, Esq. ... His Epitaph," in ibid., p. 368.

19. *Winthrop Papers*, II, 307.

20. Bradstreet, *Works*, pp. 145–6.
21. Ibid., pp. 40–2.
22. "Anne Bradstreet," in Hensley, ed., *Works*, p. xvii.
23. Consider, in this connection, the following lines from a late, untitled poem in which Bradstreet anticipates the thoughts of a "weary pilgrim" about to die:

> The burning sun no more shall heat
>   Nor stormy raines, on him shall beat.
> The bryars and thornes no more shall scratch
>   nor hungry wolves at him shall catch
> He erring pathes no more shall tread
>   nor wild fruits eate, in stead of bread,
> for waters cold he doth not long
>   for thirst no more shall parch his tongue
> No rugged stones his feet shall gaule
>   nor stumps nor rocks cause him to fall
> All cares and feares, he bids farewell
>   and meanes in safity now to dwell.
>   (*Works*, pp. 42–3)

24. Alexis de Tocqueville, *Democracy in America*, trans. Henry Reeve, ed. Phillips Bradley (New York: Vintage Books, 1945), II, 54.

Chapter 2. Brother Jonathan

1. Joseph Atkinson's play, *A Match for a Widow*, staged in Dublin, April 17, 1786, was among the first dramatic representations of the Yankee. Although it preceded Royall Tyler's *Contrast* by nearly a year, there seems to have been no direct influence. See Marston Balch, "Jonathan the First," *Modern Language Notes*, 46 (May 1931), 281–8, and G. Thomas Tanselle, *Royall Tyler* (Cambridge, Mass.: Harvard University Press, 1967), pp. 55–7.
2. John Cotton, "Gods Promise to His Plantations," *Old South Leaflet*, no. 53 (1896); rpt. in *Colonial American Writing*, ed. Roy Harvey Pearce, 2d ed. (New York: Holt, Rinehart & Winston, 1969), p. 76. Understandably, the text was a favorite with the writers of the jeremiads; see, for example, Joshua Scottow, *Old Men's Tears, for Their Own Declensions* (Boston: J. Allen, 1715).
3. William Bradford, *History of Plymouth Plantation*, ed. Worthington C. Ford (n.p.: Massachusetts Historical Society, 1912), II, 369.
4. Ibid., 316–22.
5. The body of literature devoted to aspects of the "declension" or the waning of piety is large and growing. Among the most useful works are the two volumes of Perry Miller, *New England Mind, The Seventeenth Century* (Cambridge, Mass.: Harvard University Press, 1954) and *From Colony to Province* (Cambridge, Mass.: Harvard University Press, 1953), and the same author's "Declension in the Bible Commonwealth," in *Nature's Nation* (Cambridge, Mass.: Harvard University Press, 1967), pp. 14–49; Kenneth Lockridge, *A*

New England Town, The First Hundred Years: Dedham, Massachusetts, 1636–1736 (New York: W. W. Norton, 1970); Alan Heimert, *Religion and the American Mind from the Great Awakening to the Revolution* (Cambridge, Mass.: Harvard University Press, 1967); Jack P. Greene, "Search for Identity: An Interpretation of Selected Patterns of Social Response in Eighteenth-Century America," *Journal of Social History*, 3 (Spring 1970), 189–200, and David D. Hall, *The Faithful Shepherd: A History of the New England Ministry in the Seventeenth Century* (Chapel Hill: University of North Carolina Press, 1972). The most significant recent contributions, however, are the two volumes by Sacvan Bercovitch, *The Puritan Origins of the American Self* (New Haven, Conn.: Yale University Press, 1975) and *The American Jeremiad* (Madison: University of Wisconsin Press, 1978).

Greene, in "Search for Identity," cites a number of sermons in support of the thesis that "as the clergy continued to dilate upon the theme of New England's decline, the great 'Leaders of the first Generation' assumed heroic, almost saintly proportions" (p. 192). Although Bercovitch does not share this view, he does, in *The Puritan Origins*, examine Cotton Mather's crucial development in the historical biographies contained in the *Magnalia* of the idea of exemplary American identities.

6. The phrase is the title of a sermon by Andrew Eliot (Boston: Benjamin Harris & John Allen, 1753). I base this conclusion in part on Clifford K. Shipton's thesis that the Puritans' struggle in the wilderness was primarily an effort to conserve culture; see Shipton's "The New England Frontier," *New England Quarterly*, 10 (March 1937), 25–36. Jack Greene's article (see note 5, above) seems to me to support Shipton and to dispute Perry Miller's claim that New England succeeded in working out a satisfactory synthesis. Greene claims that "far from discovering a 'deeper identity' of their own, . . . they never ceased to measure their own achievements against their idealized conception of their ancestors, and the blatant disparity between this mythic past and contemporary reality contributed to the formation . . . of what Erik Erikson has referred to as a 'guilt-culture' " (p. 199). If Greene's hypothesis is correct, then the behavior pattern coincides with the dynamic of frontier consciousness in three of its most important elements: (1) the felt need to affirm tradition, (2) the failure under frontier conditions to do so, and (3) the sense of guilt that the failure induces. Lockridge (see note 5) also confirms this view in his portrayal of Dedham, a town that, like many others, resisted the Half-Way Covenant in order to "preserve the pure church" (p. 34). This act of conservatism, like others on the frontier, was supported with difficulty and was ultimately self-defeating.

7. In *The Puritan Origins*, Bercovitch suggests that the form of Franklin's *Autobiography* entails "a mythic mode of cultural continuity" since the career of the persona "at once recapitulates the nation's past and predicates its future" (p. 143). But Franklin's future is predicated on rejecting the past and – in his southward emigration – removing himself from its constraining influence. Written by the least provincial man in America, the *Autobiography* treats only the writer's *most* provincial period and shows that the conflicts

of the "guilt-culture" can be resolved by defying the authority of the past, conceived as a force that, by constraining, provincializes.

8. Royall Tyler, *The Contrast,* in *Representative American Plays,* ed. Arthur Hobson Quinn (New York: Century Co., 1917), p. 48.

9. Manly's character is, significantly, a patchwork, and in saying that he "represents" the values of the Puritan past, I do not mean to dispute Manly's own assertion that he is imitating Washington; nor do I intend to deny the pertinence to Manly's character of Cincinnatus, who figures in the popular imagination as the antitype to the type of Washington. My point is that even the Roman-soldier aspect of Manly's character serves the larger purpose of the defense of Puritan values, and that Tyler's confusing eclecticism is simply further evidence of his view that style ought always to be subordinate to content.

10. Tyler, *The Contrast,* p. 57.

11. Ibid., p. 58.

12. See Arthur H. Nethercot, "The Dramatic Background of Royall Tyler's *The Contrast,*" *American Literature,* 12 (January 1941), 437. Nethercot shows that Tyler had some familiarity with English drama, gained either by reading playbooks or by seeing amateur performances. See also Daniel F. Havens *The Columbian Muse of Comedy: The Development of a Native Tradition in Early American Social Comedy, 1787–1845* (Carbondale: Southern Illinois University Press, 1973), pp. 8–51, Tanselle, *Royall Tyler,* pp. 49–59, and Marius B. Peladeau, ed., *The Verse of Royall Tyler* (Charlottesville: University Press of Virginia, 1968), pp. 5–7.

13. Quoted in Havens, *The Columbian Muse of Comedy,* p. 9.

14. Tyler, *The Contrast,* p. 77.

15. Ibid., p. 58.

16. Ibid., p. 68.

17. *Benjamin Franklin's Memoirs,* ed. Max Ferrand (Berkeley: University of California Press, 1949), p. 2.

18. The phrases are from James Lockwood, *Religion the Highest Interest of a Civil Community* (New London, Conn.: 1754), p. 28, quoted in Richard L. Bushman, *From Puritan to Yankee: Character and the Social Order in Connecticut, 1690–1765* (Cambridge, Mass.: Harvard University Press, 1967), p. 280.

19. Tyler, *The Contrast,* p. 67.

20. Cf. Herbert Schneider's discussion of the "loss of the sense of sin" as the crucial issue in the declension: *The Puritan Mind* (New York: Henry Holt, 1930), chap. 3.

21. Ralph Waldo Emerson, "Nature," in *The Collected Works of Ralph Waldo Emerson,* ed. Robert E. Spiller et al. (Cambridge, Mass: Harvard University Press, 1971), I, 22.

22. Constance Rourke, *American Humor: A Study in the National Character* (New York: Harcourt Brace, 1931), p. 16.

23. Tyler, *The Contrast,* p. 60.

24. Ibid.

25. *The History of New England*, ed. James Savage (Boston: Little, Brown, 1853), II, 281.

26. Tyler, *The Contrast*, p. 60. Tyler himself accompanied the expedition against Shays as aide-de-camp to General Benjamin Lincoln. Tradition has awarded much of the success of the campaign to Tyler's eloquence in addressing the rebels.

27. Ibid., p. 62.

28. Ibid., p. 66.

Chapter 3. "A musy in the thicket"

1. H. H. Brackenridge, *Modern Chivalry*, ed. Lewis Leary (New Haven, Conn.: College and University Press, 1965), p. 46.

2. Edwin H. Cady, *The Gentleman in America: A Literary Study in American Culture* (Syracuse, N.Y.: Syracuse University Press, 1949), pp. 56–7.

3. Arthur K. Moore, *The Frontier Mind* (Lexington: University of Kentucky Press, 1957; rpt. New York: McGraw-Hill, 1963), pp. 5–6. Moore's description of the situation of the conservative settler bears an interesting analogy to that of the elder Wieland in Charles Brockden Brown's novel. In *Wieland*, however, the irrational forces that violently and dramatically reject the importation of the "Old World legacy" are located, metaphorically perhaps, in the free and unformed quality of the environment itself. See A. Carl Bredahl, Jr., "Transformation in *Wieland*," *Early American Literature*, 12 (Fall 1977), 177–92.

4. "If there were such a thing as 'the genteel tradition' in America, the indomitable fight of thinking Americans against loss of the heritage of European culture would be it. Obviously, no group of people is without culture in the anthropological sense. But, as many of the vials of scorn poured upon the gentleman in America attest, what civilized persons value as civilization exists in America now in significant measure because of the traditions of the gentleman" (Cady, *The Gentleman in America*, p. 17).

5. Claude M. Newlin, *The Life and Writings of Hugh Henry Brackenridge* (Princeton, N.J.: Princeton University Press, 1932), p. 4.

6. From "A Dogrel Said to Be by Auld Brackie on the Scots-Irishman," *Tree of Liberty*, June 20, 1801; rpt. in ibid., p. 5. There is a danger, perhaps, in making too much of this brief passage, but it is worth noting that it runs counter to the ordinary preference in American pastoral for that "middle ground" which Leo Marx identified in *The Machine in the Garden* (New York: Oxford University Press, 1964). Between "places farther back" where a kind of Arcadian culture is posited (without human beings), and the amenities of a fuller civilization to the east lies the scene of the conversion of the one into the other, imaged as a rape of the land. Fenimore Cooper's romance *The Prairie* exhibits a similar preference for either wild or civilized (both, in a sense, "finished" states) over the change and disruption always already localized in the "middle ground."

7. Newlin, *Brackenridge*, p. 58. Husbands (1724–1795) was a veritable western

"character," a minor figure in the Great Awakening and a leader of the Whiskey Rebellion.

8. Moore, *The Frontier Mind*, p. 24.

9. Tocqueville noticed this tendency and (wrongly, I think) saw it as an effect of democracy rather than of cultural isolation. The example is nevertheless a good one: "When I arrived for the first time at New York . . . I was surprised to perceive along the shore, at some distance from the city, a number of little palaces of white marble, several of which were of classic architecture. When I went the next day to inspect more closely one which had particularly attracted my notice, I found that its walls were of white-washed brick, and its columns of painted wood. All the edifices which I had admired the night before were of the same kind.

"The social conditions and institutions of democracy impart . . . certain peculiar tendencies to all the imitative arts, which it is easy to point out. They frequently withdraw [their efforts] from the delineation of the soul to fix them exclusively on that of the body, and they substitute the representation of motion and sensation for that of sentiment and thought; in a word, they put the real in the place of the ideal" (*Democracy in America*, trans. Henry Reeve, ed. Phillips Bradley [New York: Vintage Books, 1945], II, 54).

10. Newlin, *Brackenridge*, p. 195.

11. James D. Hart, ed., *The Oxford Companion to American Literature*, 4th ed. (New York: Oxford University Press, 1965), q.v. Brackenridge. For a description of Andrew Jackson as a "democratic autocrat," see James Parton, *Life of Andrew Jackson* (New York: Mason Brothers, 1860), I, vii.

12. Biographical information in this chapter is drawn from Kenneth Silverman, *Timothy Dwight* (Boston: Twayne, 1969), and Charles E. Cuningham, *Timothy Dwight, 1752–1817: A Biography* (New York: Macmillan, 1942).

13. Quoted in Silverman, *Timothy Dwight*, p. 130.

14. Silverman, *Timothy Dwight*, p. 113.

15. Timothy Dwight, *Travels in New-England and New-York* (New Haven, Conn.: Timothy Dwight, 1821), II, 459.

16. Ibid., p. 460.

17. Ibid., p. 469.

18. Silverman, *Timothy Dwight*, p. 133.

19. Quoted in ibid., pp. 145–6.

20. Dwight's occasional defenses of American neologisms are evidence of this indecision. On the whole he approved the lexical inventions of his countrymen on the grounds that they were useful. "Interval," for example, seemed to Dwight an indispensable word for which the English simply had no counterpart. Likewise, the verb "progress" filled an obvious need for a "go ahead" people. His own *Travels* includes the first recorded use of the word "pioneer." But Dwight knew how these innovations were regarded in England, and he treated them gingerly, sometimes with an embarrassed awkwardness, as in this sentence from the *Travels*: "Seven men, one of them a Mr. Palmer, went into the Eastern part of the township, and, in the language of the country, *were lost*; that is, they became wholly uncertain

of the course, which they were to pursue, in order to regain their habitations" (II, 119). Dwight's own efforts at word-coinage were not happy; his use of the term "conflagrative brand" (a torch) earned him the amused ridicule of Francis Jeffrey. See Dwight's *Remarks on the Review of Inchiquin's Letters* . . . (Boston: Samuel T. Armstrong, 1815), p. 139.

21. Timothy Dwight, *Greenfield Hill: A Poem in Seven Parts* (New York: Childs & Swaine, 1794), p. 17.

22. Ibid., pp. 169–70.

23. Ibid., p. 16.

24. Ibid., p. 8.

25. Ibid., p. 140.

26. Ibid., p. 141.

27. This cyclical rise and fall cannot be squared with Dwight's progressive "frontier thesis," and therefore he regards it as pathological. Stow Persons, in "The Cyclical Theory of History in Eighteenth-Century America," *American Quarterly*, 6 (Summer 1954), esp. 153, shows that men of Dwight's generation saw in history the difficulty of sustaining the good society indefinitely, given the apparently natural tendency of civilizations to grow and decay. For Dwight, the problem seemed in large measure to consist in the difficulty of *transmitting*, intact, the normative values of the past.

28. Dwight's *Dissertation on the History, Eloquence, and Poetry of the Bible* (New Haven, Conn.: Thomas & Samuel Green, 1772), gives a hint concerning the possible origins of the inveterate proclivity of American writers to approach the largest issues through the smallest doors: "Sensible that *General History*, though in many respects instructive, is dry and unentertaining – sensible that *General Descriptions* leave very faint traces on the Memory; the writers of Inspiration, contented with giving a plain, concise account of everything of that kind necessary to be known (though even this very circumstance hath made their *General Histories* more striking than those of any other nation) hurry on to events more particular, relations more minute. Perhaps not one fourth part of the Sacred History is *General*. To interest the attention, to employ the Memory, it is necessary that we should have a clear, distinct, and perfect idea of any transaction – this can only be given by an exact relation of every minute important circumstance – and such a relation can only be made of single events" (pp. 7–8). This way of approaching the poetry of the Bible is not uniquely American, but the circumstantial outlook of frontier Americans certainly made it congenial. One is naturally reminded of Emerson's observation that "the piety of the Hebrew prophets purges their grossness. The circumcision is an example of the power of poetry to raise the low and offensive. Small and mean things serve as well as great symbols. The meaner the type by which a law is expressed, the more pungent it is, and the more lasting in the memories of men" ("The Poet," in *The Collected Works of Ralph Waldo Emerson*, ed. Robert E. Spiller et al. [Cambridge, Mass.: Harvard University Press, 1983], III, 11). This passage, in turn, is likely to remind one of Walt Whitman's observation that "the greatest poet hardly knows pettiness or triviality. If he breathes into anything that was before thought small, it dilates

with the grandeur and life of the universe" ("Preface to *Leaves of Grass*," in *The Complete Prose Works of Walt Whitman* [New York: G. P. Putnam's Sons, 1902], II, 164–5). Surely this view could not have won such wide and significant support were it not for the frontier-induced conviction that the American environment was impressively mean, trivial, and commonplace.

29.   Sir John Denham, "Cooper's Hill," in Brendan O Hehir, *Expans'd Hieroglyphicks: A Study of Sir John Denham's Coopers Hill with a Critical Edition of the Poem* (Berkeley: University of California Press, 1969), p. 139. I have quoted the text designated by O Hehir as the " 'B' text, Draft IV," which is the one "best known to subsequent generations of readers." Spelling and punctuation have been modernized somewhat for clarity.

30.   Ibid., pp. 140–1. The first line of this passage in the "B text" reads, "though," a less satisfactory reading than "Through," which O Hehir records as an MS variant (see p. 94).

31.   Dwight, *Travels*, II, 127.

32.   Denham, "Cooper's Hill," pp. 160–1.

33.   Dwight, *Remarks*, pp. 104–5; the italics in the first sentence are Dwight's; those in the next to last are mine.

Chapter 4. Geoffrey Crayon and the gigantic race

1.   Washington Irving, *Tales of a Traveller* (New York: G. P. Putnam, 1860), p. x.

2.   James Russell Lowell, "The Cathedral," in *The Writings of James Russell Lowell* (Boston: Houghton, Mifflin, 1891), X, 43.

3.   Joseph S. Buckminster's 1809 Phi Beta Kappa address indicates the Federalist view of the connections among innovation, the spread of democracy, and the general weakening of cultural institutions. The fury of the French Revolution, he wrote, "is past and spent, but its effects have been felt throughout the whole system of liberal education. The foul spirit of innovation and sophistry has been seen wandering in the very groves of the Lyceum, and is not yet completely exorcised, though the spell is broken. When we look back to the records of our learning before the American revolution, we find, or think we find, (at least in New England) more accomplished scholars than we have since produced; men, who conversed more familiarly than their children with the mighty dead; men, who felt more than we do the charm of classical accomplishments. . . . Our forms of education were becoming more popular and superficial; the knowledge of antiquity began to be despised; and the hard labour of learning to be dispensed with. Soon the ancient strictness of the discipline disappeared; the curriculum of studies was shortened in favour of the impatience or the necessities of candidates for literary honours; the pains of application were derided, and a pernicious notion of equality was introduced, which has not only tainted our sentiments, but impaired our vigour, and crippled our literary eminence" ("The Dangers and Duties of Men of Letters," in *The Federalist Literary Mind: Selections from the Monthly Anthology and Boston Review, 1803-11*, ed. Lewis

P. Simpson [n.p.: Louisiana State University Press, 1962], pp. 95–6). One notices how similar is the sense of degenerating scholarship to the perception of a decline in piety, and how in each instance the effect is to make ideal models of a previous generation.

4. Quoted in Russell B. Nye, *The Cultural Life of the New Nation: 1776–1830* (New York: Harper & Brothers, 1960), p. 151.

5. Hawthorne felt this personally when he went to England in 1853. He tried to obtain information about his English ancestors, and later attempted, without success, to embody the theme of the English inheritance in a romance. His duties as consul at Liverpool brought him in contact with many Americans who were convinced that they were rightful heirs to various English estates. In "Consular Experiences," the first essay in *Our Old Home*, Hawthorne observes that "as an individual, the American is often conscious of deep-rooted sympathies that belong more fitly to times gone by, and feels a blind, pathetic tendency to wander back again, which makes itself evident in such wild dreams as I have alluded to . . . about English inheritances" (*Our Old Home: A Series of English Sketches*, ed. Claude M. Simpson [Columbus: Ohio State University Press, 1970], p. 19). William Dean Howells felt this, too: "No American, complexly speaking, finds himself in England for the first time. . . . It is probable, rather, that on his arrival, if he has not yet visited the country, he has a sense of having been there before, which a simpler psychology than ours used to make much of without making anything of. His English ancestors who really were once there stir within him, and his American forefathers, who were nourished on the history and literature of England, and were therefore intellectually English, join in creating an English consciousness in him" (*Certain Delightful English Towns* [New York: Harper & Brothers, 1906], p. 1). This myth owed much of its vitality to the racial view of history one finds, for example, in Emerson's *English Traits*, and which was popular with historians until it was successfully challenged by Turner, beginning with his frontier thesis.

6. Washington Irving, *The Sketch-Book of Geoffrey Crayon, Gent.* (New York: G. P. Putnam, 1860), pp. 17–18.

7. Ibid., p. 86.

8. Ibid., p. 87. It may be that a slight parodic nod to Franklin saves this passage from being hopelessly smug.

9. Henry Wadsworth Longfellow, "The Building of the Ship," ll.26–39, in *The Complete Poetical Works of Henry Wadsworth Longfellow* (Boston: Houghton Mifflin, 1893), p. 100. By pointing out the architectural similarities between Old World ships and European castles, Longfellow emphasizes the need for Americans to innovate, and to do so in a way that promotes functional utility and devalues ornament for its own sake; the American ship will be "built for freight, and yet for speed" (l.40).

10. Philip Rahv, "The Native Bias," in *Literature in America*, ed. Philip Rahv (New York: Meridan Books, 1957), pp. 11–12.

11. Irving, *The Sketch-Book*, p. 82.

12. Ibid., p. 86.

13. The contradictory flavor of Irving's essay seems to have baffled William

Hedges, who, in *Washington Irving: An American Study, 1802–32* (Baltimore: Johns Hopkins University Press, 1965), p. 128, found it "confused" in its attitudes and "almost unreadable." But the significance of the essay is not that Irving's Anglophilia is at odds with his literary nationalism; it is that, given this wholly typical provincial dilemma, he made so elaborate and balanced an effort to reconcile them. The process, the movement within the essay, gives the work its meaning for us, not Irving's failure summarily to choose nativism or subservience.

14. Irving, *The Sketch-Book*, pp. 30–1.

15. Ibid., p. 34.

16. Ibid., p. 36.

17. Longfellow, "The Building of the Ship" (ll. 7–8), p. 99.

18. Irving, *The Sketch-Book*, p. 31.

19. Ibid., p. 33.

20. Pierre M. Irving, *The Life and Letters of Washington Irving* (New York: G. P. Putnam, 1862), I, 412. See also Hedges, *Washington Irving*, pp. 115–16.

21. Irving, *Life and Letters*, I, 463.

22. Enlarging on his discussion of Whittier's reading, Horace E. Scudder wrote: "Time was . . . when the Bible was read as a whole, then the effort was not so much to read it as if one were a contemporary of its scenes as to realize those scenes on the plane of the reader. The historic sense was not cultivated, but the imaginative was, and the prophets and apostles walked the streets and hills of New England, in the imagination of the people, much as they showed themselves once in Venice to painters" ("Whittier's Life and Poetry," *Atlantic Monthly*, 74 [November 1894], 695–6). I regard this hint as helpful in understanding how the scarcity of books and other amusements affected the act of reading, that is, the *quality* of reading, in rural areas and on the frontier.

23. Irving, *The Sketch-Book*, p. 15.

24. *Letters and Papers of John Singleton Copley and Henry Pelham, 1739–1776*, in Massachusetts Historical Society *Collections*, 71 (1914), 51.

25. Irving, *Life and Letters*, II, 166.

26. In *The Voice of the Folk: Folklore and American Literary Theory* (Amherst: University of Massachusetts Press, 1972), Gene Bluestein illustrated this point by quoting the following passage from Irving's *Tour on the Prairies*: "We were over-shadowed by lofty trees, with straight, smooth trunks, like stately columns; and as the glancing rays of the sun shone through the transparent leaves, tinted with the many-colored hues of autumn, I was reminded of the effect of sunshine among the stained windows and clustering columns of a Gothic cathedral. Indeed there is a grandeur and solemnity in our spacious forests of the West, that awakens in me the same feeling I have experienced in those vast and venerable piles, and the sound of the wind sweeping through them supplies occasionally the deep breathings of the organ." Bluestein remarks that "the frame of reference and the language it evokes remove us from the forest itself in an attempt to raise the scene to the level of high culture" (p. 60). Interestingly, the germ of this vignette is an equally lyrical passage from a letter of 1828 comparing the

Cathedral of Seville to an American forest scene (*Life and Letters*, II, 330–1). Perhaps, then, it is more fair to say that what Irving is doing in both is attempting to blur the strongly ingrained but inhibiting distinction between American materials and high culture. Both passages, I think, manage to convey a rather melancholy feeling of unnatural dislocation.

27. Irving, *Life and Letters*, II, 165: "I feel like a sailor who has once more put to sea, and is reluctant to quit the quiet security of the shore." Similar statements are to be found throughout the letters.

28. Perry Miller, "Afterword," in *The Sketch-Book of Geoffrey Crayon, Gent.* (New York: New American Library, 1961), p. 374.

29. Irving, *The Sketch-Book*, p. 15. This quotation seems to me to link in a single tradition Dwight's aspersions on the log cabin, quoted in the previous chapter, and Hawthorne's sense of place as expressed in "Wakefield" and again in Zenobia's remarks to Coverdale toward the end of *The Blithedale Romance* when she speaks of "the woman who goes one hair's breadth out of the beaten track . . . and never sees the world in its true aspect, afterwards!" (*The Blithedale Romance and Fanshawe*, ed. Roy Harvey Pearce [Columbus: Ohio State University Press, 1964], p. 224).

30. The two Indian sketches were written before Irving went to England.

31. Irving, *The Sketch-Book*, pp. 387–8.

32. Quoted in Irving, *Life and Letters*, I, 422.

33. Herman Melville, "Hawthorne and His Mosses," in *Herman Melville: Representative Selections*, ed. Willard Thorpe (New York: American Book Company, 1938), p. 338.

34. Irving, *The Sketch-Book*, pp. 409–10. It is customary to refer to Irving's view of the Indian in a dismissive way as "romantic," and to mean by this that its inaccuracies are traceable, ultimately, to an influence from Rousseau. Without disputing the fact of influence, I think more is to be gained by noting that the distortions in Irving's portrait of the native American can almost always be traced to a compulsion to project through it an image of himself.

35. Ibid., pp. 425–6.

36. Ibid., pp. 501–2.

Chapter 5. Hawthorne's provincial imagination

1. Nathaniel Hawthorne, *Hawthorne's Lost Notebook: 1835–1841*, ed. Barbara S. Mouffe and Hyatt H. Waggoner (University Park: Pennsylvania State University Press, 1978), p. 14; *The American Notebooks*, ed. Claude M. Simpson (Columbus: Ohio State University Press, 1972), p. 244.

2. Henry James, *Hawthorne* (New York: Harper & Brothers, 1880), p. 41.

3. Alexis de Tocqueville, *Democracy in America*, trans. Henry Reeve, ed. Phillips Bradley (New York: Vintage Books, 1945), II, 59.

4. Ralph Waldo Emerson, "The Poet," in *The Collected Works of Ralph Waldo Emerson*, ed. Robert E. Spiller et al. (Cambridge, Mass.: Harvard University Press, 1983), III, 6.

5. Quoted in Crowley's "Historical Commentary," *Twice-Told Tales*, ed. J. Donald Crowley (Columbus: Ohio State University Press, 1974), p. 516.

6. James, *Hawthorne*, pp. 30–1.

7. Nathaniel Hawthorne, "Lichfield and Uttoxeter," in *Our Old Home*, ed. Claude M. Simpson (Columbus: Ohio State University Press, 1970), p. 122.

8. See, for example, the preface to Nathaniel Hawthorne's *The Blithedale Romance*.

9. "Hawthorn[e] invites his readers too much into his study, opens the process before them. As if the confectioner should say to his customers Now let us make the cake" (*The Journals and Miscellaneous Notebooks of Ralph Waldo Emerson*, ed. Ralph H. Orth and Alfred R. Ferguson [Cambridge, Mass.: Harvard University Press, 1971], IX, 405).

10. Hawthorne, "Civic Banquets," in *Our Old Home*, p. 315. Note that Hawthorne's sense of the effect of time on materials is essentially the reverse of Irving's. The "literary nationalists" include William Tudor, William Howard Gardiner, Robert Walsh, J. G. Palfrey, and others, whose opinions are discussed in Neal Frank Doubleday, *Hawthorne's Early Tales, A Critical Study* (Durham, N.C.: Duke University Press, 1972), pp. 18–26.

11. Hawthorne, "Sir William Phips," in *Tales, Sketches, and Other Papers* (Boston: Houghton Mifflin, 1899), p. 227.

12. On "The Story Teller," see N. F. Adkins, "The Early Projected Works of Nathaniel Hawthorne," *Papers of the Bibliographical Society of America*, 39 (1945), 119–45.

13. Hawthorne, "Mr. Higginbotham's Catastrophe," in *Twice-Told Tales*, p. 107.

14. Ibid., p. 108.

15. Ibid., p. 110.

16. Ibid., p. 112.

17. Ibid.

18. Ibid., pp. 119–20.

19. Pike's deliverance contrasts sharply with the personal circumstances of the Story Teller, who leaves his home to wander about the country reciting these tales to the public. In the case of "Mr. Higginbotham's Catastrophe" he fails ludicrously to convey the meanings he wishes to. See Hawthorne's "Passages from a Relinquished Work," in *Mosses from an Old Manse*, ed. J. Donald Crowley (Columbus: Ohio State University Press, 1974), pp. 405–21. "Passages . . . " is the title Hawthorne gave to the frame of "Higginbotham" when he reprinted it separately in *Mosses*.

20. Mouffe and Waggoner, eds., *Hawthorne's Lost Notebook*, p. 36.

21. Simpson, ed., *The American Notebooks*, pp. 233–4.

22. Richard Harter Fogle, *Hawthorne's Fiction: The Light and the Dark* (Norman: University of Oklahoma Press, 1952), p. 56.

23. Horatio Bridge, *Personal Recollections of Nathaniel Hawthorne* (New York: Harper & Brothers, 1893), p. 64. Cf. Hawthorne, "The Artist of the Beautiful," in *Mosses from an Old Manse*, p. 450: " . . . the character of Owen's mind was microscopic, and tended naturally to the minute, in accordance

with his diminutive frame, and the marvellous smallness and delicate power of his fingers. . . . The Beautiful Idea has no relation to size, and may be as perfectly developed in a space too minute for any but microscopic investigation, as within the ample verge that is measured by the arc of the rainbow."

24. Washington Irving, *Bracebridge Hall, or The Humorists* (New York: G. P. Putnam, 1859), p. 79. The quality of the environment, in other words, dictates the power of what Dwight called the "minute, important circumstance" (see Chapter 3, note 28). Cf. Hawthorne's advice to Bridge about journalizing: "Begin to write always before the impression of novelty has worn off . . . else you will be apt to think that the peculiarities which at first attracted you are not worth recording; yet those slight peculiarities are the very things that make the most vivid impression upon the reader. Think nothing too trifling to write down, so it be in the smallest degree characteristic. You will be surprised to find on re-perusing your journal what an importance . . . these little particulars assume" (Bridge, *Personal Recollections*, pp. 92–3).

25. Hawthorne, "Wakefield," in *Twice-Told Tales*, p. 130.

26. In Hawthorne, "Edward Randolph's Portrait," in *Twice-Told Tales*, pp. 256–70.

27. For biological inheritance, see, for example, Hawthorne's *The House of the Seven Gables*, where the point is made as much through the Pyncheons' inbred race of chickens as through the Pyncheons themselves; for translation, see Mouffe and Waggoner, eds., *Hawthorne's Lost Notebook*, p. 19; and for imported fashions, see the reference to the "imitators of the European fine gentlemen of the period" in Hawthorne, "My Kinsman, Major Molineux," *The Snow-Image and Uncollected Tales*, ed. J. Donald Crowley (Columbus: Ohio State University Press, 1974), p. 215. One might multiply such examples indefinitely.

28. James, *Hawthorne*, p. 41.

29. Mouffe and Waggoner, eds., *Hawthorne's Lost Notebook*, pp. 21–2. The scene is of course Salem harbor.

30. "On being transported to strange scenes, we feel as if all were unreal. This is but the perception of the true unreality of earthly things, made evident by the want of congruity between ourselves and them. By and bye, we become adapted, and the perception is lost" (*Hawthorne's Lost Notebook*, ed. Mouffe and Waggoner, p. 62). Cf. the passage from *The Marble Faun* quoted by Charles Feidelson in *Symbolism and American Literature* (Chicago: Chicago University Press, 1953), p. 13: "There is a singular effect oftentimes when, out of the midst of engrossing thought and deep absorption, we suddenly look up, and catch a glimpse of external objects. We seem at such moments to look farther and deeper into them, than by any premeditated observation; it is as if they meet our eyes alive, and with all their hidden meaning on the surface, but grew again inanimate and inscrutable the instant that they became aware of our glances."

Matter and circumstance are a barrier to meaning and remain so by man's own involuntary connivance; were it not for the penalties of original sin, the universe would be alive for us at all times. Because of the peculiar nature of the frontier environment, which creates an intense sense of the intransigence of physical circumstances, American provincial artists – and Hawthorne particularly – were inclined to regard their own situation as an epitome of the general human condition. The American, in short, was effectively a symbol of Man. Cf. Tocqueville, *Democracy in America*, II, 80–1.

31. Hawthorne, *The Snow-Image*, pp. 221 and 220.
32. Ibid., p. 7.
33. Nathaniel Hawthorne, *The Scarlet Letter*, ed. William Charvat (Columbus: Ohio State University Press, 1962), p. 63. It might be pointed out that the Puritan establishment does not *want* to punish Hester: it would prefer that she had not committed her sin in the first place and that she could serve the interests of the community by upholding voluntarily her ordinary relations to it. Having, however, violated those relationships, she has (intolerably for the community) stripped herself of her social usefulness and must now have a use assigned to her. Whether one's usefulness is voluntary or assigned, the Puritan community insists that each of its members hold the entire fabric together.
34. Ibid., pp. 68–9.
35. Ibid., p. 69. The metaphor of the "stony crust" recurs frequently in Hawthorne's writing, especially toward the end of his career when he is reflecting on European scenes. Here as elsewhere it conveys his sense of the dead intransigence of the material world. For example: "Dirt . . . is plenty enough all over the world, being the symbolic accompaniment of the foul encrustation which began to settle over and bedim all earthly things as soon as Eve had bitten the apple" ("Outside Glimpses of English Poverty," in *Our Old Home*, p. 277).
36. Hawthorne, *The Scarlet Letter*, p. 65. "The Snow-Image" was the last tale Hawthorne wrote before *The Scarlet Letter* (see *The American Notebooks*, ed. Simpson, p. 627).
37. Hawthorne, *The Scarlet Letter*, p. 86.
38. Ibid., pp. 199–200.
39. Ibid., pp. 201–2.
40. Ibid., p. 216.

Chapter 6. Working in Eden

1. Ralph Waldo Emerson, James Freeman Clarke, and William Henry Channing, eds., *Memoirs of Margaret Fuller Ossoli* (Boston: Phillips, Sampson, 1852), I, 235.
2. T. S. Eliot, "Tradition and the Individual Talent," in *The Sacred Wood: Essays on Poetry and Criticism* (London: Methuen; New York: Barnes & Noble, 1964), p. 49.
3. The best known of these lists are to be found in William Bradford's *Of Plymouth Plantation*, book II, chap. 1; James Fenimore Cooper's preface to

Home as Found; Hawthorne's introduction to *The Marble Faun*, and Henry James's *Hawthorne*.

4. In *The Conservative Tradition in America* (New York: Oxford University Press, 1967), p. 56, Allen Guttmann points to the conclusion of "The Legend of Sleepy Hollow" to indicate that "The Dutch . . . have won their comic war for cultural independence," and yet it seems essential to an appreciation of the story that we not forget the historical fate of these Dutch communities, a fate sufficiently indicated in "Rip Van Winkle." What makes their resistance comic, moreover, is not the fact of victory, but their automatic recourse to legend and play in waging their defense.

5. William Dean Howells, *The Rise of Silas Lapham* (Boston: Houghton Mifflin, 1957), p. 96.

6. *The Journals and Miscellaneous Notebooks of Ralph Waldo Emerson*, ed. Merton M. Sealts, Jr. (Cambridge, Mass.: Harvard University Press, 1965), V, 395.

7. Reference to the *Oxford English Dictionary* will show that the word "culture" was in Emerson's day only beginning to take on the meaning it has now. Its primary application had been to agriculture, as in the culture of plants.

8. *Journals*, ed. A. W. Plumstead, William H. Gilman, and Ruth H. Bennett (Cambridge, Mass.: Harvard University Press, 1975), XI, 203.

9. Ibid., V, 411. Compare the passage from Irving's "Philip of Pokanoket" quoted from *The Sketch-Book* in Chapter 4.

10. R. W. Emerson, "The American Scholar," in *The Collected Works of Ralph Waldo Emerson*, ed. Robert E. Spiller et al. (Cambridge, Mass.: Harvard University Press, 1971), I, 65.

11. James Fenimore Cooper, *The Pioneers; Or, the Sources of the Susquehanna* (New York: Hurd & Houghton, 1872), p. 67.

12. Nathaniel Hawthorne, *The English Notebooks*, ed. Randall Stewart (New York: Modern Language Association of America; London: Oxford University Press, 1941), p. 197.

13. Pardon Davis, *Davis's Modern Practical English Grammar Adapted to the American System of Teaching* (Philadelphia: Uriah Hunt & Son, 1845), p. 171.

14. Emerson, "The American Scholar," p. 62.

15. Henry David Thoreau, *Walden*, ed. J. Lyndon Shanley (Princeton, N.J.: Princeton University Press, 1971), p. 6.

16. From a letter to Emerson's brother William, dated February 10, 1850; see Ralph L. Rusk, ed., *The Letters of Ralph Waldo Emerson* (New York: Columbia University Press, 1939), IV, 179.

17. Merle Curti et al., *A History of American Civilization* (New York: Harper & Row, 1953), p. 238.

18. Quoted in Benjamin T. Spencer, *The Quest for Nationality: An American Literary Campaign* (Syracuse, N.Y.: Syracuse University Press, 1957), p. 85.

19. Emerson, "The American Scholar," p. 113. Despite the elder Holmes's having called the address an "intellectual Declaration of Independence," it was in fact less a call to literary nationalism than an attack on imitation: see, for example, Ralph L. Rusk's discussion in *The Life of Ralph Waldo Emerson* (New York: Charles Scribner's Sons, 1949), pp. 262–3.

20. Henry James, *Hawthorne* (New York: Harper & Brothers, 1880), p. 43.

21. John L. Blake, *A Geographical, Chronological, and Historical Atlas* (New York: Cooke & Co., 1826), p. 165. Blake's politics, I assume, may be inferred from his habit of capitalizing the "People" and their attendant pronouns.

22. A good short treatment of the relationship between the frontier and anti-intellectualism is Merle Curti, "Intellectuals and Other People," *American Historical Review*, 60 (January 1955), 259–82.

23. *The American Notebooks*, ed. Claude M. Simpson (Columbus: Ohio State University Press, 1972), p. 308.

24. Lyman Beecher, *A Plea for the West* (Cincinnati: Truman & Smith, 1835), pp. 11, 30, 31. See also Ernest Marchand, "Emerson and the Frontier," *American Literature*, 3 (May 1931), 154.

25. This is the thesis convincingly put forth by Rush Welter in "The Frontier West as Image of American Society: Conservative Attitudes Before the Civil War," *Mississippi Valley Historical Review*, 46 (March 1960), 593–614.

26. The phrase is taken from the conclusion to Chapter 26 of *Moby-Dick*, where it is associated with Jackson.

27. The whole passage in which these phrases appear gives the contradictory flavor of Emerson's attitude: "Webster's speeches seem to be the utmost that the unpoetic West has accomplished or can. We all lean on England, scarce a verse, a page, a newspaper but is writ in imitation of English forms, our very manners & conversation are traditional & sometimes the life seems dying out of all literature & this enormous paper currency of Words is accepted instead. I suppose the evil may be cured by this rank rabble party, the Jacksonism of the country, heedless of English & of all literature – a stone cut out of the ground without hands – they may root out the hollow dilettantism of our cultivation in the coarsest way & the new-born may begin again to frame their own world with greater advantage." *Journals*, ed. Alfred R. Ferguson (Cambridge, Mass.: Harvard University Press, 1964), IV, 297.

28. Emerson, "The Poet" in *The Collected Works of Ralph Waldo Emerson*, ed. Robert E. Spiller et al. (Cambridge, Mass.: Harvard University Press, 1983), III, 22.

29. See Seymour Martin Lipset, *The First New Nation: The United States in Historical and Comparative Perspective* (New York: Basic Books, 1964), esp. pp. 1–2, for a discussion of equality and achievement as "America's key values." Lipset points out that "these values, though related, are not entirely compatible." In fact, for certain purposes it is useful to think of them as a polarity, one gaining dominance at the expense of the other, one becoming more "concentrated" at a given time and place at the expense of the other.

30. Rusk, *Life*, p. 326.

31. Stewart, ed., *The English Notebooks*, p. 367.

32. It should be pointed out that this resistance, in itself, has no particular value. It was, as I have been arguing, of great use to gifted writers, but in the vast majority it led simply to timidity and a fear of lapsing into the provincial. The predominance of the latter effect was frequently noted: Evert Duyckinck, for example, was annoyed that "our literature has, in fact, been

the very opposite of the conditions claimed by De Tocqueville. He demands originality, force, passion, fruitfulness. What have been the accepted productions of American authorship? They disclose, for the most part, just the opposite qualities, of imitation, tameness, want of passion, and poverty" ("Traits of American Authorship," *The Literary World*, April 17, 1847, p. 245).

33. Henry James, *The American*, in *The Atlantic Monthly*, 37 (June 1876), 667. James made some significant revisions in this passage in the New York edition (*The American* [New York: Charles Scribner's Sons, 1907], p. 45); Newman's retort becomes: " 'Oh come,' Newman protested; 'I'm not an honest barbarian either, by a good deal. I'm a great fall-off from *him*. I've seen honest barbarians, I know what they are.' " Told that there are "different shades," Newman replies, "I have the instincts – have them deeply – if I haven't the forms of a high old civilisation."

34. James, *The American*, pp. 668 and 669.

35. From Margaret Fuller, *Summer on the Lakes, in 1843*, rpt. in *Margaret Fuller: American Romantic*, ed. Perry Miller (Garden City, N.Y.: Doubleday, 1963), p. 122.

36. For Irving, see Chapter 4, note 25; for Bryant, see, among other poems, "A Forest Hymn."

37. James, *The American*, in *The Atlantic Monthly*, 38 (September 1876), 323–4.

38. *The Notebooks of Henry James*, ed. F. O. Matthiessen and Kenneth B. Murdock (New York: Oxford University Press, 1947), p. 24.

39. Henry Adams, *The Education of Henry Adams*, ed. Ernest Samuels (Boston: Houghton Mifflin, 1974), p. 387.

40. Margaret Fuller, "Letter XVIII," in *At Home and Abroad*, ed. Arthur B. Fuller (Boston: Crosby, Nichols, 1856), p. 252.

Chapter 7. Life as art in America

1. R. W. Emerson, *The Letters of Ralph Waldo Emerson*, ed. Ralph L. Rusk (New York: Columbia University Press, 1939), II, 41.

2. Henry James, *Hawthorne* (New York: Harper & Brothers, 1880), p. 143.

3. Ibid., p. 69.

4. James Russell Lowell, "Cambridge Thirty Years Ago," *The Writings of James Russell Lowell* (Boston: Houghton Mifflin, 1890), I, 63.

5. See her letter to Emerson, January 7, 1839, in Thomas Wentworth Higginson, *Margaret Fuller Ossoli* (Boston: Houghton Mifflin, 1884), p. 95, and Arthur W. Brown, *Margaret Fuller* (Boston: Twayne, 1964), p. 50. Fuller did, of course, contribute a paper on Allston to the *Dial* for July 1840.

6. Quoted in *Memoirs of Margaret Fuller Ossoli*, ed. Ralph Waldo Emerson, James Freeman Clarke, and William Henry Channing (Boston: Phillips, Sampson, 1852), I, 15. Higginson, in *Old Cambridge* (New York: Macmillan, 1899), p. 25, argues nevertheless that her education was no more strenuous than that given college-bound boys at the time, a view borne out

by *The Letters of Margaret Fuller,* ed. Robert N. Hudspeth (Ithaca, N.Y.: Cornell University Press, 1983), I, passim.

7. See Madeleine B. Stern, "Margaret Fuller's Schooldays in Cambridge," *New England Quarterly,* 13 (June 1940), 207–22.

8. Lowell, "Cambridge Thirty Years Ago," in *Writings,* I, 89.

9. Details for this paragraph are drawn from Lowell, "Cambridge Thirty Years Ago," in *Writings,* I, 69, 86–7, and Stern, "Fuller's Schooldays," p. 211.

10. Lowell, "Cambridge Thirty Years Ago," in *Writings,* I, 95.

11. Ibid., I, 91. Possibly the reference is to James Otis.

12. Quoted in Russell E. Durning, *Margaret Fuller, Citizen of the World* (Heidelberg: Carl Winter, 1969), p. 45, with this comment: "One's life should be poetry made visible in words and deeds, but the disturbing influences of circumstance and the actions of others made such a goal impossible at times."

13. Fuller to Sophia Ripley, in *Memoirs,* I, 324.

14. Fuller, quoted in *Memoirs,* I, 250 (italics in the original).

15. Ibid., I, 141. Durning considers this passage in *Margaret Fuller,* p. 35, where he regards it as a call to the vocation of teaching. For Bell Gale Chevigny (*The Woman and the Myth: Margaret Fuller's Life and Writings* [Old Westbury, N.Y.: Feminist Press, 1976], p. 167), it "demonstrates how the frustration of her position and the discipline of repressed desire and ambition could explode in a vision of the self subsumed in the 'All.' "

16. Cf. Emerson: "The man must be so much that he must make all circumstances indifferent" ("Self-Reliance," in *The Collected Works of Ralph Waldo Emerson,* ed. Robert E. Spiller et al. [Cambridge: Harvard University Press, 1979], II, 35); and Thoreau: "If a man should walk through this town and see only the reality, where, think you, would the 'Mill-dam' go to?" (*Walden,* ed. J. Lyndon Shanley [Princeton, N.J.: Princeton University Press, 1971], p. 96).

17. Fuller, quoted in *Memoirs,* I, 99. The allusion is to Matthew 8:20; when a scribe offered to follow Jesus, he was told, "The foxes have holes, and the birds of the air have nests, but the Son of man hath not where to lay his head."

18. Ibid., I, 149.

19. Ibid., I, 25. She later had the same objection to Balzac: see Fuller, "French Novelists of the Day," in *Life Without and Life Within,* ed. Arthur B. Fuller (Boston: Brown, Taggard & Chase, 1860), pp. 158–68.

20. Fuller, quoted in *Memoirs,* I, 228–9. One is curiously reminded by the syntax and rhythm of this sentence, corresponding as it does to a certain sort of experience, of Anne Bradstreet's response to the shock of relocation: "I . . . came into this Country, where I found a new world and new manners, at which my heart rose. But after I was convinced it was the way of God, I submitted to it and joined to the church at Boston" (see Chapter 1, note 6).

21. Margaret Fuller, *Summer on the Lakes, in 1843* (Boston: Charles C. Little & James Brown, 1844), p. 5. She seems to have been enchanted because she

could "sit on Table Rock, close to the great fall . . . [where] all power of observing details, all separate consciousness, was quite lost" (p. 6).

22. Quoted in Durning, *Margaret Fuller*, pp. 84–5.

23. Fuller's reading in German at this time is briefly summarized in Durning, *Margaret Fuller*, p. 85. The subject of her knowledge of German literature has received considerable attention: see, for example, Frederick O. Braun, *Margaret Fuller and Goethe* (New York: Henry Holt, 1910); Henry Pochman, *German Culture in America: Philosophical and Literary Influences, 1600–1900* (Madison: University of Wisconsin Press, 1957); Arthur R. Schults, "Margaret Fuller – Transcendentalist Interpreter of German Literature," *Monatshefte für Deutschen Unterricht*, 34 (April 1942), 169–82; Harry Slochower, "Margaret Fuller and Goethe," *Germanic Review*, 7 (April 1932), 130–44; Stanley M. Vogel, *German Literary Influences on the American Transcendentalists* (New Haven, Conn.: Yale University Press, 1955); and René Wellek, "The Minor Transcendentalists and German Philosophy," *New England Quarterly*, 15 (December 1942), 652–80.

24. James Freeman Clarke, in *Memoirs*, I, 114.

25. Emerson, in ibid., I, 164.

26. Ibid., I, 147.

27. Fuller to Richard Fuller, August 11, 1842 (in the Houghton Library, Harvard University, Cambridge, Mass.).

28. Ibid.

29. James, *Hawthorne*, pp. 68–9 and passim.

30. Emerson, in *Memoirs*, I, 266.

31. Ibid., I, 267.

32. Fuller, quoted in ibid., I, 189. John Flaxman, the English artist, was a friend of William Blake and an important figure in the Greek revival. Fuller's final word on Flaxman is contained in a highly interesting sonnet published in *Life Without and Life Within*, ed. A. B. Fuller, p. 371:

> We deemed the secret lost, the spirit gone,
>   Which spake in Greek simplicity of thought,
>   And in the forms of gods and heroes wrought
> Eternal beauty from the sculptured stone –
> A higher charm than modern culture won,
>   With all the wealth of metaphysic lore,
>   Gifted to analyze, dissect, explore.
> A many-colored light flows from our sun;
> Art, 'neath its beams, a motley thread has spun;
>   The prison [prism?] modifies the perfect day;
> But thou has known such mediums to shun,
>   And cast once more on life a pure white ray.
> Absorbed in the creations of thy mind,
> Forgetting daily self, my truest self I find.

33. James, *Hawthorne*, pp. 68–9.

34. Reliable means of reproducing color were, of course, not available; not even chromolithographs had yet appeared.

35. Americans have frequently defended their critical judgments on the grounds
     that their provincial isolation filtered out extraneous considerations. Ben-
     jamin Franklin claimed that Americans "are a kind of Posterity in respect
     to" English writers because, "being at too great a Distance to be bypassed
     by the Fashions, Parties and Prejudices that prevail among you," Americans
     can "read their Works with perfect Impartiality." Moreover, knowing
     "nothing of [the] personal Failings" of British authors, "the bright and
     amiable part strikes us with its full Force" (see *The Papers of Benjamin
     Franklin*, ed. Leonard W. Labaree [New Haven, Conn.: Yale University
     Press, 1961], III, 13). In an unsigned review of "Mrs. Hemans' Poems"
     (*North American Review*, 24 [March 1827], 463), George Bancroft makes
     much the same sort of claim: "The voice of America, deciding on the
     literature of England, resembles the voice of posterity more nearly than
     anything else, that is contemporaneous, can do." Yet another example in
     this tradition may be found in "Home Criticism," in W. Alfred Jones,
     Essays upon Authors and Books (New York: Stanford & Swords, 1849), pp.
     28–9. Fuller was undoubtedly aware that the idea of the superiority and
     permanence of form as opposed to color was central to the aesthetic theories
     of Johann Joachim Winckelmann.
36. James, *Hawthorne*, p. 101.
37. Emerson, "Nature," in *Collected Works*, I, 37–8.
38. Fuller, *Summer on the Lakes*, p. 6.
39. "It is so true that a woman may be in love with a woman, and a man with
     a man. I like to be sure of it, for it is the same love which angels feel"
     (Fuller, quoted in *Memoirs*, I, 283). The idea is less biblical than Miltonic
     (cf. *Paradise Lost*, VII, lines 618–29). Hawthorne expressed a similar idea in
     an early letter to Sophia: see *Love Letters of Nathaniel Hawthorne* (Chicago:
     Society of the Dofobs, 1907), II, 74–5.
40. Margaret Fuller, *Woman in the Nineteenth Century* (New York: Greeley &
     McElrath, 1845), pp. 105–6.
41. Ibid., p. 162.
42. *Margaret Fuller: American Romantic*, ed. Perry Miller (Garden City, N.Y.:
     Doubleday, 1963), p. 202. Miller's view is somewhat less generous than
     that of most other commentators.
43. *Love-Letters of Margaret Fuller, 1845–1846* (New York: D. Appleton, 1903),
     p. 21.
44. Ibid., pp. 150–1.
45. Emerson, "Nature," *Collected Works*, I, 23.
46. Margaret Fuller, "A Short Essay on Critics," *Dial*, 1 (July 1840), 6.
47. Margaret Fuller, Review of Charles Anthon, *A System of Latin Versification,
     New-York Daily Tribune*, May 12, 1845, p. 1; rpt. as "A Transcendental
     Defense of Classical Metres," in *Margaret Fuller*, ed. Miller, pp. 205–7.
48. Fuller, "A Short Essay on Critics," p. 5.
49. The way in which this peculiarly American condition might of itself affect
     one's style of perception, and thus one's values and tastes, is indicated
     obliquely in Fuller's review of Henry Taylor's *Philip Van Artevelde*, in a
     passage explaining her admiration for Alfieri. Notice in particular the last

term of the explanation: "We hold that if a vagrant bud of poesy here and there be blighted by conforming to . . . rules, our loss is more than made up to us by our enjoyment of the plan, of symmetry, of the triumph of genius over multiplied obstacles" (see *Western Messenger*, 1 [December 1835], 401).

50. Fuller, "A Short Essay on Critics," p. 5.
51. Ibid., p. 8.
52. Ibid., p. 10.
53. Fuller, *Summer on the Lakes*, p. 61.
54. Ibid., pp. 62–3.
55. Ibid., p. 63.
56. Ibid., pp. 63–4.
57. Margaret Fuller, "Thom's Poems," *New-York Daily Tribune*, August 22, 1845, p. 1; rpt. in "Poets of the People," *Papers on Literature and Art* (New York: Wiley & Putnam, 1846), II, 1–14, from which all subsequent quotations are taken.
58. Fuller, *Woman in the Nineteenth Century*, p. 163.
59. *At Home and Abroad*, ed. Arthur B. Fuller (Boston: Crosby, Nichols, 1856), p. 250.
60. Ibid. Compare Emerson's response to the Athenaeum statuary, cited above.
61. Fuller, quoted in *Memoirs*, II, 224–5.
62. Fuller looked for this hero, modestly, in others for a time before becoming convinced of the need to be one herself. Her career as a teacher and as a leader of Conversations gradually accustomed her to the role. But she realized that education was not sufficient, the role of the teacher too local. See her letter to Emerson, June 1, 1843, in *Memoirs*, I, 263, on the function of the hero in the cultural awakening of the people. The letter was written from Niagara Falls.
63. Emerson, in *Memoirs*, I, 238; I follow Perry Miller who, in quoting this passage (*Margaret Fuller*, p. xvii), corrects a printer's error. Miller, however, misleadingly attributes the language and the harshness of the opinion to Emerson, who in fact indicates that he is merely repeating something.
64. Emerson, in *Memoirs*, I, 238.

Chapter 8. Reading God directly: the morbidity of culture

1. R. W. Emerson, "The American Scholar," in *The Collected Works of Ralph Waldo Emerson*, ed. Robert E. Spiller et al. (Cambridge, Mass.: Harvard University Press, 1971), I, 57.
2. *The Letters of Ralph Waldo Emerson*, ed. Ralph L. Rusk (New York: Columbia University Press, 1939), V, 86.
3. Emerson, "Song of Nature," lines 37–44, in *The Complete Works of Ralph Waldo Emerson* (Boston: Houghton Mifflin, 1904), IX, 245. The earliest version of these lines, more hopeful and expectant than the text first published in 1860, is preserved in *The Journals and Miscellaneous Notebooks of Ralph Waldo Emerson*, ed. William Gilman and J. E. Parsons (Cambridge,

Mass.: Harvard University Press, 1970), VIII, 464 (hereafter cited as *JMN*). The notebook version may have been written as early as the mid-1840s.

4. *JMN*, ed. A. W. Plumstead and Harrison Hayford (Cambridge, Mass.: Harvard University Press, 1969), VII, 17.

5. William Bradford, *History of Plymouth Plantation*, ed. Worthington C. Ford (n.p.: Massachusetts Historical Society, 1912), I, 155.

6. Emerson, *Collected Works*, I, 209.

7. The line is given in Edward Emerson's note to the poem: see Emerson, *Complete Works*, IX, 490.

8. Emerson, "Nature," in *Collected Works*, I, 7.

9. "Our Native Writers" does not appear in any of the standard collected editions; all quotations are taken from its first printing in *Every Other Saturday*, I (April 12, 1884), 116–17.

10. Bowdoin College, where Longfellow had just spent four years, was in a sparsely populated area in Maine. Some indication of the isolation of the school and of the curious mix of sophisticated and rustic manners to be encountered there may be had from Hawthorne's fictional re-creation in *Fanshawe*. William Charvat, in his chapter on Longfellow in *The Profession of Authorship in America, 1800–1870* (Columbus: Ohio State University Press, 1968), pp. 106–54, speaks of many practical difficulties in the way of Longfellow's becoming a professional man of letters. Only a year before he delivered the "Native Writers" address, his father had written to inform him that "there is not wealth & munificence enough in this country to afford . . . patronage to merely literary men" (quoted on p. 118).

11. Cf. Alexis de Tocqueville, *Democracy in America*, trans. Henry Reeve, ed. Phillips Bradley (New York: Vintage Books, 1945), II, 80–1.

12. The close association of the artists of the Hudson River school, America's first group of landscape painters, and the Knickerbocker writers in particular is examined by James T. Callow in *Kindred Spirits: Knickerbocker Writers and American Artists, 1807–1855* (Chapel Hill: University of North Carolina Press, 1967).

13. *The Notebooks of Henry James*, ed. F. O. Matthiessen and Kenneth B. Murdock (New York: Oxford University Press, 1947), p. 24.

14. W. C. Brownell, *American Prose Masters* (New York: Charles Scribner's Sons, 1909), p. 164. Floyd Stovall has objected that in this contention Brownell "is surely going too far" ("Emerson," in *Eight American Authors: A Review of Research and Criticism*, ed. Floyd Stovall [New York: W. W. Norton, 1963], p. 61).

15. *JMN*, VIII, 175.

16. *JMN*, VII, 7.

17. Emerson, "The American Scholar," in *Collected Works*, I, 52.

18. Ibid., I, 65.

19. Ibid., I, 53.

20. Such references are a notable feature of all of Emerson's better-known essays and addresses. The theory is set forth in *Nature* in Chapter 7 and again in Chapter 8. In "The Divinity School Address," Emerson asserts that "the absence of this primary faith" in the unity of consciousness "is the presence

of degradation . . . . Once man was all; now he is an appendage, a nuisance" (in *Collected Works*, I, 80).

21. Hawthorne's treatment of history in *The House of the Seven Gables* as *essentially* cyclical but at the same time capable of being "straightened out" by moral affirmations is, I think, a suggestive analogue to Emerson's idea. In his lecture on "Education" (1840), Emerson argued that "deliberate, premeditated, organized instruction" necessarily failed "because of its low aim. It aims to make amends for the Fall of Man by teaching him feats and games" (*The Early Lectures of Ralph Waldo Emerson*, ed. Robert E. Spiller and Wallace E. Williams [Cambridge, Mass.: Harvard University Press, 1972], III, 293, 299). Emerson felt that education *ought* to have the effect of reversing human degradation, but that it could not so long as it concerned itself with trifling externals.

22. Emerson, "The American Scholar," in *Collected Works*, I, 66.

23. The phrase occurs in *JMN*, VII, 15, where Emerson observes that "Goethe hates dissection, hates the sundering of a thing from the universal connexion of nature." In terms of their attitudes toward foreign culture, one way to distinguish Emerson from the Longfellow of "Our Native Writers" and from the literary nationalists in general is to note that Emerson's disapproval was reserved for the sundering process and not, as with the others, for the culture that is received *as* sundered.

24. Emerson, "Self-Reliance," in *Collected Works*, II, 46.

25. Ibid., II, 35.

26. Emerson, "The Divinity School Address," in *Collected Works*, I, 77.

27. *JMN*, VII, 280, written October 26, 1839.

28. For a quite literal test of this proposition, compare the 1857 letter with a journal entry composed twenty years earlier (*JMN*, V, 377) which Emerson was perhaps half remembering.

Index